SOCIAL POLICY AND WELFARE PLURALISM

Selected writings of Robert Pinker

Edited by John Offer and Robert Pinker

First published in Great Britain in 2017 by

Policy Press
University of Bristol
1-9 Old Park Hill
Bristol BS2 8BB
UK
t: +44 (0)117 954 5940
e: pp-info@bristol.ac.uk
www.policypress.co.uk

North American office:
Policy Press
c/o The University of Chicago Press
1427 East 60th Street
Chicago, IL 60637, USA
t: +1 773 702 7700
f: +1 773-702-9756
e:sales@press.uchicago.edu
www.press.uchicago.edu

© Policy Press 2017

British Library Cataloguing in Publication Data
A catalogue record for this book is available from the British Library.

Library of Congress Cataloging-in-Publication Data
A catalog record for this book has been requested.

ISBN 978-1-4473-2355-6 hardcover
ISBN 978-1-4473-3535-1 ePub
ISBN 978-1-4473-3536-8 Mobi
ISBN 978-1-4473-2356-3 epdf

The right of John Offer and Robert Pinker to be identified as editors of this work has been asserted by them in accordance with the 1988 Copyright, Designs and Patents Act.

Cover design by Hayes Design
Front cover image © October 2017 Derby Museums Trust, painting by Joseph Wright of Derby (1734–97), 'The Alchemist Discovering Phosphorous', 1771
Printed and bound in Great Britain by Clays Ltd, St Ives plc
Policy Press uses environmentally responsible print partners

Contents

Acknowledgement

John Offer acknowledges with gratitude the financial assistance of the British Academy in undertaking the research on which this book is based.

Preface

Bob Pinker and John Offer have known each other since the late 1970s. However, the plan to collaborate on *Social Policy and Welfare Pluralism: Selected Writings of Robert Pinker* dates back to only February 2011. Then, Pinker, although retired from the London School of Economics as Professor of Social Administration, was still engaged with the Press Complaints Commission, and Offer was Professor of Social Theory and Policy at the University of Ulster, and about to embark on a stint as Chair of the Editorial Board of *Sociology* which met in London. Meeting from time to time at Pinker's home in Blackheath, two complementary ideas began to take shape. Offer believed that the breadth of Pinker's thought on social policy, which extended well beyond his very influential book of 1971, *Social Theory and Social Policy*, was in need of a detailed reappraisal, and Pinker had written a range of essays over recent years which we both felt amply justified being revised into the form of a book.

The most welcome award of a British Academy Small Research Grant in 2011 enabled Offer to take forward the first idea, itself now represented here as 'Robert Pinker on rethinking approaches to welfare', a general introductory review of Pinker's contribution to thinking about the study and practice of social policy. This essay is an extended and thoroughly revised version of an article called 'Robert Pinker, the idea of welfare and the study of social policy: on unitarism and pluralism', published in 2012 in the *Journal of Social Policy* (vol 41, no 3, pp 615-34). The second idea has now matured after due gestation in the shape of the remainder of this book.

Throughout the preparation of the book, we have each read and commented on the other's drafts. We had to agree, of course, on the outputs by Pinker to be included, and under what thematic groupings they were best ordered. On these matters, our discussions covered many memorable and convivial afternoons. On other matters, the aim has been to strive for clarity, not overall agreement for its own sake; although we should say that we knew already that in broad terms there was little likelihood of serious friction between us. And so it has proved. However, we should record in the interests of transparency that Offer takes primary responsibility for the introductions, general and sectional, and Pinker for the selected writings in question which the book contains.

The essays by Pinker which we have selected for inclusion fall under three thematic headings, representing a good cross-section of, in the main, his relatively recent output. The sections are 'On social policy studies', 'On social care, communities and the conditions for well-being' and 'On welfare pluralism'. The third section concludes with a substantial new essay from Pinker, 'The prospects for social policy in the UK after the 2015 General Election', especially written for the appearance of the book. There is a post-Brexit Afterthought in which the implications for social policy are discussed, with fears raised for the future of the UK itself as a political entity.

Five of the essays have not been previously published. For some of the others which were published, it has not proved possible to contact the publishers. We are grateful to John Wiley for permission to include 'Golden Ages and welfare alchemists', first published in *Social Policy & Administration* in 1995 (vol 29, no 2, pp 78-90), and 'From gift relationships to quasi-markets: an odyssey along the policy paths of altruism and egoism', first published in *Social Policy & Administration* in 2006 (vol 40, no 1, pp 10-25). We are also grateful to Taylor and Francis for permission to include material from *Social Work in an Enterprise Society*, and to include 'Citizenship, civil war and welfare: the making of modern Ireland' from *21st Century Society* (2006, vol 1, no 1, pp 23-38).

We are deeply grateful to Elizabeth McNeill of Portrush whose word-processing skills contributed hugely to the polishing of our text to make it presentable to Policy Press. At Policy Press, Emily Watt and Laura Vickers deserve thanks for their faith in the project, especially as illness and other events caused substantial delays to the schedule. Our production editor, Jo Morton, has been an unfailing source of excellent guidance on presentational matters. Bob Pinker thanks his partner, Mimi O'Keeffe, for her unfailing support and encouragement throughout these setbacks and delays. His essay on 'The ends and means of social policy', which is published in Part One of this collection, concludes with a tribute to his wife, Jennifer, who died in 1994. John Offer thanks his wife Janet Mackle-Offer for countless helpful things connected with seeing the preparation of the book through to completion.

John Offer
Robert Pinker
30 May 2017

Robert Pinker on rethinking approaches to welfare

John Offer

Introduction

Robert Pinker began writing on social policy in the 1960s, when the publications of Richard Titmuss at the London School of Economics (LSE) were the dominant influence on the study of social policy in the UK.[1] He is still writing on social policy today. His earliest research work concerned the development of health care within the poor law (with Brian Abel-Smith) and also, with Peter Townsend, the experiences of the staff and 'inmates' of local authority 'care homes' for elderly people, into which form many former poor law institutions had mutated (see Johnson *et al*, 2010).[2] When his *Social Theory and Social Policy* appeared in 1971, it rapidly became essential reading where social policy or 'social administration' was studied, influencing students for many years. As Anthony Forder noted, *Social Theory and Social Policy* 'was the first major British book in the field of social administration to examine the theoretical perspectives underlying the study of the subject' (Forder *et al*, 1984: 230).[3] Two further books were published devoted to social policy, *The Idea of Welfare* (1979) and *Social Work in an Enterprise Society* (1990), together with many articles on complementary topics.[4]

Pinker's overarching concern was to rethink the *study* of social policy, drawing initially and in a general sense on the non-structuralist and phenomenological sociological perspectives explored in Berger and Luckmann (1966). Although the teaching of sociology and social administration was often, if sometimes uneasily, the responsibility of one department in universities at the time, Pinker's *Social Theory and Social Policy* was the first book to map what the 'sociology of welfare' might study (what the sociology of religion comprised, for instance, was by comparison already well established). It was also the first to assess the potential of classical theorists (Durkheim, Spencer, Marx and Weber in particular and, to a lesser extent, Simmel) to contribute to the development of the specialism, and the first to criticise from a sociologically informed position the traditional range of topics taught and investigated within social policy studies. Pinker's criticisms followed three guiding principles. First, a focus in the study of welfare and policy on the 'welfare state' was not in itself sufficient. Second, 'theory' should not be confused with ideology or rhetoric. Third, how people in their everyday lives thought about and practised securing the welfare of themselves and others deserved close attention: this area was important both in its own right and because it yielded insights which were of assistance in understanding the differing principles, ends and means displayed in comparative and historical terms in 'welfare states', themselves at the time not well understood.

In important respects, Pinker's work presented novel and fundamental challenges to the framework for social policy studies associated with Titmuss (that other writers pursued different lines of criticism, often drawing on Marx, is not here in dispute [see Wilding, 1983]).[5] On many occasions when familiarity with Pinker's work would enhance new contributions to the subject areas, it now seems to be often overlooked.[6] With this context in mind, a new appraisal of his writing, past and present, is seriously overdue.

Social theory and policy

One focus of Pinker's attention was the distinction commonly made in social policy analysis between 'residual' and 'institutional' conceptions of the role of the state in the provision of welfare. Pinker accepted that this essentially individualistic/collectivist binary division relating to the aims of social policy captured real normative differences held by academic analysts of the 'welfare state'. He also accepted that in practice actual policies and provisions in a country might be categorised in terms of one or the other, or as a mixture of both, depending on historical and cultural experience and the contrasting complexions of the political parties forming governments over time. The problem was that these academic perceptions and analyses of social reality had become confusingly equated with the social reality of *actual* service users and members of a society in general. In the process, assumptions were being made about the motivations and moral dispositions of persons. For Pinker, a new generation of specialists in social policy and administration had grounds for being 'disturbed' by its 'persistent lack' of rigorous 'conceptual and theoretical foundations' (1971: 13). To advance a contextualised understanding of social policy itself, the pressing need was to renounce a reliance upon assumptions, and undertake instead the actual study of the applications of altruistic thought and practice by ordinary people in their everyday lives, in their aspirations for social change and in their conceptions of for what and on what principles the state, as opposed to markets, families and community organisations, should assume responsibility.[7] Pinker returned to this theme, perhaps most memorably, in his 1996 lecture 'The experience of citizenship: a generational perspective' (1996; included as **Chapter Eleven** in **Part Three** of this book). At informal levels of social life, he remarked (**Chapter Eleven, p 236**):

> the plans we make for the future are shaped by the values and meanings we have developed on the basis of our past and present experience. What we expect from our own efforts, from our family members and friends and from the provisions of social policy are salient elements

in these plans. They are not greatly informed by theory. They are profoundly influenced by practical experience. Consequently, the more general and comparative our approach, the more difficult it becomes to take these informal dimensions into account. Welfare theorists who seek the comparative 'way to the stars' will never escape into the firmament of cold abstractions while they are weighed down by the multitudinous sands of autobiographical and cultural detail.

This is exactly what happens in much of what passes for comparative welfare theorising. As the details of the really interesting cultural and subjective variables are jettisoned, the models become so abstract and formal that they amount to little more than collections of institutional platitudes. Any reasonably competent social scientist should be able to produce up to ten different models of 'welfare state regimes' in as many minutes. Unfortunately, they do.

The really challenging and difficult task is not to identify the apparent similarities in different 'welfare states', but to explore the nature and causes of the dissimilarities in securing welfare between areas or countries. And this is a task that requires analysis of the informal as well as the formal ways of securing well-being.

One way of demonstrating the impact of *Social Theory and Social Policy* at the time is to glance at *Society and Social Policy*, a book by Ramesh Mishra with some clearly similar objectives, which first appeared later in the decade in 1977. Thus, Mishra recognises that Pinker perceived the debate over residual and institutional models of social policy – central to social administration – as a case in which the protagonists should 'come clean with [their] value judgements' (1977: 11). It is curious, then, that Mishra then adds the criticism that 'in defining and conducting the debate in terms of the two models, certain other ways of looking at welfare tend to be ruled out' (1977: 11). For one of Pinker's central contentions beyond doubt both in *Social Theory and Social Policy* and subsequently was that the two models are conceits of academics, and seriously unreliable guides to altruism and associated values as practised in everyday social life.

By thus contending, Pinker was not advocating 'going native' in terms of the content or reach of the social policy which might be prescribed, but seeking a richer and more sociologically grounded kind of inquiry into how welfare (and not just a 'welfare state') was reasoned about and came to possess the meanings it did in everyday life.[8] The development of research and social theory in this manner would redirect the discipline away from one in which 'too much is prescribed, too much indicted and too little explained' (1971: 166).

While Pinker acknowledged that user consultation and local participation had merits in connection with the evaluation of the aims and provisions of services, he noted there was a linked risk of introducing further forms of unexamined and possibly oppressive normativity (1971: 130–2). The position he adopted was neither a dogmatic anti-statism nor an apologia for any normatively popular status quo: it was held because he anticipated that the study of 'subjective states of social consciousness' would facilitate a supply of evidence enabling a genuine dialogue to arise about perceptions in conflict, offering, in turn, enhanced legitimacy to the development of social reform in democracies (1971: 131–2).

Pinker pointedly distanced himself from the argument, advanced by the then in-vogue radical polemics of Herbert Marcuse's *One-Dimensional Man* (1964), that 'the map of social consciousness cannot be expected to delineate the true profiles of human discontent and frustration, for it is in the nature of capitalism that the masses do not know the difference between true and false consciousness' (1971: 125). Concepts associated with an intellectualist ideology, in this case, 'false consciousness', could serve to define away or devalue what might be ideologically uncomfortable evidence in a manner such that, in effect, it ceased to signify as evidence at all.[9] For Pinker, it was important to distinguish the untestable propositions of ideology from the propositions of theory which, properly understood, fell short of certainty, were subject to disconfirmation and were held by those who advanced them in an open, even sceptical, frame of mind. Normative theory in particular was closely associated with ideology, but a distinction could nevertheless be maintained, as he noted in 1982: 'The distinction between normative theory and ideology is especially difficult to draw because it is a matter of degree as well as of kind. I think there are two relevant criteria: first, the general Popperian point as to whether or not the theory is set out in a testable and falsifiable way and, secondly, the degree of unprejudiced consideration that is given to new evidence and alternative explanations' (1982a: 7).

Pinker's orientation was to give him a focus not on 'individualism' or 'collectivism', but on aspects of social life in general which gathered together such themes as stigma, giving and receiving, conditional altruism, access to land and property, and migration and civil war. He believed that this kind of focus on concerns of the middle range would make more accurate and useful our understanding of whatever principles might be advanced to improve policy and whatever actions might be adopted to deliver benefits when well-being or welfare was in question.

The analytical explorations which Pinker envisaged at this time were also discussed outside of *Social Theory and Social Policy*: thus, he distinguished between ideas of a 'welfare state' and a 'state of welfare' in his James Seth Memorial lecture of 1972, *The welfare state: A comparative perspective* (1973; the lecture is included as **Chapter Four** in **Part One** of this book). The first concept concerned specified forms of intervention by governments in the processes and outcomes of unregulated or 'inadequately' regulated market operations, while the second referred 'both to the subjective feelings of ordinary people about the nature of welfare, and to the complete range of activities by which they seek to enhance their own well-being through individual and collective endeavour'. In the interests of understanding and explaining faring well as a social phenomenon, '[t]he way in which ordinary citizens define and seek to enhance their own state of welfare merits as much attention as the ways in which academics define the welfare state' (see **Chapter Four, p 70**).

These points, for Pinker, applied to the study of any one country and to comparative studies. More was required by way of change than ecumenical nods towards the mere existence of differing ideas of moral or social progress. What Pinker regarded as essential was encapsulated in his distinction between 'those modes of enquiry which seek to establish the criteria by which one system of welfare can be deemed morally superior to another and those which seek to explain why there are similarities and dissimilarities between the welfare systems of different countries' (**Chapter Four, p 70**). While it is difficult in practice to keep them apart, the fact of their qualitative difference needed to be borne in mind. Within social administration and policy in the 1970s, Pinker detected a default normative position, 'strongly collectivist in value orientation', in which 'social welfare is assumed to be almost synonymous with institutional variants of what we term "the welfare state"' (**Chapter Four, p 70**). Many historical accounts of social policy had fallen into line, describing its growth as a 'kind of pilgrim's progress towards a promised land' (**Chapter Four, p 70**).[10] A consequence of conflating the perspectives Pinker had distinguished was to mistake judgement for social explanation. As a result, the academics' conception of the 'real' 'moral society', in itself unexceptionable, had led them into assuming for themselves 'the role of public guardians against the immoralities of the economic market', while overlooking in their perspective both that 'some citizens believe that the social market generates its own forms of injustice' and that there is 'a vastly complex range of human aspirations and activities … within and between different societies' (**Chapter Four, p 76**).

At the time, Roy Parker (1974) highlighted the value of Pinker's distinction between concepts of the 'welfare state' and 'states of welfare': 'Whereas the notion of a welfare state may provide a unified and unifying concept, states of welfare are individual and often irreconcilable. As he goes on to say, social administration has not shown much interest in this distinction, nor in the subjective definition of well-being'. Were the interest to grow, 'some challenging discoveries might be made obliging us to reconsider conventional views on how improvements in "welfare" might best be achieved' (1974: 568). As Pinker had already observed in *Social Theory and Social Policy*, we lack an understanding of 'why individuals define their needs as they do, and why these definitions so often appear to be at variance with those of the social scientists' (1971: 106).

Pinker, in *Social Theory and Social Policy*, singled out as exceptional the contribution of W.G. Runciman's *Relative Deprivation and Social Justice* (1972). Runciman had substantiated empirically the 'distance' between occurrences of low levels of grievance or resentment expressed by persons over their situation in respect of inequality when the rectification of the actual inequality involved was justified by appeal to Rawlsian 'social justice' (1971: 108–15). As Pinker noted, deeper insight into subjective levels of meaning may call into question some of the assumptions about the meanings of specific social conditions underpinning reformist normative preferences. Nevertheless, a focus 'on the subjective states of consciousness and expectations of the poor is necessary … if the concept of relative poverty is to have any meaning at all' (1971: 115). Valuing the ideas of one group above those of another in this kind of context would constitute a distortion of the truth about the meanings attached to social life by its participants.

Pinker indeed emphasises that we need to improve our understanding of public attitudes towards social services. To achieve this, we need 'better maps of the current levels of satisfaction and discontent and more convincing explanations of why people hold the range of attitudes and expectations they do' (1971: 110). This way, social theory and intellectual ideologies remain distinct, making it possible that a well-grounded understanding of social life may over time bring a change in everyday public understandings and meanings: 'Sociological theory does not enable us to distinguish "goodness" from "badness", although it may provide new forms of knowledge and insight which can be used for a variety of moral purposes' (1971: 130).[11]

In *Social Theory and Social Policy*, Pinker drew attention to the evident distinction in social life ('akin to a psychological proposition') between 'givers' and 'receivers'. In varying degrees, states of dependency and a shortage of resources can compromise the status of the receiver and act as widespread sources of stigmatisation (1971: 170). What citizens may expect of social services:

> is greatly affected by their prior experience of economic situations. A large proportion of those who use social services do so after having been stigmatized by adverse experiences in the economic market. Inequalities of knowledge and expertise also serve to reinforce feelings of inferiority and dependence, and these kinds of inequality persist in welfare relationships. Whenever self-help and independence are powerfully sanctioned values, the subjective facts of social consciousness impose inferior status on the dependent. (1971: 167–8)

As it happens, Pinker added, there are often contexts in which persons perceive themselves as solely receivers or givers, even though they are both, as in the case of the benefit claimant who pays Value Added Tax or the charitable donor eligible for tax relief.

It may be seldom that the explicit aim of social services is to perpetuate or extend stigma. However, the need to ration provision or the normative orientations of staff may be experienced as forms of coercion by the users of a service, and this subjective experience, whether intended or unintended, generates self-reinforcing perceptions of inferiority. Indeed, Pinker suggested, services may be stratified by the levels of dependency with which they deal (1971: 201, 207). Stigma itself will vary in its intensity among receivers of 'gifts' according to the variables of depth, distance and time. For the relatively young and fit, their prospective periods of independence serve to prevent any categorisation of them as in a state of dependency in relation to the fields of acute illness and education, whereas dependency is firmly associated with chronic illness in old age.

Pinker's treatment of stigma attracted comment. Julia Parker observed: 'Pinker has argued that stigma – the denial of citizenship – attaches most firmly to those states of dependency which are most complete and prolonged, such as old age and chronic mental or physical incapacity, precisely because the possibilities of services being reciprocated are so remote, and has suggested that this may help to explain the poor quality of public care for these particular groups' (1975: 175).[12] Anthea Tinker enlarged upon the experiences of older people in the context of Pinker's treatment of stigma and the exchange relationship (1992: 209–11).[13] Pinker himself also added that reparations and rewards for past service 'thin' the feelings of dependency. When social or spatial distance leads to remoteness and unfamiliarity, stigma may be more strongly enforced and felt. If dependence is of long duration, a person may adopt an identity very largely determined by the form of dependency in question. According to Pinker, the imposition of stigma 'is the commonest form of violence used in democratic societies ... it can best be compared to those forms of psychological torture in which the victim is broken psychically and physically but left to all outward appearances unmarked' (1971: 175). The phenomenon of stigma is of key significance in understanding the forms and aims of social services and the power imbalances in democratic societies in which, for the most part, conflict is institutionalised.[14]

Beyond question, then, one important achievement of *Social Theory and Social Policy* was to establish a framework for thinking about welfare and policy in which it became obligatory to consider familial and other sources of 'informal care' as priority areas of research.[15] At this stage, however, Pinker had specified few of the details of what kinds of research were required.

Social policy, a sociology of morals and marrying formal and informal care

During the 1970s, Pinker made explicit the areas of study he had in mind, under the heading of what he described as a 'sociology of morals':

> One of the tasks of a sociology of morals would be to clarify the nature and consistency of individual and public attitudes towards the varieties of mutual aid practised ... within families. We need to know far more about the preferred and actual forms of reciprocity and obligation which occur between strangers sharing a common citizenship and members of the same kin. A second task would be to re-examine the extent to which the values and assumptions which are implicit in social legislation support, weaken or modify the moral beliefs and practices of ordinary people. (1974: 8–9)

In *The Idea of Welfare*, Pinker maintained his argument that policy makers, welfare professionals and academics often adhere to ideas of social and individual welfare that are substituted for but in fact related problematically to the ideas of social and individual welfare held in ordinary life. There is a tendency to ascribe moral and epistemological superiority to particular ideas of welfare. However, the approach most likely to advance our understanding of the meaningfulness of social reality for the actors involved is the non-normative and sociologically descriptive study of *the plurality* of ideas, with each idea accorded an equal epistemological status. If the basic point was an amplification of his earlier position on the concept of welfare, this position was now complemented by a body of literature displaying contextual sensitivity in relation to cognate concepts. Robert Dingwall had argued the case in respect of the concepts of health and illness in his *Aspects of Illness* (1976), and others, notably Carrier and Kendall (1973, 1977, 1986), had treated a range of policy-related concepts similarly. Reservations, though, were expressed by Pinker that ideology was displacing theory in sociology (1979: 244). In his writing, Pinker always eschewed explicit references to 'phenomenology' and 'ethnomethodology' as models but an underlying concern with everyday meanings and practices, on 'the meanings of morality – and rules in general – in everyday life' (Douglas, 1970: 9), was nonetheless shared. In a review of the book at the time, it was shrewdly remarked that it is 'his maintenance of several conceptual themes (altruism; collectivism; the linkages between economic and social markets) which make it an intellectually stimulating and challenging book. It is his attack on the ideologies of the right and the left which makes it a brave book' (Jones, 1980: 598; see also Weale, 1980). Martin Knapp went a step further. He credited Pinker as being one of a select group of writers who, in his *The Idea of Welfare*, had responded critically to Titmuss's *Commitment to Welfare*. Pinker was instrumental in showing that Titmuss had 'generated a deal of confusion with his false dichotomy between "economic markets" and "social markets", a view which now seems to have been largely dispelled' (Knapp, 1984: 10; compare Pinker, 1979: 247).

Pinker discussed in specific terms the topics which an approach focused on a 'sociology of morals' illuminated. Family life might give unique 'affective support' (Goodin, 1985: 34), but Pinker also noted it as a realm in which desert as well as need were followed as principles of resource allocation, and it was adjudged in *The Idea of Welfare* as 'one of the most potent sources of what might be called the "counter-policies" of social welfare' (1979: 41). It can be added that neighbours might also be such a source, as Rex and Moore had noted in their study of Sparkbrook in Birmingham. Sometimes neighbours 'protected' each other by turning away unwanted visitors, 'a custom which was not very helpful to social workers' (1967: 70). In some detail, Pinker explored the conditions of reciprocity, in particular, how the interplay 'of self-interest and familial, communal and national loyalties places institutional limits on people's notions of felt obligations and entitlement. These loyalties', he added, 'will be seen to have a limiting effect if the idea of welfare is defined in internationalist terms, but from an alternative and more conditional point of view they can be seen as providing the moral justifications and the welfare resources by which our boundaries of obligation and entitlement can be extended from the narrowest of familial loyalties to include at least an awareness of national interests' (1979: 66). Under such scrutiny, a universalisable 'welfare ethic' appeared to be more of an aspiration than a reality (see also 1990: 45). As Forder observed: '[s]ome writers on social administration (e.g. Titmuss, 1970) believe that altruism can and should be fostered; others (e.g. Pinker, 1979) stress the importance of recognising the limits of altruism' (Forder, 1984: 49).

Arising from Pinker's review of the history of these sentiments and loyalties and the well-being associated with them, which covered chapters on Russia and America as well as his material on the UK, two important themes emerged. These were the salience of access to land and its ownership, and migration. Both themes were in due course developed in his later work. On the first, Pinker observed: 'in Russia the question of land reform dominated all other issues of social welfare. Matters such as the creation of modern forms of social service were of relatively marginal importance not only in what was achieved by the government but also in what was expected by the mass of the population. As late as 1917 eighty per cent of the Russian population were still peasants for whom the ultimate form of welfare was the possession of land' (1979: 142). On migration, Pinker concluded that for ordinary people, emigration was a traditional means by which they 'tried to provide for their own welfare on their own terms' (1979: 230). At the level of government action, discriminatory migration policies, together with tariff policies, may be counted as among the means by which 'modern welfare states continue to enhance the well-being of their subjects' (1979: 230).

Pinker's themes resonated with Pat Thane, who invoked them in the concluding 'Assessment' to her popular book *The Foundations of the Welfare State*. In particular, she accepted his position on the limits to altruism (1982: 289–90), and then drew on his idea that at the heart of the development of state welfare 'lies nationalism and the urge for national survival, which is acute not only in wartime but in periods of economic and social crisis' (1982: 293).

During the 1970s, therefore, Pinker had theorised the space on which he hoped that substantive research studies, on informal welfare practices and everyday attitudes towards and expectations of 'formal' social welfare services, would come to shed light. Jones, in his review for the *British Journal of Sociology*, questioned whether it would be a popular perspective because 'not only is Pinker bidding for the middle ground within social ideology, he is also bidding for a redirection of the discipline of social policy' (1980: 598). Some such research was indeed undertaken and published in a short span of time (see Parker, 1990; Offer, 1999a), and, on occasion, Pinker's discussions were acknowledged as a factor shaping the research (for example, Cecil *et al*, 1987: 2, 14–15). A new vocabulary had developed around discussions of informal welfare practices, including 'informal care' and 'carer' (see Twigg, 1994: 290–1). In social policy studies, knowledge was growing about a 'hierarchy of caring obligations' utilised in everyday theorising and practice by family members as they negotiated their caring responsibilities, and about the 'costs' and 'satisfactions' of 'caring'. It was beyond doubt that caring responsibilities fell mostly to women, though research also highlighted the contribution of young carers and married men caring for chronically ill wives. There was, though, less research than might have been expected centrally concerned with the interactions which families had with social workers, nurses based in communities and the police; also, 'networks' of advice-giving and general support remained in general at the margins of study.

Shortly after *The Idea of Welfare* had appeared in 1979, Pinker served as a member of the team chaired by Peter Barclay which was tasked in 1980 by the Conservative government to prepare a report on the future of social work, published in 1982 as *Social Workers: Their Role and Tasks*. The previous years had seen the performance of social work and the chief employer of social workers, local authority social service departments, become the target of sustained criticism, notably in Brewer and Lait's *Can Social Work Survive?* (1980). At the time, Harry Specht noted that this book had been 'warmly received by those who support the monetarist policies of the Thatcher government', and feared it could have 'a devastating effect on the quality and availability of services' (1981: 593). In the event, the Barclay Report was supportive of social work but urged the development of 'community social work', with a new focus and local mode of delivery: 'If every client, family and social problem is seen as a need requiring formal social work help or intervention, social workers will always be expected and expecting to do too much. If, however, social workers see and draw out the potential in others, their ability, in conjunction with others, to respond to need will be enlarged' (1982: 111). In particular, the Report advised that social workers should 'tap into, support, enable and underpin the local network of formal and informal relationships which constitute our basic definition of community' (1982: xvii).

Pinker declined to sign the main Report. An Appendix, 'An alternative view' (Pinker, 1982b; included as **Chapter Six** in **Part Two** of this book), recorded his reservations. He found the main Report naive in its presumption that with the notion of 'community' as its banner, agreement and harmony rather than conflict and alienation would result (a verdict that Geoffrey Pearson [1983] soon explicitly endorsed in *Critical Social Policy*). Roger Sibeon, in his *Towards a New Sociology of Social Work*, often cited publications on social work by Pinker in the 1980s, usually with references in one way or another to the modest esteem in which the profession held research, including his indictment that in professional social work, 'social work theory is rarely presented in testable form' (1991: 28; the Pinker source is Pinker, 1989: 86). According to Pinker, the most disadvantaged, stigmatised and excluded in society could become invisible to 'community social work', the privacy of clients and others might be jeopardised, and it appeared 'a romantic illusion' that locally based social workers alone could 'miraculously revive the sleeping giants of populist altruism' (see **Chapter Six, p 130**).

Later, Pinker (1990; in a chapter, 'The quest for community', reproduced as **Chapter Seven** in **Part Two** of the present book) expanded on his concern over the lack of evidence to justify the Report's confidence in 'the universal strengths of communities and the feasibility of harnessing them to the ends and means of formal social policy' (see **Chapter Seven, p 153**). The research of Philip Abrams (see

Bulmer, 1986) and others on neighbourhoods and care in the UK indicated that a policy of 'closer interlinkage between formal services and informal care' risked the creation of tensions, through the formal sector "colonising" the informal sector' (**Chapter Seven, p 154**). Attempting to 'interweave' the contrasted nature of 'natural' Gemeinschaft and bureaucratic Gesellschaft, social relationships might yield mutual incomprehension and dysfunctional consequences (Pinker, 1982a: 12). As Bulmer well knew, Pinker had already underlined (in 1979) that mutual aid in the family 'occurs within complex networks of interdependency involving power relations between and within generations and the sexes' (Bulmer, 1986: 116). These are features still apparently having to be independently rediscovered today, as in Nast and Blokland, 2014). A similar hiatus had also been pinpointed in one American study sensitive to the sociology of moral categories in ordinary life (Wellman, 1981: 185; the reference to Jack and Jill is to the traditional English nursery rhyme):

> overall ties link persons and not specific strands. The link between Jack and Jill encompasses more than just help with carrying a pail of water, and the specific kind of help given should be interpreted in the content of their overall relationship.

It may be added that, at this time, a further finding of significance to emerge from research into neighbourhoods and care was that 'natural helping networks' (the title of an early American study, [Collins and Pancoast, 1976]), as opposed to care provided primarily by one (often female) individual, were comparatively rare, at least in the UK (Allan, 1983).

On the foundations of welfare pluralism

Pinker's next book, *Social Work in an Enterprise Society*, appeared in 1990. It reflects, to a large extent, the development of his interests following his appointment as Professor of Social Work Studies at the London School of Economics in 1978. Some parts of the book focus on topical issues at that time, including the nature of the role of the Central Council for Education and Training in Social Workers and its emphasis on genericism (a full discussion of Pinker's sometimes controversial contribution to issues around social work education would require a separate book-length study), but there are sociologically and historically informed discussions of several themes of wider significance for social policy studies that cannot be omitted here.

Thus, in respect of the treatment of conceptions of agency and 'the personal', Pinker considered that in social administration and social work, difficulties arose over an 'excessive' disposition 'to attribute causation to structural rather than personal factors and to look for remedies in increased levels of equality and expenditure. To suggest that on occasion individuals can be the architects of their own misery would be labelled "judgemental", "pathologising" or "stereotyping"'

(1990: 44). In connection with the organisation of social work and training for social work, there had arisen, in contrast to the time of their origination in the Charity Organisation Society in the 19th century, a marked isolation from industrial and commercial concerns, and an institutionalised hostility 'to the competitive values of the economic market' (1990: 34). This isolation and hostility had left social workers with 'a distinctive set of social market values which reflect an unhelpful sense of moral superiority in the context of entrepreneurship, self-help, the profit motive and capitalism in general' (1990: 75). Yet, participation in economic markets enhances personal freedom, which is 'intrinsic to the idea of welfare' (1990: 130). (Pinker also viewed both Keynes and Beveridge as including the idea of freedom in their ideas of welfare [1979: 117].)

However, the first of his two chief concerns, mirroring the greater visibility of informal care as a topic, was to examine the growing trend to refer to 'welfare pluralism' or a 'mixed economy of welfare' (an approach Pinker had described as 'mercantilist' in 1979, to signal, with approval, its pragmatic, situation-based approach to matters of welfare). He took these expressions as equivalent, but suggested an important distinction about the underlying idea involved:

> It can refer to a system in which the range and variety of service providers is increased while the statutory authorities of central and local government retain the main responsibility for funding through transfer payments of one kind or another. It can also refer to the development of a new plurality of service providers as an alternative to statutory funding, with the ultimate goal of privatising the entire financial structure of social welfare. (1990: 126)

The idea, Pinker observed, was thus adaptable to both institutional and residual patterns of normative or ideological thought about social welfare (for Pinker, forms of selectivity and universalism in statutory services were compatible with either pattern of thought [1979: 7]). Pinker in fact concentrated on the review of policy proposals to 'mix' formal and informal forms of care contained in the Report by Sir Roy Griffiths, *Community Care: Agenda for Action*, in the process expanding on his reservations over the Barclay Report. The benefit of a wealth of recent research into informal care was now to hand. 'The quest for community', included as **Chapter Seven** in **Part Two** of the present book, was delivered initially as a plenary paper at the University of Ulster, Coleraine, for a conference launching a book portraying the results from a participant observation study funded by the DHSS, Northern Ireland. This book was *Informal Welfare* (Cecil, Offer and St Leger, 1987), a study of informal care in a town (Garvagh) in County Londonderry. Pinker's paper drew into the discussion research from across the UK. He identified the chief weakness of the Griffiths Report as:

> its explicit assumption that formal social services can be interwoven with informal networks of support, in conformity with entrepreneurial

and management requirements. Although there is evidence that informal care is sustained as much by egoistic as altruistic motives, it could still prove difficult to protect the distinctive character and integrity of informal care if it came under the regulation of professional social workers and formal care agencies. In addition there is no way of knowing how the incorporation of an entrepreneurial and managerial ethos will affect the values and practices associated with family and neighbourhood care.... Every generation has its own way of renewing the quest for community and the Griffiths Report is a significant step in that direction. Progress will depend on the extent to which entrepreneurial and managerial objectives can be reconciled with the values and practices of family and neighbourhood life. (**Chapter Seven, p 167**)

The other and related theme of most significance was Pinker's own exploration of his own relationship to the thought of Titmuss. In his Preface to Reisman's (1977) book on Titmuss, Pinker suggested that Titmuss's polarisation of economic interests and social interests, with social interests regarded by Titmuss as morally superior because of their intrinsic altruism, was misleading and unfortunate. In *Social Work in an Enterprise Society*, he regarded it as prompting social policy analysis to give, firstly, 'undue attention to the redistribution of wealth and not enough to the creation of wealth', with social policies thus expected to aim 'at greater equality ... based on the assumption that economic growth could be taken for granted', and, secondly, to neglect the possibility that 'through a competitive market economy ... both freedom and welfare could be enhanced' (1990: 40–1).

Pinker added that, although Titmuss was in favour of 'community care', 'he would have had little time for our present notions of decentralised, participatory community action which must be based on the assumption that equitable policies of positive discrimination and redistribution can be realistically pursued in the absence of firm administrative direction and control' (1990: 37). Indeed, Titmuss, in his famous essay 'The social division of welfare' (1958a), had distinguished statutory social services, occupational welfare (work-placed benefits) and fiscal welfare (allowances and concessions through the tax system), but took no account of either the voluntary or the informal sectors of care (**Chapter Seven, p 151;** see also Pinker, 1985: 101). In fact, in his commitment to an institutionalist philosophy of welfare provision, Titmuss was a welfare unitarist (though within the framework of universal unitarist provision, there was scope for selectivity). It was his view that the statutory social services 'constituted the most important institutional feature of a civilised society because the egoism of the private market alienated people from each other whereas the altruism embodied in the statutory public services united and elevated them' (Pinker, 2008; included as **Chapter Five** in **Part One** of the present book, **p 99**).

As Pinker noted, this was a form of analysis which Titmuss developed in depth in his *The Gift Relationship* (1970). Titmuss was convinced that the state should be the main funder and provider of social services 'because only the state had the authority to implement, without fear or favour, the redistributive policies that he considered necessary' (**Chapter Five, p 99**). In Pinker's judgement Titmuss's 'hostility to the mixed economy of welfare was uncompromising'; it would 'undermine the principle of equity, increase inequalities and weaken social solidarity' (1992: 276). When Pinker later reviewed *The World of the Gift* by Godbout and Caille, he noted sympathetically their view, contrary to Titmuss's analysis of statutory social services as embodying a gift relationship, that in such circumstances, the 'gift relationship' becomes 'an anonymous circulation network between strangers' (2000: 151). For Pinker, Titmuss was not a specialist in anthropology, sociology or economics. He had drawn on anthropology, sociology and economics selectively, mining them for certain theoretical perspectives and empirical findings which appeared to offer support rather than the opportunity to test out his normative commitment to welfare unitarism and its expansion. He was not a polymath. In similar vein, Fontaine has pointed out that Titmuss 'liked to describe himself as "a student of society"' (Fontaine, 2002: 418).

The freedoms and benefits offered by markets and the need to recognise the contextual and conditional nature of altruism in all social life, including statutory services, remained unexamined in Titmuss's form of idealist social analysis: the structural composition of his way of thinking focused on the means to the end of what he took to be 'moral growth' and the 'good society' and seemed to preclude engagement with the everyday production by people in their ordinary lives of what they regarded as their own and others' welfare (Offer, 1999a, 2006; Mann, 2009). For Pinker, Titmuss was adamant that freedom as a value was secondary to a guarantee of material welfare by the state (1995a). He was to suggest that Titmuss's ideal of social welfare:

> would impose nothing less than an intellectual and normative straightjacket on the diversity of policy ends and means that ought to characterise a free society. I preferred the idea of a pluralist mixed economy of welfare which took more account of the ambiguities and paradoxes of human nature and gave more opportunities for us all to pursue what *The Book of Common Prayer* describes as 'the devices and desires of our own hearts'. Titmuss, in his preoccupation with 'opportunities for altruism', would undoubtedly have endorsed the whole of this quotation which goes on to confess that 'we have followed too much the devices and desires of our own hearts'. (**Chapter Five, p 108**)[16]

The model of formal services provided in the form of a pluralist mixed economy of welfare, with appropriate regulation and safeguards, thus appealed to Pinker, provided that the 'mix' did not extend to familial care being coerced or colonised (1985: 117). Pinker has often noted the value for his own work of the precedent set by T.H. Marshall (Pinker, 1981, 2006a, 2006b, 2011; all included in the present book) in finding a path between the polarities of collectivism and individualism (and welfare and freedom) with his concept of 'democratic-welfare-capitalism' (Marshall, 1972).[17] The underpinning ideas for this reflective normative outlook, taken from John Stuart Mill's philosophical liberalism and fuelled by Pinker's own emphasis on the sociology of morals and cultural diversity, complemented the broader understanding of welfare matters for which he argued, including the scrutiny of the normative preferences of professionals and social policy academics themselves. This all came to the fore, for example, in the context of developing a comparative understanding of welfare in Japan and the UK:

> The way in which the provision of social welfare is organised and located in particular institutional settings is an integral part of the culture of a society, and such national characteristics should be taken seriously not only by upholders of the *status quo* but by those who hope to change it. The conservative tendency to defend traditional patterns of obligation and entitlement takes insufficient account of the extent to which tradition is the outcome of change. The radical challenge to traditional patterns of obligation and entitlement takes insufficient account of the extent to which they reflect authentic and popular beliefs about social welfare. A well-formulated theory of welfare gives as much attention to the distinctive features of national culture and tradition as it does to the formal context of social policy. (1986: 114–5)[18]

This outlook had indeed been a feature of the critical comments in *Social Theory and Social Policy* on both conservative and radical tendencies in intellectualist ideologies (1971: 146). With the passage of time, it is possible, as Baldock has implied, to find a degree of affinity between Pinker's critique on the Titmussian approach to social policy studies and latterly a more generic concern to criticise a culture of 'progressivism':

> Today, with the benefit of hindsight, it is clearer that the creation of state welfare systems during the twentieth century has been a typically modernist enterprise. The 'idea of social policy', as Robert Pinker (1979) so aptly called it, is not a populist one but is of a piece with Bauhaus, the social architecture of Le Corbusier, the urban planning movement and the conception of 'new towns'. These in their turn are all classic representations of a wider modernist movement represented in art, literature and, in different forms, in the ideas of socially responsible natural science and in utopian socialism. Twentieth-century modernism was the apogee of rationalism, the triumph of human knowledge over nature and of humane sentiments over brutishness and base instinct. The ideals of modernist social policy were not the product of the existing culture, as represented in established religion,

mass politics or the accepted tastes and manners of the day. Modernist thought, in all its forms, has always been elitist and self-consciously progressive – seeking to triumph over the limiting culture and prejudices of the present. Modernism, in so far as it was an ideology, was very much the province of intellectuals and their attempts to understand and control the modernity they saw developing around them. (Baldock, 1999: 468–9)

In this context, a rather peculiar assessment of Pinker's position on thinking about welfare was advanced by Lee and Raban (1988) and deserves some discussion. Lee and Raban viewed the early 1970s as a time when critical social analysis, generally drawing its strength from Marx's views on economics and society as displayed within capitalist social relations, began to focus on what were argued to be shortcomings of both the 'welfare state' and the study of 'welfare' itself. Social administration as a nascent academic discipline, heavily indebted to Beatrice and Sidney Webb and then to Richard Titmuss, had, by the early 1950s, become firmly established as the principal discipline of the social sciences concerned with welfare matters – coupling its hallmark empirical orientation with a precarious mixture of normative and social-scientific theories. Lee and Raban's primary concern was in fact to help in constructing a coherent fusion of the radical Marxist perspective with the milder reformist and revisionist aspirations characteristic of this Fabian socialist tradition or 'orthodoxy' which they had detected in social administration as a subject. However, in pursuing this objective, they needed to assess what Pinker had written.

Lee and Raban took the view that within the discipline it seemed that the post-war 'welfare state' 'had brought the "real" into closer approximation to the "ideal": post-war Britain was seen as being, in every essential respect, "the good society itself in operation". In these circumstances it was hardly surprising that academic commentaries on welfare had been largely conducted within a pragmatic, empirical and particularising idiom. This basically conservative idiom served, in turn, to mask the underlying assumptions of a consensus theory of welfare, politics and contemporary social problems' (1988: 2-3). Lee and Raban believed that the development of the Marxist critique prompted 'doyens of orthodox social administration' (1988: 3) to react in a somewhat hostile manner. In this context, Pinker is described as mounting a 'rearguard defence of "orthodox" social administration' (1988: 5).

This assessment radically distorts and undervalues the core of Pinker's contributions. Although he was adopting a perspective very different to that adopted by Lee and Raban, Pinker was himself calling into question premises of 'orthodox' social administration. By confronting social administration with the conditionality of altruism in ordinary life and the reality of everyday familial welfare practices, with their own culture and logic sometimes running counter to the normative assumptions of the discipline, Pinker was being uniquely heterodox, and proving in the process to be of real significance in the paths adopted in the longer term within social policy studies. His target was as much the normative theories prevalent in the discipline and what they served to eclipse from the research agenda as any difficulties which might be associated with the revival of interest in Marxist perspectives on welfare matters and, one might add, dogmatic marketisation.

Lee and Raban have not been alone in misreading Pinker. It should also be added that in an article on the post–1945 era called 'The changing face of social administration', the author, Robert Page, notes Pinker's advocacy of the need for more theory in the subject (Pinker, 1971, 1993) but makes nothing of his early and wide-ranging criticisms of Titmuss's perspective and what it eclipsed from view, such as everyday familiar practices associated with welfare and well-being (Page, 2010).

In a nutshell, Pinker wanted neither muffled nor megaphone ideology, but theory. Ideological forms of discourse, with their campaigning imperatives, were prone to the imprecision and subjectivity associated with conceptual ambiguities and mutation as circumstances changed. For Pinker, it was rigorous theory that was needed, theory which was genuinely broad enough to accommodate in its analyses and empirical understanding the actual ethical imperatives and welfare practices embedded in the social reality of a complex and pluralist society such as the UK. At a normative level, Pinker emphasised strongly that social policy studies in this mode did not entail a commitment to lowest-common-denominator populism (1984), but indicated rather that a plurality of providers was desirable if the needs of ordinary people were to be met. If an expression such as 'meeting needs' was to be meaningful, opportunities must be readily available such that the possibly conflicting values and voices associated with professional judgement, the availability or otherwise of resources, and the lived social reality could best find mutually acceptable resolutions and outcomes. Those opportunities were most likely to flourish in conditions where a plurality of welfare providers, cooperating as circumstances might suggest, pertained. Seen in this light characterisation of Pinker whereby he 'appears as an ideologue of the "common sensical" centre' (Pope *et al*, 1986: 110) seems only to discredit the authors.

It is worth recording too that after *The Idea of Welfare* had been published in 1979, with its discussion of the mixed economy of welfare and pluralism, , a second edition of Mishra's *Society and Social Policy* appeared in 1981. In it, Mishra declared: 'Pinker does not tell us what the objectives of such a mixed system might be and how it might be successfully established – in normative as well as institutional terms. His notion of a "middle path" of "conditional altruism" turns out to be rather vague as a normative proposition. ... In short, Pinker fails to provide a convincing "logic" of the mixed system – the institutional model – in which a predominantly market economy is underpinned by a system of social welfare in a stable and harmonious manner' (1981: 15). But if the basic arguments really were not already clear, Pinker subsequently provided generous further elaboration of the 'logic' involved, as we have seen.

Once the pendulum of political fashion swung away from welfare unitarism in the early 1990s, it should not be a matter of surprise that Pinker focused his attention on those policy analysts who wanted to replace it with a similarly unitarist model based on theories of competitive market individualism. David Green had set out the case for returning 'much of what we call the welfare state to civil society', which he saw as 'the realm of free choice and conscience as opposed to the realm of government command' (Green, 1993: 152–3). In Pinker's view, this claim served to exaggerate 'the civic virtues of private enterprise and voluntary service at the expense of the public sector in exactly the same way as Titmuss used to exaggerate to the opposite effect' the virtues which are inherent also 'in the long tradition of public service and statutory welfare provision that has its modern origins in nineteenth-century Britain' (1995b; included as **Chapter Nine** in **Part Three** of the present book, **p 199**).

More recently, Pinker has explored what we may call the necessary conditions in social life for welfare. In a sense, though, this interest in part again harks back to *Social Theory and Social Policy*, in this case, his concern that 'public utilities and services' such as 'libraries, museums parks and other freely available services' were routinely excluded from definitions of social policy, but that the distinction was arbitrary 'if the aim of a social service is the enhancement of individual or collective welfare' (1971: 147). A free public transport system, he mused, might even do more for individual welfare and community relations than increases in social security benefits (1971: 150). The point here was that the conceptualisation of 'welfare' had to move beyond the then conventional boundaries of social policy studies, even just to understand 'welfare' as construed within those normative boundaries (a point Rowntree had made less directly in *Poverty and Progress* [1941] and discussed in his portrayal of everyday recreational activities in *English Life and Leisure* [Rowntree and Laver, 1951]).[19] Once planted, the seed grew quickly. By 1973, Pinker considered that perhaps the 'most neglected index of popular welfare preference has been the private ownership of land'. While kinship is the first focus of altruism, it is predicated on security: the acquisition of property and its transmission across generations (with an associated sense of patriotism) is a search for security 'which can only be checked or denied by force' (1973; **Chapter Four, p 86**). Moreover, as noted when discussing *The Idea of Welfare*, he recognised a connection between the possession of land and everyday ideas of welfare. Later, he felt, I think judging himself ungenerously, that he had then failed to grasp 'the connections between the idea of land *as* welfare, citizenship, sovereignty, and nationhood and the impact of wars, notably civil wars, on the growth of citizenship and welfare' (2004a: 7). By 2006 Pinker was in any case describing land as a 'unique' aspect of welfare:

> Conventional theories of welfare fail to take these kinds of issue into account because they are based on conventional definitions of welfare that typically include essential goods and services like health care, social security, education and housing. The land on which these amenities stand

is, more or less, taken for granted. When matters of national sovereignty are involved, however, land becomes a unique welfare good. It represents the beginning and end of all our welfare aspirations. (2006b; included as **Chapter Eight** in **Part Two** of the present book, **p 186**)

Pinker considered now that, while the 20th century had created the concept of welfare rights, the secure ownership of land 'has always been a key determinant of status, wealth and the prospect of welfare' (**Chapter Eight, p 174**). Conventional issues about social welfare do not cause civil wars.

If the secure possession of land is absent, and thus a condition for welfare is not fulfilled, the phenomenon of migration becomes an issue. The control of immigration and the access of refugees and immigrants to the welfare arrangements of the host nation then arise as concerns related to the maintenance of the institutions of welfare in that nation, of considerable interest but probably less noticed than the plight of the refugees and immigrants themselves.

In the most recent years since his retirement from academic life, one of the driving forces behind Pinker's commitment to the work of the Press Complaints Commission has been his view that privacy requires protection, unless there is convincing evidence to the contrary, since privacy too serves as a condition and source of personal and social welfare (in Deacon *et al*, 2010: 66). A full assessment of this aspect of Pinker's contribution to public life, however, would need specialist consideration in a separate review beyond the limits of this Introduction.

Conclusion

Pinker characteristically insists on the disinterested excavation rather than normative or ideological interpretation of the everyday ideas and practices of altruism and welfare. This led him to conclude that, in the context of a parliamentary democracy, these everyday felt duties and obligations and the social understanding which they embody would place a brake on radical proposals for social reform, whether possessing collectivist or individualist origins: 'social services can only function effectively when their policy ends and means are based on, and developed out of, the customary values and expectations of the particular nation and people they serve' (2004a: 6). Pluralist rather than unitarist forms of welfare action were most likely to connect with and foster informed popular sentiment. In a democratic and open society, they offer the best prospect of finding negotiated and sustainable, if pragmatic, compromises between the ineluctably contested valuations of personal freedom and collective well-being.

Pinker in fact identified not one, but two 'great unitary ideologies that have dominated welfare theory for the past two centuries' (1995b; included as **Chapter Nine** in **Part Three** of the present book, **p 202**). On the political right, some theorists of competitive market individualism were ideologically committed to residualising the statutory social services and creating a unitary system of privatised welfare. On the left, anti-market socialists and collectivists were committed to residualising the private sector and creating a unitary system of statutory welfare.

As a pluralist, Pinker argued that all such ideological approaches to policy making were 'subject to a law of diminishing returns'. It was not possible for any single political ideology to encompass or reconcile the diversity of human principles and desires which find expression in the institutions of a free society. Such diversity is best met by following a middle way between these extremes, by sustaining a mixed economy of formal social services and respecting the distinctive institutional characteristics of the informal networks of mutual aid.

Pinker himself considered his two books of the 1970s, *Social Theory and Social Policy* and *The Idea of Welfare*, to have been written 'largely as critiques of Titmuss's analysis of the moral dynamics of welfare institutions, the uncompromising distinction he drew between egoism and altruism, and the unitary model on which his analysis was based' (2008; **Chapter Five, pp 107–8**). While Pinker respected Titmuss's pioneering contributions to the study of social policy, he was, from *Social Theory and Social Policy* onwards, elaborating in a variety of ways the drawbacks as he saw them to the normative assumptions which had framed Titmuss's choice of topics to be studied in detail and the analytical point of view which he had adopted.

New areas for research beckoned offering new kinds of evidence on conditional altruism and the 'forms of reciprocity and obligation'. Pinker's efforts to alter the intellectual foundations of social policy studies redirected attention towards the moral sentiments constitutive of everyday family and social life. In this way, we could improve our knowledge about the users of services as and when changes in those services were made once welfare-pluralistic perspectives were adopted. In particular, we should understand how 'users' can act as informed agents, putting together their own family's best outcome in term of its well-being from the range of resources that can be accessed. In the process, of course, these agents will need to make more or less successful adaptations to the unpredictable and possibly turbulent circumstances that form their environment. Pinker's efforts in this direction, this chapter has argued, contain insights we can ill-afford to ignore.

Julian Le Grand, the Richard Titmuss Professor of Social Policy at the London School of Economics since 1993, came to a similar conclusion in the 2006 edition of his *Motivation, Agency, and Public Policy*. In that version, he included within a Postscript a substantial extract from Pinker's essay 'From gift relationships to quasi-markets: an odyssey along the policy paths of altruism and egoism' (2006a; included as **Chapter Ten** in **Part Three** of the present book). 'Until I read Robert Pinker's essay', Le Grand now wrote (2006: 208):

> I had not realised the extent to which his two seminal works – *Social Theory and Social Policy* (1971) and *The Idea of Welfare* (1979) – had prefigured mine, and I am glad to have the opportunity to acknowledge this. He criticised simplistic notions of altruism and egoism, pointing out that most people are driven by a combination of altruistic and egoistic motives and that this fact must be taken into account in any

development of social policy. He emphasised that the extent of the sacrifice involved in an altruistic act is an important test of the scope and limits of altruism as a moral motivator. He was an early advocate of pluralistic systems of welfare – at a time when it was deeply unfashionable to do so. He argued that the most authentic rights that we have are those of the market place, and, in a phrase that has echoes of the pawn/queen analogy but that has a quality all of its own, points out that in unitary or state monopoly systems welfare users of social services are 'paupers at heart'.

Pinker also makes two points that I do not, but that I am happy to appropriate. First, familial altruism is a key element in overall welfare provision, driving as it does arguably the most important element of that provision, *viz* family support for those in need. This has just as strong a moral claim as Titmuss's altruism to strangers, and, moreover, has an essential practical value – probably more than does the kind of altruism that involves gifts to strangers. Second, monopolies, or unitary systems in Pinker's terminology, are poor at meeting the diversity of human needs and aspirations. Even more importantly, all systems of welfare provision create dependency, but that dependency is total when the provider is a monopoly. This is bad psychologically for users, but also carries major risks for them in the case of provider failure. Pluralism of providers (quasi-markets in my terminology) reduces the risk both of total dependency and of the distress created by total system failure.

Indeed, by way of a postscript here, we might introduce the case of a more recent challenging and potentially influential book on policy and theory by Graham Room, entitled *Complexity, Institutions and Public Policy: Agile Decision-Making in a Turbulent World*. In a discussion of poverty in this context, Room alerts us to the world of 'welfare policy from below'. Households at risk of poverty, as a consequence of benefits reforms, are 're-weaving the *bricolage* of their resources and relationships, in an effort to resist exclusionary pressures' (2011: 258). Here is the householder as 'agile institutional entrepreneur', reconfiguring 'the complex web of formal and informal social affiliations' in which they are enmeshed (2011: 257). There is, though, no mention of the path-breaking work by Pinker in opening up this territory to our gaze. Room also shows how *social institutions* themselves adapt to the terrain they are faced with, and that 'risky' decisions create turbulence, with unequal costs falling on the least agile. But again, here, while Room cites the essay 'The Irresponsible Society' by Titmuss (1963) on the growing power and influence on public policy of pension funds (2011: 295), there is no acknowledgement that *Pinker* had graphically shown that the entrepreneurial agility of kin was, as quoted earlier, 'one of the most potent sources of what might be called the "counter-policies" of social welfare' (1979: 41).

Notes

[1] In his academic career, Pinker was successively Head of the Sociology Department, Goldsmiths College London 1964–72, Lewisham Professor of Social Administration, Goldsmiths and Bedford Colleges London 1972–74, Professor of Social Studies, Chelsea College London 1974–78, Professor of Social Work Studies at the London School of Economics 1978–93, and Professor of Social Administration at the LSE 1993–96.

[2] Pinker's first book was *English Hospital Statistics 1861–1938* (1966).

[3] References to Pinker became frequent: the index to Taylor-Gooby and Dale (1981), for instance, lists a dozen entries, mostly pointing to significant engagements with his ideas. *Social Theory and Social Policy* was translated into Dutch, Serbo-Croat, Japanese and Korean.

[4] *The Idea of Welfare* was one volume (the ninth) in an influential series of 'Studies in Social Policy and Welfare' of which Pinker was Series Editor from 1975 to 1985, published by Heinemann of London. T.H. Marshall's *The Right to Welfare and Other Essays* (1981), to which Pinker contributed, was the fourteenth volume in the same period. Pinker was editor of the *Journal of Social Policy* from 1977 to 1981 and Chair of the Editorial Board from 1981 to 1985.

[5] Howard Glennerster, also at the LSE, has seen Pinker's reservations about Titmuss as 'emerging from within the social policy community itself': 'Bob Pinker was critical of Richard's brand of social administration (Pinker 1971; 1979). It was too prescriptive and it was too dismissive of any kind of market exchange. Yet, social policy depended for its revenue on the success of that despised economic sector' (2014: 3). A few other social policy specialists pursued broadly complementary and independently formed lines of thought. The writings of Joyce Warham, for example, displayed on occasion a cognate intellectual disquiet (1970, 1973, 1978). Warham was concerned with the systematic mapping of the social contexts and matters of moral judgement influencing the formation and implementation of social policy, and with the relationships between sociology and the study of social policy. For Warham, what may be defined as 'welfare' by policy makers 'may not be perceived as such by many of those who are at the receiving end of social services' (1978: 61). On the life and work more generally of Titmuss, see his daughter's study (Oakley, 2014).

[6] As, for instance, by Daly (2011).

[7] Deacon and Mann curiously describe Pinker as 'almost wholly' neglecting 'agency' (1999: 415). A no less questionable claim about social policy and administration in general has been made: 'in the 1960s and 1970s', Welshman reported, 'the notion of human agency was ignored' (2004: 226).

[8] Pinker's 'Populism and the social services' (1984) recorded reservations about appeals to an alleged populist 'consensus' as a sound basis for policy.

[9] Pinker also expressed reservations over the inference drawn from the utopia-regarding concept of 'alienation' that alienation was all-pervasive under capitalist social relations, as proposed by the 'young' Marx in the 1840s and made influential in part by a recent selection of Marx's writings edited by Bottomore and Rubel (Marx, 1963).

[10] It is only comparatively recently that this historiographical approach has been challenged comprehensively (see Finlayson, 1994; Harris, 2002; see also Offer, 2006a).

[11] Given that Pinker had established his position with careful argument, it was difficult to see a just basis for charges that Peter Leonard advanced against him, of an 'emphasis on the *moral rather than the social science* base of the discipline of social policy and administration' and '*frantic attacks* on Marxism and the radical Left in general'. Leonard admitted, however, 'the controlled rationality of most of the book' (1972: 91, italics added). The discussions of Pinker in Plant, Lesser and Taylor-Gooby (1980: 133-9) and Taylor-Gooby (1981) appear to interpret arguments

that he had advanced for the repositioning of the *focus of study* of social policy as entailing moral prescriptions about what 'welfare' and 'need' *ought* to mean, whereas Pinker had taken pains to establish that this normative concern should be regarded as a distinct question to be answered separately.

[12] Julia Parker felt that the hypothesis might be 'difficult to prove'. In this connection, she pointed out that it 'also seems likely that the inherent nature of severe mental or physical handicap may inhibit or deter the concern or attention both of the medical profession, who can expect little improvement in the condition of their patients, and of social workers, who may also find their attempts to help unrewarding. From the public at large the chronically disabled tend to be hidden away but, so far as they are visible, they often fail to arouse sympathy' (1975: 175). However, she added a point which Pinker would endorse fully: even if his hypothesis were correct as a matter of empirical fact, 'that is not to say that such a situation is unchangeable. The problem becomes one of how the attitudes and values which operate to deny citizen status to dependants can be modified and altered' (1975: 175).

[13] George and Wilding related the value placed on 'individualism' in social life to Pinker's treatment of stigma and the exchange relationship (1976: 121–24).

[14] Titmuss responded somewhat sharply to Pinker's observation that 'Public services may have a greater propensity to stigmatise' (1971: 175): 'Greater than what? Private enterprise? Private markets? We are not told. What may be true is that "Public services have a greater propensity to be criticised"' (Titmuss, 1974: 45–46). In fact, Pinker had specified the 'private sector'. Plant, Lesser and Taylor-Gooby contended that in Pinker's discussion of stigma, the concept was 'reduced to the social psychology of stigma' (1980: 133), but this verdict does not accord with the significance he bestows on power imbalances.

[15] While Pinker carefully studied Spencer as a sociological theorist relevant to social policy studies, he overlooked his typological 'division of welfare' by source. 'We have', Spencer had written in his *Principles of Ethics* of 1892/93, 'the law-established relief for the poor by distribution of money compulsorily exacted; with which may fitly be joined the alms derived from endowments. We have relief of the poor carried on by spontaneously organised societies, to which funds are voluntarily contributed. And then, lastly, we have the help privately given – now to those who stand in some relation of dependence, now to those concerning whose claims partial knowledge has been obtained, and now hap-hazard to beggars' (1910 [1893]: 376). In 1984, A.W. Vincent challenged Pinker's claim (1971: 29–30) that 'Spencer's vigorously individualistic doctrines of self-help found expression in the work of the COS [Charity Organisation Society]' (1984: 353). Vincent is correct in that most of the COS leadership owed little to Spencer (Thomas Mackay is an exception), although a recent interpretation of Spencer (Offer, 2010) suggests that both Pinker and Vincent fail to allow in their characterisations of his social theory that it explicitly bestows upon individuals a *social* self-consciousness.

[16] See Pinker (2011; included in **Chapter Two, Part One** of the present book) for his associated views on the extensive and collectivist social and economic reorganisation envisaged in Peter Townsend's (1979) *Poverty in the United Kingdom*.

[17] Low (2000) has reappraised Marshall on 'citizenship' and 'class' (alongside of the Idealist philosopher Henry Jones).

[18] The layers of cultural meaning associated with 'need' and the 'meeting' of 'need' are discussed further in Ignatieff (1984; see also Dean, 2010).

[19] The Arts Council of Great Britain, created in 1946, has been viewed as 'a minor aspect of the welfare state' (Hewison, 1995: 29). Interestingly, John Maynard Keynes, who, as Chairman of the Council for the Encouragement of Music and the Arts (CEMA), played a large role in fostering its successor, the Arts Council, was worried that in CEMA's policies '"welfare" was

being developed at the expense of standards' (Hewison, 1995: 39; see also Leventhal, 1990). Keynes preferred metropolitan aesthetic excellence over the cultivation of popular culture.

On social policy studies

John Offer

Pinker's best known book is *Social Theory and Social Policy*, published in 1971. Its primary task was to review the problematic assumptions and methods in the study of social policy which Pinker found in the new academic subject of what was then called 'social administration'. Later, in 2000, Pinker gave a lecture offering a bird's-eye view of some of the formative influences he experienced as a Research Officer and student from the mid-1950s at the London School of Economics, which gave him his abiding interest in the broad field of social policy studies.[1] The same lecture also introduced some of the chief research concerns which were to occupy him when he launched himself on his subsequent career in academic life. It does seem appropriate, therefore, that this lecture, 'The ends and means of social policy: a personal and generational perspective', should, in this selection of Pinker's writings, substitute for the full elaboration of his ideas which *Social Theory and Social Policy* provides. So we have placed it first as **Chapter One** in this selection. It provides a basic context in which all the other material included in this volume can be located.

As far as the discussion in this first chapter is concerned, neither Pinker nor those whom he was criticising were particularly wedded to the expression 'the Welfare State' as an attempt to describe the nature of what they were studying. Both Pinker and Richard Titmuss considered that this expression was so lacking in clear meaning that it should be only introduced into analysis to be discarded as unfit for purpose (the origins of and difficulties with the expression 'the welfare state' are extensively discussed in Veit-Wilson, 2000 and Wincott, 2003, 2015). However, for Pinker, there was a particular difficulty about the meaning of the idea of 'welfare' itself, which he felt was being taken for granted and thus left unexamined in the academic subject's own deliberations. In place of a focus on building up pictures of 'need' as theorised and met in everyday life, and how in interactions between people, the nature of what was to be accepted as 'well-being' was routinely negotiated and accomplished, the subject itself was in effect imposing on social reality an interpretation of what it believed 'welfare' and associated ideas *ought* to be taken to mean.

It might be imagined that Pinker's line of criticism owed something to postmodernist ideas. However, this would be a false idea. Some of the important points against and for a postmodernist perspective were reprised in Peter Taylor-Gooby (1994), and also Sue Penna and Martin O'Brien (1996). A fairly typical claim on behalf of a postmodernist perspective on social policy is that it gives us the opportunity to interrogate *the assumptions about the identity* of situations or persons that come to be embedded deep down in the structure, architecture and applications of a policy. It does this 'in a way that enables us to rethink and resist questionable distinctions that privilege some identities at the expense of others. A postmodern policy analysis would not take identity as pre-given', but would see it as constructed in the narratives, texts and discourses associated with policy; it thus 'holds out the prospect of highlighting how policy discourses and public policies themselves are implicated in the construction and maintenance of identities in ways which have profound implications for the allocation of scarce resources' (Schram, 1993: 349).

However, Pinker's criticisms were voiced significantly earlier in their date than these comments. He was without doubt calling into question beliefs which in some quarters were taken as being *universally* shared. But it seems to me that he was doing so in a manner that did not involve a loss of faith in 'rationality' and 'science' in general. Instead, he was pointing out that in specific cases where an 'expertise' in knowing about what it was that counted as 'welfare' was claimed, there had arisen a confusion between (contestable) judgements of value, or normativity, and what could be taken as *description*. Moreover, this was occurring in a context in which it was simply important that the two needed to be distinguished.

Another way of expressing this point is to say that, for Pinker, Titmuss was *not*, on reflection, focused on trying to describe as objectively as possible how 'welfare' and related ideas such as 'need' were used, and the conditions in which altruistic acts were regarded as called for. But this focus was, for Pinker, a legitimate and desirable focus, and would build up much-needed knowledge on to what he elsewhere referred to as the 'sociology of morals' (1974: 8–9). In contrast, Titmuss had, in effect, endeavoured to identify an underlying, more 'real' and perhaps more 'objective' and 'universal' meaning for 'welfare' and similar ideas. But, in fact, this attempt was doomed to fail. All it could yield was an additional normative claim about what 'welfare' *ought* to mean, and not an 'objective' claim reflecting the condition of the 'sociology of morals' in the UK or elsewhere. And this neglected point was the one that Pinker was emphasising.

Thus, Pinker was criticising simply this *particular* attempt to discount diversity and enthrone in its place (a dubious) 'rationality' and 'universality'. As is probably already apparent, Pinker is in favour of welfare pluralism, not for any broader commitment to postmodernism, whether as a theory or an ideology, but for the reasons outlined above.

Like many others who were encountering sociology and social science generally for the first time in the late 1960s and the 1970s, Pinker's reading of *The Social Construction of Reality* by Peter Berger and Thomas Luckmann, originally published in 1966, was a significant influence on his thought. This book argued that the morals, values and beliefs shared among people in social life are products of everyday, common-sense knowledge. It is by the construction, and reconstruction, of inter-subjectively shared meanings that we achieve mutual understanding and by which concepts such as 'welfare' are given their meanings and their legitimacy. Through his familiarity with that book, Pinker could go on to apply insights relevant to understanding social policy from the phenomenology of Alfred Schütz (1972) and symbolic interactionism, as developed by George Herbert Mead (1967). When reflecting on the sociology of everyday life, Sarah Neal and Karim Murji recently wrote that:

> in everyday life social relations, experiences and practices are always more than simply or straightforwardly mundane, ordinary and routine. Rather, everyday life is dynamic, surprising and even enchanting; characterized by ambivalences, perils, puzzles, contradictions, accommodations and transformative possibilities. Focusing on what the ordinary is involves an immersion in the seemingly unremarkable and routine relationships and interactions with others, things, contexts and environments. (2015: 811–12)

When compared with other writers on social policy matters at the time, a hallmark of Pinker's thinking was that he too experienced everyday life as enchanting. It was his familiarity with perspectives on 'the everyday' derived from sociology which inspired much of his writing. This feature was then unusual, but it is one of the features which is a thread recurring in the chapters in this section, and his work as a whole.

This book should indeed provide abundant evidence that while Pinker readily acknowledged the significance of the work done on policy matters by such key figures as Titmuss and Peter Townsend, he was pioneering a broader, more pluralistic conception of what the field of social policy studies should embrace, including the differing points of view provided by some other social science disciplines. It should also show that Pinker was developing a research programme different to the 'political economy' approach that perhaps was epitomised in the late 1970s by Ian Gough's *The Political Economy of the Welfare State* (1979) and Norman Ginsburg's *Class, Capital and Social Policy* (1979). Within the frameworks of the sweeping structural narratives they adopted, everyday experiences received short shrift. In that regard, the approach was reductive. For Pinker, it was at fault in that it eclipsed from view the social significance of everyday life. For some time now, however, the time has been ripe for Pinker's own voice on how the study of social policy should be advanced to be retrieved. As Pinker himself said, such a reductive approach shifted too far 'the focus of the debate about social welfare from micro to macro issues' (1983: 154).

It is fair to claim, then, that Pinker was an early and influential advocate of the view that invaluable knowledge was to be gained from ethnographical studies in the advancement of the understanding of social policy and ideas of welfare as features of social life. That Pinker may not himself have undertaken ethnographic fieldwork is a side issue. The fact of key significance is that he had been convinced that the approach adopted by ethnography was able to yield unique insights. These were capable of being set against less directly faithful accounts derived from other sources which were more concerned with theoretical and/or ideological beliefs, which might run the risk of giving a *reinterpretation* to the social reality in question, in the process losing sight of the meaning that it possessed at the outset.

In this regard it is interesting to note that as recently as 2014, in the neighbouring discipline of public administration, we can encounter an urgent plea from Rhodes that the insights available from ethnographic research are still not universally shared: 'ethnographic fieldwork provides texture, depth and nuance, and lets interviewees explain the meaning of their actions. It is an indispensable tool and a graphic example of how to enrich public administration' (2014: 317). So, Rhodes continues (2014: 321):

> the task is to unpack the disparate and contingent beliefs and practices of individuals through which they construct their world; to identify the recurrent patterns of actions and related beliefs. The resulting narrative is not just a chronological story. Rather, narrative refers to the form of explanation that disentangles beliefs and actions to explain human life. Narratives are the form theories take in the human sciences, and they explain actions by reference to the beliefs and desires of actors. People act for reasons, conscious and unconscious (Bevir, 1999: chs 4 and 7).

'Social theory and social policy: a challenging relationship' forms **Chapter Two**. It is an essay especially written for the present book, although some parts were delivered at conferences and a section also originally appeared in 2011 in *The Greek Review of Social Research*. In this chapter, Pinker embarks on more thoroughgoing discussion of the role of and difficulties faced by social policy research in democratic societies. In the process, he discusses the work of the philosophers Karl Popper and Hilary Putnam. According to Pinker, theories are highly summarised versions of reality to begin with, and when they are shielded from full exposure to the evidence of the social world, they become ideologies. Therefore, our methods and conduct of enquiry must be based on accuracy of statement, objectivity of description and dispassionate weighing of evidence. Pinker takes issue with writers who insist that *all* knowledge is made relative by the normative contingencies of given times and places. With reference to Durkheim, Pinker goes on the make a key distinction between descriptive theory (concerned with what *is*) and normative theory (concerned with what *ought to be*). Pinker cautions us that:

> Drawing distinctions between scientific theories, normative theories and ideologies is a difficult task because it involves matters of degree as well as of kind. The first distinction to be drawn is whether or not the theory is set out in a testable and falsifiable form. The second concerns the degree to which unprejudiced consideration is given to new evidence and possible alternative explanations. (**Chapter Two, p 53**)

For Pinker, the theoretically informed understanding that is required in particular, and as distinct from ideology, embraces the relationship between the elements of the 'mixed economy of welfare': private, statutory and voluntary sources of social service provision. Pinker also briefly indicates how imperatives of security and control coexist with those of freedom and risk, both within and beyond the sphere of welfare activities. However, the detailed nature regarding what Pinker has to say about these particular matters, and about the nature of felt obligation and familial altruism and how these informal welfare practices are strengthened, weakened or modified by formal social services, is of course to be unfolded in subsequent chapters.

Another key concern of 'Social theory and social policy – a challenging relationship' is to discuss afresh, as two 'case study' illustrations of the relationship, the 'personal culpability' thesis on the causation of poverty (based on 'behavioural' explanations which pinpoint the personal shortcomings of the poor themselves) and the contrasting 'victim' thesis (based on 'structural' explanations which focus on the disadvantages that the unequal distribution of wealth, income and life chances impose on the poorest members of unequal societies). In this connection, Pinker reviewed Peter Townsend's work in *Poverty in the United Kingdom* (1979) and its use of the 'victim approach'.

On the central topic of the causation of poverty, Pinker is not persuaded by the strongly ideological forms of either the individualistic 'personal culpability' thesis or structural 'victim' thesis. He aligns himself with what he understands T.H. Marshall's position to be (Marshall, 1981: 119) in which collectivist social services contribute to the general enhancement of social welfare as long as their interventions do not subvert the system of competitive markets. Indeed, Pinker argues that Townsend's action plan to try to combat inequality in the UK entailed 'an awesome concentration of coercive powers in the institutions of central government' (**Chapter Two, p 56**), and took no account of its likely and negative impact on wealth creation, without which there would be no resources available for distribution or redistribution.

Pinker also introduces a brief discussion of the work of Amartya Sen on the capability approach and its relevance to poverty analysis. Sen was awarded the Nobel Prize for Economics in 1998. Since this approach is attracting rapidly increasing interest, we should perhaps expand a little more on what Pinker has to say. The capability approach is primarily concerned with what people are able to do and become, in terms of their freedom to achieve well-being, not what resources they have, or how they feel. In analysing well-being, Sen believes we should shift our primary focus from income to the actual functionings that motivate people and the capabilities they substantively possess. Here, 'functionings' refer to the various things a person succeeds in doing, while 'capabilities' refer to a person's real or substantive freedom to achieve such functionings (Sen, 1992, 1993, 1999; Nussbaum 2000; Clark, 2005).

Thus, according to Hick's recent assessment:

> The capability approach offers a framework for poverty analysis which prioritises capabilities (ends) over resources (means), adopts a multidimensional perspective and takes a broad focus on the constraints that may restrict human lives … [It] can provide additional coherence to the concept of deprivation, not because the concept of capabilities should replace that of deprivation but because the concept of deprivation should focus on people's capabilities. (Hick, 2012: 301)

Although the question of how people have come to acquire the functionings and capabilities needs to be left open, the capabilities approach of Sen does allow us to distinguish between cases where we choose the outcome and cases where we have no opportunity to make a choice. Townsend's work has attracted criticism for not having this feature (Offer, 1999b), although, as it happens, this is not an argument that Pinker himself develops when he comes to consider Townsend.

Chapter Three, 'Stigma and social welfare', was originally published in *Social Work* in 1970 (vol 27, no 4). At that time, the concept of 'stigma' was frequently being referred to in social policy discussions, particularly in association with the potentially demeaning process of proving a person's eligibility in the UK for certain social security benefits by undergoing a 'test' of (low) income (Kay, 1972). The concept had recently gained expanded general currency through the popularity of the book by the sociologist Erving Goffman *Stigma: Notes of the Management of Spoiled Identity* (1968a; see Offer, 1999b, ch 5). Pinker's treatment of the concept, here and in *Social Theory and Social Policy*, was original. In essence, he was setting out the need for research which would show whether, in everyday life, there is a distinction made between 'givers' and 'receivers' of services, in which the values of the economic market are also reflected in social welfare systems. Thus, again, issues of felt obligation, or its absence, are significant. Given those connections, he cautions that stigmatisation is 'a highly sophisticated form of violence in so far as it is rarely associated with physical threats or attack. It can best be compared to those forms of psychological torture in which the victim is broken psychically and physically but left to all outward appearances unmarked' (**Chapter Three, p 67**). Robert Walker's *The Shame of Poverty* (2014) has recently explored this landscape from within a comparative perspective.

Chapter Four is Pinker's James Seth Memorial lecture of 1972 delivered in Edinburgh, entitled 'The welfare state: a comparative perspective' (originally published in 1973 in London by Bookstall Publications). This lecture functions as a bridge between the earlier *Social Theory and Social Policy* (1971) and *The Idea of Welfare* (1979). The problems which the first book exposed, particularly in regard to an assumption by many British social policy scholars that there was an bottomless reservoir of individual altruism waiting to be channelled by the state towards meeting the collective needs of 'strangers', was now being partnered by a searching international and comparative curiosity about the sociology of morals as embedded in welfare activities. Pinker was charting some of the main historical currents which differentiated the experiences of Britain, America and Russia in the 19th and 20th centuries.

Through exploring the contrasting popular cultures and the political and moral values involved, he was contributing to explaining their diverse social welfare provisions, especially over the balance between provisions based on self-help and those emanating from the state. On America, for example, Pinker chiefly attributes the relative lack of collective welfare provision to 'the sheer success of capitalism in America' (**Chapter Four, p 78**). In America, 'the social theories of Spencer and Sumner have proved more reflective of popular opinion than either the reformist tradition in American sociology, which originated in the Chicago school, or in its more radical manifestations' (**Chapter Four, p 79**). In Pinker (1979), a focus in an expanded form on internationalist themes indeed became one of its principal features. That book deliberately aimed to advance comparative research. Such research was still in its infancy, and perhaps conducted with an arguably and regrettable Anglocentric accent. For instance, Asa Briggs had noted already that specialists in social administration 'have collected comparative data, but they have naturally enough used them more frequently for practical than for historical purposes. The "uniqueness" of Britain has been emphasized to the neglect of the study of trends and tendencies in other countries' (1967: 27–8).

The Seth lecture also touched briefly on migration, immigration and imperialism. As we will see, Pinker took up such themes several years later in more detail. Here, for now, we might just underline one prescient observation from this lecture. For Pinker, 'perhaps the most neglected index of popular welfare preference has been the private ownership of land, either as a means of livelihood or as a location for property' (**Chapter Four, p 86**).

A notable feature of the lecture is that, as Pinker mention in the text, it was written at the time when the UK was joining the Common Market. Now of course, over 40 years on, the UK is preparing to make its exit. In the UK back in the 1970s, the European Communities Act 1972 provided for the UK's accession to the Common Market (now the European Union [EU]) under the Conservative Prime Minister Edward Heath on 1 January 1973. The opposition Labour Party led by Harold Wilson was much more deeply split about joining than the government. For Ken Clarke, then a junior member of Heath's government, 'the most numerous opponents were from the anti-capitalist left who regarded the whole European project as some kind of capitalist plot which they rightly felt would prevent any further movement towards the central command economy to which the Labour Party aspired' (2016: 66). Although at no point was a referendum required, when Labour formed the government in 1974 Wilson had already promised a referendum on the UK's membership, given Labour's internal splits over the Common Market. This referendum was held on 5 June 1975. Across the UK the resulting vote was clear. Overall the vote was 67% for staying in, and 33% for leaving.

For this printing of the Seth lecture, over 40 years on from its original appearance, Pinker has added a brief *Afterword*. In particular, he explains how his reading of Titmuss led to the contrast he develops in the lecture between the ideas of a 'welfare society' as opposed to a 'welfare state'.

The Seth lecture is followed by 'Richard Titmuss and the making of British social policy studies after the Second World War: a reappraisal', which forms **Chapter Five**. This was originally a lecture delivered in Norway, at the University of Bergen, on 5 December 2007. It draws quite extensively on Pinker's own earlier essay of 2006, 'From gift relationships to quasi-markets: an odyssey along the policy paths of altruism and egoism' (thus only non-overlapping parts of that earlier essay are reproduced in **Chapter Ten**, in **Part Three** of this collection, including Pinker's discussion of the ideas of Julian Le Grand).

In the Titmuss essay, Pinker begins with his impressions of the man and his early experiences, and how his thoughts on the ends and means of social policy developed to maturity. Titmuss possessed no university degree, yet the London School of Economics appointed him to the new Chair of Social Administration in 1950, when he was 42 years old. Beyond question, Titmuss's study of the wartime history of the health and social services, *Problems of Social Policy*, which appeared earlier in 1950, was received so well that the transition was a smooth one. With his wife, Kay, he had already published in the area of demography, *Parents' Revolt*, on the declining birthrate, in 1942. It seems to have been only after his appointment that his knowledge of economics, for example, was subjected to some scrutiny (see Fontaine, 2002). Note that among the publications by economists which did make a favourable impression on Titmuss in, for example, *Social Policy* (1974), were those of Kenneth Boulding (1967, 1968) and John Kenneth Galbraith (1970).

Pinker pinpoints a number of distinctive and often controversial features which are characteristic of Titmuss's collectivist and unitary approach to the discussion of social policy and social problems. These include a framework of universal services in which there was a place for selectivity, which would foster the aims of enhancing social integration and social solidarity and reducing inequality.

The essay also explores the 'conditional' as opposed to, for Titmuss, the open-ended nature of altruism and reciprocity in everyday life. The main focus of attention in this respect is *The Gift Relationship* (1970). An article by the economist Kenneth Boulding (1967) had already stimulated Titmuss. Boulding had discussed the boundary between 'the economic' and 'the social', and the socially integrative role, and therefore the moral superiority, of social policy as opposed to economic policy. In *The Gift Relationship*, Titmuss uses voluntary blood donations as a case study to provide a test of where the 'social' begins and where the 'economic' ends. Titmuss tapped into French social anthropology for the title of this study, in the shape of *The Gift* (*Essai sur le don*) by Marcel Mauss (1990), originally published in 1925. It was Robin Oakley, his son-in-law, and a sociologist at Bedford College, who introduced Titmuss to this book in 1967, and to other anthropological writings on the gift relationship (Fontaine, 2002: 419). For Titmuss, the study gives us a lesson in how we can provide and extend 'opportunities for altruism in opposition to the possessive egoism of the market place' (Titmuss, 1970: 13).

The anthropologist Mary Douglas believed that Mauss would have disapproved of the use Titmuss made of his work. According to Douglas, Mauss would have said 'Nonsense!' to Titmuss's idea 'that the archetypal pure-gift relationship is the anonymous gift of blood, as if there could be an anonymous relationship. Even the idea of a pure gift is a contradiction' (Douglas, 1990: x; see also Fontaine, 2002: 424).[2] In a recent review of Mauss's work, Hart has observes that 'Mauss's chief ethical conclusion is that the attempt to create a free market for private contracts is utopian and just as unrealizable as its antithesis, a collective based solely on altruism' (2014: 41). Thus Mauss himself rejects the Titmussian binary opposition for which Titmuss uses Mauss as a source. Hart adds that, for Mauss, there are

> two prerequisites for being human: we must each learn to be self-reliant to a high degree and to belong to others, merging our identities in a bewildering variety of social relationships. Much of modern ideology emphasizes how problematic it is to be both self-interested and mutual. Yet the two sides are often inseparable in practice, and some societies, by encouraging private and public interests to coincide, have managed to integrate them more effectively than ours. Human institutions everywhere are founded on the unity of individual and society, freedom and obligation, self-interest and concern for others. The pure types of selfish and generous economic action obscure the complex interplay between our individuality and belonging in subtle ways to others. (2014: 41–42)[3]

In this context, Pinker himself believed there was the risk that when the state 'becomes directly involved in the informal sector of social care and sets out to create partnerships with family members and other volunteers, it tends to reduce disinterested acts of altruism to the status of "unpaid work", regulated by bureaucrats and professionals' (2000: 151): Titmuss had not foreseen that the state could swiftly superimpose its own order on informal and communal gift relationships, to the extent that they are usurped by a network of formal rights and obligations.

For Pinker, however, a potentially open-ended commitment to altruism would lead to the collapse of the wealth-creating capability of competitive markets, with the paradoxical consequence that 'gifts' to 'strangers' would in all likelihood disappear. Indeed, Pinker concluded that Titmuss was trapped in this position, flying in the face of what all moral decision-making demands, of wanting to prohibit people from making the 'wrong' choice so that they could be 'free' to make the right choices.

Pinker has also added his own *Afterword* to this chapter. In this, he shares with us his own unique insights into the character of Titmuss in the context of a full review of the recent book by Ann Oakley, Titmuss's daughter, *Father and Daughter: Patriarchy, Gender and Social Science* (2014).

Notes

[1]   Pinker's research work on residential care for older people for Peter Townsend's (1962) book *The Last Refuge* is discussed in Johnson, Rolph and Smith (2010: 7–8). For his work for Brian Abel-Smith, see Sheard (2013).

[2]   In the introductory essay to this book on 'Rethinking approaches to welfare', we saw Pinker making clear that Godbout and Caille in *The World of the Gift* (1998) adopted a similar position.

[3]   A recent introduction to Mauss's thought and its Durkheimian context is Hart and James, 2014.

ONE

The ends and means of social policy: a personal and generational perspective*

Robert Pinker

Introduction

I have been asked to tell you what it was like to be a social policy student at the London School of Economics (LSE) in the mid-1950s, to describe some of the scholars who taught me and to recount how my views on the subject have changed during the intervening years. Preparing this kind of lecture at the age of 69 has led me to reflect on the ways in which different generations of students perceive the history of social policy, and the different vantage points in time from which each of us look back on our own lives.

The age range of a typical academic department extends over several generations. The oldest staff who taught me at LSE in the mid-1950s had been born before the First World War – a time when the Poor Law was the main provider of relief to the destitute. The events that had shaped their lives were, for my generation, already a part of history. Of course, we also shared some memories because we had all lived through the experiences of the Second World War and the creation of the post-war British welfare state.

The memories passed on across the generations can reach far back in time. As it happened, William Beveridge was still alive and visiting LSE when I was appointed to my first junior post in 1961. Beveridge had a study in the same building where I worked. He was then in his 82nd year, a small, physically frail man but manifestly still intellectually alert and active. He was busily engaged in trying to complete a major work on the history of wages and prices that he had started during the 1930s. It was one of my duties to keep a discreet eye on his welfare, making sure he had his morning cup of tea and helping him into his taxi when he wanted to go to the House of Lords. I still remember the kindness and consideration he showed me. On two occasions, he advised me on my research and talked at length about his early experiences as a social worker at Toynbee Hall, as a journalist and as a civil servant helping to set up a national system of labour exchanges. He told me that those years between 1904 and 1914 was the

* Transcript of a lecture given at the London School of Economics and Political Science in August 2000, not previously published.

best and most productive decade of his life. He showed little interest in talking about the great report for which we all remember him today. So much, then, for the differences which arise between the judgements of history and the ways in which the makers of history judge themselves!

The passing of time and the process of ageing inexorably affect the manner in which we reflect on our past and speculate on what the future holds for us. The older we become, the less we have to anticipate. As Francis Bacon once observed, hope is a good breakfast in our youth but a poor supper in old age. Nevertheless, if we have children and grandchildren, our hopes for the future can still reach out beyond the limits of our own mortality. In reflecting on these generational continuities, Edmund Burke once described society as 'a partnership between those who are living, those who are dead, and those who are to be born' (Burke, 1982, 194–95).

Academic influences – the 1950s onwards

I was a student in Richard Titmuss's department at LSE and subsequently a member of his research staff between 1956 and 1962. During this period, I was employed on several research projects under the supervision of Peter Townsend (1962) and Brian Abel-Smith (1964). From 1958 to 1961, I worked as a full-time research officer while studying as a part-time student for my first degree. I was still a diploma student in Titmuss's department when he offered me a junior research appointment. At the time, he advised me to complete a first degree if I wanted to become a university teacher. As it happened, Titmuss had been appointed to his Chair at LSE without any formal academic qualifications. He had, however, published *Problems of Social Policy* and other highly regarded texts and papers (Titmuss, 1950).

Throughout the 1950s and 1960s, Richard Titmuss had been widely recognised as Britain's most distinguished social policy scholar. The extent of his influence ranged far beyond the LSE where he held his Chair. More than 20 of the staff who taught in his department during this period went on to hold professorial appointments at the LSE and other universities. Titmuss was a lifelong admirer of Tawney's work. He wrote a long and sympathetic introduction to the 1964 edition of *Equality* after Tawney himself had declined to do so because of his advancing years. In 1950, Tawney had written a laudatory review of Titmuss's *Problems of Social Policy* for *The New Statesman and Nation* (Tawney, 1950; Deakin and Wright, 1995).

T.H. Marshall was the second major social policy scholar of this period. He was, however, 15 years older than Titmuss and he had taken early retirement in 1956. His first collection of essays was published in 1950 under the title *Citizenship and Social Class* (Marshall, 1950). These essays were subsequently reprinted in a larger collection, *Sociology at the Crossroads*, which was published in 1963 (Marshall, 1963). Marshall's seminal work on *Social Policy* did not appear until 1965 (Marshall,

1965a). His most influential essays on social policy issues were not published in book form until 1981 under the title of *The Right to Welfare* (Marshall, 1981).

This sequence of events gives some insight into the pattern of generational linkages that helped to shape the development of social policy studies in Britain. In a longer essay, it would be possible to extend and explore these linkages in greater breadth and depth. Titmuss, for example, worked closely for many years with younger departmental colleagues like David Donnison, Brian Abel-Smith and Peter Townsend. Howard Glennerster, David Piachaud, Adrian Webb and Roy Parker also began their careers as junior members of Titmuss's department at LSE.

Similar cross-generational networks developed in other major social policy centres at Nottingham, Edinburgh, Glasgow, Birmingham, Newcastle, Southampton and Bristol during the 1950s and 1960s. Within the University of London, a second important department of policy studies developed at Bedford College under the leadership of Professor O.R. McGregor (later Lord McGregor of Durris). McGregor's department specialised in socio-legal studies and medical sociology. My own Chair of Social Administration at Goldsmiths' was originally invested at Bedford College because Goldsmiths' was not a constituent School of London University at the time when the Chair was established.

Of all the scholars who influenced my approach to the study of social policy, Richard Titmuss, Brian Abel-Smith, T.H. Marshall and O.R. McGregor made the most powerful and lasting impression. They influenced me, however, at different stages in my career and in different ways. I began my studies in Titmuss's department when he was the acknowledged *doyen* of the discipline.

Titmuss thought that collectivist values ought to inform and direct the ends and means of social policy. He was an unapologetic unitarist insofar as he believed that the state should be the major funder and provider of social services. He was opposed to the growth of occupational and other private sector services on the grounds that they fostered economic inequality and social divisions. He wrote very little about the voluntary sector and never envisaged it playing more than a peripheral role as a service provider. His strong political convictions sometimes caused him to confuse moral theories with social theories, and to use empirical evidence to justify his moral beliefs about what constituted good social policy (Titmuss, 1958a, 1968; Wilding, 1995).

Although I respected the quality and originality of Titmuss's scholarship, I could not accept the normative assumptions that shaped his approach to social policy. I have always worked from the premise that when theories of any kind are used to defend a particular point of view, they become indistinguishable from political ideologies.

Social theories should be treated as provisional assertions about causal relationships between social phenomena. They should, therefore, be set out in forms which are testable and open to refutation. In this way, they can be revised, or even abandoned, in the light of new evidence which challenges the original premise. *Social Theory and Social Policy* (Pinker, 1971) was written, in large part, as a critique of the discipline of social policy as it had developed during the years of the Titmuss ascendancy.

I was always a pluralist and a pragmatist in my appraisals of the relative merits of statutory, private and voluntary forms of welfare provision. I was sceptical of claims that there were irreconcilable conflicts between collectivist and individualist values. I could find no evidence to support the view that the great majority of citizens were primarily motivated by either altruistic or egoistic sentiments – or that governments had either the mandate or the ability to create a welfare state or society which was either predominantly collectivist or individualist in character.

Nevertheless, I still remember Titmuss as a remarkably engaging, challenging and likeable teacher. He fired my enthusiasm for the subject. He had a genius for identifying and exploring the key issues of equality, universality and selectivity in ways which highlighted the moral dilemmas that are intrinsic to the study of social welfare institutions. He died in 1973.

I served my academic apprenticeship with Brian Abel-Smith and Peter Townsend as a research worker and higher degree student. With Abel-Smith, I wrote *English Hospital Statistics* (Pinker, 1966) and several other papers. He taught me how to undertake archival research and structure an academic article. He was a brilliant lecturer, an incisive commentator and policy analyst, and a most supportive supervisor. We remained good friends until his death in 1996 (Abel-Smith, 1964, 1994).

T.H. Marshall never attracted a coterie of younger academics during his years as a professor. He retired in 1956 and, with the exception of *Citizenship and Social Class*, most of his best social policy essays were published after 1965. He is perhaps better known and more widely read today than he was during his lifetime.

I first met Marshall in 1971, shortly after the publication of *Social Theory and Social Policy*, when he invited me to lunch with Professor Donald MacRae at the Athenaeum Club. I had always admired Marshall's writing and in the course of our discussions over lunch, we found that we shared a wide range of interests and affinities. Our meeting proved to be the start of a friendship that was to last until his death in 1981.

Marshall was a sociologist of welfare and a theorist of the middle ground. As I wrote in an earlier essay, he was 'almost the only major contributor to social policy studies to express the view that a modified form of capitalist enterprise is not incompatible with civilized forms of collectivist social policy. Indeed, it appears to be central to his thesis that the creation and enhancement of welfare depend on the existence of a free economic market' (Pinker, 1995: 104).

In contrast to Titmuss, Marshall was a pluralist. He defined the concept of citizenship in essentially pluralist terms, exploring the extent to which the elements of civic, political and social rights complemented and conflicted with each other. His primary interest was focused on the positive and compensatory status that social rights conferred on citizens in democratic countries. In *Social Theory and Social Policy*, I had given more attention to the stigmatising propensities of social welfare policies. In this respect, we found that our interests complemented each other.

Although, in some respects, we approached our subject from different start points and perspectives, we soon learned that we shared a tendency to reach similar conclusions. Since we were never disposed to write co-authored papers, we agreed not to compare notes while we were writing our own. We only discussed and exchanged comments after we had finished whatever we were doing.

It was, however, Marshall's concept of 'democratic welfare-capitalism' that helped me to connect my analyses of social policy issues with their broader political and economic contexts. Titmuss wrote about social welfare institutions as if they were the moral exemplars of their societies and the agencies through which radical social change could be achieved. Titmuss started me thinking about the causal relationships between social policy and social change. Marshall helped me to understand the true direction in which this causal process moved. Important though they are, changes in social policy are more often contingent on the broader processes of political and economic change. Without the prior extension of civil and political rights and the growth of wealth-creating economic markets, the subsequent extension of social rights would never have been possible.

Towards the end of his life, Marshall asked me to help produce what was to be his last collection of essays. He was ruthless when it came to excluding all but the best of his most recent work. He added 'afterthoughts' to the essays he decided to include. He lived just long enough to see this collection published in 1981 under the title of *The Right to Welfare*. In my introduction, I wrote that 'After re-reading Marshall's works I am left not so much with a sense of completion but with a feeling of renewal, a stimulus to think again about the perennial issues of social welfare' (Marshall, 1981: 26).

O.R. McGregor was the last of my British academic guides and mentors. He held the Chair of Social Institutions at Bedford College from 1964 to 1985. We first met when I was interviewed for the post of departmental Head at Goldsmiths' College. McGregor was a member of the appointing board. At the time, I was an assistant lecturer in a small polytechnic with one year's teaching experience. After my appointment, McGregor helped me in many different ways as I began the task of developing a third centre of social studies in the University of London.

McGregor was born in 1921. He read economic history at the LSE and taught briefly at Hull University before his appointment at Bedford College in 1947. He wrote widely on the history of social policy, on the socio-legal aspects of social welfare and on family policy (McGregor, 1957, 1970; Finer and McGregor, 1974).

In addition to his academic eminence, McGregor was a leading authority on self-regulatory institutions. He chaired the Royal Commission on the Press, which reported in 1977. He served successively as Chairman of the Advertising Standards Authority and of the Press Complaints Commission from 1980 to 1994. In 1978, he was created a Labour Life Peer, and he subsequently served as an active reforming cross-bencher in the House of Lords.

McGregor's command of 19th century social history and his understanding of legal process were memorably impressive. He was a brilliant stylist who wrote with cogent insight, transparent clarity and engaging wit. Over the years, we became close friends. He gave me invaluable commentaries and advice when I was writing *Social Theory and Social Policy* and *The Idea of Welfare* (Pinker, 1979). I have never known anyone who knew so much, who wore his knowledge so lightly and who shared it so generously with his friends.

Most of all, McGregor was a tireless defender of civil liberties and advocate of social reform. He believed that in a well-ordered society, it was possible to reconcile the claims of personal freedom and collective welfare. As a social reformer, he followed the middle way between the extremes of individualism and collectivism. As a scholar, he was scrupulously impartial and open-minded He died in 1997.

In this short essay, I have tried to describe the academic context in which I started my career and wrote *Social Theory and Social Policy*. I have written about four scholars, each of whom, in their different ways, greatly influenced my approach to the study of social policy and administration. The passage of their lives spanned several generations. Marshall was born in 1893, Titmuss in 1907, McGregor in 1921 and Abel-Smith in 1926. Titmuss and Abel-Smith shared the closest bonds of intellectual affinity. Titmuss and Marshall knew each other but they made remarkably few references to each other in their respective publications. McGregor and Titmuss shared some common interests in the field of social policy, notably with regard to single-parent families. But they were never close colleagues.

What is remarkable is that all four of them shared the same commitment to the development of an academic discipline which did not exist as an undergraduate field of study when they were students. Titmuss, indeed, had never been a university student. He left school at 15 to work as an office boy before making a career in the world of insurance, where he rose to the rank of inspector. He did not hold a university post until he was appointed Professor at LSE in 1950. He was 42 years old at the time.

Marshall read history at Cambridge. He was first appointed to a tutorship in social work at LSE in 1925 and four years later transferred to the Sociology Department. Up to that time, he had written mainly on topics in the field of economic history. McGregor also read economic history and he developed his interests in sociology and social policy after his appointment at Bedford College. Abel-Smith read economics at Cambridge and became an authority on social policy after he joined Titmuss's department at LSE.

Theories and models of welfare

As late as 1956, social policy and administration was taught at LSE only as a two-year non-graduate certificate course and as an option in the sociology degree programme. These were the courses of study that I followed between 1956 and 1961. Social policy and administration did not become established as a degree subject in its own right until the mid-1960s. As a distinctive community of scholars, it came of age when the Social Administration Association was formed in 1967 and I subsequently had the honour of serving as its Chairman from 1974 to 1977.

By the early 1970s, there were many younger academics who wanted the subject to develop a distinctive intellectual identity. In *Social Theory and Social Policy,* I wrote of 'the poverty of Social Administration as a theoretical discipline' (1971: 5). As Ramesh Mishra has noted: 'the missionary aspect of the discipline was very prominent at this time. The field of social policy came to be defined in terms of a struggle between the forces of good and evil – the institutional and residual approach to social policy. With its predominantly collectivist values social administration was on the side of the "good" while individualism and *laissez faire* represented the "evil" side. With the arena of social policy defined in this way, "moral rhetoric and fact-finding" in the pursuit of equity and justice loomed large. Academic development, on the other hand, seems to have received less attention' (Mishra, 1989: 77).

Mishra's analysis of the situation as it was in the late 1960s was entirely accurate. The main reason why I wrote *Social Theory and Social Policy* was to challenge this state of affairs and to assert the claims of impartial scholarship against those of moralising partisanship. Nonetheless, I never argued that social policy should seek to become a 'value-free' discipline. I believed then, as I do now, that 'the first function of any kind of scientific theory is not to criticise what exists, or to "transcend" what exists, but to help us distinguish correct from incorrect knowledge. Sociological theory does not enable us to distinguish "goodness" from "badness", although it may provide new forms of knowledge and insight which can be used for a variety of moral purposes. As it finds new applications in the field of social welfare, it may indicate new possibilities for social change and improvement' (Pinker, 1971: 130).

Developing theories and models of social welfare for purposes of historical and comparative research has always been a dominant interest in my academic life. Teaching and learning from my students has been its complementary delight and privilege. My theoretical interests led me on to explore the ethical and practical dynamics of social welfare – what motivates us to develop systems of mutual aid and formal social services in making provision for social needs? And how can these services be best organised with regard to their efficiency, their coverage and their responsiveness to individual and collective needs as they change over time? What causes them to change?

In *Social Theory and Social Policy,* for example, I set out a model of social welfare as a system of exchange relationships between providers and recipients. At that time, I was particularly interested in exploring the ways in which different methods of organising and delivering social services and meeting needs encouraged or discouraged people from using them.

More recently, I have been writing about two forms of service organisation – unitarism and pluralism – and two forms of social service delivery – universality and selectivity – and their impact on the status of citizenship. In a unitary model of social welfare, the state is the main provider of formal social services with additional support from the informal networks of mutual aid based on family and neighbourhood relationships. In pluralist, or mixed, economies of welfare, there is much more scope for cooperation and competition between statutory, voluntary, private and occupationally-based providers who make up the formal sector. These services are, again, supplemented by the care and support provided by the informal networks of mutual aid.

A universalist social service is one which is provided to everyone who falls within a formally defined category, like old people or children. It is provided on proof of need and without reference to a selective test of means or income. A selective service is provided on proof of need and subject to a test of means or income. In practice, these two modes of service delivery often overlap.

Pluralist models of welfare offer people a choice of statutory, voluntary and private sector social services. The ideal pluralist model is one in which statutory agencies can act as both direct providers and purchasers of voluntary and private sector services.

The typical unitary model of welfare is one in which either the statutory or the non-statutory agencies are the main service providers. Such quasi-monopolistic models cannot respond with sufficient sensitivity to the diversity of human need and preferences. When choice is denied because there is only one kind of service provider, the risks of total dependency and stigma are maximised.

The variables of depth, time and distance mitigate and sometimes remove the risk and experience of stigmatising dependency. The depth of felt dependency is eased when we feel that the services received are a compensation for some past injustice, a restitution for some past injury or a provision that will enhance our future economic and social independence. Distance between the giver and receiver eases the stigma that is always inherent in one-way exchange relationships. And short-term dependency is always preferable to long-time dependency.

Over 25 years ago, I drew attention to Eugene Litwak's model of exchange relationships and shared welfare functions. Litwak advanced the thesis that 'the norms of equivalency and reciprocity are most likely to pertain when the individual is totally dependent upon neither primary groups nor formal organizations. Dependencies of a stigmatising or humiliating nature are most likely to be avoided when the individual receives aid of a partial nature from a number of providers' (Pinker, 1971: 160). Indeed, total dependency on the informal networks of familial or neighbourhood care may be potentially more stigmatising than dependence on formal welfare agencies because we have no formal or legal rights to care from our relatives or friends. Even if we possessed such rights, the very act of *having* to assert them would be the most humiliating of all.

Given the diversity of human values and aspirations, it is therefore essential that the component rights and duties that make up the concept of citizenship are grounded in a similar diversity of social institutions and personal experiences and sentiments. Unitary models of welfare, whether they are ideologically driven by individualist market values or collectivist welfare values, ignore this diversity, increase the risks of total dependency and thereby impoverish the status of citizenship.

My interest in the relationship between modes of service delivery, dependency and the status of citizenship led me on to explore the moral dynamics of welfare institutions and, more specifically, the respective roles of egoism and altruism. Every normative model of welfare means and ends rests on certain assumptions about the moral qualities of human nature. On the basis of the relevant empirical evidence, I rejected those models which drew sharp distinctions between our propensities for egoism and altruism. I argued that if people were predominantly altruistic, compulsory forms of social service would not be necessary; conversely, if people were exclusively self-regarding, such compulsion would be impossible. Egoism is often equated with self-interest but it is also associated with the positive qualities of self-help and a willingness to accept responsibility for one's own welfare.

As we grow up, we learn to accept restraints upon our more selfish dispositions and show consideration for other people. We become moral beings in the context of family life through example and the lessons of experience. Familial altruism is the first and most natural way in which we express our concern for other people's welfare. Our sense of personal responsibility grows out of the love and affection we feel for our closest relatives but it is also sustained by the imperatives of duty and the expectations of society.

Familial altruism may be a limited form of altruism, restricted to those we know and love, but it is the mainspring from which all our other moral concerns for other people's welfare flow. As we mature and become citizens of a wider community, our notions of obligation and entitlement also grow more extensive and take on the formal character of social rights and duties.

Once again, this extension in the range of our awareness is driven by a combination of egoistic and altruistic motives. We learn from personal experience that familial altruism alone cannot guarantee our welfare in an uncertain world. We learn that collective forms of social provision – statutory and voluntary – are sensible ways of helping each other in times of need, and pooling risks (a Beveridge concept). The compassion we feel for those less fortunate than ourselves is also an important factor but, as I once wrote, the welfare institutions of a society can best be understood in terms of 'an unstable compromise between compassion and indifference, between altruism and self-interest' (Pinker, 1971: 211).

Politicians of all parties, however, tend to exaggerate the strengths and virtues of the family as a social institution. It is certainly the case that where members of a family are disposed to help each other, they often provide some of the most devoted and intense forms of care but their boundaries of obligation are as narrowly drawn as they are deeply felt because they are based on *personal* relationships. Nevertheless, because informal systems of care based on kinship are governed by personal qualities, they are likely to be less enduring and less reliable in the long term; members of a family may quarrel, move away or die, and there are people who have no family.

It is also unfortunately the case that a minority of families are grossly dysfunctional, characterised by episodes of domestic violence between spouses and partners and the abuse of children by their parents.

In more general terms, the family, as a social institution, is undergoing some fundamental processes of change. At the present time, nearly one in three of all births in Britain take place outside marriage. The annual rate of divorce has risen sixfold over the past 35 years and four in every 10 marriages contracted will end in divorce if current trends persist. One in five of all British families with dependent children are headed by a single parent and one in 12 are living with step-parents.

These changes in the patterns of family life have given rise to much debate. On the right, traditionalists lament the decline of the two-parent family and naively claim that it can be checked and reversed by a combination of legal and policy changes which will make divorce more difficult and discourage the future formation of extra-marital unions by cutting off welfare support. There is, however, no evidence to support the view that the passing of stricter divorce laws and the reinvention of old forms of stigma will have much effect on what ordinary people do. If *de jure* divorces are made more difficult, then the number of *de facto* separations will increase. And no one has yet invented a family policy which punishes extramarital unions without inflicting great hardship on their innocent offspring.

Some policy analysts claim that what matters is the quality of family life enjoyed by its members rather than the formal structure of the family itself. A happy one-parent family, they suggest, is better for the children than an unhappy two-parent family. It would, of course, be difficult to argue otherwise. Nevertheless, despite much tendentious reinterpretation of research evidence, it is undeniable that happy two-parent families are generally more successful than even happy one-parent families in bringing up well-adjusted children in conditions of economic security.

There are other features of modern family life to be considered, notably the impact of demographic and economic change. Average family size is smaller than it was, say, 50 years ago. There is generally more geographical and social mobility; people are consequently less likely to live close enough to other members of their family to care for each other in times of adversity. In modern families, it is common for both spouses to go out to work, so that fewer women can undertake the long-term care of dependent relatives without continuous support from the social services. There is now a large number of families that would experience a sharp drop in living standards if they had to relinquish one of their two regular incomes.

The continuities of familial altruism both complement and conflict with the formal redistributive ends of statutory social policies. Through acts of voluntary saving, we give substance to the hope of leaving wealth to those we know and love. Through the processes of redistributive taxation, we make provision for the welfare of total strangers who lack the means to help themselves.

Conflicts of interest and loyalty are bound to arise when taxpayers start complaining that the government is leaving them with insufficient income and wealth for the welfare needs of their own families. Nevertheless, democratically elected governments would find it difficult to stay in office if they tried to raise taxes for collective needs without some measure of voluntary compliance on the part of the general public. All governments have to live with the difficult task of striking the right balance between the conflicting claims of familial and collective altruism.

It is, however, important to remember that what we call collective altruism is also tempered with a measure of self-interest, which is not surprising since it has its origins in the mainsprings of familial altruism. Governments can pass laws to extend the boundaries of social welfare and protect the family as a social institution. They can compel citizens to obey their laws but they cannot compel them to be moral because acts of duty are only moral if they are voluntarily undertaken.

A welfare society – as distinct from a welfare state – is a society in which people assume a substantial degree of responsibility for their own welfare and the wellbeing of their families. These informal networks of concern and social care provide the moral and cultural foundations on which the formal structures of statutory and voluntary social services develop. Taken together, these interactive networks and structures make up the institutional elements of welfare pluralism. Although conflicts of interest frequently arise between these institutional elements, they are, in the last analysis, dependent upon each other. The welfare of many individuals and families would be jeopardised if statutory social services were to disappear. Conversely, the statutory social services could not compensate or provide adequate substitutes if the structures of familial altruism ceased functioning.

Conclusion

Theories of social welfare need to be tested on a comparative basis and I have always been keenly interested in the social service arrangements of other countries. Over the years, I have supervised doctoral and post-doctoral scholars from countries as diverse as Norway, Germany, Canada, South Korea, China and Japan. In our tutorials, we shared our insights and added something of value to each other's stores of knowledge and understanding.

In this lecture, I have described some of the people who have helped and encouraged me over the years The greatest debt I owe is to my wife, Jennifer. We met in 1954 and were together for 40 years before she died in 1994. Jennifer typed and edited all my work. She was my wisest critic and my constant support and inspiration. Whatever we achieved, we achieved together. The memories of the life we shared, our two daughters, their partners and their children are one more instance of the sustaining power of those generational continuities that I have talked about today.

For each one of us, the families to which we belong and the memories we share are special. In terms of their generality, they are commonplace – which leads me to conclude on an optimistic note that in our supposedly secular and uncertain world, small miracles of constancy and continuity are happening all around us, all the time.

TWO

Social theory and social policy: a challenging relationship*

Robert Pinker

In this chapter, I will try to answer the following three questions. What do we mean by 'theory' in the applied discipline of social policy? How do we distinguish between scientific theory, normative theory and ideology? Is it possible – or desirable – to design and implement rational social policies in the fractious world of democratic party politics where partisanship and passion are more evident than scholarly impartiality and rationality is in short supply?

The role of theory in social research

The development and testing of theories is an essential element in the conduct of social research. Theories set out explanatory and predictive propositions about the causal relationships between phenomena, such as the characteristics and incidence of poverty and the processes by which people become poor, remain poor and escape from poverty.

Deductivists and inductivists hold differing views about the sequence in which scientific research should be conducted. Deductivists start by formulating a theory and then proceed from this general proposition to a consideration of particular cases in order to test their theory. Inductivists start by drawing inferences from particular cases from which they proceed towards the formulation of a theory.

The central assumption of the inductivist approach is that 'scientific knowledge grows out of simple unbiased statements reporting the evidence of the senses' (Medawar, 1984: 98). 'In real life', however, as Peter Medawar suggests, 'discovery and justification are almost always different processes', and researchers seldom, if ever, start their enquiries with a clean sheet. They begin with a review of the relevant literature, and some provisional ideas, or hypotheses, about the subject they wish to investigate. Medawar's reductivist approach to the conduct of research shares much in common with Karl Popper's hypothetico-deductive method of scientific enquiry.

In Popper's approach, we must rely 'upon the best tested of theories, which are the ones for which we have good rational reasons, not of course good reasons for believing them to be true, but for believing them to be the *best available* ... the

---

* Not previously published but incorporating material from Pinker, 1995b, 2004b and 2011.

best among competing theories, the best approximations to the truth' (Popper, 1978: 95; emphasis added). On this basis, scientific knowledge will continue to advance through a 'method of bold conjectures and ingenious and severe attempts to refute them' (Popper, 1978: 81).

Popper's views have, in turn, been subjected to critical reappraisal by other philosophers. His claim that falsifiability is the hallmark of a scientific theory has been challenged on a number of grounds – as has his dismissal of inductivism. Not all scientific theories are predictive in character and it does not always follow that one negative finding invalidates a theory.

Hilary Putnam reminds us that, in the real world of policy making, people do make inductions and draw inferences from available evidence without reaching unwarranted conclusions about the truth or falsity of their theories. Putnam suggests that Popper draws an unnecessarily sharp distinction between the worlds of theory and practice. In doing so, he overlooks the fact that ideas are 'not just ends in themselves'. They also 'guide practice' and 'structure whole forms of life' (Putnam, 1979: 374). In his study of *The Structure of Scientific Revolutions*, Thomas Kuhn (1996) offers an alternative explanation of the way in which scientific knowledge develops which I will discuss towards the end of this chapter.

There are, however, a number of good reasons why Popper's approach to scientific enquiry can improve the quality of social policy. First, the ends and means of social policy are shaped by value judgements which often conflict with each other. Policy researchers often hold strong moral and political beliefs about the subjects they wish to investigate. Popper's injunction that theories are propositions to be tested is a useful corrective against value bias and partisanship in the conduct of research. Secondly, Popper's approach leaves open the alternative possibilities that theory can generate research and research can generate theory since hypotheses can emerge at any point in either of these two interactive processes.

Thirdly, Popper reminds us that, however rational and well-intentioned our social policies may be, they are always hostages to errors of judgement and unintended outcomes that have adverse consequences for service users. Large-scale policy initiatives frequently result in large scale errors of judgement.

Popper was a rationalist, but he was a 'critical rationalist' in the sense that he recognised that, in the world of politics and policy making, there are limits to the exercise of rationality. Future policy outcomes cannot be predicted in accordance with rational scientific procedures. Piecemeal incremental policy changes are less likely to result in large-scale errors of judgement.

Predictive theories in the social sciences are much more open to error than their physical science counterparts because the subjects of social research – unlike atoms, molecules and planets – are thinking, sentient beings with motives and intentions of their own. In planning the domestic economies of our everyday lives, we are all micro-policy makers in our own right.

Policy making, policy research and public opinion

These considerations make it all the more imperative that social researchers should rely only on those theories for which they have 'good rational reasons' for believing that they are the 'best tested' and the 'best approximations to the truth' among all the other theories competing for their attention. This ongoing scholarly quest for scientific objectivity is sustained, not only by the professional integrity of individual researchers, but by the continuous exposure of their findings to informed debate and rigorous peer reviews within the wider community of scholars to which they belong.

Nevertheless, this is not the only context in which social policies, and the evidence on which they are based, are subjected to critical appraisal. In democratic societies, the effectiveness of social policies is ultimately judged in the court of public opinion through the ballot box. Democratic societies are 'open societies' in which the right to freedom of expression and the public's right to know and be kept informed are protected under the law.

It follows, therefore, that although social policies are informed and influenced by the findings of social research, the policies *as such* are made, unmade and remade in the fractious world of democratic party politics. This is a world in which partisanship and passion are more evident than scholarly impartiality and, most certainly, it is not one in which the dictates of reason reign supreme.

Conversely, it can be argued that, in a society that adopted a model of rational social policy, democratic values would *not* reign supreme. As Becker and Bryman point out, such a model would rest on the highly questionable assumption that policies 'can be defined rationally and unambiguously, with clear goals, aims and means, which are acceptable to, and accepted by, all parties and players' involved in or affected by the policy-making process (Becker and Bryman, 2012: 32–33).

The policy-making process simply does not work like that in democratic societies. The ends and means of new policy proposals are always subjected to a diversity of conflicting value judgements. The existence of political parties and a plurality of interest groups ensures that a consensus is rarely, if ever, achieved. Compromises are reached through complex processes of negotiation, bargaining and 'partisan mutual adjustments'. The outcomes can seldom be described as 'rational' (Becker and Bryman, 2012: 33).

The relationships that hold between policy makers, policy researchers and public opinion are shaped as much by the strengths and diversity of moral sentiments and value judgements as they are by the dictates of reason. In general elections, governments defend their legislative track records, present new policy proposals and promise to implement them if they are re-elected. They publish a wealth of research-based evidence that gives voters ample opportunity to make appraisals of their fitness to continue in office.

Opposition parties seeking to become the next government campaign in exactly the same way. Their own research evidence will be critical of the government's past performance and the evidence it presents. Even in cases where political parties agree that a set of research findings are reliable, they may disagree about their significance because they hold different views about what the ends of social policy ought to be.

There may, for example, be general agreement that a data set accurately describes the distribution of the nation's wealth and income. Viewed from one value perspective, the distribution may be interpreted as a fair and morally defensible allocation of material resources. Viewed from another perspective, it may be seen as unfair and morally indefensible. In the world of social policy, the facts do not always 'speak for themselves'. If facts of this kind had feelings, they would undoubtedly suffer from bouts of identity crisis.

Nevertheless, it remains a fact of political life that, in democratic societies, governments and political parties invest large sums of money in the conduct of social research. They do so because they want their policy initiatives to be as effectively designed, implemented and monitored as possible. And since it is also possible for people to have both strong convictions and open minds, political parties hope that – after studying the relevant evidence – their traditional supporters will remain loyal and that some of those who previously voted for other parties will change their minds and vote for them.

The media play a vitally important role in fostering informed public debate about the ends and means of social policies and as social investigators in their own right. How effectively they perform these roles would be the topic for another occasion. I would only add, in passing, that, in the UK at least, they do it a lot better than they are given credit for.

Democratic societies foster institutional diversity but, if they are to survive as *democracies*, this diversity must be held together by a cultural framework of values with which people can identify as members of the same nation while remaining free to advocate their own views on the ways in which their nation ought to be run.

Value judgements, and the moral convictions on which they are based, provide the normative and emotional driving force that triggers and gives momentum to the progress of both policy making and social research.

Reason provides the logical and evidence-based guidance towards identifying the most effective ways and means by which the chosen ends can be achieved. Scientific research cannot tell policy makers what is wrong 'or what *ought to be done*; it can only provide factual information about the effects of an intervention' (Hammersley, 2012: 45; emphasis added).

For illustrative purposes only, I will briefly review the ways in which sharply divergent normative theories have polarised the debate about *why* poverty persists in even the wealthiest nation states and *what* policy makers *ought* to be doing with regard to its elimination or relief.

Behavioural and structural models of poverty

The ongoing debate about the causes of social inequality and poverty has always been polarised between the policy makers and theorists who believe that the poor are largely the culpable architects of their own misfortunes and those who believe that they are largely the innocent victims of adverse social circumstances and changes beyond their control.

The 'personal culpability' thesis is based on 'behavioural' explanations which attribute the causes of poverty to the personal shortcomings of the poor themselves. The very poor are defined as people who lack the necessary intelligence, competence or motivation to make sensible choices in the management of their daily lives. They grow up in dysfunctional families, live dysfunctional lives and pass on their dysfunctional values from one generation to the next. They have a marked preference for idleness and would rather live on welfare benefits than work for a living. They are the self-perpetuating members of an unregenerate underclass and the agents through which the 'cycle of deprivation' repeats itself.

The 'victim' thesis is based on 'structural' explanations which focus on the massive disadvantages that the unequal distribution of wealth, income and life chances impose on the poorest members of class–based societies. For the greater part, the very poor are defined as people who are forced by adverse circumstances to live out their lives excluded from the activities of the societies to which they 'belong' only in notional terms. In reality, they are a socially excluded underclass.

From the early 20th century onwards, structural explanations of the causes of poverty became more influential in the making of social policies and more popular with voters. In Britain, they played a key role in the gradual processes of political change that resulted in the eventual abolition of the Poor Law and the creation of what came to be called the British 'welfare state'.

In recent times, policy makers and advisors have grown more circumspect in their use of terms like the 'deserving' and the 'undeserving' poor. They do not wish to appear overly patronising or disparaging in their judgements about benefit applicants. Nevertheless, in the court of popular opinion, many people still believe that such moral distinctions ought to be drawn with greater authority and force than is currently the case. They remain convinced that those who are able to help themselves ought to receive substantially less than those who are unable to do so.

A growing number of European governments are also becoming convinced that unemployed benefit claimants ought to be required to enrol in work or retraining programmes as a condition of receiving benefit. Failure to do so should entail denial or deduction of benefit. We live in more democratic and humanitarian times, and workfare policies have come to be seen as morally preferable to workhouse tests.

Moral imperatives and the relief of poverty

In their more radical forms, both the 'personal culpability' and 'victim' theses offer uni-causal explanations of the causes of poverty which take little or no account of the empirical evidence which shows that poverty is a multi-causal phenomenon and that there is no such homogeneous entity as *the* poor. The various causes of poverty are interactive over long periods of time and 'it is possible for them all to apply simultaneously' in particular cases (Spicker, 2006: 71).

Unravelling these causal processes is a difficult task which is just as likely to end in accusations of unfair treatment when a person's entitlement to help is confirmed as when it is denied. In any system of exchange relationships, both welfare recipients and taxpayers, as welfare providers, make comparisons and judgements about the relative justice of these outcomes.

Most people will readily agree that justice is synonymous with fairness but, in the context of welfare exchange relationships, they find it much harder to agree on what counts as fairness. Need and desert are the key criteria by which welfare entitlements are decided. As moral precepts, however, they embody conflicting interpretations of what counts as fairness, and people of different political convictions disagree about which of these precepts should carry the greater moral authority in the assessment of welfare entitlements.

The concept of poverty itself is also charged with powerful moral connotations. As Paul Spicker notes, 'poverty consists of serious deprivation and people are held to be poor when their material circumstances are declared to be morally unacceptable'. In this respect, he shares David Piachaud's belief that the concept of poverty 'carries with it an implication and moral imperative that something should be done about it. Its definition is a value judgement and should be clearly seen to be so' (Spicker, 1999: 157; Piachaud, 1981: 421).

It is not, therefore, surprising that policy makers and their advisors seldom agree on *what* should be done about poverty, *who* should do it and at *what levels* of deprivation it becomes morally imperative that something 'ought' to be done. Amartya Sen argues that the most serious and incontestable level of deprivation is the condition of absolute poverty in which it becomes impossible for people 'to meet their nutritional requirements, to escape avoidable disease, to be sheltered, to be clothed, to be able to travel, to be educated ... to live without shame'. Some moralists, however, contend that the undeserving poor ought to feel ashamed of the conduct that rendered them destitute. Nevertheless, most people would share Sen's view that there is 'an irreducible absolutist core in the idea of poverty. If there is starvation and hunger then, no matter what the relative picture looks like there clearly is poverty' (Sen, 1983: 153–69).

Our two explanatory models of the causes of poverty are located on what might be called the polar extremes of welfare ideology. Relatively few policy analysts feel completely at home in these chilly intellectual domains. Most of them, however, attach greater heuristic significance to one or other of these models. When governments seek their advice they offer more temperate versions of the one which they prefer. The policies which they recommend will, therefore, lie somewhere between the ideological extremes of left-wing collectivism and right-wing individualism.

Social policy theorists often hold strong political and moral beliefs about the issues they investigate, notably with regard to the causes of poverty and the ends and means of social policy itself. They develop theories which embody normative critiques of the political status quo and policy prescriptions for changing it. The distinction between non-normative and normative social theories was very clearly drawn by Émile Durkheim. He suggested that, 'Social theories separate themselves at once into two large categories. One seeks only to express what is or what has been; it is purely speculative and scientific. Others, on the contrary, aim to modify what exists; they propose, not laws, but reforms. They are practical doctrines' (Durkheim, 1967: 51–2).

Normative theorists tell us what will happen if we do x rather than y but they also leave us in no doubt as to which option we *ought* to choose on moral grounds. Drawing distinctions between scientific theories, normative theories and ideologies is a difficult task because it involves matters of degree as well as of kind. The first distinction to be drawn is whether or not the theory is set out in a testable and falsifiable form. The second concerns the degree to which unprejudiced consideration is given to new evidence and possible alternative explanations.

As long as there is open debate between open-minded theorists, the avenues for falsification and correction will remain open. The more general social theories become, the more likely they are to be overloaded with normative convictions and the less likely they are to be presented in falsifiable forms. Paradoxically, general theories of radical social change tend to be most resistant to falsification and their advocates most resistant to changing their minds when new evidence challenges their most cherished convictions.

The general theories that underpin our explanatory models of poverty are based on fundamentally different beliefs concerning the causal links between poverty and inequality, the relative importance that should be accorded to the criteria of need and desert in the allocation of welfare resources and the kinds of distributional relationship that ought to hold between the principle of equity (or fairness) and the social ideals of equality and inequality as policy objectives.

Liberal individualism, social inequality and poverty

Behavioural explanations of the causes of poverty are philosophically grounded in the classical theories of economic market liberalism. This form of liberalism, or 'neo-liberalism, as it is sometimes called, lies further to the right of the political spectrum than traditional conservatism.

Liberals, in this sense, argue that the key role of the state is to maintain the rule of law with as little arbitrary governmental interference as possible. Leaving competitive economic markets to the workings of the price mechanism and the 'invisible hand' of supply and demand will result in a natural reconciliation of individual and collective interests and the most efficient allocation of resources under what Adam Smith once described as an 'obvious and simple system of natural liberty' (Heilbroner, 1986: 289).

Under conditions of market freedom, the benefits of economic growth and wealth creation will trickle down to the poorest members of society and the incidence of poverty will diminish. Removing 'the mainly political obstacles to the work of the market under capitalism would hasten the rate at which incomes and wealth trickled down from the richer to the poorer' and assist in the creation 'of a more egalitarian society based on the natural or acquired ability of individuals to enrich one another' (Seldon, 1990: 196–7).

Neo-liberals like Hayek reject the idea of 'social justice' as being 'necessarily empty and meaningless' because it can only be achieved by political and bureaucratic ordinance. The idea of social justice can only have meaning in a 'command' economy and a centrally controlled society. Policies based on principles of redistributive social justice constitute 'one of the greatest obstacles to the elimination of poverty' because they undermine the effective workings of the competitive market and wealth creation. In Hayek's view, they have 'probably produced more injustice in the form of new privileges, obstacles to mobility and frustration of efforts than they have contributed to the lot of the poor' (Hayek, 1982: 139–40).

Hayek was convinced that, sooner or later, such policies result in the breakdown of competitive markets and a slackening in the rate of economic growth and wealth creation. In the political sphere, the inexorable growth in the regulatory powers of the state deprives us all of our basic rights and liberties.

Socialism, collectivism, social inequality and poverty

Structural explanations of the causes of poverty are philosophically grounded in theories of socialism and other more pluralist versions of social-democratic left-wing collectivism. In the classical traditions of Marxist and non-Marxist socialism, the causes of poverty are attributed to the unequal distribution of wealth, income and power that the free play of competitive market forces produces in capitalist societies (Freedman, 1962; McClelland, 1996, 543–612; Marx and Engels, 1998).

Nothing less than radical structural change will abolish the economic and social inequalities of class-based capitalist societies. Changes of this order will require the nationalisation of the means of production and distribution under a system of common ownership, the creation of a centralised command economy and radical policies of social redistribution from rich to poor (George, 2010: 202–32).

So far, no society has come remotely near to realising this egalitarian ideal in the form that Marx and Engels envisaged. Their predictions that capitalism would eventually collapse under the weight of its own inner contradictions have not been vindicated by events. Neither has their belief that planned economies would prove to be more efficient and egalitarian in the production and distribution of goods and services than competitive market economies. (It should be noted, however, that without swift governmental intervention, the 2007/08 banking crisis might well have ended with the near-total collapse of the global financial markets.)

An increasing number of democratic socialist and social-democratic parties have come to terms with the ethos of competitive markets and rested their hopes for achieving more egalitarian societies through the agencies of social reform and redistributive social policies.

T.H. Marshall stands out as the foremost advocate of these kinds of political compromise between individualist and collectivist policy ends and means. In discussing the ends of social policy, he separated the abolition of poverty from the abolition of inequality, on the grounds that, 'Poverty is a tumour which should be cut out, and theoretically could be; inequality is a vital organ which is functioning badly' (Marshall, 1981: 119). In Marshall's preferred model of 'democratic-welfare-capitalism', his idea of welfare rests on a balance struck between the claims of different kinds of right and the satisfaction of different kinds of need. Political, social and economic rights expressed different but complementary dimensions of welfare which were brought together in the status of citizenship. It was not possible to go on extending 'any one of these rights at the expense of the others without crossing the critical threshold at which the relationship between freedom and security becomes one of diminishing marginal utility' (Pinker, 1995c, included in **Part Three** of this volume as **Chapter Twelve, p 249**).

The ends and means of social policy are defined in progressively more egalitarian terms as we move further to the left along the party political spectrum. In democratic societies, increasing importance is attached to the criteria of need in assessing entitlement to welfare benefits. Entitlements are endowed with the status of social rights which, in turn, are linked into the 'idea that full citizenship requires not only the rule of law and political democracy, but guaranteed entitlements to social welfare, health care and education' (Dean, 2002: 239).

In theory, at least, this degree of egalitarianism might be accommodated within Marshall's middle-of-the-road model of democratic-welfare-capitalism. A Hayekian liberal would describe it as a collectivist's itinerary for navigating 'the road to serfdom'. A radical socialist would question whether any significant degree of equalisation could ever be achieved without the effective abolition of competitive market capitalism.

This indeed was the conclusion that Peter Townsend reached in his monumental study of *Poverty in the United Kingdom*, which was published nearly 40 years ago. He began his enquiry with the assertion that 'poverty can be defined objectively and applied consistently only in terms of the concept of relative deprivation'. Individuals and households were in poverty when 'they lack the resources to obtain the types of diet, participate in the activities and have the living conditions which are customary, or at least widely encouraged or approved, in the societies to which they belong. Their resources are so seriously below those commanded by the average individual or family that they are, in effect, excluded from ordinary living patterns, customs and activities' (Townsend, 1979: 31).

Townsend lists 60 indicators of 'styles of living', or 'living patterns', which include whether or not households have a refrigerator, the frequency with which families entertain relatives and friends and children have cooked breakfasts. He hypothesises that a particular point is 'reached in descending the income scale' when 'a significantly large number of families reduce more than proportionately their participation in the community's style of living. They drop out or are excluded. These income points can be identified as the poverty line' (Townsend, 1979: 249). The 'objective' status of these indicators has been called into question by a number of other social policy scholars, most notably by David Piachaud (1981: 421).

Townsend sets out three 'alternative policies for dealing with large-scale deprivation or poverty' which he describes as 'a) conditional welfare for the few; b) minimum rights for the many; and c) distributional justice for all' (Townsend, 1979: 62). He chooses the 'distributional' option, which he transforms into a radically egalitarian model of a socialist welfare state without once mentioning the 's' word. The structural preconditions for implementing this model are 'the destratification of society through economic, political and social reorganization and the equal distribution and wider diffusion of all kinds of power and material resources' (Townsend, 1979: 64).

In his conclusion, Townsend outlines his polices for 'an effective assault on poverty'. They include the abolition of 'excessive' wealth and income with 'a statutory definition of maximum possible earnings (and income) agreed' backed up by a 'comprehensive income policy'. The 'abolition of unemployment' would be achieved by introducing a 'legally enforceable right to work' and 'a corresponding obligation on the part of employers to provide alternative types of employment' (Townsend, 1979: 926).

Whatever we may think about the viability and desirability of these proposals, there can be no doubt that they can only be implemented if the radical structural preconditions that Townsend outlines were to be met. The likelihood that the electorates of any democratic societies would vote for structural changes of this order is, to say the least, remote.

Townsend, for his part, says little or nothing about their political and economic implications. Implementing his policies would require an awesome concentration of coercive powers in the institutions of central government. All the institutions of civil society would have to be micro-managed on a continuous basis.

No consideration whatever is given to the impact such policies would have on the processes of wealth creation without which there would be no resources available for distribution or redistribution. All the historical evidence shows that, in highly centralised command economies, most of the population ends up with equal shares in relative poverty – relative, that is, to the standards of living they previously enjoyed in competitive market economies.

In the distant days of the Cold War, the most noteworthy difference that emerged between the nation states with competitive market economies and those with centralised command economies was that the former had to cope with the flow of refugees from command economies, while the latter built walls and watch-towers to prevent them leaving. In today's newly emergent global economy, democratic–welfare–capitalist societies are still struggling to cope with the flow of refugees in search of freedom and a better standard of living.

It is becoming increasingly evident that the processes of wealth creation cannot be safely left to the spontaneous operation of competitive market forces under 'light touch' systems of financial regulation. Under such conditions, 'booms' can turn into 'busts' with alarming speed and the benefits of economic growth do not 'trickle down' to the poorest members of society.

Conclusion

Karl Popper, as we have noted, described the growth of scientific knowledge in terms of a gradual evolutionary progress towards the truth. In the early 1970s, Thomas Kuhn set out an alternative way of conceptualising the development of scientific knowledge.

In his study of *The Structure of Scientific Revolutions,* Kuhn claimed that science develops in a sequence of 'phases' (or distinct stages) within communities of scholars who share a common intellectual framework which he describes as 'a paradigm' or a 'disciplinary matrix' (see Kuhn, 1996: 10 *passim*; Preston, 2008: 23; Naughton, 2012: 14).

In the first phase, which Kuhn describes as the period in which 'normal science' prevails, scholars concentrate primarily on making incremental and peripheral changes to the paradigm they share. *Pace* Karl Popper, they do not challenge and seek to falsify the fundamental premises on which their paradigm rests.

With the passage of time, however, the number of unresolved anomalies and discrepancies increase within the paradigm until a point is reached when 'some scientists begin to question the paradigm itself'. In his brilliant review of a new edition of Kuhn's book, John Naughton summarises what happens next. 'At this point', he writes, 'the discipline enters a period of crisis' characterised by a 'willingness to try anything' and to 'open a debate on fundamental issues'. 'In the end, the crisis is resolved by a revolutionary change in world view in which the now deficient paradigm is replaced by a newer one.'

As Naughton adds, 'This is the paradigm shift of modern parlance and after it has happened the scientific field returns to normal science, based on the new framework. And so it goes on' (Naughton, 2012: 14).

Kuhn challenged Popper's account of the nature of scientific knowledge and the methods by which it advances. Popper claimed that the only theories that count as scientific are those which are set out in a testable form and survive the scrutiny of objective criticism. Kuhn 'suggested that the last thing normal scientists try to do is to refute the theories embedded in their paradigm' (Naughton, 2012: 14).

Whether or not Kuhn's notion of a 'paradigm shift' explains why and how conceptual revolutions happen in the physical sciences, it may help to explain why they are *not* happening in the field of social welfare theory. The debate about the causal links between social inequality and poverty has been largely stuck fast for decades in the normative grip of the two great unitary ideologies that resemble Kuhn's paradigms, at least with regard to their durability.

The collectivist paradigm of a benevolent, rationally planned and radically egalitarian society is still cherished by small coteries of social policy scholars. As far as serious policy makers are concerned, this paradigm has passed its crisis point, been overtaken by catastrophic events and abandoned. In democratic societies, it simply does not win votes.

By contrast, the individualist paradigm still holds the imaginations and retains the trust of some of the world's most powerful politicians and policy makers. Despite all the evidence that unregulated market forces behave in highly unpredictable ways, nothing seems to shake their belief that the imperatives of globalisation will bring forth a more perfectly competitive world order in which the benefits of wealth creation eventually trickle down to the poor of every nation.

One feature contributing to 'this normative grip of the two great unitary ideologies' is that there is no commonly agreed meaning to the widely-used expression 'the welfare state'. I have made detailed comments about that expression at several points in this book. The point to emphasise now, however, is that the expression can be and is invoked by both ideologies, although on reflection in quite different ways. In this connection we may note that John Veit-Wilson has pointed out that the expression 'the welfare state' can be applied so broadly that it can become impossible to identify *any* country which *cannot* be so described (Veit-Wilson, 2000: 1, 4). Such fuzzy rhetoric seems to have obscured the need for conceptual and theoretical precision.

However, from the late 1890s onwards, we have witnessed the gradual evolution of a third social welfare paradigm of theories and policies that have steered a middle way between the extreme versions of individualism and collectivism. The mixed economies of today's pluralist democracies are underpinned by a matrix of policy compromises between these more radical options. Policies based on ideological compromises, however, do not evoke strong feelings of normative commitment and partisanship. They tend to be looked down on as the base metals of normative theory in contrast to the noble ones that promise future Golden Ages of either perfect competition or benevolent egalitarian collectivism.

Policy makers and theorists of the middle way, however, need not become ideological prisoners of their own paradigm. Social policies of the middle way are, by their very nature, the outcomes of incremental change and piecemeal social engineering that proceeds in an ongoing evolutionary manner. They have less need of – and are less prone to – the long overdue radical 'paradigm shifts' that Kuhn describes.

Policy makers and theorists of the middle way are 'critical rationalists' in Popper's meaning of the term. They remain aware of the limits of rationality in the making of social policies and the need to reach compromises between the dictates of reason and those of custom, sentiment and public opinion.

Finally, it should be noted that theories of the middle way *can* be set out in forms which allow them to be tested and falsified. Scholars who treat their theories as propositions open to critical scrutiny rather than defended against all comers need never become ideological prisoners of their own paradigms.

THREE

Stigma and social welfare[*]

Robert Pinker

The contribution of social theory to the field of social policy is too often one which begins in ideology and ends in rhetoric. The subject matter of social policy contains many of the most urgent problems of our time. Consequently theories and models of social welfare tend to be highly normative, explaining how men ought to behave if they wish to accomplish certain results, as discussed in Horton (1966).

Currently the two most influential theoretical formulations in social policy are based respectively on the 'institutional' and the 'residual' models of social welfare.[1] Both models draw on historical and sociological evidence to predict future trends in social policy. The residual model rests on moral assumptions about the self-evident virtues of competition and self-help. The institutional model rests its moral case on the ethics of co-operation and mutual aid.

In both cases psychological assumptions are made about the attitudes of individuals towards welfare provision. Their common weakness is a tendency to confuse academic perceptions of social reality with those of the ordinary users of social services. There is, however, no firm evidence as yet that sizeable sections of the community are strongly committed either to the ethic of mutual aid or to the liberties of the free market.[2] The end result for the discipline of social policy and administration is that too much is prescribed, too much indicted and too little explained.

The central and unresolved issue in this debate has been defined by Richard Titmuss as the problem of developing socially acceptable selective services within an 'infrastructure of universalist services' in such a way that stigma is reduced to a minimum.[3] This approach correctly focuses attention upon the subjective realities of everyday life for those in need.

The aim of this paper is to set out a number of empirically testable hypotheses in the form of a model of social welfare. If substantiated, the model could be used to classify welfare systems in terms of their stigmatising propensities. It should then be possible to formulate a theory explaining why people are elevated or debased in exchange situations and which conditions of provision and usage are most likely to engender stigma in industrial societies.

---

[*] Article originally published in (1970) *Social Work*, vol 27, no 4, pp 13-17, and subsequently included in my *Social Theory and Social Policy* (1971).

It is postulated that a sharp distinction exists in the consciousness of ordinary people between 'givers' and 'receivers' of social services whose respective statuses are elevated or debased by virtue of their exchange relationship. It is self-evident that citizens are sometimes subjected to humiliation in the supposedly therapeutic context of social services. This paradox arises because the values of the economic market are always reflected in social welfare systems. The extent to which this occurs in a given society influences the degree to which welfare systems are required to impose sanctions upon users. In so far as social services also operate as agents of social control they combine both therapeutic and stigmatising functions (Berger and Luckmann, 1967: 87).

In relatively simple societies systems of exchange are more likely to be based on norms of reciprocity between equals. Awareness of kinship obligations will be almost the same as awareness of total social obligations. So long as the norms of reciprocity are maintained, there will be almost perfect congruence between the individual's consciousness of his expectations and obligations and much less likelihood of stigma.

In complex industrial societies, by contrast, consciousness of kinship obligations may not go far beyond the scope of the privatised nuclear family. The growth of social inequalities also weakens notions of social reciprocity. The relationship between givers and receivers in the welfare context of industrial societies is always inherently an unstable and unequal one. As we are socialised into the economic ethos of such societies we learn to equate money with the protection of individual autonomy and the postponement of dependency. We might argue that it is as blessed to receive as to give, but there seems little evidence to support this view at the level of daily life in industrial societies.

The expectation which citizens have of social services is greatly affected by their prior experience of economic situations. A large proportion of those who use social services do so after having been stigmatised by adverse experiences in the economic market. Inequalities of knowledge and expertise also serve to reinforce feelings of inferiority and dependence and these kinds of inequality persist in welfare relationships. Whenever self-help and independence are powerfully sanctioned values, the subjective facts of social consciousness impose inferior status on the dependent.

The relationship between class structure and social consciousness manifests itself in social policies. The agreed levels of social provision reflect both the coercion of the privileged by the deprived and the resistance of the privileged to such coercion.[4] The levels and intensities of this conflict will be determined by the way in which people learn to define their welfare roles. What matters is the extent to which individuals and groups define themselves predominantly as 'givers' or 'receivers', and the extent to which the needful believe they have the right to demand from the privileged. The privileged must also define their position in relation to the poor. The imposition of stigma by the privileged can be seen as a means of self-protection from the 'excessive' demands of the poor, while preserving their own sense of moral rectitude.

We must, however, account for the fact that expectations and demand for social welfare appear to increase in industrial societies despite the revulsion people learn to feel for stigmatising dependency. This may be explained by the fact that although stigma does inhibit demand, biological needs frequently outweigh cultural sanctions. At the same time, other cultural factors such as rising expectations reduce tolerance of felt deprivation. The unemployed labourer would suffer the indignity of the workhouse test in Victorian England because he was starving. He would none the less endure hunger before he applied. Some did choose to starve. Today the *expectation* of hunger rather than starvation will normally cause the needful to ask for help despite their feelings of stigma.

We need to know much more about how people define their roles in welfare. It is hypothesised that, within the context of social services, much sharper contrasts are drawn between 'givers' and 'receivers', or 'providers' and 'users', than is the case in other situations such as work or leisure. However crude these distinctions may seem to specialists, they may still be very much a part of the 'common-sense' view of both the man in the Rover 2000 and the old-age pensioner on the Clapham omnibus.

Clearly these two roles are not so easily separated. The giver, for example, is often a receiver in other situation. People act, however, according to what they think they know, or need to know. What matters is the authenticity of the experiences on which the truths and fallacies of conventional wisdom are based. The authenticity of being in receipt of a 'free' prescription is more real to most recipients than an awareness of having paid a tax when purchasing a bar of soap in the same shop. The model therefore makes no reference to any kind of reciprocal 'feed-back' through taxation or rates, because it is hypothesised that such phenomena are not a significant part of ordinary social consciousness.

Two levels of administrative process are involved, namely, the major protective institutions of central and local government and their bureaucratic sub-units staffed by various professionals and other specialists. The moral component of these welfare systems expresses the criteria of social evaluation which determine the allocation of available resources.

There can be marked variations in the degree of consistency with which these evaluative criteria are applied at different levels of action. In the poor law where professional workers like relieving officers tended to support the deterrent ideologies of the central authority, there was always a minority of relatively lenient local Boards of Guardians. Today similar variations occur at local government level, and social workers are gaining much greater autonomy in their professional roles. Social workers are, therefore, better able to act as intermediaries between 'givers' and 'receivers'. Halmos (1967) refers to them as 'moral tutors', whose professional ideology stresses the qualities of compassion and acceptance. Of equal relevance are the professional expectations and attitudes of doctors, nurses, teachers and other 'personal service' professions.

The most obvious fact of social welfare, however, still tends to be misconstrued. The existence of vast welfare bureaucracies in industrial societies suggests not so much that these societies are uniquely compassionate, but a recognition of the fact that the spontaneous dictates of compassion consistently fail to meet the volume of unmet human needs. Only by taking a simplistic view of democratic processes is it possible to describe the recognition of these needs and our compulsory levels of provision as expressions of the popular will. Few of us, given the choice, would match our present compulsory level of taxation with voluntary donations. For every one of us some group of sufferers exists so different or distant from ourselves that our compassion is not aroused in any purposive way.

Our major premise is akin to a psychological proposition, namely, that in systems of exchange it is always less prestigious to receive than to give. The main hypotheses put forward in the model are that a significant proportion of citizens draw a sharp distinction between the welfare roles of 'giver' and 'receiver'; that exchange relationships in the public welfare sector are more stigmatising than those pertaining in the private sector; but that all such exchange relationships are inherently stigmatising in so far as they involve common cultural and biological factors defining and relating to dependency in industrial societies.

There are, none the less, a number of important qualifications which must be added to the above statement and these can be identified as the variables of *depth, distance* and *time*, to which some passing reference has already been made. The first variable of *depth* refers to the extent to which the recipient is made aware of his dependence and sense of inferiority and accepts the definition of his status as legitimate. The status of a recipient may be enhanced when what he receives is recognised as being a restitution for earlier service, or a compensation for disservice previously suffered. This principle is exemplified in many forms of social insurance provision where war pensions and industrial injuries benefits are paid on a more generous scale than other benefits.

Secondly, the status of the recipient may be enhanced when the gift is recognised as being likely to enhance his future gift-giving potential (or his propensity for reciprocity). For this reason, education is normally provided on a more generous basis than the other social services, and when means tests are used in relation to the actual educational provision, rather than supplementing welfare provisions like food, the experience of stigma is not common. Similarly, the medical care of the young is generally given priority over that of the aged, when resources are limited. The poorer quality of medical care given to the aged, especially in institutional contexts, reinforced the feelings of stigma experienced by the recipients. In the same way, diseases and handicaps having the best prognosis for recovery will be least stigmatising to the sufferer.

Whenever such arguments are publicly credible, voluntary associations for the handicapped stress the potential usefulness of their clientele when appealing for funds. Straightforward appeals to human compassion are normally the last resort of fund raisers working on behalf of groups with an apparently hopeless prognosis. The less likely the recovery prospects the more likely it is that stigma, intentionally or unintentionally, will be imposed on the group in question. The mentally subnormal, for example, suffer such marked discrimination that even their institutional diets are costed more cheaply than those of other National Health Service patients.

When the factors of incurability and age are combined, we recognise in the chronic sick a social group highly exposed to the risks of stigma. Their potentiality for restitution or reciprocity is zero. As we have seen in special cases, recognition of past service or gift ameliorates the sense of stigma. Such cases are becoming more exceptional in major fields of welfare provision like pensions. Graduated pension schemes on a national basis represent the extension of market criteria of evaluation in a life span. Despite the publicity given to the element of redistribution in this scheme, its net effect must be to legitimate the market evaluations of a person's worth. If this were not so, there would be no point in graduation. Although any element of redistribution amounts to a measure of social rather than economic recognition of worth, in any graded hierarchy of persons, some group must come bottom.

The facts of ageing and mortality ensure that all men will end their days in conditions of dependency. The only exceptions to this proposition would seem to be forms of sudden death and altruistic suicide. In the first case the practice of modern medicine has the effect of frequently postponing death but increasing the likelihood of very long periods of dependency. The younger victims of traditional agents of sudden death such as war and epidemic disease are less likely to die at once. The same is true of road injury victims.

It may be that the universal fear of death as an objective certainty for us all impels men to impose some of the most hurtful forms of stigma on the dying and even upon the dead themselves. The last page in each man's autobiography will always be written by someone else. Consequently an ability to stigmatise the dying is a sanction available to all societies. The ultimate stigma of the poor law – the pauper's funeral – was so effective because it symbolised a public defacement of a person's last page of life in the red ink of civic debt, overdraft and humiliation. Each pauper's funeral was intended as the public debasement of a human identity. Even today old people will go without in life to save money for a dignified funeral.

Every dependent group in society can be seen as a threat to the autonomy of the self-supporting (Matza, 1967: 296.If the dominant human impulses were compassionate, we could expect that the greatest of human tragedies such as irretrievable loss, chronic dependency, the process of dying and death itself, would attract a prior claim on welfare resources. This is clearly not the case.

Stigmatised people may, however, reject the dominant criteria of social evaluation. Their propensity to do so ultimately depends on the factor of power. Elderly, infirm citizens receiving the lowest graduated pension payable are unlikely to challenge effectively the low esteem in which they are held. They lack both the political and physical power to demand a greater economic reward for past services, none of which are viewed as exceptional and all of which have already been evaluated retrospectively in market terms. Over their working lifetime they have already become habituated to a place of lowly social esteem. If they failed to challenge this evaluation in their prime of life, such pensioners are unlikely to do so in their declining years. The facts of relative poverty will reinforce the sense of social distance from prospective givers, as will their high propensity for institutionalisation. The physically and mentally handicapped will be still more adversely affected by these factors.

Groups exposed to short-run risks of dependency, such as redundant able-bodied workers and minority groups with a high proportion of young members, are more likely to reject or be indifferent to prevailing forms of stigma. The counter claims of such minority groups take the form of a demand for civil rather than social rights. As Marshall suggests, the contemporary demands for power amongst black Americans express a demand for something more basic than additional social rights to better health, welfare and educational provisions.[5] One of our main arguments has been that people's estimation of themselves is not necessarily enhanced if their claims to social welfare are more liberally met. It is the status of recipient or dependent which is intrinsically humiliating.

The second major variable is that of *distance*, which may be social or spatial. We have noted that the problems relating to distance are central to an understanding of welfare provision in industrial societies. It has been suggested that the more distant the recipient is from the giver, the less is he likely to receive. Social distance, measured in terms of economic inequality or status differences, may be reinforced by powerful ideological factors. In Victorian England paupers were outside the social hierarchy altogether, and their social remoteness made their sufferings seem less real. Today, ethnic differences are identified and used in the same way.

Institutionalisation reinforces the effect of distance in spatial terms. Once groups like the aged and mentally handicapped are isolated they are both more easily forgotten and made aware of their stigmatised identity, even when material amenities are relatively generous.[6] There is no clear evidence to support the view that creating new forms of welfare provision on a smaller scale at local level will necessarily reduce stigma. The English poor law was, at all times, a very local service and also a very stigmatising one. Account must be taken not only of social and spatial distance but the ideologies which reinforce awareness of distance.

The third variable is that of *time*. The longer the period of dependency persists, the more likely the dependant is to redefine his total social life in terms of the stigma. Goffman's concept of 'spoiled identity' illustrates this phenomenon with regard to personal handicap.[7]

Processes of secondary socialisation and resocialisation reinforce feelings of inferiority in so far as they have more time in which to take effect. Institutionalisation adds the dimension of intensity to that of time. Stigmas deriving from ascribed forms of inferiority such as ethnicity or religion provide the greatest scope for reinforcement. Similarly, the process of pauperisation is complete when those affected have 'adapted to their poverty' and have become 'apathetic regarding their condition' (Matza, 1967: 292). Paradoxically, the long-term effect of stigmatisation is to cause the despised to accept their dependent status. In this way the therapeutic aims of those who impose stigma are defeated.

The sanction of stigma fails to inspire greater efforts at self-help. The importance of chronological age has already been noted in our discussion of the variable of *depth*.

In the long run most of us will experience extreme dependency, a condition we are socialised to equate with stigma. This relationship is not immutable, but it will certainly not be changed by the mere rhetoric of social reformers. Concepts like 'the caring society' and the 'welfare state' are subjectively meaningless to those who have not achieved citizenship in an authentic form. It may be that effecting changes in the social consciousness of ordinary people is now becoming more important than further changes in the statute book.

This model of social welfare can be applied to exchange situations in both the public and private sectors. Public services may have a greater propensity to stigmatise. The most profound humiliation of all, however, may be experienced in learning that only money can preserve self-respect in conditions of dependency. In both fields of welfare, the quality of compassion always appears to be in short supply.

In the public sector, however, stigma becomes an administrative technique for rationing scarce resources. It also expresses the nature of the relationship between the privileged and the underprivileged. The majority of people are disposed to give less voluntarily than they will give up under coercion. They are equally disposed to coerce others in order to retain what they believe is rightly their own. In this sense, coercion is also definable as a rationing device. And stigmatisation is a most effective form of coercion.

The imposition of stigma is the commonest form of violence used in democratic societies. Stigmatisation is slow, unobtrusive and genteel in its effect, so much so that when the stigmatised hit back physically in Londonderry or Chicago they can technically be accused of being the first to resort to force. Stigmatisation is a highly sophisticated form of violence in so far as it is rarely associated with physical threats or attack. It can best be compared to those forms of psychological torture in which the victim is broken psychically and physically but left to all outward appearances unmarked.

The phenomenon of stigma is therefore a central one, both for understanding the structure and aims of welfare services and the balance of power within societies where most forms of conflict have become ostensibly institutionalised.

Notes

[1]   A useful summary of the present state of debate about selectivity is given in Kaim-Caudle (1969); also in Seldon (1966). See also Friedman (1968).

[2]   Amongst the most useful studies in this field are P.E.P. (1961); Heywood (1962); and I.E.A., Harris and Seldon (1965). See also Runciman (1966/1972), esp. p. 285 passim.

[3]   Titmuss (1968), p. 135. See also **Chapter Five** of the present book.

[4]   Discussed in Lenski (1966), p. 313 passim.

[5]   Marshall (1969). See also especially **Chapters Eleven** and **Twelve** of the present book.

[6]   See Townsend (1962), especially ch. 8; Morris (1969); and Goffman (1968b), p. 15 passim.

[7]   Goffman (1968a), p. 11 passim.

FOUR

The welfare state: a comparative perspective[*]

Robert Pinker

I am greatly honoured by your invitation to give the James Seth Memorial lecture for 1972 in this university. James Seth, I know, is remembered with affection in Edinburgh not only for his outstanding contributions as a scholar and teacher, but for his lifelong involvement in the social welfare services of Edinburgh. James Seth was an example of that honourable tradition in academic life which holds that a university can and ought to contribute to the social well-being of its local community. His achievements in the practical tasks of social welfare are a testimony to his generosity of spirit. I hope that the subject of this lecture will have some relevance to those academic and social issues which concerned James Seth during his lifetime.

Over forty years ago, Elie Halevy delivered the third series of Rhodes Memorial lectures on the subject of 'The World Crisis of 1914–1918'.[1] His concern was 'to define the collective forces, the collective feelings and the movements of public opinion, which, in the early years of the twentieth century, made for strife'.[2] I shall attempt in this paper, with far less qualification for the task, to make a similar analysis of those collective forces which have been most instrumental in the making of social welfare. In doing so, I shall also be examining the extent to which the same collective sentiments and opinions which have been most influential in the creation of modern welfare states have also served to inhibit the growth of international systems of welfare. I begin with some comments on the traditionally collectivist bias and narrowly drawn boundaries of our subject. In the second part, I outline an analytical framework which may assist in the development of comparative welfare studies. The third section of the paper presents some evidence concerning the development of welfare policies within three major industrial nations – Britain, the United States and Russia. The fourth section is concerned with the international implications of these developments, with particular reference to trends in migration and migration control.

This paper does not presume to be more than an exploratory exercise. Its coverage is limited to three major industrial nations and even this degree of restriction is an affront to intellectual modesty. Far more detailed work on

---

[*] James Seth Memorial lecture of 1972, originally published in 1973 by Bookstall Publications for the Department of Social Administration, Edinburgh University.

a still broader scale will be necessary before the comparative study of social administration achieves the authority and assurance of its national counterparts. We begin with the handicap that although so many specialists in social policy are internationalist in outlook, the subject has been largely taught and studied within exclusively national contexts.[3] This is the legacy which we inherit and the paradox from which we start.

The moral basis of social welfare

The development of social policies in different countries embodies various notions of social and moral progress. We need to distinguish, however, between those modes of enquiry which seek to establish the criteria by which one system of welfare can be deemed morally superior to another and those which seek to explain why there are similarities and dissimilarities between the welfare systems of different countries. These two forms of intellectual enterprise are both equally necessary, and while it is difficult in practice to keep them apart, the fact of their qualitative difference needs always to be borne in mind.

At the present time, the orthodox academic consensus in social administration is strongly collectivist in value orientation. Social welfare is assumed to be almost synonymous with institutional variants of what we term 'the welfare state'. For this reason, most historical studies of social policy describe a kind of collectivist pilgrims' progress towards a promised land. The danger in such approaches is that, in comparative studies, a vastly complex range of human aspirations and activities tends to be overlooked or undervalued both within and between different societies. Social administration has developed as a field of academic study largely in democratic capitalist societies. It has therefore been too easy for social administrators to assume the role of public guardians against the immoralities of the economic market and to overlook the fact that some citizens believe that the social market generates its own forms of injustice. Comparative studies will lead us to consider a wider range of possible connections between welfare and justice. The range of debate becomes extended to include not only societies in which social policies are used to reduce inequalities and compensate the victims of social change, but countries in which social market values are so dominant that economic criteria are invoked to justify compensating the victims of egalitarianism.

We need, in short, to remind ourselves that there is an important distinction between what may be termed a welfare state and a state of welfare. The first concept is concerned with specific forms of government intervention in the free play of market forces. The second concept refers both to the subjective feelings of ordinary people about the nature of welfare, and to the complete range of activities by which they seek to enhance their own well-being through individual and collective endeavour. The way in which ordinary citizens define and seek to enhance their own state of welfare merits as much attention as the ways in which academics define the welfare state.

Comparative studies imply a concern for both the international and national aspects of welfare policies, the implications of which go beyond those statutory and voluntary forms of social service which have been our traditional concern. The welfare of every citizen is profoundly affected by such matters as the scale and incidence of tariffs and the conditions under which labour is allowed to move between one country and another. The current debate about entry into the Common Market has, for example, revealed how rigid are our value assumptions and how narrow our concerns in British social administration. The main instruments of debate have been political manifestos waving from the ends of slide rules.

A comparative typology of social welfare

One of the problems which arises in the comparative study of social welfare stems from the lack of a classificatory framework which would help us to identify the key institutional and normative features of different kinds of welfare system from the mass of descriptive data which research is making available for study. The classificatory framework outlined in this paper should be treated as a set of working hypotheses about the development of social welfare systems and the reasons for their apparent similarities and dissimilarities.

Nearly all the societies which currently lay claim to the title 'welfare state' are either highly industrialized or in the process of becoming so. The way in which social policies have developed in different societies has been profoundly influenced not only by the process of industrialization, but by the kinds of political context within which such changes occurred. A valid distinction can be drawn between those societies in which industrialization took place without the extensive intervention of the government and those in which it was imposed on the population by a small ruling elite. A second distinction can usefully be made between those societies in which the gradual extension of the franchise made it necessary for governments to create the broadest possible basis for social consensus and those societies in which governments ruled by force and needed only to generate sufficient public loyalty and support to enable them to continue doing so.

Sharp distinctions of this kind are of analytical value if they are treated as extreme types, located at the ends of their respective continua. Most societies come within the middle ranges, and their positions are subject to change over time. Nor does it follow that the position of a society on one of these scales necessarily determines its place on the other. Democratically accountable governments may sometimes attempt to lead public opinion and set aside popular expressions of short-term preference in the pursuit of what they define as long-term national interests. Nonetheless, some account will always be taken of the variety of beliefs concerning social justice and welfare priorities out of which a measure of consensus has to be created – even in totalitarian societies. An effective classificatory framework must also enable us to specify the relative importance of the criteria employed by the government in the allocation of welfare resources.

There would seem to be three major criteria by which material welfare goods and services are allocated in social life. In the economic market, the criterion is one of utility, or price; in the social market, the criterion is one of need. There is, however, a third criterion – that of political desert – which also operates in all societies.[4] Within the economic market, there is discrimination between like cases of need in terms of price. Those with an equal ability to pay can enjoy equality of provision. Within the social market, the allocation of welfare provision is governed by the principle that like cases of need should be treated in a like manner. Political criteria may take the form of ideological, religious or ethnic discrimination. Within groups whose members share the same publicly recognized need, such as the need for housing or health care, some individuals will receive more or less provision without regard either to their similarity of need or their ability to pay – because they fail to meet one or more of the criteria of political desert.

The operation of these systems of exchange, with their different criteria of entitlement, are of central importance in the study of social policy. In each society, the conflict between these criteria is posed and resolved in a different way, according to the extent and type of governmental intervention in the process of economic change and according to the quality of the relationship between rulers and ruled. Since a concern for welfare is not the prerogative of governments, some account must also be taken of the role of public opinion and community sentiment.

Comparative studies of social policy are, of necessity, often focused at such an abstract level that they fail to take account of the growth of mutual aid interactions and welfare sentiments at the level of everyday life. Our comparative analysis should try to rediscover something of the experience of those ordinary people who laid the foundations of mutual aid and local participant forms of democracy in both long-established and new communities, taking account of the social processes by which ordinary people made their own welfare before the term 'welfare state' was invented, and continue to do so in the present time.

At the same time, it has to be recognized that the values of local community impose their own limits upon the scope of welfare altruism. Industrialization weakens the moral framework of traditional forms of mutual aid which are rooted in local loyalties and the bonds of kinship. It is all too easy to become sentimental about these attachments after their demise, to forget that while the new values of the economic market distinguish between 'givers' and 'receivers' on the basis of a dispassionate utilitarianism, the older values of local community often discriminated with equal harshness between members and strangers.[5]

Any programme of social development and reform carries with it connotations of sacrifice made by one generation on behalf of another. Within the context of nuclear and extended families, altruism finds its most natural and total expression in the deference which one generation shows to the needs of the next. Shared experiences and common endeavours over long periods of time can inspire similar but less unconditional forms of altruism between members of small local communities. At a national level, these altruistic qualities remain an authentic part of human consciousness. But the idea of welfare at this level is always the product of varying degrees of compromise between numerous sectional interests, including those of family, locality and class affiliations. The nature of these compromises is expressed in the ordering of welfare priorities and in the kinds of criteria employed in this ordering. Consensus in such matters is always of a provisional kind.

We must also take account of those societies in which industrialization was imposed by governments ruling by force rather than popular consent and where it frequently happens that the government defines industrialization not as an end in itself, but as a means to creating or confirming a new kind of political order. Ideological considerations will determine the extent to which a competitive market economy is allowed to operate, but in the absence of democratic political institutions, the scope for government intervention is wide and the disposition to intervene is generally strong. In practice, all the major societies which experienced periods of forced industrialization of this kind did so with the aid of high tariffs and policies designed to regulate emigration and internal labour mobility. This was true at various stages in the industrial development of Germany, Russia and Japan.

In societies where industrialization is imposed, and where there is a high degree of centralized economic planning, social policies are often used as a means of securing and reinforcing the loyalty of one group at the expense of another. The privileged minorities will be just sufficiently large to ensure the survival of the regime and the efficient pursuit of its various political objectives.

Since the giving and the withholding of welfare goods and services are such effective instruments of labour discipline, collectivist social welfare policies become component features of economic life at a very early stage in processes of forced industrialization. As the process of industrialization succeeds in generating greater wealth, social services may be used to enhance the welfare of a larger proportion of citizens and, in this way, the social basis of a genuine consensus can be greatly extended. As this process occurs, the economic criterion of utility will become increasingly important in the allocation of welfare goods and services. Nonetheless, the criterion of political loyalty will still operate to exclude hostile groups and individuals. In this respect, the key distinction between democratic and non-democratic societies is that in a democracy, once a contingency such as illness or old age has been taken into consideration in the allocation of welfare resources, for economic and/or social reasons, political criteria *are not subsequently used to discriminate between like cases of need.*

Social welfare in Britain

Britain and the United States were the first great nations to become industrialized. Such government intervention as occurred was designed to give greater scope for the free play of market forces. The governments of both counties, for example, resorted to coercive poor laws which were intended to create a mobile and industrial labour force. It also became British policy to encourage emigration, preferably of paupers and other persons of low economic market value. Successive American governments encouraged immigration and increasingly gave preference to those who appeared to be potentially the most economically productive. (This flow of emigrants was contingent upon the export of British capital, without which economic expansion in the United States could not have been sustained.)[6]

In Britain, collectivist forms of welfare provision appeared at a relative late stage of industrialization. These provisions were in part a response to the gradual, if partial, democratization of political life, the dangers of social conflict and a growing uncertainty regarding the capability of a free economic market to meet essential welfare needs. In their much abused and seldom read account of Soviet Communism, the Webbs compared the miseries of forced collectivization with 'the statutory "enclosure of commons"', and 'the eviction of the Scottish crofters in favour of sheep and grouse ...' with the deporting of paupers to their parishes of origin.[7] In this sense, it can be argued that so many of the labouring poor had to be coerced into the freedoms of the economic market and suffer its criteria of evaluation that the basis of political consensus was placed in jeopardy.

I have reviewed elsewhere the workings of the Poor Law Amendment Act of 1834 and the collectivist reaction against its aims and consequences.[8] In so doing, I stressed the pragmatic nature of this response and its lack of any explicit ideology. In this brief section, I wish only to add some further observations on the connection between social reform and the search for political consensus in Britain, suggesting that in the democratic context of this country, political forces worked for compromise between the claims of the economic and social markets without imposing discriminatory criteria of their own.

In mid-nineteenth-century Britain, there was a conservative reaction against the excesses of *laissez-faire* doctrines and the 1834 Poor Law Amendment Act which influenced welfare policy long before socialism became an effective political force. The paternalistic welfare policies of successive Tory ministries can be seen as attempts to mitigate the sufferings of those who were forced to seek their own welfare in the bleak economic market of the 1840s and 1850s. This reaction was given coherence and a clearer sense of broad political purpose by Disraeli. In making the Conservatives the 'patriotic party' and the party of social reform, he recognized the need to recover a sense of national unity. The wounds of class conflict were to be healed by social reform at home and imperialism abroad. We should note, however, that Disraeli's Crystal Palace speech of 1872 came four years after the publication of Dilke's *Greater Britain,* in which very similar views were put forward.[9]

Between 1880 and 1910, both major parties had their imperialist lobbies, urging the need for social reform in the interests of national efficiency.[10] It was the conflict between the principles of free trade and protection – deemed to be of crucial relevance to social welfare – which prevented a coalition between these Tory and Liberal imperialists. Among the Fabians, there was a sizeable group of imperialist social reformers, including the Webbs and Shaw, who sought to influence the two major parties and seriously considered establishing their own party of national efficiency.[11] This tendency to associate patriotic interests with social reform is manifest in the writings of many of the most widely read social scientists of the period, including Benjamin Kidd and Karl Pearson.[12] Economists and economic historians such as William Cunningham, Sir William Ashley and Sir Halford McKinder were influenced by the nationalistic welfare programmes of the German Association for Social Policy.[13] Although the making of social policy was left largely to Lloyd George and other radical members of the Liberal Party between 1905 and 1914, the reform movements of the time were greatly assisted by a flood tide of patriotic sentiment which was both intellectually and popularly respectable.

There were also working-class socialists, such as Blatchford, who claimed to be 'Britons First and Socialists next'.[14] In his popular weekly, *The Clarion,* Blatchford ridiculed those 'cosmopolitan friends who are so cosmopolitan that they admire everything but their own, and love all men except Englishmen'.[15] The outbreak of war in 1914 was to reveal how shallow were the roots of international working-class solidarity amongst the European proletariat. In his study of Salford life between 1905 and 1914, Roberts observed that throughout these years of working-class militancy, 'the ultra patriotic mass remained intensely loyal to the nation and the system as a whole'.[16]

In the subsequent making of the British welfare state, we should take note of the way in which the connection between social welfare and political stability became especially evident in times of national crisis. The poor health of Boer War recruits intensified concern about the physical state of the poor. During both the First and the Second World Wars, the promises of post-war reform and the immediate recourse to rationing, price control and rent restrictions are obvious examples of the way in which governments used social policies to ensure the patriotic loyalty of their citizens.

It can be argued that in no other country were the values of self-help and independence as sensitively adapted to the claims of social need and political consensus as they were in Britain. The stigma of pauperism was preserved, but the alternative principle of insurance became the linchpin of collectivist welfare provision. The reforms of 1902–14 and 1944–48 were not attempts to change the social consciousness of the British people; they were the outcome of democratic processes which created over time a measure of congruence between government policies and popular expectations. While the continuing dominance of economic market values in the United States indicated the survival of unqualified trust in free enterprise, the rise of collectivism in Britain was a symptom of doubt rather than a gesture of confidence in the future. Both Britain and the United States typify the kind of society described by Marshall as 'democratic–welfare–capitalist'.[17] Nonetheless, the compromises effected in each country between the claims of the economic, social and political criteria were of a significantly different nature.

Social welfare in America

In the United States, it is arguable that democratization hindered rather than helped the development of collectivist social services. The absence of a traditional land-owning class and the apparently limitless scope for self-help tended to foster attachment to the values of the economic market amongst new and old immigrants alike. During the greater part of the nineteenth century, 'The poor in America considered themselves merely impoverished entrepreneurs, not as an independent class. Opportunity, not support, was their goal'.[18] For example, even that majority of settlers who became wage labourers rather than independent farmers eventually formed their unions in the spirit of potential entrepreneurs rather than socialists.[19] The immigrants who survived were those who acquired most swiftly the qualities of self-help and independence which were to inhibit the growth of public social services in the succeeding decades.

By the middle of the nineteenth century, the majority of white American males were enfranchised without regard to property qualifications.[20] Yet there was neither a democratic nor a paternalistic reaction against either *laissez-faire* doctrines or the Poor Law which America inherited from colonial times[21] and subsequently rendered still more a deterrent in imitation of the English act of 1834.[22] The key differences between these welfare policies began to emerge during the last quarter of the century. As the rigours of English public relief were mitigated and the welfare functions of the central government extended, the autonomy of local authorities in the United States was strengthened and their public relief systems were administered with greater stringency. Education was an exception to this trend because it was considered to be the most effective means of preventing pauperism and encouraging self-help.[23]

The Atlantic migration to America was the most dramatic expression of the search for welfare in modern times. The United States was built on the hopes of the thirty-three million immigrants who came to its shores between 1821 and 1924.[24] F.J. Turner, in his 'frontier thesis', suggests that westward migration provided a 'safety valve' for the tensions and frustrations of the new American cities[25] and that the availability of frontier lands ensured the survival of local democratic communities against both collectivism and competition.[26] There are certain affinities between Turner's thesis and those of the early Russian social and political theorists who looked to the village commune for moral salvation. Both were in the populist tradition.

Amongst the many criticisms of this thesis, it has been suggested that the cities, rather than the rural frontier lands, provided until recent years the 'safety valve' for popular discontents.[27] Nonetheless, the alliance between capitalists and workers which was to make possible the victory of the North in the Civil War found its most dramatic expression in the Homestead Act of 1862. The availability of free land contributed to giving both rich and poor a common commitment to the values of entrepreneurship and the economic market.[28]

In comparison with Britain, the creation of new forms of community organization and consensus can be interpreted as following a more democratic course, unaffected by paternalistic concern or intervention by central government. Houses, schools and churches had to be built, local defence organized, law and order enforced. The process of establishing these basic services and resolving local conflicts of interest helped to create structured communities out of scattered homesteads and establish a tradition of participant democracy.[29] Inter–state migration initially engendered strong local ties of community, but with the passage of time, it also created a new sense of national identity.[30] The social problems and challenges arising from immigration were, however, manifested more dramatically in the cities than in the frontier regions.

It was to study such problems that Thomas and Znaniecki prepared their classic study, *The Polish Peasant in Europe and America*.[31] The majority of these peasants came from village communities in which even the totally helpless or destitute were accepted and cared for within a traditional system of mutual aid.[32] Wherever a Polish settlement occurred in the Chicago of the late nineteenth century, new 'societies' for mutual aid were established against sickness, unemployment and death.[33] Znaniecki and Thomas describe how within the immigrant communities, hostility towards their own 'inefficient and misadapted' members increased as insurance contributions rather than membership of the community became the criterion of entitlement[34]: whoever accepted public relief was 'considered not only disgraced as a pauper but as disgracing the whole Polish colony'.[35] The immigrants came to equate economic dependency with stigma and self–help with full membership of a new Polish–American way of life.[36]

In such ways were the foundations laid both for a national consensus and for a variety of ethnic conflicts. The societies provided a training in local leadership, a focus of community organization and a framework for cultural assimilation.

A similar trend can be observed in the farmers' cooperative movements such as the Grangers, the Southern Alliance and the National Farmers' Alliance, which grew up in the populist mid–western states of the 1870s.[37] These movements encouraged the cooperative pooling of capital resources and began campaigns for such objectives as railway nationalization and monetary reform. Turner emphasizes two features of this reconciliation between individualism and collectivism – the desire to make a reality of the 'ideals of democracy' and the willingness of the pioneers to sacrifice 'the ease of the immediate future for the welfare of their children'.[38] But the forms of collective intervention were of a kind fundamentally different from those which occurred in Britain, and the key differences lay in the fact that welfare provision remained a strictly personal concern. The role of government was to ensure the individual entrepreneur a fairer chance in the competitive struggle for survival.

These cooperative movements found their urban counterpart in the reformist programmes of the Progressive Party during the 1880s and 1890s. Despite the introduction of local schemes of social insurance and factory legislation in cities such as Madison, Cincinnati and Cleveland, 'progressivist' ideas influenced federal policy for only a brief period during the presidency of Theodore Roosevelt, who won a massive presidential victory in 1904 with an electoral programme of imperialism and social reform. It was, in part, Roosevelt's inability to carry through these social reforms that caused him to adopt a more radical position and stand unsuccessfully as presidential candidate for the Progressives in 1912.[39] His successor, Woodrow Wilson, carried on the progressive tradition of American politics in a more moderate form. The main beneficiaries were railway workers and seamen, whose conditions of work were improved, as well as the independent farmers, who secured government aid for land improvement and road construction. The economic market was more carefully regulated but remained largely uncomplemented by social service provision.

The almost total inadequacy of public social services was revealed during the depression of the 1930s. Nonetheless, even during the peak years of unemployment, 'An interesting feature of popular discontent was a tendency towards self help in contrast to the emphasis on assistance'.[40] Protest organizations like the Bonus Army, the Townsendites and the Old Age Pensions Movement campaigned for limited objectives based largely on self-help principles. Franklin Roosevelt's New Deal was a programme to save capitalism, not to destroy it. The Social Security Act of 1935, while compromising between the claims of the economic and social markets, emphasized 'contractual' rather than 'social' rights.[41]

Piven and Cloward argue that the primary function of the American public relief system was and continues to be that of preserving the efficiency and continuity of the economic market, either by alleviating conflict or by forcing men to work 'on any terms' when employment is available.[42] The thesis is an interesting one but it neglects what seems to be the most interesting and obvious points of all. Despite the eagerness with which social scientists diagnose and publicize the gross injustices and inadequacies of American society, no other country has had to protect itself so thoroughly against such a legion of prospective new members.

Despite the persistence of racial and ethnic discrimination and residual poverty in America, the relative lack of collective welfare provision has been as conducive to consensus as has been its increasing availability in Britain. The American Supreme Court was for many decades an impediment to social reform[43] but the major obstacle has been the sheer success of capitalism in America. Neither socialism nor the social gospel movement made any substantial impact on this general attachment to economic market values.[44] The socially deprived in both societies have been gradually reduced through economic progress or social reform to a residual minority. Sociologists may question the evidence regarding the process of embourgeoisement. The fact is that if the deprived and the despised were not a residual minority in most Western democracies, it would not be necessary for social scientists and other pressure groups to urge their claims with such vigour. In America, the social theories of Spencer and Sumner have proved more reflective of popular opinion than either the reformist tradition in American sociology, which originated in the Chicago School, or its more recent radical manifestations.

Social welfare in Russia

In the case of Russia, we must chart a social process in which appeals to patriotic sentiment were never effectively complemented by social reform, and the traditional forms of self-help and mutual aid based on local communities were transformed by revolution into agencies of centralized control and coercion. In pre-revolutionary Russia, the village commune, or *mir*, was the main unit of self-help and mutual aid. The commune represented a compromise between individualism and collectivism and had long been a focus of both conservative and radical interest.[45]

In their intense patriotism, the Slavophil writers argued that the village commune was a form of social organization morally superior to any Western institutions. They contrasted its collectivism and mutual aid with the ruthless competitiveness of Western capitalism. Many of the early Russian populists and socialists shared the belief that capitalism could be avoided and poverty alleviated in Russia by a strengthening of the commune as a social institution.[46]

But the commune system restricted the free movement of labour and discouraged efficiency and individual initiative in agriculture. The political architects of economic change in tsarist Russia – Witte and Stolypin – saw no prospect either of their country continuing to be a great power or of the alleviation of poverty without industrialization. They therefore used the power of an autocratic state to impose industrialization on a largely parasitic nobility and a deeply conservative peasantry, who constituted 80 per cent of the total population. The costs of industrialization were to be paid for by the peasants through high rates of indirect taxation and increases in agricultural exports. The growth of domestic industry was to be protected by high tariffs. Between 1880 and 1911, the levels of taxation, exports and tariffs steadily increased.[47]

Stolypin's land reform of 1906 was 'a wager on the strong', designed to undermine the traditional egalitarianism of the commune, to create a class of wealthy peasants and to encourage labour mobility, including voluntary migration to Siberia. The peasants were given the chance as individuals to buy their own land. They did so in great numbers, but only a minority possessed the initiative and ability to succeed in a competitive struggle for survival. A small class of peasants did become wealthy, but many more were reduced to the status of hired agricultural labourers or forced to move permanently to the towns in search of work.[48] These new criteria of entitlement and reward were, however, in conflict with the traditional belief of the peasants that they all had an inalienable right to possess the land.[49]

Throughout the last quarter of the nineteenth century, a modest range of public health and other social services was developed by the new system of local government created by the *zemstvo* reforms of 1874. These provincial and municipal *zemstvos* continued, however, to be seriously handicapped by lack of revenues and adequately trained personnel.[50] Between 1886 and 1912, a government-sponsored social insurance scheme was introduced which was largely copied from Germany and Austria, but its modest provisions were restricted to about 20 per cent of the urban labour force in the larger towns.[51]

The land reforms satisfied the welfare aspirations of only a minority of peasants, and the 'losers' were left to the mercies of the economic market. Within a context of rapid industrial growth and growing political unrest, the limited measures of social reform were totally insufficient. In the absence of a widely based popular consensus or a representative system of government, the regime suppressed protest or criticism. Account must also be taken of the government-sponsored schemes of discrimination against Jews and other national minority groups which offended against both the criteria of political justice and economic efficiency.[52]

Nonetheless, there is evidence to show that despite their depressed conditions, the majority of the urban and rural poor wanted social and economic reform rather than radical political change. This remained true up to and after the outbreak of revolution. The poorest class of peasant wanted land, food and an end to the war;[53] the urban workers wanted better living conditions and a greater degree of control over their own lives.[54] It was the unequivocal Bolshevik promise to meet these limited demands which gave them a sufficient popular base from which they won the revolution. After the interim of the New Economic Policy, the peasants bitterly opposed the decision to collectivize agriculture and destroy that 'compromise between individual and collective behaviour on which the commune was based'.[55] The conflict between popular definitions of welfare and the long-term political objectives of the Bolsheviks was resolved at the cost of economic efficiency, the living standards of the rural poor and the popularity of the regime.

The decisions to build socialism in one country, to give total priority to rapid industrialization and the development of military power were in effect decisions to postpone improvements in living standards for all but a minority of the population. Stalin's decision to place the aim of national security above that of national welfare was practical mercantilism without a trace of social conscience. As Nove observes, 'the new men were remarkably indifferent to the welfare of the masses'.[56] The peasants were forced into collectives 'in order to make them the main basis ... of the socialist version of primary capitalist accumulation'.[57]

A new minority of highly privileged citizens was created and its membership was decided in terms of political loyalty and, in special cases, of economic utility. Since the regime lacked widespread popular support, Soviet social services were used to win and preserve this loyalty; they were used also as positive and negative instruments of labour discipline amongst the masses. As Rimlinger concludes, 'No other country has ever exploited its system of social protection in such a blatant fashion.'[58] Workers in vital sectors of industry, and especially those with scarce skills, were given generous economic incentives and welfare privileges. Malingerers and other 'hostile' citizens were punished by the withdrawal of the most basic amenities. Since the party had subsumed all secondary associations under its control, the trade unions were used for the administration of these sanctions. This system of 'comradely courts' was a novel form of community participation in which the workers were required to discipline and supervise one another.[59]

As these processes of political discrimination became intensified during the 1930s, the economic market, already disrupted by war and administrative chaos, was rendered incapable of maintaining, let alone enhancing, standards of living. Failure to meet even modest social expectations necessitated further coercion and a still greater reliance on political criteria in the allocation of what little welfare provision was available. It is significant that the *Kolkhoz* [collective farm] peasants remained largely excluded from the benefits of the Soviet social security system until the Kruschev period of reform between 1956 and 1964.[60]

The fact that Soviet Russia has always been a one-party state ought not to obscure the extent to which the government has been able to transform public values and use various forms of community participation as means of social control. During the last decade, there has been a vigorous campaign against 'parasites, vagrants and beggars' who by all accounts still constitute a major problem in Soviet Russia. We can only surmise that some of these vagrants and beggars are the victims of earlier political discrimination. The parasite laws of 1960 empowered local associations such as street committees and resident associations to constitute *ad hoc* public trials of such offenders.[61] The traditions of communal participation and control which derive from the pre-revolutionary *mir* now appear to be used in enforcing the strictest criteria of the economic market within a socialistic context.

In the post-Stalinist era, the successful inculcation of a strictly utilitarian work ethic in the mass of the population has contributed to a more equable compromise between the claims of the political, economic and social markets. There have recently been significant improvements in levels of social welfare provision, and there is evidence to suggest that these welfare measures have done much to widen the basis of a genuine political consensus. In nineteenth-century Britain and America, those who accepted the popular versions of *laissez-faire* asserted with confidence that no man need remain unemployed in a free economic market. Poor Law officials were employed to teach this lesson to the idle. In Soviet Russia today, it is asserted with equal confidence that under socialism, unemployment cannot exist, and the belief is now sufficiently widely shared for local community associations to be entrusted with the task of teaching the same lesson to the indolent.

International aspects of social welfare

The political variable also determines to a great extent the relationship between national and international welfare provision.

Governments will frequently advance the welfare interests of one section of their population at the expense of another. They will also, under certain circumstances, insist on the subordination of all immediate and personal welfare preferences to the pursuit of what is defined as a national interest or a long-term political or economic objective. What governments will not do – irrespective of their political type – is to jeopardize what are popularly defined as national welfare interests in order to enhance the welfare of any other society. Some marginal account is taken by most governments of the claims of international welfare, but in these cases, it can be argued that any such concessions are made despite rather than because of the popular will. Account must also be taken of the extent to which the majority of citizens will set aside their domestic disagreements regarding internal issues of social justice and combine to invoke the sovereign power of the state to protect and enhance their collective welfare interests, if need be, at the expense of other nations.

There is indeed evidence to suggest that at an international level today, the dominant trends in the development of welfare services, the revision of tariff preferences and the regulation of migration are still operating in favour of richer nations and at the expense of poorer ones.[62] Titmuss suggests that the notion of a welfare society expresses a more altruistic spirit than that of a welfare state, insofar as a welfare society is more clearly committed to the ideals of an international community.[63] In welfare terms, we suggest, such a community has yet to find its founding member.

We would appear, therefore, to be faced with the paradox that at a time when most advanced industrial societies can lay some claim to being 'welfare states', the ideals of international welfare are still very far from realization. This truism has inspired more moral indignation than systematic analysis. We have already implied that there is a close connection between the search for internal political consensus and the enhancement of welfare. But the point of central importance is that rulers and ruled are never in such close agreement as they are at a time when decisions are taken which affect the balance of welfare advantages between their own nation and the outside world.

The comparative study of social welfare draws attention to the exclusive as well as the inclusive features of social policy. The criteria of eligibility for social services provide both an index of community membership and an indication of those who are defined as internal and external strangers or deviants and are denied such membership. One of the tasks of comparative study is to describe and analyse the forms of external discrimination, thus complementing the exhaustive work which has already been carried out on discrimination within nations. Patterns of migration provide one of several possible indices for measuring the scope and limits of social altruism.

Compared with other industrial societies, Britain has been slow to impose controls on immigration as a means of preserving standards of living. The imperial tradition and a lingering sense of commonwealth unity and obligation may have helped to delay this process. Nonetheless, as early as 1870, an Extradition Act was passed qualifying the rights of refugees to claim political asylum. The Aliens Acts of 1905, 1914 and 1919 regulated the entry of East European refugees.[64] Although there were no further major extensions of control until 1953, the recent upsurge of legislation reflects a variety of long-standing and widely shared anxieties – the fear of 'cheap labour', the 'abuse' of welfare services and the subversion by aliens of our British way of life. In practice, the operation of these Acts has been highly selective and attentive to the manpower needs of the national economy and especially those of our social services. The most significant feature of these legislative trends during the last ten years is that government immigration policies have been based on the assumption that they enjoy a wide measure of public support. It is currently most unlikely that either of the two major political parties would risk a return to more liberal policies or that any other party would achieve electoral success by promising to do so.

The history of modern British social services began in a period of imperialist expansion. The socially adverse consequences of industrialization were mitigated in a piecemeal way which did not prevent the achievement of a reasonably popular balance between the claims of the economic and social markets. For a brief period after the Second World War, the British, in their insular manner, assumed that the welfare state was a phenomenon unique to the British way of life. And in the dying days of Empire, relatively little attention was given to the question of which members of the Commonwealth were uniquely British. In recent years, a heightened consciousness of our diminished national territory and vanished imperial destiny has brought the question to a more central position in the debate about welfare priorities and immigration control. The process of adjustment has also left us psychologically ill-prepared for re-entry into any community wider than our own.

It is possible that the strength of popular commitment to laissez-faire in the United States can be explained at least in part by the existence of free land. Not until the end of the nineteenth century were the frontiers completed and the supply of free land exhausted. The myth of free competition and the eternal frontier in one sense outlasted the reality, acting as an ideological barrier to collectivist social reform. But in another, sense there had always been premonitions regarding the finite nature of the nation's resources. The early settlers, for example, never considered that there was enough land to share with the two million Native Americans. And as early as the 1830s the maritime states had begun to impose controls on immigration.[65]

Throughout the nineteenth century, there was increasing popular pressure to have the flow of immigration checked. Congress passed its first major acts in 1882. Some of these restrictions were based on principles of individual selection. They singled out those in greatest social need – or those likely to become a charge on public funds – paupers, lunatics, criminals and prostitutes.[66] The Chinese Exclusion Act of the same year singled out the first of the social groups to become the subject of discrimination on ethnic grounds.

There were a number of reasons for this policy of restriction. The trades unions feared that cheap labour would reduce wage levels. But it was the arrival of so many destitute immigrants which alarmed local authorities and rate-payers. Immigration control was a response to those European governments who, from mid-century onwards, adopted the policy of 'shovelling out' their paupers.[67] During the 1850s and 1860s, certain groups of immigrants became increasingly defined as a threat to the American way of life, as American nativism became a more influential force in local political life.[68] In academic circles, writers like John Fiske and Herbert Adams identified themselves with these anxieties and gave them a more articulate expression. This growth of patriotic sentiment helped to create widespread fears of politically subversive immigrants from Germany and Eastern Europe.[69] Further restrictions were imposed in the twentieth century, including literacy tests and a quota system.

A similar trend towards restriction occurred in Canada, Australia, New Zealand and South Africa.[70] The criteria of exclusion were almost identical. The process was, as Richmond suggests, 'a logical concomitant of any nation state's claim to autonomy and some control over its economic and social policies'.[71]

In a similar manner, the ideal of *laissez-faire* was gradually restricted to national frontiers. As the terms of trade became less favourable to America during the nineteenth century, an influential section of the public began to campaign for tariff protection. The dilemma throughout the period was that of reconciling the farmers' interest in low tariffs and the need of 'infant industries' for protection.[72]

After the Civil War, America became increasingly protectionist. The anti-trust Sherman Act of 1890 was complemented by the McKinley Act of the same year, which imposed high levels of tariff. This act was followed by economic recession and a high incidence of bitter labour disputes. The initial response to these social troubles was a vigorous imperialist foreign policy initiated by McKinley and carried on by Theodore Roosevelt during his term of office.

Despite its formal commitment to the values of individualism and free enterprise, there has been a gradual if uneven extension of collectivist social services in America. The persistence of ethnic discrimination and disadvantage has done as much violence to economic criteria of justice as it has to the claims of social need and political justice. The continuing strength of local and state governments within a federal system has also helped to create sharp disparities in welfare policy and provision which make generalizations difficult and usually misleading.

What we cannot reliably assess is the range and depth of popular commitment to the values of the economic market amongst the underprivileged in the United States. In a society in which the consensus of popular opinion favours the enhancement of welfare in the economic market and equates citizenship with economic independence, social welfare becomes intrinsically stigmatizing to its recipients. In this kind of society, it may be a genuinely equal right to compete in the economic market rather than an equal right to share in the social market which is most conducive to social consensus.

Patterns of migration provide a poor guide to the expression of welfare preferences in both tsarist and Soviet Russia. The traditional restraints on labour mobility obstructed but did not entirely prevent either emigration or the internal movement of labour. Approximately one million Russians emigrated to the United States between 1873 and 1902, the majority leaving after 1890.[73] Most of these emigrants were Jews. As the pace of land reform increased, the movement of population to Siberia also grew in volume after 1900. Between 1900 and 1914 – approximately 3–5 million Russians migrated east of the Urals – almost as many as those who had done so throughout the preceding century.[74] We should, however, note that despite the political, legal and social disadvantages suffered by them, the indigenous populations of Siberia and central Asia were not subjected to extreme treatment such as mass deportation or genocide. Russians settled in these localities but were rarely allowed to usurp the land and means of livelihood belonging to the native peoples.[75]

Immediately after the Bolshevik revolution, there was a sizeable exodus of political emigrants. By the early 1930s, the regime had imposed stringent and effective controls on emigration. And the most widely publicized welfare state of all time has never been seriously troubled by immigration. Internal movements of the Russian population have been largely determined by political decisions rather than voluntary choice in the search for welfare. If the ultimate expression of negative discrimination under democratic welfare states is the ghetto, under Stalin's form of totalitarianism, it became the labour camp. In more recent times, coercion and terror as means of enforcing labour mobility have been largely replaced by economic incentives and additional welfare inducements such as housing and preferential social security benefits. With regard to negative sanctions, it is significant that the punishment for parasites, vagrants and beggars remains the traditional one of enforced exile – for periods of up to five years. And the Soviet government has recently surprised the world by seeking to impose a levy on prospective Jewish emigrants which is based on their estimated value in the economic market.

Conclusion

One of the future tasks of social analysis will be to explore more thoroughly the scope and limits of altruism as it is manifested generationally over the dimension of time, and also as it is revealed throughout the various levels of social organization – familially, locally, nationally and internationally – at any one point in time.

One of the dominant assumptions in the study of social administration has been that men and women are by nature communally orientated and altruistically motivated, and that the process of democratization makes manifest these natural and public virtues. From these assumptions, it becomes possible to argue that the welfare state is a staging post along a path which leads upwards from one form of collective enterprise to the next. In this sense, liberal reformers cling to their trust in the inevitability of community with the same fervour as that with which radical Marxists believe in the inevitability of class war.

In this paper, I have suggested an alternative hypothesis which questions this 'optimistic' collectivist view of social policy development at both national and international levels. In Britain and America, where democratic choice has existed, it can be argued that economic rather than social criteria have accorded most closely with popular notions of welfare and justice. Collectivist welfare policies were adopted as a last resort in Britain when confidence in the free play of economic market forces was undermined, although the eventual compromise between individualism and collectivism was a more equable one than that which occurred in the United States. In both cases, the balance struck made for consensus rather than conflict. The nature of these compromises suggests that whilst the enhancement of welfare has been a primary concern of both governments, collectivist social policies have never had more than a residual function in either society. Even in Britain, the compromise leaves the claims of social need subordinate to those of the economic market. In tsarist Russia, the attempt to create a property-owning autocracy came too late, and the Bolsheviks never submitted their revolutionary programme to a popular vote. Despite the rejection of the profit motive, Soviet social policies have continued to display highly utilitarian criteria of evaluation.

If, as Dicey has suggested, 'a collectivist never holds a stronger position than when he advocates the enforcement of the best ascertained laws of health',[76] the individualist, for his part, is never so universally popular as when he advocates in the name of welfare the extension of private ownership of property and its protection in law. Perhaps the most neglected index of popular welfare preference has been the private ownership of land, either as a means of livelihood or as a location for property. If kinship remains the natural focus of altruism, the commonest expression of this familial search for security is the acquisition of property and its transmission from one generation to the next. It is a search which can only be checked or denied by force.

There would also seem to be good reasons for giving to patriotism as much attention as we have given to socialism in welfare studies. It is arguable that there has never been a natural affinity between the values and aims which inspired the growth of welfare states and the ideals of international welfare. The balance of evidence supports a contrary view – that these two manifestations of human altruism are in many respects mutually antipathetic.

Before the emergence of the modern welfare state, emigration was a traditional means by which people tried to provide for their own welfare on their own terms. Migration serves as a catalyst in the creation of community and national sentiments which, in turn, redefine the limits of social altruism. But these migratory processes and the growth of new community and patriotic feelings interact with each other, making the enhancement of social welfare a predominantly national concern.

To countless Europeans, America offered throughout the eighteenth and nineteenth centuries a prospect of relative welfare, freedom and justice, although it was not a welfare state in social market terms. Many were driven out of their homelands by the harshness and persecution of others. There are few immigrants who, once they were established in new lands, hesitated to persecute, displace or destroy indigenous communities. The treatment of Native Americans and slaves, African Bushmen, Hottentots and Bantus, Australasian Aborigines, Tasmanians and Maoris serves as a counterpoint to the history of social welfare. In post-revolutionary Russia and in Nazi Germany, the same human propensities for discrimination were expressed in political, racial and religious terms.

As new nations discovered a sense of national identity and achieved a measure of prosperity, they sought to preserve them by regulating migration and erecting tariffs. Their criteria of selection encouraged the immigration of those with scarce economic skills and discouraged the entry of those who were in the greatest social need. The new nations built mainly from immigrant stock have long ago ceased to accept the 'bad risks' and 'failures' of the older nations; and as the supply of free land decreased, the controls became still more stringent. As emigration rates have declined and the standard of living has improved in the older nations, similar policies have been adopted with regard to under-developed countries.

If war is the natural extension of diplomacy carried on by 'other means',[77] discriminatory migration and tariff policies are the other means by which modern welfare states continue to enhance the well-being of their subjects. Trends in migration control would appear to be a significant index of the way in which both governments and popular opinion have come to share a common definition regarding the proper scope and limits of welfare altruism. Tariff protection has always been a more contentious issue, but both protectionists and free-traders have based their arguments, in popular debate, upon nationalist rather than internationalist premises. The modern systems of welfare provision which have developed in both the new and the older nations have become objects of financial anxiety as well as comfort to their members, resources to cherish rather than share. Viewed in comparative perspective, the internationalist ideals of social welfare seem almost to become ambivalent corrections scribbled in the margins of history.

Afterthoughts

9 February 2016

The text of this lecture was published in 1972 by Bookstall Publications on behalf of Edinburgh University's Department of Social Administration. It subsequently became the genesis of *The Idea of Welfare*, which was published by Heinemann Educational Books in 1979.

With the passage of time, the concepts we use in the study of social policy have changed and, in this respect, readers of an essay published over 40 years ago may be puzzled by the distinction Richard Titmuss drew between a 'welfare state' and a 'welfare society', which I cite in the section on 'International Aspects of Social Welfare' (**p 81**).

The essay in which Titmuss discussed the 'use or misuse' of these two concepts was published in *Commitment to Welfare* under the title 'Welfare State and Welfare Society' in 1968.[78] He begins with the following disclaimer: 'I did not choose this title. It was chosen for me. Despite this assistance, I must say that I am no more enamoured today of the indefinable abstraction "The Welfare State" than I was some twenty years ago when ... the term acquired an international as well as a national popularity'.[79]

Titmuss goes on to deliver a swingeing critique of the way in which rich countries like the UK and the US were developing their healthcare systems 'at the expense of poorer countries' throughout the world.[80] In his view, Britain was becoming increasingly dependent on recruiting doctors and nurses from poor Third World countries because of its failure in the past to train enough health workers for our own national needs.

Titmuss went on to suggest 'one criteria for the definition of a "welfare society"; namely, a society which openly accepts a policy responsibility for educating and training its own nationals to meet its own needs for doctors, nurses, social workers, scientists, engineers and others'. In his view, one of the dangers in the use of the term 'welfare state' was that it restricted the scope of welfare altruism 'solely within the limited framework of the nation-state'.

This was the specific issue I had in mind when I suggested that, for Titmuss, 'the notion of a welfare society expresses a more altruistic spirit than that of a welfare state insofar as a welfare society is more clearly committed to the ideals of an international community'. If Titmuss was alive today, he might well agree with my suggestion that – with regard to the recruitment of health care staff from Third World countries, 'such a community has yet to find its founding member'.

In concluding this essay, I also suggested that 'collectivist welfare policies were adopted as a last resort in Britain ... although the eventual compromise between individualism and collectivism was a more equable one than that which occurred in the United States'. The compromises in question were the British social policy reforms of 1902–14 and, in the US, Rooseveldt's New Deal and the 1935 Social Security Act.

In my conclusion, I said that 'collectivist social policies have never had more than a residual function in either society. Even in Britain, the compromise leaves the claims of social need subordinate to those of the economic market'. On reflection, I ought to have said, 'Until the passage of the British social policy reforms of 1902–14 and the US 1935 Social Security Act, collectivist social policies had never had more than a residual function in either society. Even in Britain, the compromise left the claims of social need subordinate to those of the economic market.'

Notes

[1]   Halevy (1930).

[2]   Ibid., p. 5.

[3]   Recently, there have been encouraging signs of a developing interest in comparative social administration. See especially Titmuss (1970); Rimlinger (1971); Rodgers (1968).

[4]   T.H. Marshall uses very similar criteria in his essay, 'Value Problems of Welfare-Capitalism', (Marshall, 1972). In this paper, I have laid much greater emphasis on the significance of political variables, including in this category a wider range of discriminatory criteria.

[5]   See Pinker (1971), pp. 165–75, for a more detailed analysis of this distinction.

[6]   See Jenks (1938); Brebner (1946), pp. 109–10 & 120; Thomas (1954), pp. 30–4.

[7]   Webb and Webb (1944), pp. 490–2.

[8]   Pinker (1971), pp. 48–94.

[9]   See Blake (1970), pp. 130 & 270 and Thornton (1963), p. 21.

[10] Semmell (1960), pp. 26 & 81.

[11] McBriar (1962), pp. 119–45 and Semmell (1960), p. 73.

[12] See Kidd (1894) and Pearson (1905).

[13] Semmell (1960), pp. 202–4.

[14] Blatchford (1931), p. 199.

[15] *The Clarion*, 28 October 1889, p. 37.

[16] Roberts (1971), p. 69.

[17] Marshall (1972), p. 18.

[18] Mencher (1967), p. 237. See also Handlin (1953), pp. 217–19.

[19] Thistlethwaite (1955), pp. 256 passim.

[20] Beard and Beard (1944), pp. 117 & 209–13 and Hofstadter et al (1959), pp. 390–3.

[21] Coll (1972), p. 130.

[22] Mencher (1967), pp. 131 passim & 148–51.

[23] Ibid., p. 151.

[24] Moller (1964), pp. 73 passim. See also Thistlethwaite (1960), pp. 32–60.

[25] Turner (1962).

[26] Ibid., p. 286.

[27] See Hofstadter and Lipset (1968) and Noble (1965), and especially in Hofstadter and Lipset: Lee (1968), pp. 66–8; Shannon (1968), pp. 172 passim; and Hofstadter (1968), p. 7. Shannon suggests that the 'frontier thesis' may be most usefully treated as 'a special case of a more general theory of migration', p. 66.

[28] Beard and Beard (1927), pp. 648–9, and Moore (1970), p. 130. Mencher (1967) describes the Homestead Act as 'the American counterpart to British concern about the poor laws' (p. 238).

[29] Elkins and McKitrick (1968), p. 127 and Boatright (1968), p. 48.

[30] Turner (1962), p. 30.

[31] Thomas and Znaniecki (1958), p. 350.

[32] Ibid., pp. 1,500 & 1,698.

[33] Ibid., pp. 1,698 & 1,518.

[34] Ibid., pp. 34, 1,586 & 1,688.

[35] Ibid., p. 19.

[36] Ibid., p. 1,602.

[37] Thistlethwaite (1955), pp. 259–62.

[38] See Turner (1962), Ch. XI & pp. 346–9.

[39] There are useful summaries of the rise and decline of the Progressive Party in Thistlethwaite (1955), pp. 268–72 and Fine (1956).

[40] Rimlinger (1971), p. 201.

[41] Ibid., pp. 204–5 & 230.

[42] Fox Piven and Cloward (1972), pp. xiii & 33.

[43] Fine (1956), pp. 126 passim & 140 passim.

[44] Hopkins (1961).

[45] Venturi (1964), pp. viii & ix (Preface by Isaiah Berlin); Stephenson (1969), p. 16; Joubert (1905); Troyat (1961), pp. 102–3; Wallace (1912), pp. 120 passim.

[46] Venturi (1964), pp. viii, xxix & 147, 150 & 160 and Wallace (1912), pp. 143, 411 & 497.

[47] Nove (1969), pp. 13–19; Seton-Watson (1960), pp. 109–10 & 287–90; von Laue (1969), pp. 127–35; Wallace (1912), pp. 660–2.

[48] Carr (1969), pp. 21 passim; and Hill (1971), pp. 66 passim. The phrase used by Stolypin in explaining his policy objectives is given by Carr as 'The government has placed its wager, not on the needy and the drunken, but on the sturdy and the strong' (1969, p. 22) (quoted from G. T. Robinson, *Rural Russia under the Old Regime* (1932), p. 194). There is an extensive literature on Stolypin's land reform policies. Carr provides an excellent summary of trends between 1906 and 1917 in Ch. XV.

[49] Wallace (1912), p. 505.

[50] Seton-Watson (1960), pp. 289–90. See also Madison (1960) and Vucinich (1960).

[51] Rimlinger (1971), p. 249 and Milligan (1969), pp. 370–4.

[52] See Seton-Watson (1960), pp. 158–64, 243–4 & 303–9; Joubert (1905), pp. 84–137; Byrnes, (1968), p. 207.

[53] Pipes (1968): see articles by Marco Ferro, pp. 147–8; G. F. Kennan, p. 13; R. Pipes, pp. 39–40. See also Nove (1969), pp. 30–1.

[54] Moore (1970), p. 481.

[55] Pitcher (1964), p. 173.

[56] Nove (1969), p. 376.

[57] Moore (1970), pp. 481 & 498–9.

[58] Rimlinger (1971), p. 245.

[59] See Rimlinger (1971); Madison (1960); Conquest (1968).

[60] Rimlinger (1971), p. 292.

[61] Beermann (1958a; 1958b; 1961).

[62] On general trends in trade policies and capital movements, see Myrdal (1971), pp. 280 passim. See especially Titmuss, *Commitment to Welfare* (1968), Ch. XI, for a general review, and Gish, (1971), for a more detailed study of trends in medical care services. There is a useful article by Tom Soper, 'Western Attitudes to Aid' (Soper, 1969). The case for a more generous provision of foreign aid is developed in the work of Gunnar Myrdal, and Jack L. Roach and Janet K. Roach, who provide an introduction to the work of other authorities in Roach and Roach (1972). An alternative view is presented by P.G. Bauer in *Dissent on Development: Studies and Debates in Development Economics* (Bauer, 1972a), summarized in an article in *The Listener* (Bauer, 1972b).

[63] Titmuss (1968), p. 127.

[64] See Thornberry (1964); Stephens (1970); Garrard (1971).

[65] Beard and Beard (1944), p. 418; Coleman (1972), p. 232; Hansen (1961), pp. 256–60.

[66] James-Davis (1970), pp. 296–8.

[67] Beard and Beard (1944), pp. 412–13. As late as 1959 four-fifths of the states were found to impose residence qualifications for poor relief in the hope of discouraging domestic and foreign immigrants (Mencher, 1967, p. 385).

[68] The intense xenophobia of the Know Nothing Party was one of its more dramatic if transient manifestations. A number of towns and states began to deport undesirable immigrants. See Terry Coleman (1972), Ch. 14.

[69] Hansen (1961), p. 272; Thistlethwaite (1955), p. 210.

[70] See Carr-Saunders (1964), pp. 211–16.

[71] Richmond (1969), p. 240.

[72] The 1850s were the heyday of the Democrat free-traders, and although Lincoln won the presidency in 1860 on a protectionist programme, he secured only a minority of the votes. The other two features of his electoral programme were free homesteads and opposition to slavery. This programme represented two of the three main centres of capital growth in the republic – the industrial North-east and the free-farm areas of the West (Moore, 1970, p. 115). The slave-based cotton industry of the South, representing the third area, was anti-protectionist but also opposed to the extension of independent farming into the West. Slavery was an obstacle not only to democracy but to the operation of a free economic market based on equal opportunity and competition (ibid, pp. 150–3).

[73] See also Davis (1922), p. 10.

[74] Carr-Saunders (1964), p. 56 and Stephenson (1969), pp. 94–96.

[75] Seton-Watson refers to protest movements and revolutionary activities amongst various national minority groups in Siberia during the years 1905–6 (1960, pp. 24–2).

[76] A. V. Dicey, *Law and Public Opinion in England During the Nineteenth Century*, Macmillan, London, 1962, p. lxxiv.

[77] Von Clausewitz (1940): '… war is nothing but a continuation of political intercourse, with a mixture of other means' (p. 121).

[78] Titmuss (1968), pp. 124–37.

[79] Ibid, p. 124.

[80] Ibid, p. 126.

FIVE

Richard Titmuss and the making of British social policy studies after the Second World War: a reappraisal*

Robert Pinker

Fifteen years ago, I was fortunate enough to hear Professor Friedrich von Hayek deliver a public lecture at the London School of Economics (LSE). That evening, the Old Lecture Theatre was packed with students and faculty members. Hayek had served as a Professor at the School and the University of London from 1931 to 1950. He had been awarded a Nobel Prize for his contributions to Economic Science in 1974.

Fifteen years on, I still see him standing at the lectern, ninety years old, six foot tall, spare of build and straight as a ramrod. I cannot recall the exact topic on which he spoke but I have never forgotten his introduction. 'This occasion', he said, 'is undoubtedly the first and last time that any of you will receive a lecture on economics from a former artillery officer of the Austro-Hungarian Empire'. And it probably was.

I draw this comparison only to make the point that occasions like this give us an opportunity to reaffirm the continuities of scholarship in our chosen fields of study. We gather together in a ceremonial laying on of hands across the years when our memories become the generational fingertips by which we keep in touch with each other. Some of our recollections will be recorded in biographies and history books. Others will disappear into what Shakespeare called 'the dark backward and abysm of time'.

I happen to be still young enough to have missed the First World War by a very generous margin of time. Nevertheless – in addition to having heard Hayek – I am still old enough to have taken morning coffee with Lord Beveridge and known most of the leading scholars – including Professor Tom Marshall – who were trailblazers and pioneers in the making of British social policy studies from the mid-1950s onwards. My one-time professor and teacher, Richard Morris Titmuss, was in the front rank of that vanguard.

---

*   Lecture delivered at the University of Bergen on 5 December 2007, published in 2008 in *Sosiologisk tidsskrift* (*Journal of Sociology*), 16: 2, 167–84. The second part of this lecture is based largely on the article 'From gift relationships to quasi-markets: an odyssey along the policy paths of altruism and egoism' (Pinker, 2006a).

The early years

I will start by saying something about Titmuss, the man, the place and time in which he worked as an academic, and the changing political and social background against which his thoughts about the ends and means of social policy developed to maturity. I will also add some passing comments on other British social policy luminaries of the period.

Titmuss was born in the county of Bedfordshire in 1907, the son of a tenant-farmer. His mother also came from a farming family. He left school at the age of fourteen and briefly attended a commercial college before starting work as an office boy. He then decided to make a career in the world of insurance, where he rose to the rank of Inspector. His marriage to Kay Miller in 1937 was generally regarded in academic circles as a model of its kind. Their daughter, Ann Oakley, offers her own distinctive interpretation of their relationship in her memoir *Man and Wife*. She acknowledges that 'Richard and Kay undoubtedly loved each other', but goes on to suggest that over the years of their marriage, Kay disappears 'as a public figure' in her own right while Richard went on to fulfil his destiny as a scholar. The one half of the partnership is remembered and celebrated in many articles and memorials. The other is largely forgotten or listed in the footnotes of her husband's biographies. And their daughter goes on to suggest that women like Kay Titmuss, living in the times and social milieux that they did, were often 'reticent about their own wish for some sort of memorial' (Oakley, 1997, 10–12, 298).

Throughout the 1930s and 1940s, the Titmusses carried on their part-time research and writing on family planning, eugenics, health care and poverty. Their co-authored book, *Parents' Revolt: A Study of the Declining Birth-rate in Acquisitive Societies,* was graced with a Preface by Beatrice Webb (Titmuss and Titmuss, 1942). It was during this period that the Titmusses became active members of the Eugenics Society, where they established friendships with some of the leading demographers and policy analysts of the time.

As it happened, their involvement in the activities of the Eugenics Society was to became Richard's path of transition from the world of insurance to the world of academia. In 1941, the British government commissioned an Australian economic historian, Sir Keith Hancock, to supervise the production of a mammoth thirty-volume official history of the Second World War. Hancock let it be known among his circle of friends that he was having difficulties finding a good person to write the volume on the wartime history of the health and social services. One of these friends was a member of the Eugenics Society. She knew and admired Richard Titmuss and recommended him to Hancock. Within weeks, Titmuss was appointed to his team of official war historians (Abel-Smith and Titmuss, 1956).

When *Problems of Social Policy* appeared in 1950 (Titmuss, 1950), it was received with general acclamation. He had written a work that is still recognised as the definitive study of the impact of war on British civil society and the response of the social services. The narrative and analysis is focused on three salient issues –

wartime evacuation, the reorganisation of the hospital and medical care services, and the problems of homelessness. In a laudatory and lengthy review published in 1950, R.H. Tawney described *Problems of Social Policy* as 'this brilliant book'. In 1975, T.H. Marshall considered it to be 'a flawless masterpiece' and, in my own judgement, it still remains 'his masterpiece' (Wilding, 1995, 162).

A few months later, the LSE appointed Titmuss to a newly established Chair of Social Administration. He was 42 years old, he did not hold a first degree and had no previous experience of university life and work. His brief was to transform a department that was primarily concerned with the training of social workers into a leading centre of social policy teaching and research. Apart from having a sympathetic Director in the person of Sir Alexander Carr-Saunders, he had very few other friends and allies in the School.

As is so often the case with truly memorable people, Richard Titmuss was a paradoxical man. He had an engaging and fluent style of writing but he was never the best of public speakers. Like Sidney and Beatrice Webb, he was both a student of the social causes of ill-health and a lifelong dedicated smoker of cigarettes. He was also a dedicated egalitarian but as his daughter, Ann, observed, 'you didn't have to be a detective to discern my father's concealed adulation of certain unsocialist institutions'. As A.H. Halsey notes, he agreed to be made a CBE in the Queen's Honours List of 1966 but he declined the offer of a peerage and the membership of the House of Lords that went with it. (Oakley, 1997, 3; Halsey, 2007, 59).

Most of all, the people who knew Richard, and especially those who were taught by him, remember his unfailing kindness and gentle disposition. I was still a Diploma student when he offered me a junior research appointment. He persuaded the Home Office to release me from my contract and shortly afterwards took me to one side and advised me to study part-time for a first degree if I wanted to became a university teacher. 'You mustn't take me for a precedent', he said. 'I don't think anyone else will ever be appointed to a Chair without a first degree.' So I studied part-time until he persuaded my local authority to give me a grant so that I could go full-time for my final year. And, even in those far-off days, we didn't always see eye to eye on issues like the ends and means of social policy.

What kind of expertise and convictions did Titmuss bring with him to confront the challenges we faced at that time? He was widely recognised as an accomplished, self-taught demographer and epidemiologist but, as Vaizey points out, 'he knew no economics and next to no sociology' (Vaizey, 1983, 69). In *Problems of Social Policy*, he had already demonstrated his 'ability to master an enormous and complex mass of material, to infuse the narrative and analysis with his own deep concern and draw out the central issues' (Wilding, 1995, 162).

As for his convictions, we must go back in time to the early 1930s when Richard and Kay were becoming 'passionately involved [in the politics of the Liberal Party] and in the peace and anti-rearmament movement' (Oakley, 1997, 64). The British Liberal Party at that time was still a party committed to social reform, but it was no longer the political force that it had once been in the years prior to and during the First World War. Kay had been the prime mover in engaging Richard in these activities but he soon became a dedicated Liberal Party activist in his own right.

In 1938, Richard and a charismatic Liberal MP, Sir Richard Acland, discovered that they shared the same interests in health and unemployment policies and the campaign against rearmament. Acland, however, was already in the process of becoming a socialist and a practising Christian.

In 1942, Acland broke away from the Liberals and established a new party called Common Wealth which was committed to nothing less than the moral regeneration of British political society. As Oakley observes, 'The two driving forces of Richard's intellectual and political life at this time were concern for the future of population and [a] distaste for the culture which produced the Second World War' (Oakley, 1997, 152).

Titmuss joined the Common Wealth movement because it seemed to offer solutions to these and other urgent social problems of the time. Common Wealth was committed to the common ownership of the means of production and distribution, and the moral regeneration of British political and social life. Its programme of reform was based on the principles of altruism and Christian socialist ethics. It was unequivocally opposed to the acquisitive values of capitalism, competitive markets and the profit motive.

Common Wealth went on to win three wartime by-elections but, after its eclipse in the 1945 General Election, Acland rejoined the Labour Party and Titmuss subsequently became one of the party's key advisers on social policy issues. In many respects, however, it can be argued that Common Wealth remained his spiritual home for the rest of his working life. The concept of altruism recurs again and again in all of his books and essays and reaches its apotheosis in his last work, *The Gift Relationship* (Titmuss, 1970).

In many respects, the development of Titmuss's ideas about the nature of the good society and his philosophy of welfare seemed to have travelled a full circle that began and ended in the ethical affinities he shared with Common Wealth. To the best of my knowledge, however, he never shared an affinity with the Christian ethos of that movement. Although he was to become what we now call an ethical socialist, he never became a Christian socialist. And, it is also worth noting that, in a recent collection of his essays, co-edited by Ann Oakley and other colleagues, there are no references at all to his brief membership of Common Wealth (Alcock et al, 2001).

At this point in time, however, we can only speculate about the lines of attachment that might have held between the altruistic principles that motivated Common Wealth and those that found expression in *The Gift Relationship*. As T.S. Eliot wrote in the last of his *Four Quartets*:

> We shall not cease from exploration
> And the end of all our exploring
> Will be to arrive where we started
> And to know the place for the first time.

It is just possible that Titmuss's intellectual odyssey followed a similar kind of trajectory.

The political and social background

I began my academic life in 1956 as a student at the LSE, funded by the Home Office and contracted to become a Probation Officer. Titmuss's first six years in post had been a time of radical change in British social policy, following the creation of the post-war welfare state between 1944 and 1950. A Conservative government had been in office since 1951 and, because concern was mounting about the rising cost of the National Health Service, Titmuss, with his colleague and close friend, Brian Abel-Smith, had been asked to review its funding and expenditure.

We lived in a world dominated by the politics of the Cold War. Europe was divided between East and West by an ideological and military Iron Curtain. By the time that the hot war between North and South Korea had ended in 1953, Britain had possessed the atom bomb, the USA was a nuclear power and the USSR was about to become one. As the churchman, Archbishop of Canterbury Michael Ramsey, wrote, the great political paradox of the mid-1950s was that 'the security of the welfare state [was] crossed by the radical insecurity of a world that might suddenly be blown to bits' (Hennessy, 2007, 132).

At home, the government remained committed to policies of maintaining full employment and holding down inflation as levels of welfare and defence expenditure rose inexorably. In 1956, this economic balancing act went out of kilter when Britain, France and Israel invaded Egypt and occupied the Suez Canal. At the same time, an armed rebellion in Hungary was brutally crushed by the Red Army.

The Suez venture ended in failure. A new Prime Minister, Harold Macmillan, took office and faced up to the aftermath of a major economic crisis. Long before, in the 1930s, Macmillan had campaigned for policies of national reconstruction and increased social service expenditure. His own finance ministers now told him that cutbacks in the defence and welfare budgets would have to be made as a precondition for economic recovery. These demands were rejected and the dissident ministers resigned.

Within months, the government was reflating the economy and the British people were once again living beyond their means. This was the time when Macmillan made his famous observation that 'most of our people have never had it so good', although he also went on to ask whether it was all 'too good to be true?' Thereafter, Britain entered the 1960s, still a nuclear power, still a welfare state and still paying off a massive burden of overseas debt.

Similar policies were to be pursued by successive Labour and Conservative governments until economic nemesis struck in the form of the 1978–79 'Winter of Discontent' which followed a Labour government's belated decision to impose a 5% ceiling on pay awards. The trade unions went on strike, major public services closed down and the economy stuttered to a halt. In the ensuing General Election of 1979, Margaret Thatcher led the Conservatives to victory. The long years of cross-party political consensus about the ends and means of British social policy were well and truly over.

As I will seek to show, Titmuss's whole approach to social policy was based on the premise that no such consensus had ever existed. He remained convinced that the institutions of the welfare state were under continuous threat from a host of political enemies, but he did not live long enough to witness the demise of what some of us, at the time, might have mistaken for a consensus.

Titmuss's social policy

There was, undoubtedly, a *collectivist* consensus *within* the discipline of social policy about what its ends and means *ought* to be. This consensus, with which Titmuss was closely identified, was never total, even during his lifetime, but it was to have a lasting impression on future developments in the discipline.

Some measure of Titmuss's influence on these developments can be inferred from the fact that more than twenty of the academics who taught in his department during the 1950s and 1960s went on to professorial appointments at the LSE and other British universities. His influence on the international development of the discipline was just as impressive.

Seven features stand out in Titmuss's approach to the study of social policy and administration. First and foremost, Titmuss defined the objectives of social policy in terms of their moral purposes. Unlike economic policy, which dealt in exchange relationships and bilateral transfers, social policy was primarily concerned with 'gift relationships' and 'unilateral transfers' directed towards meeting a complex and ever-changing range of social needs. Its moral purposes were egalitarian and redistributive in character. The equally complex set of statutory social services that served these needs operated 'outside or on the fringes of the so-called free market, the mechanisms of price and tests of profitability'. Social policy, he went on to say, 'is thus concerned, for instance, with different kinds of moral transactions, embodying notions of gift-exchange, of reciprocal obligations', whose purpose is 'to bring about and maintain social and community relations'. The overriding objective was 'to foster integration and discourage alienation' in society (Titmuss, 1976, 20–21, 131).

In this respect, contemporary readers of Titmuss will probably note that the issues of gender and ethnic inequality are rarely touched on in his writings – apart from an interesting essay on 'The Position of Women' written in 1952 and published in 1958 and some positive references to 'coloured workers' in his essay on 'The Irresponsible Society'. As has often been observed, Titmuss's approach was, in some respects, 'embedded in a traditional view of gender roles' and the issue of ethnic inequalities was not as prominent in social policy literature as it is today (Titmuss, 1958a, 88–103; Alcock et al, 2001, 149, 15).

Secondly, the clear-cut moral distinction that Titmuss drew between the values and purposes of economic and social policy runs like a motif through the three alternative models of social welfare that are set out in his posthumous work, *Social Policy, An Introduction* (Titmuss, 1974). The first of these is described as a 'residual model' in which a minimal range of statutory social services leave the majority of needful people dependent on self-help, their families and the private sector. Next, there is the 'industrial achievement–performance model' in which priority is given to maintaining a reasonably educated and healthy workforce and social services are seen largely as an adjunct to the economy.

Titmuss then goes on to define an 'institutional–redistributive model' of social welfare which 'sees social welfare as a basic integrated institution in society providing both universal and selective services outside the market on the principle of need'. These services, he states, will be able to foster and promote 'the values of social solidarity, altruism, toleration and accountability' (Titmuss, 1974, 30–32).

These three models can also be seen as stages of moral development starting from the narrowest forms of egoistic self-interest and proceeding through the prudential manifestations of reciprocal exchange to the higher forms of gift relationship encompassing the 'universal stranger' portrayed in Titmuss's last major empirical study, *The Gift Relationship* (Titmuss, 1970).

Titmuss's conceptual analysis of the dynamics of giving and receiving was shaped and driven by the two convictions that underpinned his philosophy of welfare – namely, that greater equality means greater equity (or fairness) and that the wider the institutional range of our benevolence, the more morally commendable it becomes.

Thirdly, Titmuss was an unequivocal welfare unitarist and never more so than when he was denouncing the moral shortcomings of welfare pluralism, as he did in his essays on 'The Social Division of Welfare' and 'The Irresponsible Society' (Abel-Smith and Titmuss, 1987). While T.H. Marshall looked on competitive markets as an essential element in his own model of "democratic welfare capitalism", Titmuss believed that the statutory social services constituted the most important institutional feature of a civilised society because the egoism of the private market alienated people from each other whereas the altruism embodied in the statutory public services united and elevated them. It followed from this, in Titmuss's view, that the state should be the main funder and provider of social services because only the state had the authority to implement, without fear or favour, the redistributive policies that he considered necessary.

Fourthly, Titmuss believed that universalist social services were far less likely to stigmatise their users than selectivist ones. A universalist social service is provided to everyone who falls within a formally defined category, like old people or children. It is provided on proof of need without resorting to a selective test of income and other means. A selectivist service is provided on proof of need *and* is subject to a test of income and other means. In practice, these two modes of service delivery often overlap. An elderly person, for example, may be receiving a universalist state pension that is insufficient to meet her needs. She may, therefore, have to apply for additional and selectively means-tested assistance in order to make ends meet.

Titmuss recognised that there had to be a place in the social security system for exceptional and unexpected kinds of need. 'The real challenge', as he saw it, resided 'in the question: what particular infrastructure of universalist services is needed in order to provide a framework of values and opportunity bases within and around which can be developed socially acceptable services aiming to discriminate positively, with the minimum risk of stigma, in favour of those whose needs are greatest' (Titmuss, 1976, 135).

In other words, as long as universalism remained the dominant principle in service delivery, some selective means-tested services could be provided for people with special needs in ways that did not stigmatise them, lower their self-esteem and status as citizens, and thereby discourage them from applying for help.

Fifthly, Titmuss was an internationalist, although he was also, paradoxically, something of what we now call a 'Euro-sceptic'. In 1962, he opposed Britian's application to join what was then the European Economic Community on the grounds that the social services of member states did not match up to the standards of their British counterparts. He was dedicated to improving living standards in the Third World. He served as a consultant to various overseas governments, notably those of Tanzania, where he became close friends with Julius Nyerere, and Mauritius, where he advised on issues of population control. He undertook this work with James Meade, a Nobel Prize-winner for Economics and Brian Abel-Smith (Alcock et al, 2001, 169–74).

In Howard Glennerster's opinion, Titmuss 'was not just an international figure' in the world of social policy. 'He also made the academic subject of social policy international' (Alcock et al, 2001, 169). That judgement, in my view, is absolutely correct – Titmuss played a key role in adding an international dimension to the discipline throughout the 1960s. I would only add the thought that his most distinctive contribution derived from his conviction that gift relationships directed towards meeting the needs of 'universal strangers' were of an intrinsically superior moral significance than those directed towards the needs of the people we know and live amongst.

Sixthly, Titmuss's definition of the subject field of social policy and administration in terms of its distinctive and superior moral purposes did not encourage the growth of closer relationships with other social sciences during the 1950s and 1960s. While occasional excursions were made into sociology, anthropology, economics and law, they were largely undertaken in the spirit of missionary visitations to heathen parts. At the same time, it is worth noting that a large number of converts from these other parts became social policy scholars during his lifetime and after. He also played a major role in helping to establish what is now the UK Social Policy Association (Pinker, 2006a).

Despite his injunction to social administrators to draw liberally on the methods and perspectives of the other social sciences, Titmuss himself did so with some caution. He elicited from the sociology of Emile Durkheim and the anthropology of Marcel Mauss certain theoretical perspectives and empirical findings that appeared to be compatible with his own philosophy. He was equally selective in his approach to economics, admiring, in particular, the work of Kenneth Boulding, J.K. Galbraith, James Meade and Gunnar Myrdal, whose views on competition and capitalism were similar to his own. And Gunnar Myrdal, it should be noted, received his Nobel Prize at the same time as Hayek (in 1974). As for the law and lawyers, Titmuss had little sympathy with what he once described as 'the pathology of legalism' (Carrier and Kendall, 1992, 61–87).

At the time of Titmuss's death, the discipline of social policy was still normatively isolated from the main currents of economic, sociological and legal thought, although there were closer links with social history, social statistics and some aspects of moral philosophy. Shortly before his death, Titmuss describes how he took a copy of Rawls' *A Theory of Justice* into hospital with him and, after reading it, concluded that it was 'one of the most important books published in the field of social philosophy for the last twenty-five years' (Titmuss, 1974, 149–50).

Finally, it should be added that Titmuss's philosophy of welfare was explicitly political. Although he was not a member of the Fabian Society, his democratic, incrementalist, empiricist brand of socialism had a distinctly Fabian character. Such theory as he espoused was ideological in character, insofar as he used empirical evidence to substantiate rather than test out his own normative theories and to indict those of his critics. As Arthur Seldon pointedly remarked in his review of *Commitment to Welfare*, 'The difficulty of conducting an academic debate with Professor Titmuss is that he makes his adversary feel not only wrong but also wicked' (Seldon, 1968, 196–200).

A summary of Titmuss's philosophy of welfare might read as follows. He defined the subject in terms of its egalitarian and redistributive moral purposes. He argued that the values shaping these purposes were morally superior to those of the economic market. He was committed to a unitary model of social welfare in which the government would provide most of the funding and administrative expertise and the statutory social services would function as key agents of redistribution, social integration and social change.

He believed that the creation of a broad framework of universalist social services was the best way of ensuring that selective services did not stigmatise and discourage people in need from using them. In his approach to comparative welfare, Titmuss was both an internationalist and a Little Englander. He was also something of an isolationist in his dealings with other social sciences. These key aspects of Titmuss's writings will serve as starting points for a review of their continuing significance and relevance to current policy debates.

Reviewing the contribution

In the following review of Titmuss's contribution, I will range in no particular order across the seven key features which I identified as the key principles that underpin his philosophy of welfare. My purpose in doing so will be to explore the extent to which these principles complement each other and constitute a unitary approach and a coherent body of thought.

At the time when I wrote *Social Theory and Social Policy*, I was becoming increasingly disenchanted with Titmuss's unitary model of social welfare or, to use his own terminology, 'the institutional Redistributive model of Social Policy' (Pinker, 1971). It is important to note that concepts like 'unitary' and 'pluralist' models of welfare were not generally used by social administrators in the 1970s. In terms of his ideology and interests, however, Titmuss was undoubtedly a unitarist. He wrote very little about the voluntary sector and it is scarcely mentioned in his benchmark essay on 'The Social Division of Welfare'. The occupational and fiscal welfare sectors are, however, subjected to much closer scrutiny but they are conceptualised in largely negative terms – as institutional obstacles to the creation of a more unified and egalitarian welfare state (Titmuss, 1958a, 34–55).

The problem with unitary models of social welfare is that they cannot respond with sufficient sensitivity to the diversity of human aspirations and needs and this will be the case irrespective of whether the sole providers of services are statutory, voluntary or private sector agencies. Most significantly, the risks of total dependency are maximised when there is only one provider of social services and support.

By contrast, a pluralist system of welfare is less likely to generate stigma and undermine the authenticity of citizenship than a unitary system – irrespective of the relationship that holds between universality and selectivity. Not all universalist services enhance the status of citizenship. Not all selectivist services debase it. Too much universality can leave the residual means-tested minority profoundly stigmatised. Too much selectivity can residualise the welfare state altogether. The ideal compromise is a pluralist model in which the state is both a direct provider and purchaser of non-statutory social services and selectivity operates within a broadly universalist structure. At times, dependency is an inescapable fact of life but partial dependency is preferable to total dependency. For most people, complete independence is an unattainable and unattractive condition. The same may be said of complete dependency.

Good social policies ought, therefore, to be designed to complement and reinforce the qualities of interdependence and reciprocity. These are the ideals by which most people try to order their social relationships. Welfare pluralism optimises opportunities for interdependence and reduces the risks of total dependency. The greatest risks of stigma arise when the dependency is total and only one set of welfare agencies – public or private, formal or informal – has a monopoly or near-monopoly of service provision. In a pluralist mixed economy of welfare, there is a diversity of service providers, which greatly reduces the risk of total dependency and, of course, the risk of total system failure.

Given the diversity of human values and aspirations, it is, therefore, essential that the component rights and duties that make up the concept of citizenship are grounded in a similar diversity of social institutions and personal experiences and sentiments. Unitary models of welfare, whether they are ideologically driven by individualist market values or collectivist welfare values, ignore this diversity, increase the risks of total dependency and thereby impoverish the status of citizenship.

Nevertheless, Titmuss was absolutely right in his contention that welfare needs could only be met with effectiveness and humanity by simultaneous reliance on the two forms of service delivery – universality and selectivity – provided that the overall framework was universalist. Past experience throughout the democracies of Western Europe and elsewhere has demonstrated that exceptional and unanticipated needs cannot be met effectively unless scope is left for the exercise of discretion on the part of service administrators and providers.

Titmuss's definition of social policy in terms of a set of distinctive egalitarian and redistributive purposes is more open to question. As we have already noted, he defines the discipline as 'the study of a range of social needs and functioning, in conditions of scarcity, of human organizations, traditionally called social services or social welfare systems, to meet those needs. This complex area of social life lies outside or on the fringes of the so-called free market, the mechanisms of price and tests of profitability.' It therefore followed that social policy was concerned 'with different types of moral transactions, embodying notions of gift exchange, of reciprocal obligations, which have developed in modern societies in institutional forms to bring about and maintain social and community relations'(Titmuss,1974, 20–21).

The subject of Titmuss's last major work, *The Gift Relationship* (1970), is the role of altruism in modern society, taking the example of voluntary blood donorship as one of the ultimate tests of where the 'social' begins and the 'economic'ends in order to demonstrate the potential scope for 'providing and extending opportunities for altruism in opposition to the possessive egoism of the market place'(Titmuss, 1970, 13). It is also a passionate indictment of the corrupting influence of competitive markets across the whole field of social policy.

There are a number of reasons why I find Titmuss's analysis of the moral qualities that underpin exchange relationships deeply unconvincing. In the first instance, he uses the terms 'altruism' and 'egoism' in such as a way as to describe a polarity of antipathetic sentiments and motives which, in the real world, are more likely to be interactive and conditional. In their extreme forms, altruism and egoism are marginal phenomena.

As I suggested in *The Idea of Welfare*, 'for the egoist social life is meaningless, and for the altruist it is impossible. The egoist could be likened to a black hole in the social universe, devouring everything which comes within its range, while the altruist may be compared to a brightly burning star, ineffectually striving to illuminate and warm a dark and limitless universe' (Pinker, 1979, 10).

As for the welfare claims of Titmuss's 'universal stranger', I can think of no reason why we should treat them as being self-evidently more morally deserving of our attention than those of our closest relatives and friends. There is no master principle by which the claims of one social group may be measured against the claims of others, once we abandon the crude utilitarian principle of seeking the greatest good for the greatest number. This is not to deny that the claims of Titmuss's universal stranger merit our consideration but only to point out that they are a part of a highly complex network of claims and obligations.

Even if we were to make unconditional altruism the crowning glory of our moral sentiments, it would still be as well to remember that crowns are reserved for special occasions, and that most good deeds are done in the fustian of a more homespun philosophy. Titmuss invests his concepts of the 'unnamed' stranger, the 'universal' stranger and 'stranger' relationships with immense moral significance. Giving to strangers and, in particular, the 'universal' stranger is his ultimate touchstone of altruism and the good society. It is as if the virtue intrinsic to the act of giving grows exponentially as the recipients become more anonymous, more scattered and more distant from the giver.

In addition, Titmuss's concepts of altruism and egoism so elevate the institutions of the social market and debase those of the economic market as to give the impression that the main effects of competition and entrepreneurial activity have been the infliction on humanity of diseconomies, diswelfares, social disintegration and alienation. Much of Titmuss's published work can be read as a continuous indictment of the values of private enterprise and the profit motive. It is, therefore, easier for us to form an impression of the kind of economic system which he would have eschewed than the one he would have preferred. More radical socialists than Titmuss would have agreed with his views on the corrupting values of competitive markets and the acquisitive society. They might, however, have gone further and recommended that large sectors of the economy should be taken into public ownership and institutionally transformed by the uplifting power of altruism. Such a bold initiative would, at the same time, have put paid to the acquisitive society since, thereafter, there would have been much less in the supermarkets for its shopaholic members to acquire.

Titmuss, however, leaves us in ignorance about the system of values and means by which wealth is to be created and goods and services are to be produced. Competitive markets are demonstrably more effective in the continuous creation of wealth than any other known system of economic organisation. Globalisation may well have inflicted 'diseconomies' on the poorest nations of the Third World but these failures are open to remedy. It remains the case that without the wealth-creating capability of competitive markets, the whole structure of international aid, both statutory and voluntary, would swiftly collapse and the needs of countless 'universal strangers' would go unmet (Pinker, 1977, vii–xvi).

Titmuss's distinctive views on the nature of altruism are complemented by his equally distinctive views on the nature of moral choices. In *The Gift Relationship*, he came to the conclusion that, in the interests of freedom, altruism and public safety, the buying and selling of blood should be prohibited by law and that the resolution of this matter 'has to be a policy decision; in other words it is a moral and political decision for society as a whole'. He justifies this conclusion on the grounds that, 'In a positive sense … policy and processes should enable men to be free to choose to give to unnamed strangers. They should not be coerced or constrained by the market. In the interests of the freedom of all men they should not, however, be free to sell their blood or decide on the specific destination of the gift' (Titmuss, 1970, 242).

It would, therefore, seem that Titmuss wanted to prohibit people from making the 'wrong' choices so that they could be 'free' to make the right choices. The alternative was to leave them at the mercy of the 'atomistic private market' which 'freed' men from 'any sense of obligation to or for other men regardless of the consequences to others …' (Titmuss, 1970, 239). People's opportunities for altruism are ultimately determined by the type of society in which they live. They become more altruistic only in societies where needs are met primarily by reference to the collectivist values of the social market. They inevitably become more egoistic in societies where the individualist values of the economic market prevail.

Rather than leaving people to make their own decisions as to where the path of duty lies, Titmuss wanted to compel them to be moral. He did not seem to recognise that acts of duty are only moral acts if they are voluntarily undertaken. Throughout *The Gift Relationship*, he frequently refers to the problem of alienation in capitalist societies. Marx's remedy for this state of mind was the abolition of private property, social classes and the division of labour. Titmuss's remedy appears to be the creation of a unitary welfare state and a drastic reduction in the range of consumer choice in the use of social services. All these considerations led me to the conclusion that the philosophy of *The Gift Relationship* is based on a double oxymoron – namely, that, in policy terms, we are 'free' to choose between compulsory altruism in the social market and compulsory egoism in the economic market.

Finally, we return to Titmuss's first assumption – that the statutory social services ought to act simultaneously as institutional exemplars of social solidarity and shared moral purposes *and* as agencies of wealth and income redistribution. Their overriding objective should be to 'create integration and discourage alienation'.

All of our normative models of welfare ends and means rest on certain assumptions about the moral qualities of human nature. On the basis of the relevant empirical evidence, I have always rejected those models which draw sharp distinctions between our propensities for egoism and altruism. I have argued that if people were predominantly altruistic, compulsory forms of social services would not be necessary. Conversely, if people were exclusively self-regarding, such compulsion would be impossible.

Egoism is often equated with self-interest but it is also associated with the positive qualities of self-help and a willingness to accept restraints on our more selfish dispositions and show consideration for other people. Familial altruism is the first and most natural way in which we express our concern for other people's welfare.

Familial altruism may be a limited form of altruism, restricted to those we know and love, but it is the mainspring from which all our other moral concerns for other people's welfare flow. As we mature and become citizens of a wider community, our notions of obligation and entitlement also grow more extensive and take on the formal character of social rights and duties and are thereby subsumed under the broader category of what I have described as conditional altruism (Pinker, 1979, 39).

Once again, this extension in the range of our awareness is driven by a combination of egoistic and altruistic motives. We learn from personal experience that familial altruism alone cannot guarantee our welfare in an uncertain world. We learn that collective forms of social provision – statutory and voluntary – are sensible ways of pooling risks and helping each other in times of need. The compassion we feel for those less fortunate than ourselves is also an important factor but, as I suggested in *Social Theory and Social Policy*, the welfare institutions of a society can best be understood in terms of 'an unstable compromise between compassion and indifference, between altruism and self-interest' (Pinker, 1971, 211).

It is the case, however, that the continuities of familial altruism both complement and conflict with the formal redistributive ends of statutory social policies. Through acts of voluntary saving, we give substance to the hope of leaving wealth to those we know and love. Through the processes of redistributive taxation, we make provision for the welfare of total strangers who lack the means to help themselves. All governments have to live with the difficult task of striking the right balance between the conflicting claims of familial and collective altruism.

And this brings me to the fundamental issue that Titmuss never faced up to. Given the claims of familial altruism and their own rights to a measure of consideration, many voters do not equate fairness with achieving a greater equality of wealth and income. They accept the need for a measure of redistribution but as levels of taxation rise, they will undoubtedly decide that 'enough is enough' long before Richard Titmuss would have done.

For this reason alone, the more radical policies of income redistribution become, the more likely they are to generate conflict than consensus and to encourage rather than discourage alienation. And this principle, I suggest, will hold whether the direction of distribution is from the richer to the poorer or from the poorer to the better-off.

Fortunately, there is a middle way because most democratically elected governments and their voters recognise that, in the last analysis, we *are* all dependent on each other. They know that the living standards and welfare of many individuals and families would be jeopardised if statutory social services were to disappear. Conversely, they accept that the statutory social services could not compensate or provide adequate substitutes if the structures of familial altruism ceased functioning.

In summary, I rejected the idea of a unitary model of welfare on the grounds that it took insufficient account of the diversity of human preferences and needs and increased rather than reduced the risks of people experiencing conditions of stigmatising dependency. I also concluded that a model of human motivation based on a sharply drawn distinction between the qualities of egoism and altruism bore little or no relationship to what we know about human nature and the realities of the world in which we live. By contrast, pluralist approaches which conceptualised social policies *in terms* of a mixed economy of welfare are more likely to generate useful explanatory theories *and* the provision of better-quality social services.

Throughout *The Gift Relationship* and many of his other works, Titmuss's approach is charged with the intensity of his moral commitment to a vision of collectivist social progress. As I wrote nearly two decades ago, it is really a book about the possibility for human redemption and its message, like that of John Bunyan's *Pilgrim's Progress*, is advanced in the form of an allegory.

Apart from both being Bedfordshire men, Bunyan and Titmuss shared the same unmistakably English quality of moral earnestness in the pursuit of self-improvement. Bunyan was driven by religious and Titmuss by secular convictions, but both were sustained by a distinctive vision of salvation. Bunyan's pilgrim, Christian, confronts the 'foul fiend, Apollyon' and scorns the material temptations of Vanity Fair (Bunyan, 1965, 90, 124). Titmuss confronts the menace of predatory competitive markets and exposes the falsity of the promises that they can deliver greater freedom of choice. Christian sets out for a heavenly Celestial City. Titmuss tells us what kind of social institutions we must establish in order to build a more just and compassionate society here on earth. And it is this visionary quality that explains why *The Gift Relationship* is still read while better works of scholarship have slipped into obscurity.

Conclusion

When we look for coherence and continuity in Titmuss's writings, we will find them in his commitment to a clearly stated set of values and social policy objectives. Most of his conclusions about the objectives of social policy follow logically from his original principles and premises about the qualities of human nature. Like many dedicated social reformers, he believed that if our social institutions were changed for the better, then our natures and our propensities for altruism would change in like manner. He also believed that the agencies of the statutory social services had a vitally important role to play in bringing about this transformation. My views about the paths that lead to social betterment are less visionary.

Both *Social Theory and Social Policy* and *The Idea of Welfare* were written largely as critiques of Titmuss's analysis of the moral dynamics of welfare institutions, the uncompromising distinction he drew between egoism and altruism, and the unitary model of social policy on which his analysis was based. I thought that his ideal of social welfare as 'a major integrated institution' – were it ever to be realised – would impose nothing less than an intellectual and normative straightjacket on the diversity of policy ends and means that ought to characterise a free society. I preferred the idea of a pluralist mixed economy of welfare which took more account of the ambiguities and paradoxes of human nature and gave more opportunities for us all to pursue what *The Book of Common Prayer* describes as 'the devices and desires of our own hearts'. Titmuss, in his preoccupation with 'opportunities for altruism', would undoubtedly have endorsed the whole of this quotation which goes on to confess that 'we have followed too much the devices and desires of our own hearts'.

But academic disciplines thrive on disagreements and Richard Titmuss, who was a modest man, might be pleasantly surprised to know that the issues he raised are still the subject of intense and lively debate.

In such ways, the continuities of scholarship are reaffirmed and the man who was the subject of these lectures will, most assuredly, *not* be consigned to 'the dark backward and abysm of time' that is the fate of all forgotten scholars.

Afterthought

As many readers in the community of social policy scholars will know, Richard and Kay Titmuss had a daughter, Ann Oakley, who grew up to become a highly regarded sociologist in her own right. In 2014, she published a memoir entitled *Father and Daughter* in which she set out 'to investigate two intellectual and social biographies: my own and my father, Richard Titmuss's'. She goes on say that she tried 'to show ... how these biographies are connected and also disconnected, how who he was and what he did intersects with the trajectory of my own work and identity' (Oakley, 2014, xi–xii).

The narrative of *Father and Daughter* takes the form of a thematic synthesis of personal memoir, soliloquy and policy analysis. Oakley's biographical odyssey begins some years after her father's death in 1973, on a day when her friends and surviving relatives gather outside the house that had once been the Titmusses' home. They are there in order to witness the placing of a Blue Plaque on the external wall of the house in which she grew up.

As Oakley explains, in British public life, 'The blue plaque shouts legendary and symbolic status: Such an honour is conferred only on people who have achieved great eminence in public life and made some important contributions to human welfare and happiness' (2014, 243). In her view, 'Richard Titmuss's writings justly made him famous'.

His fame was such that one of his distinguished obituarists, S.M. Miller, described him as '"the premier philosopher and sociologist" of the welfare state' (2014, 3).

In Oakley's view, however, the 'legendary status' of Richard Titmuss was based, not only on the record of his academic achievements, but on the personal qualities of the man himself – how he had risen from humble origins by 'transcending his own impoverished background through sheer hard work' and becoming 'a truly self-made man' (2014, 40). She also draws attention to the numerous obituaries following his death which in her words 'are striking for their religious imagery' and their descriptions of him as 'the welfare saint, the quiet saint, the high priest of the welfare state' (2014, 33).

The evidence Oakley uncovered in her exhaustive search of personal and public archives, however, confirmed that her mother, Kay, played a key role in fostering what she describes as the 'legend' of Richard's humble origins and saintliness. His parents had been relatively prosperous farmers and there was nothing in the evidence to suggest that he was particularly saintly in his familial, personal and professional relationships.

Propagating the 'legend' enabled Kay to demonstrate 'how important she had been to [Richard's] success'. Kay abandoned her own career as a social worker because she believed she had found her true vocation in being her husband's helpmate. Oakley says that Kay 'never admitted … that had she not married Richard Titmuss she might have had a satisfying career of her own'. In her view, Kay 'was an able woman in the competencies that languished in the confines of that marriage and that home'. Oakley goes on to claim that 'her mother's sense of incompleteness and my failure as her only child to be the product she wanted (conformist, domestic) dominated not only my childhood, but my whole life. This was the greatest conundrum of my childhood: *her* secondary citizenship versus *their* profession of equality' (2014, 68).

Richard and Kay (like Ann herself) professed the same egalitarian beliefs about what the ends and means of social policy ought to be. Ann, however, could not understand how her father was able to uphold 'a socialist view of inequality but one that excluded gender'. In his domestic life, he saw nothing that was intrinsically inegalitarian in Kay's self-adopted status of 'secondary citizenship' as a housewife dedicated to the task of making him famous (2014, 18, 97). In his social policy publications, Richard seldom, if ever, addressed issues of gender inequality.

When Ann presented Richard with a copy of her first book, *Sex and Gender in Society*, 'He said nothing, he looked at it, then laid it to one side'. He read the manuscript of her second book when he was terminally ill and, according to Ann, he 'found the subject uncongenial' (2014, 18).

Their fraught familial relationship eventually broke down in the late 1960s by which time Ann was married with two small children. After receiving a diagnosis of postnatal depression (which she challenged) she turned to her parents for 'support' and they responded with 'embarrassment'. Ann says that this unfortunate incident coincided with her father's 'move to the political right in the student demonstrations of 1968 and other matters. I told them both that I had nothing more to say to them'. She recounts how, 'many years later', her mother told her that her father 'wanted nothing more to do with me and would leave me nothing in his will' (2014, 16–17).

Oakley maintains that placing highly personal material of this kind in the public domain was justified on the grounds that 'what is private, the life of the home and of children and women, is also a matter of great public importance' (2014, 18). With this consideration in mind, it was necessary to unravel the enigma of Richard's persona as an eminent figure in the discipline of social policy who 'took a socialist view of inequality, but one which excluded gender' (2014, 18).

Oakley concludes that her father's views on gender and gender inequality had their genesis in the patriarchal domestic economy of his family life. Unfortunately for Richard and Kay, however, they had a rebellious daughter who 'joined the women's liberation movement', marched with the campaign for Nuclear Disarmament and went on to become an eminent feminist and sociologist in her own right (2014, 202).

There does not appear to have been any mutual forbearance or meeting of true minds in the Titmuss household. Ann complains that her parents could never accept her for the kind of person she was. For her part, however, she never seems to have considered the possibility that her mother genuinely believed she had found her true vocation in being Richard's helpmate and that there was nothing intrinsically reprehensible in following such a calling. Ann says that her parents wanted her to be 'a conformist daughter' but it never crossed her mind that there may have been moments when Kay was thinking 'my daughter wants me to be a conformist mother and follow a career as she is doing but I would rather she wanted me to be myself'.

There are passages in *Father and Daughter* where Oakley speculates on the origins of her father's morality and the intensity of the normative convictions that underpinned his beliefs about what ought to be the ends of social policy. With regard to the issue of gender inequality father and daughter were implacably at odds with each other. With regard to the passionate intensity with which she defended and advanced her countervailing feminist views on the issue I was left with the impression that she was very much a chip off the old paternal block.

Oakley draws attention to the fact that at LSE all of the 'Titmice' who belonged to the inner circle of Richard's working colleagues were men and none of them challenged him openly on gender issues. She cites Roy Parker's assessment that 'Richard Titmuss was more at ease with men because they were more deferential. They admired him, they looked up to him, he was a kind of paternal figure. And the women didn't in the same way' (2014, 159).

In *Father and Daughter*, Oakley extends her critique of gender exclusion practices at LSE into a wide-ranging and excoriating review of the ways in which male social scientists have marginalised their female colleagues with regard to their career prospects and consistently undervalued their contributions to the advancement of social science knowledge (2014, 215–37). She acknowledges – with many qualifications – the progress that has been made since the early 1960s, while drawing attention to the significant gender inequalities that survive in what she describes as the British 'patriarchal academy' (2014, 235).

In the penultimate chapter of her memoir, Oakley describes the ceremony at which an Honorary Degree of Doctor of Science in Social Science of Edinburgh University was conferred on her. In her speech of thanks she observes that this was 'quite possibly the first case of an academic father and his academic daughter both being honoured by the same university'. She ends her account of the event with the acknowledgement that 'the honours of a patriarchal academy still mean something to me' and an affirmation that 'I am still proud to be my father's daughter' (2014, 237).

Oakley makes it clear from the start that the purpose of her book was 'not to settle old accounts or contribute to the sad genus of whistle-blowing memoirs' (2014, 3). Nevertheless, *Father and Daughter* is very much a whistle-blower of a memoir insofar as Oakley effectively debunks the legend of Richard Titmuss's 'saintliness'. In doing so, however, she shows that her father was, in reality, a far more interesting, paradoxical and fallible man than the legend portrayed.

Kay Titmuss may have fostered the legend but it was the community of social policy scholars who adopted and passed it on from generation to generation down to the present day. Oakley refers frequently to the intensity of her father's moral convictions and, in particular, his fervent belief in 'the capacity of social policy to create the good society' (2014, 247). From the 1950s onwards, the legend gave the emergent discipline of social policy a moral compass to steer by. The trouble with moral compasses, however, is that they point in only one normative direction. The normative identity that Titmuss gave the discipline was a commitment to the creation and defence of a unitary and collectivist model of social welfare in which statutory agencies were the main service providers and the reduction of social inequalities was the primary objective.

Titmuss provided a normative framework within which the discipline could develop but it was not the kind of framework within which a diversity of other possible welfare models could be dispassionately compared and tested. Titmuss believed that the ends and means of social policy – as he defined them – were manifestly morally superior to those postulated in other social science disciplines and also by dissenting social policy analysts.

In this respect Oakley cites John Vaizey's claim that 'the particular logic that eluded him was that the goals of social policy must include economic growth' (2014, 187). Titmuss conceptualised competitive market forces in largely negative terms. They inflicted what he called 'diswelfares' on the poor and fostered rather than reduced inequalities. Oakley also cites my suggestion that one reason why the legend survives today is that it provides 'a rallying point and grounds for hope to an increasingly embattled enclave of collectivist and egalitarianly minded scholars' (2014, 243).

In my back-cover endorsement of *Father and Daughter* I said that 'this superbly researched memoir will become a classic of its kind – albeit a highly controversial one'. Legends can rarely be debunked with impunity and Oakley is as likely to be condemned for her indiscretions as congratulated for her courage in 'setting the record straight'. Oakley's memoir provides telling evidence in support of Leo Tolstoy's claim that 'each unhappy family is unhappy in its own way'.

Opinions will differ regarding her claim that 'what is private, the life of the home and of children and women, is also a matter of great public importance'. These were certainly matters of great importance to Oakley in helping her unravel 'the greatest conundrum' of her childhood which was her 'mother's secondary citizenship' versus 'the profession of equality' that her parents publicly espoused.

As Ann Oakley moves back and forth between past and present in her narrative, an invisible hand seems always to be drawing her back to the time-warp of her 'Blue Plaque house' and her dissonant familial relationships. We are not told whether she was able to solve the 'conundrum' that has haunted her over so many years but we are given many new insights into the enigma of her father's persona and the extent to which his views on social policy and inequality might have been grounded in the domestic economy of his everyday family life.

On social care, communities and the conditions for well-being

John Offer

Social policies concerned with the areas of social care and of social work as a profession have always been topics on which Pinker has made significant contributions. His writings more frequently and in more detail dealt with what are often referred to as the 'personal social services' than those of, say, T.H. Marshall, Richard Titmuss or David Donnison. In this book, we are covering, among other matters, Pinker's contributions to the interpretation of *social policies* affecting social work. However, his extensive contributions on what may be called the politics of social work as a profession or its governance will not be central to this study.

The Conservative Party won the general election in 1979 under Margaret Thatcher. At that time, some communitarians, notably Roger Hadley and Stephen Hatch in *Social Welfare and the Failure of the State* (1981), wanted to enhance personal social services budgets in order to increase support for informal networks. Other social researchers simply called for more prominence to be given to the *study* of informal care, and to what extent 'networks' of care could be said to exist. Within this general context, the Conservative government set up a working party in 1980 to review the role and tasks of social workers.

As explained in the **General introduction**, Pinker was directly involved, being made a member of this working party (as was Hadley, with whom he disagreed on some key matters). Chaired by Peter Barclay, it completed its report, *Social Workers: Their Role and Tasks*, in 1982. Pinker's own contribution to that report was in fact a note of dissent, 'An alternative view'. It became Appendix B (pp 236–62) of the report, and it summarised the reasons why Pinker dissented from the main recommendations. Pinker's dissent is frequently cited in discussions relating to the historical and current practices of social care and social work, and now arguably more so than the main report itself. Since 'An alternative view' is no longer at all easy to obtain (nor indeed is the main report), we have made a point of including the full text of 'An alternative view' in this part as **Chapter Six**.

However, before presenting Pinker's own contribution to Barclay, some background will be helpful. The significance of the Barclay Report itself is difficult to gauge without some appreciation of the recommendations of its predecessor, the Seebohm Report, just 14 years earlier. A lot had changed in a short period. For Pinker, writing in 1980 in 'The enterprise of social work', his inaugural lecture as Professor of Social Work Studies at the London School of Economics

(LSE), 'the Seebohm ideal of a universalist and preventive system of personal social services looks like a manifesto from another time and country' (in Pinker, 1990: 4). Accordingly, this Introduction will give a flavour of developments in what came to be called 'the personal social services' in the UK in the second half of the 20th century.[1]

By the early 1960s, the nature of existing social service provision by local authorities for groups like frail older people was coming under review. In particular, differing perspectives were emerging between the Home Office and Ministry of Health over the desired future form of the 'personal social services', in particular, over whether there should be a focus on family (the Home Office preference) or on community (the Ministry of Health preference).

In this context, the Committee on Local Authority and Allied Personal Social Services was set up in December 1965. The Chairman was Frederic Seebohm. It was asked 'to review the organisation and responsibilities of the local authority personal social services in England and Wales, and to consider what changes are desirable to secure an effective family service'. When the Committee's report appeared in July 1968, however, it commented: 'We could only make sense of our task by considering also childless couples and individuals without any close relatives: in other words, everybody' (Seebohm Report, 1968: 18). The Committee had changed its own terms of reference.

The report recommended that each local authority should have a single, unified social services department, replacing a range of separate committees, including each authority's Children's Committee (dating back to 1948). A generic approach to the skills training of social workers was recommended, with a focus on communities as well as 'families'. While the issues of increasing resources and raising the status of statutory social work services exercised the Committee to a marked degree, the future roles and contribution of the voluntary sector and, in particular, informal care attracted much less comment.

In November 1968, the Ministry of Social Security was amalgamated with the Ministry of Health, to form the Department of Health and Social Security, with Richard Crossman becoming Secretary of State for Social Services. Pinker had lunch at this time with Crossman, who thought that the Seebohm Report was 'needs-driven, over-optimistic and uncosted' (email to Offer from Pinker, 13 January 2016).[2] Yet, delays over National Health Service reform and anxieties about how best to implement general local government reform, for example, opened up a window of opportunity for the report to be translated into legislation. It was also fortuitous that Baroness Serota, a supportive member of the Seebohm Committee, was made junior minister at the Department of Health and Social Security early in 1969, and thus able to encourage the adoption of the Committee's recommendations. Phoebe Hall summarised the position well (1976: 97):

> Crossman's indifference to the committee's proposal might have condemned the report to a dusty shelf had there been no vociferous groups and powerful individuals able to persuade him otherwise. The

social work pressure groups were undoubtedly helped by the influence of the civil servants in the welfare divisions of the DHSS. The latter were firmly of the opinion that the Seebohm proposals should be implemented. In turn, they were supported by Baroness Serota without whom, Crossman has argued, he would have remained unconvinced.

It should be noted that, in citing here Phoebe Hall's *Reforming the Welfare*, reference is being made to one of the important series of books known as *Studies in Social Policy and Welfare*, published by Heinemann, which Pinker was editing at the time.

In May 1970, the Local Authority Social Services Act was passed under Harold Wilson's Labour government. The Act's implementation began the following year, under Edward Heath's Conservative government.[3] Quite quickly, it became apparent that there were serious problems confronting the new and integrated local authority departments. The Maria Colwell case of 1973 in Brighton, when the child died of injuries received at her home although her general situation was already known to social workers, was much publicised and raised questions regarding their professional competence.[4] In many places, new local government boundaries were introduced in 1974, which required a reorganisation and relocation of a significant number of the social service departments. Social workers were also being rapidly involved with additional responsibilities relating to the Children and Young Persons Act 1969, the Health Services and Public Health Act 1968, the Chronically Sick and Disabled Persons Act 1970 and the National Health Service Reorganisation Act 1973.

Coupled with a daunting workload, the new service had to endure the more general challenges of industrial conflict and high inflation, and also the suspicion in some quarters that the Seebohm reforms had from the outset made paramount the self-interests of a new profession rather than the needs of service users (Brewer and Lait, 1980). The authors of the report had declared: 'We were, regrettably, unable to sound consumer reaction to the services in any systematic fashion … we made no attempt to organise a research programme as this would have delayed publication' (Seebohm Report, 1968: 21). However, at this distance, a less-discussed point seems of more interest, for within a historical perspective, it may be claimed that Seebohm was in 1968 completing business left unfinished in the 1940s. The Children Act of 1948 had implemented strongly welfare-enhancing measures for children deprived of a normal home life. This was in line with the recommendations of the *Report of Care of Children Committee* of 1946, chaired by Myra Curtis (Parker, 1983). In the event, this gave Seebohm a well-qualified cadre of staff to incorporate into the new departments. But other 'client groups' of the personal social services had fared less well during and after the 1940s. The National Assistance Act of 1948 did not replicate the quality of care for them which Curtis had secured for children in care. At last, the new Seebohm departments now had the opportunity to improve the standard of the services for these neglected groups.

However, by 1980, with a new Conservative government in place, a fresh review of social work was felt necessary. At the time, as we have seen, there was a background of scepticism about the value of social work. The National Institute for Social Work, at the Conservative government's request and with government funding, set up a working party in 1980. The chairman was Peter Barclay, and there were 17 other members, including Pinker and Hadley. The terms of reference were: 'To review the role and tasks of social workers in local authority social services departments and related voluntary agencies in England and Wales and to make recommendations' (Barclay Report, 1982: vii). As it happened, the main report itself includes a further quotation from Pinker to underline the distance travelled since the Seebohm Report: 'the personal social services, once envisaged by the Seebohm Report as the last major addition to a generously funded system of social welfare, have been transformed from a first resort to the last ditch' (Barclay Report, 1982: 108).[5]

The main report from Barclay saw social work as necessary, but a new emphasis on 'community social work' was urged. The report believed that the function of social workers 'is to enable, empower, support and encourage, but not usually to take over from, social networks' (Barclay Report, 1982: 209). Thus, it placed a firm focus on partnerships with informal carers, and voluntary organisations. Here was an immense contrast with the focus of the Seebohm Report (1968), which was on social workers as themselves providing the service. For Barclay, social workers were to work to an extent at local or 'patch' level, with social care planning and the promotion of networks of care as central tasks, although it was appropriate that social workers should continue in a 'social policing' role (Barclay Report, 1982: 48–9), with, for example, children at risk.

Roger Hadley, who was Professor of Social Policy at the University of Lancaster, dissented, with two others (Mrs P. Brown and Mr K.J. White). They urged that reorganisation and decentralisation of the organisation of social work down to neighbourhood level was required for 'community social work' to work well in practice.

Pinker disagreed with the main report and also with Hadley. Thus, the first chapter in this Part (**Chapter Six**) reproduces Pinker's dissent from the main Barclay Report, as contained in Appendix B, 'An alternative view'. Pinker feared that the future of professional social work was being placed at risk, and that problems of social work accountability were being fudged. It was not clear whether they were primarily accountable to the local authority (their employer), the community or their service user. He argues that the report's proposal was a prescription for managerial chaos. Pinker saw threats to social work values such as ensuring privacy in the context of developing networks of care. He also argued that 'The most vulnerable, disadvantaged and stigmatised clients will be at greatest risk in the community-based models of social work since they give greatest offence to local norms of behaviour and are often rejected by their local communities' (**Chapter Six, pp 133–4**). In addition, Pinker noted the general and problematic assumption of the existence of 'networks' of informal care. There was little evidence of 'networks' of care, as opposed to individual carers with usually limited help. Such points were also underlined in contemporary research-based articles in the *British Journal of Social Work* (Allan, 1983; Graycar, 1983; Offer, 1984). Finally, he was also concerned about unresolved problems for social workers, such as when the values of a community, a neighbourhood or a family were in conflict with social workers' professional values with regard to the promotion of racial and gender equality. It is not possible, Pinker argues, to define the concept of 'community' with enough precision for it to serve as 'a framework for formal and equitable social policies' (**Chapter Six, p 128**). Specialist social work skills ran the risk of being neglected in these new models of social work. Overall, Pinker urged the need for more specialisation in the context of general social work teams.

Pinker has now added a new Afterthought to **Chapter Six**, which deals with privacy and social policy and social work.

In the discussion of Pinker's *Social Policy and Social Theory* in 'Robert Pinker on rethinking approaches to welfare' (**General introduction**), reference has already been made to the fact that he explicitly distanced himself from the adoption of a normative position which might described as 'populist'. In an article Pinker published in the aftermath of the Barclay Report, 'Populism and the social services' (Pinker, 1984), it is notable that he was at that time already detecting tendencies towards populism in the Report and the associated debates. In what he referred to as a period of 'welfare disillusionment' with big government he found it unsurprising that 'not only frustrated collectivists but hopeful individualists are beginning to revive old populist traditions as a panacea. Both of these populist groups are looking to the community, one as an alternative ground base for a political challenge to welfare cuts, the other as a largely untapped source of voluntary service to fill the gaps left by a contracting statutory sector' (1984: 91).

In such climates, anti-elitist and anti-bureaucratic sentiments and demotic language take root. Pinker wryly noticed that the content of the 'populism' that was a virtue according to one political party was a vice to another. Now, with the 'Brexit' majority vote in the UK as a whole to pull out of membership of the European Union in the June 2016 referendum (though with significant majority votes for 'remain' in Northern Ireland and Scotland), it is beyond doubt over 30 years later that explanations of Brexit have routinely invoked as a cause the resurgence of (usually right-wing) 'populist' traditions. As a consequence, the 'frustrations' of regions and people 'left behind' by the rapid and percussive impacts of worldwide changes in economics and social life are fingered as 'culprits'. Perhaps, although it is in reality unlikely, there is now more solid unanimity on the actual substance of the meaning of 'populism' than when Pinker consulted Ionescu and Gellner (1969), when agreement was conspicuous by its absence. The study by Pinker himself, however, concluded 'Populism and the social services' in 1984 by raising a more fundamental issue affecting the aspirations of 'populist' politicians. Even if the populists were successful in returning power to the people:

they would find that there was still no consensus among 'the people' as to how that power should be used, how priorities should be ordered or what objectives should be pursued. In a democratic sense there is no such thing as 'the people'. All that unbridled populism does is to reduce the conflict of interest which characterize all industrial societies to the level of the parish pump. At that primitive level of political life the long haul back to national parties, formal procedures, rule and legislation and bureaucracy begin again. (1984: 94)

Pinker is clear that a populist approach which appears to put its trust in purely local initiatives to achieve shared or communitarian ends provides no reasonable alternative to the rigours of hard democratic decision-making.

No legislation followed from Barclay, though there was some local experimentation. However, as will be commented on shortly, later legislation on community care developed the theme of a focus on supporting informal care. It should be noted that Pinker's comments include the criticism that the Barclay Committee did not unequivocally recommend the establishment of a social work council for the purpose of formal professional regulation. The General Social Care Council (GSCC) was not, in fact, established until after the Care Standards Act 2000, which came into being in 2001. Prior to the creation of the GSCC and its sister bodies in Scotland, Northern Ireland and Wales, social work training was regulated by the Central Council for Education and Training in Social Work (CCETSW). The social work profession, however, was not subject to formal regulation on a par with other professions until the creation of the GSCC. In that respect, social work was the first profession within social care to be subject to regulation. In 2012, the Health and Care Professions Council (HPC), formerly the Health Professions Council, assumed responsibility for the regulation of social workers in England from the GSCC, which was abolished on 31 July 2012 (social work regulation is a devolved matter in the UK; thus, there are three other social work regulators based in Northern Ireland, Scotland and Wales).

Chapter Seven is 'The quest for community: from the Settlement Movement to the Griffiths Report'. As the title suggests, the subject matter broadens out here, engaging with more recent debates about 'community care' as a key idea in policy for social care. This essay was originally a plenary paper presented at a Social Service Inspectorate DHSS (NI) Conference at the Riverside Theatre, University of Ulster, Coleraine on 23 March 1988, to mark the publication of Offer, St Leger and Cecil, *Aspects of Informal Care: Some Results from a Study of a Small Town in Northern Ireland* (1988). It was first published in Pinker's *Social Work in an Enterprise Society* (1990: 96–121).[6]

Pinker describes the recovery and cultivation of community as on display in London in the 1880s in the Settlement Movement, and, in particular, at Toynbee Hall. There was intellectual input here from Idealist thinkers, including Thomas Hill Green at Oxford. Social regeneration was the aim, to be achieved through the building of closer links with the local community. Yet, this concern with community suffered in comparison with the intellectual predispositions and superior connections to government of Beatrice and Sidney Webb, and also William Beveridge. Such writers favoured central government intervention and the making of policy by 'experts'. Efforts to bring about social reform by means of voluntary action, or improvements in individual well-being by encouraging informal care, were marginalised by the ascendency of this approach. Yet, by the 1970s, new stirrings were, of course, apparent in communitarian thought. Pinker insists that his dissent from the main Barclay Report 'was not hostility to the idea of community but scepticism about the Report's confident assertion of the universal strengths of communities and the feasibility of harnessing them to the ends and means of formal social policy' (**Chapter Seven, p 153**).

Pinker then considers difficulties in relations between formal and informal care, and the recommendations of *Community Care: Agenda for Action*, the Griffiths Report (Griffiths, 1988) (itself prompted by criticisms of existing policy by the Audit Commission [1986] and National Audit Office [1987]). On the relations between formal and informal care, he refers in particular to Bulmer (1985, 1986, 1987), Cecil, Offer and St Leger (1987), Offer, St Leger and Cecil (1988) and Challis and Davies (1985a, 1985b, 1986). The work of Challis and Davies reported on a highly innovatory programme of community care in Kent, aiming to provide a decentralised network of care for frail elderly people allowing them to live in their own homes, which was managed out of a shadow budget given to a key worker. It seems that decentralisation of this kind worked successfully, provided it was partnered by inter-professional collaboration (**Chapter Seven, p 167**). On the recommendations of the Griffiths Report, Pinker was supportive of the idea that local authorities should cease to be the main providers of care, but should design, organise and purchase packages of care from a mixed economy of agencies.[6] With some reservations, chiefly over its explicit assumption that formal social services can be interwoven with informal networks of support, Pinker regards this injection of managerial objectives into care provision as having the capacity to reach many of the Kent experiment's aims.

Chapters Six and **Seven** show Pinker as concerned with aspects of the *sociality* of people and how, in social interaction, it take various forms and is shaped by various cultural influences. As discussed earlier, Pinker approached social policy with a discerning sociological imagination. This approach to his studies led to Pinker's familiarity with the work of Norbert Elias, best known for *The Civilizing Process* (2000).[8] Pinker shared Elias's rejection of any crude ontological divide between the atomistic 'individual' and the 'social'. Both share a sense of the mutability and unpredictability of social change and see everyday experiences and practices as always amounting to more than the simply or straightforwardly mundane. Pinker and Elias appear to concur in seeing the current characteristics of what we call the 'social' as made up by the actions and choices of countless social individuals. The characteristics of the 'social', including the conflicts between groupings which it involves, are thus largely the spontaneous and unplanned consequences of the cooperative interactions among social individuals. The success of the outcome of no one particular cooperative interaction is to be taken for granted.

The focus on sociality and welfare continues in **Chapter Eight**, the last chapter of this section, 'Citizenship, civil war and welfare: the making of modern Ireland'. The essay first appeared in 2006 in *Twenty-First Century Society: Journal of the Academy of Social Sciences* (vol 5, no 1, pp 23-38). Pinker turns to the conditions in which the advancement of welfare or well-being is likely to be seriously disrupted. While *The Idea of Welfare* had introduced the topic, now Pinker gave it sustained discussion. As is often the case with Pinker, it was his reflections on the writing of T.H. Marshall which prompted the essay (Pinker's broader treatments of Marshall's work are contained in **Part Three**). In Marshall's theory of citizenship and welfare, citizenship means that all who have that status are equal in respect of the rights and duties which come with that status. Marshall describes three key elements in the status of citizenship: civil rights, which embraces personal liberty; political rights, which embraces the right to vote and to be a representative; and social rights, which have regard for certain entitlements to standards of living which have become popularly associated with aspects of modern 'welfare states' since the Second World War. However, Marshall did not discuss how the impact of conventional or civil war might disrupt what he tends to portray as a gradual and linear process.

Pinker's account of the history of the often conflictual relationship between England and Ireland is intended to repair a gap in Marshall's theory of citizenship and welfare, rendering it open to criticism (by Turner, 1986, as Pinker notes). Pinker surveys the periods both before and after 1921, when Northern Ireland as a political entity was formed. Pinker draws out the important lesson that civil wars 'are not fought over the conventional issues of social welfare. Ordinary people are not prepared to kill or be killed in the cause of better social services' (**Chapter Eight, pp 185–6**). And he adds:

> They are only prepared to do so once they are convinced that they will never become citizens on their own terms until they have won their national independence and the exclusive possession of whatever territories they associate with their ideal of nationhood. Since the land in question will always be the prime subject of dispute, neither side will ever enjoy the full benefits of freedom, welfare and peace until they are prepared to settle for some kind of territorial compromise.

Our ordinary theories of welfare and how we might go about securing it take little or no account of land. Access to it is taken for granted. But this cannot be so in times of unrest or civil war. Both sides in civil wars and unrest will have an interest in denying or harming the progress of each other's civil, political and social rights. So, for example, Pinker shows how, after the partition of Ireland, the minority nationalist population in the North had, in effect, weaker social rights in areas such as social housing under the Stormont government well into the 1960s than the majority loyalist population. Indeed, this eventually became the catalyst of the civil rights movement, seeking extensive social and political reform, including anti-discrimination legislation (Birrell, 1972; Birrell and Murie, 1975). As 'the Troubles' intensified, however, it was the case, as Pinker also shows, that Protestant Unionists 'feared the loss of their own civil rights in the event of their being abandoned by the British Government' (**Chapter Eight, p 184**).

It might now be added that the current and often perilous migrations from Syria and elsewhere to Europe must surely underline Pinker's contention that when it is insecure, 'land becomes a unique welfare good. It represents the beginning and end of all our welfare aspirations'(**Chapter Eight, p 186**).

Notes

[1]   See also Cooper, 1983.

[2]   See also Hall, 1976: 82–4.

[3]   Useful contemporary sources on the Committee and its report are Hall, 1976; Sinfield, 1970; Townsend, 1970.

[4]   See Butler and Drakeford, 2011.

[5]   Again, the quotation is from Pinker's inaugural lecture in 1980 as Professor of Social Work Studies at LSE, entitled 'The enterprise of social work'. It is reprinted in his *Social Work in an Enterprise Society* (1990: 12).

[6]   Pinker has had a long association with the University of Ulster, including periods as external examiner and visiting professor.

[7]   For an overview of the development of social work services from 1974 to Griffiths, see Evandrou, Falkingham and Glennester, 1990.

[8]   Pinker twice reviewed writings by Elias for the *Times Literary Supplement*: first, *The Society of Individuals*, on 6 September 1991; and second, *On Civilization, Power and Knowledge: Selected Writings*, on 15 May 1998.

SIX

Report of the Working Party on the Role and Tasks of Social Workers: an alternative view*

Robert Pinker

I am not able to sign the Report of the Working Party on the Role and Tasks of Social Workers. I have therefore written this note setting out the main reasons for my dissent. I am equally critical of the community social work model which has the support of the majority of the members and of Professor Hadley's neighbourhood, or patch model. If either model was adopted, I believe it would be detrimental to the quality of social work services in England and Wales.

I shall argue that these two community-based models share a common perspective with regard to the crucial issues of generalism and specialism, and hence with regard to the distinctive features of the role and tasks of professional social work, as well as the nature of accountability and its implications for resource allocation and the exercise of discretion. The two models differ mainly in degree on these issues. The supporters of the community social work model reach their conclusions by default, while the advocates of the neighbourhood, or patch model do so by intent. Both approaches are seriously flawed.

The main observable difference between the community social work model and the neighbourhood model described in the Report is that the former retains the area team as the working unit while the latter does not, and the size of its catchment area lies somewhere between those of the traditional client-centred model and the neighbourhood model. The average number of team members is not specified, but as a rule it would again be on the small side.

The Report states that the community social work approach calls for highly localised and smaller area teams, working more closely with local community networks and with a greater, if limited, degree of control over resources. Both community-centred models, it is argued, would greatly augment the flow of information about local needs. The roles of local authority social services staff would be more openly defined, and each team would have its own budget and a greater degree of autonomy and discretion. Both models recognise the need for some specialised social workers, but in the neighbourhood, or patch model they will be located away from the frontline teams in some unspecified 'second tier'.

---

* First published as Appendix B of the Barclay Report (1982), *Social Workers: Their Role and Tasks*, London: Bedford Square Press, pp 236–62.

In the neighbourhood model it is assumed that there is considerable scope for increasing community participation through the use of more ancillary workers. This model looks forward to the integration of all field staff, including social workers, in small locally based teams. The teams will enjoy a much greater degree of autonomy and discretion in organising their work and managing their own budgets. At the same time we are assured that a very high degree of devolution and decentralisation would be compatible with the maintenance of a strong central organisation.

Defining social work

What then are the essential role and tasks of social workers, and how can social work activities best be organised? Our present model of so-called client-centred social work is basically sound, but in need of a better defined and less ambitious mandate. Social work should be explicitly selective rather than universalist in focus, reactive rather than preventive in approach and modest in its objectives. Social work ought to be preventive with respect to the needs which come to its attention; it has neither the capacity, the resources nor the mandate to go looking for needs in the community at large.

It is more practical to define the role and tasks of social work in terms of the range of activities which social workers undertake in response to certain institutional imperatives. The first set of imperatives derives from the range and variety of needs that confront social workers. The second is contained in the legislation that defines their mandatory local authority obligations and also indicates the range of their permissive undertakings. The third relates to the employers – statutory or otherwise – to whom social workers are accountable, who are themselves accountable in the discharge of their mandatory and permissive undertakings. The fourth set of imperatives derives from the professional standards and values to which social workers may individually and collectively subscribe.

What kinds of knowledge and skill do social workers need in order to do their job, and how should the job be defined? Many social work skills are the normal skills of sociable living, although it would be misleading to labour this point. The crucial difference arises from the distinctive use to which social workers put these skills, the type of clientele they serve, the type of context in which they work, and the nature of the mandate by which their work is authorised. These are the factors that shape the role and tasks of social workers, and accordingly the skills of social work are informed by a great deal of specialised knowledge. The skills of social workers include the ability to assess needs and situations with insight, efficiency and impartiality, including the ability to make judgements about the capacities and the intentions of clients; the ability to formulate feasible methods of response to clients' problems, preferably with the clients' co-operation, but without it if necessary; and the ability to put such plans into effect and to obtain the necessary resources if they are available. The Report calls these basic skills the 'social care planning' part of social work.

The other part is social casework, which the Report describes as counselling. The term 'social casework' would be more appropriate because it is a broader term, describing a method of work which, as Yelloly points out, takes account of not only the personal but the social aspects of human problems which are so severe that they threaten or destroy clients' capacity to manage their own lives or to function effectively as members of society (Yelloly, 1980, pp.125–30). The basic skills which the report puts under the heading of 'social care planning' are general skills employed by the entire personnel of the personal service professions. They only become a part of social work when they are related to a process and method of intervention which is distinctive to social workers in response to a distinctive clientele with a particular set of needs.

This is not just a semantic difference; it is one which directly affects the focus and emphasis of concern in social work. The Report appears to attach equal importance to 'social care planning' and counselling. In fact it diminishes the significance of the counselling element in social work by conceptually separating it from the social implications of casework. The Report shows that, contrary to popular belief, social casework is not the chief activity of social workers. Nevertheless social casework is an essential part of social work, and it seems unnecessary to give it a new label.

On the rare occasions on which it uses the term, the Report caricatures social casework. For example it defines social casework in the past tense, as if it were an obsolete practice, and suggests that 'Many social workers now feel somewhat embarrassed or ambivalent about the term' (10.19). In contrast, the Report asserts that social workers should see themselves as '... upholders of networks. This may make clear our view that the function of social workers is to enable, empower, support and encourage, but not usually to take over from social networks' (13.43). Since the Report's definition of social casework seems deficient, I shall give an alternative one, which will also make plain the reason why I could not sign the Report.

Social casework is the fundamentally distinctive method of social work which is derived from social work's concern with helping individuals and families with their problems in social living. Social group work is a logical extension of this concern because it pursues the same objectives through different means. Therefore the affinity between social casework and social group work is close. The same cannot be said of community work, which is primarily concerned with needs of a more general kind. The contribution of community work is therefore largely indirect, and the broader its scope of operation, the more pronounced this characteristic becomes. All social workers undertake some indirect work, but that is not what makes them social workers.

In my view, therefore, social work and social casework are virtually synonymous, but my definition of social casework is a broad one which includes counselling and various practical tasks. The counselling part of social casework is carried out through the use of a professional relationship between the social worker and the client (and other people who are immediately affected) as the means of helping the client to manage his own life.

Interviews are a prominent feature of social casework; they are the means by which the relationships are developed and the setting in which support and advice can be offered. The aim of counselling is to help clients to understand the nature and causes of their distress and discover their personal strengths and weaknesses, and to encourage them to find the will and capacity to help themselves – if necessary by changing their attitudes and behaviour. The problems of social work clients have a great variety of causes, including bereavement, illness, handicap, mental difficulty and breakdown, criminal behaviour, and so on.

There is nothing mysterious or esoteric about social casework. It requires certain qualities of character which are common to most people, but which can be developed through training and experience. It would be wrong to dismiss social casework as nothing more than giving help, support and advice to clients, since we all give and receive help from time to time. If social work has a quality of strangeness, it is because social work is concerned with relationships between strangers.

Social workers are professional people. They cannot choose their clients and they certainly should not discriminate between clients on the basis of personal likes and dislikes. They will naturally welcome the gratitude of their clients but they have no right to expect it; indeed they have to be prepared to put up with a great deal of aggression and exposure to other people's misery. As Davies points out, at some time or other we all take part in interviews, but in doing so we seldom have to 'cope with verbal aggression, threats of violence, tears, total silence or more bizarre behaviour' (Davies, 1981, p.48) as ordinary events in the average day's work.

In addition social workers are accountable to their agencies and employers for what they do. Davies is right in saying that 'social work *can* have no existence independently of the agencies in which it operates.' The powers and responsibilities of social workers cannot be brushed under the carpet of egalitarianism. Davies lists some of their duties, which include supervising children and young persons who are at risk in the locality, or containing them in residential settings; advising courts on children who are the subject of care proceedings; making fostering and adoption enquiries; acting *as guardians ad litem;* making pre-release reports on people in various forms of custody; allocating scarce resources in cash and kind; arranging accommodation for the elderly; and advising on admissions in to psychiatric care (Davies, 1981, p.8 ff). In personal terms this means working with people who are vulnerable, damaged, distressed or dangerous.

The efficient and humane discharge of social work duties calls for specialised legal, psychological and social knowledge. Apart from practice skills, social workers must have clear and detailed knowledge of the aspects of the law which affect their dealings with child protection, care and supervision; mental illness and mental subnormality; and the care and rights of the elderly, the chronic sick and the disabled and separated, divorced or violent spouses; and they must know the relevant court procedures. They need some knowledge of welfare legislation in the fields of housing and rates, educational welfare, income maintenance and health care, and they need to know how their own agencies work, and something about the nature and scope of external local resources in both the statutory and the voluntary sectors. They must also be given the chance to acquire expertise and experience in some particular aspect of human need, and to make this available to their colleagues. Finally they must be able to put all this information to practical use in the service of their clients. Consequently they need to be familiar with the knowledge and insights which academic disciplines can give them concerning human nature and society.

The Report reviews the available evidence on the effectiveness of social work intervention. Davies reminds us how easy it is for social workers – and their critics and defenders – to exaggerate the extent to which people or situations can be changed by social work intervention. Very often the situation of the client is one in which 'The social worker couldn't make it worse, because it couldn't *be* worse' (Davies, 1981, p.116), and it would be unrealistic to expect the social worker to make it better. Some problems have no solution, and all too many tragedies cause permanent grief.

In practice a great deal of social work is a task of 'maintenance', containment, control and support (Davies, 1981, p.137 ff), so it is inevitable that social workers will find numerous examples of misery and injustice in the course of their work, but that does not justify switching the focus of social work from personal to political objectives. They already have at their disposal the normal channels of communication and influence in their agencies through which to get a better deal for their clients, and they have their professional associations through which to inform public opinion about the shortcomings of social policy. Social workers have to accept the fact that demand for their services is connected with the failures rather than the successes of social policy, whatever type of society they may work in. Their view of social life is both a special and a partial one.

Because of the enormous complexity, variety and range of needs calling for social work intervention, the case for specialisation is self-evident. The important question is, can specialisation be developed in such a way that appropriate attention will be given to each individual client as a whole person rather than as a collection of separate problems? There is no reason why the demands of generalist and specialist social work cannot be reconciled within a properly organised system of care based on adequately staffed generic area teams in which there is a sensible division of labour.

The notion of community

Before attention is given to some of the other implications of the Barclay proposals, the notion of community should be briefly considered. It is one of the most stubbornly persistent illusions in social policy studies that eventually the concept of community – as a basis of shared values – will resolve all our policy dilemmas.

The very fact that this notion is cherished from left to right across the political spectrum makes it highly suspect. There is no unitary definition of community because, like the concept of equity, it is open to various interpretations. The idea that in a complex industrial society the notion of community could provide a basis for shared values (and hence for consistent social policies) is erroneous.

It seems that when our policy-makers reach an intellectual impasse they cover their embarrassment with the fig leaf of community. It happened in the case of the Seebohm Committee, when it failed to discover a specific definition of 'the family' and immediately proceeded to extol the virtues of 'the community', which, for the purposes of that Committee, came to mean everybody and everything. Consequently the personal social services throughout the past decade have had to carry the burden of universalism implied in this definition.

The definition of community given in the Report is neither better nor worse than most of its kind. However, the concept of community can never be sufficiently well defined to serve as a framework for formal and equitable social policies, and consequently policies based on this concept are bound to be inadequate. In fact the Report itself explains why this is the case in its concluding paragraphs, where it admits that 'We still know too little about what determines the shape and style of informal networks or what constitutes a "healthy" community... The evidence reaching us, similarly, abundantly attests that there is no one way of knowing or serving communities' (13.70). I agree.

However suspect, it is not surprising that community-based approaches to social work evoke, albeit for different reasons, the approval of radicals and conservatives alike, since the idea of community is both intangible and paradoxical. It is intangible because it has not yet been satisfactorily defined in the setting of an industrial society, and paradoxical because historically it has inspired some of the most paternalist philosophies of social welfare and some of the most libertarian ones. I am aware that my view goes against the current of fashionable opinion. Whether the concept of community should be described as the Coronation Street or the Ambridge complex of sociology depends perhaps on whether the academic concerned is an urban or a rural sociologist.

Accountability

Three main dimensions of accountability are referred to in the Report, but none of them is consistently analysed. The first is accountability in a broadly political sense; the second, deriving from the first, is accountability for the use of resources, and the third is accountability for the exercise of professional discretion.

In Chapter 13 the Report touches on the issue of accountability and political control, stating that there must be a willingness on the part of social service managers to devolve 'as fully as possible decisions about resources and decentralising organisational structures' (13.50). At the same time the Report recognises that social workers may often have to take decisions which conflict with the preferences of local communities, but that 'In these circumstances particularly social workers will look to management for support' (13.57). In addition we are reminded that 'ultimate authority is vested in elected members' (13.62).

The advocates of the neighbourhood model believe that significant movement towards more community-orientated methods of social work can be achieved within the existing political system, but go on to argue that in the longer term it will be necessary to develop new political institutions like neighbourhood councils at a local level, with powers of management. Changes of this order would require new legislation.

The Report states with regard to the political element in the role of social workers that they should have a greater say in policy-making, but it neglects some of the effects it would have on representative local democracy if frontline social workers – or any other occupational group – were given a more authoritative role in policy-making. Local authority councillors are the *elected* representatives of citizens, and they are accountable to the citizens for their decisions. This is not true of social workers, nor was there any detectable enthusiasm in the evidence received by the Working Party for the view that if social workers were made more accountable to their clients and at the same time more influential in policy-making they should then become subject to the ordinary electoral sanctions characteristic of representative democracies.

The Report is generally in favour of giving both clients and local 'communities' a greater say in decision-taking, but it does not adequately analyse the conflict between accountability to clients and accountability to local 'communities'. In the context of the personal social services it is very likely that sharp conflicts would arise between clients and communities because the two groups have differing expectations of social workers.

The following quotation from the Report gives some idea of the confused pattern of accountability devised by the Working Party for the community social work model: 'In any form of community social work, social workers will be subject to multiple accountability. Primary accountability will remain to the elected members (or the council members of voluntary agencies) who employ them and can call them to account: but they will also have a duty to give an account of their actions and decisions not only to individual clients or client groups, but also to informal carers with whom they are in partnership' (13.63).

This does not exhaust the complexities of the community social work model, since we are also assured that 'It is vital that a social services department should carry the ultimate residual responsibility for seeing that social care networks are maintained' (13.67). As the Report observes, optimistically, 'It will need to be made as explicit as possible who is accountable ... to whom for which aspect of his work', although we are reminded that 'No one can remove from social workers the burden of managing ensuing tensions' (13.63).

The neighbourhood model, as mentioned above, is less equivocal about the issue of accountability. Its supporters regret the fact that political authority is vested solely in local authority councils and their committees, and see this as an impediment to greater local autonomy at neighbourhood levels. They favour 'participatory' rather than representative forms of democracy, with social workers – and their clients – as very active participants.

The first duty of a social worker is to do his job within the terms of reference presented by his local authority, and he is solely accountable to his local authority in a legal and contractual sense. If his job gives rise to conflicts of loyalty which make him feel less capable of serving his clients' needs, then he ought to resign, although it is very doubtful whether many social workers spend their working lives moving from one crisis of conscience to another. This would be much more likely if social workers were made significantly more accountable to their clients and their local neighbourhood councils as well as other informal carers.

It is not enough simply to disentangle the various strands of political accountability from the community social work and neighbourhood models; the resource implications of accountability are also important enough to merit further discussion. In both community-centred models the local communities are presented as the major untapped social care resource. Insufficient account is taken of the likelihood that the capacity of local communities to provide sustained patterns of informal care may be exaggerated, especially in areas where the needs are greatest.

Formal systems of social service delivery developed because the informal networks of mutual aid in local communities were manifestly incapable of meeting the kinds of personal need which arise in complex industrial societies. It is a romantic illusion to suppose that by dispersing a handful of professional social workers into local communities we can miraculously revive the sleeping giants of populist altruism. The most localised system of 'social' service in the history of British social policy was the Poor Law. Its relieving officers and guardians all served localities and constituencies that were sufficiently small to be intimately known. It was just this distinctive quality of parochial social service that added a uniquely hurtful dimension to the experience of stigma among the recipients of poor relief.

The idea of investing local communities with a measure of real control over the use of resources and the ordering of welfare priorities leaves open both the question of general financial accountability between local communities and their local authorities and the questions of accountability and equity among the local communities. By what criteria are resources to be allocated to patch teams, for example, and by what criteria are they to be distributed within the patches? By what criteria are the boundaries of the patches to be drawn, for example in local authorities with marked geographical variations in social class, including wealth and income? How many additional bureaucrats will be required to ensure that justice is done between the various groups of local lobbyists? Are there any reliable inferences that can be made about the self-interest or altruism of these local constituencies? And how is a community to be defined? The literature advocating community-centred models of social work does not provide satisfactory answers to these questions.

The Report is strongly in favour of giving experienced social workers more autonomy and more scope for the exercise of their own judgement and discretion. It is also in favour of enhancing the rights of clients and carers. How are these two objectives to be made compatible? The exercise of discretion is primarily required in the interpretation of regulations in particular cases and in the case of idiosyncratic needs which have not been anticipated in the regulations. It is difficult enough when the pattern of accountability is unequivocal; none the less the Report signally fails to relate its recommendations about accountability to its recommendations about social workers' use of their own discretion.

We are asked to accept a model of 'multiple accountability' in which social workers will remain primarily accountable to elected members of the local authority, but additionally accountable to council members of voluntary agencies, individual clients or client groups, neighbourhood councils or mutual aid associations and informal carers (13.63). A statement of this kind is too vague for policy purposes, especially when it is considered in relation to the Report's appeal to employers to review their management systems in order to ensure a clear organisational structure with a minimum number of layers of decision–making. In addition the due process of accountability, with the element of consultation it involves, directly affects the speed and cost of service delivery; yet, on top of its failure to differentiate the types of accountability, the Report does not seriously analyse this consideration either, which detracts from its claim that community social work is a viable method for organising the personal social services.

Generalism and specialism

Both community-based models effectively relegate specialist expertise to a residual role. The two models are based on a threefold division of labour between generalists, specialists and managers (team leaders). The generalists would continue to do counselling work, but more of their time would be given to community orientated work involving negotiation, bargaining, advocacy and teaching others 'how to find their way within the social services' and how to use social care networks (13.49). There would be no increase in the total number of professional social workers – generalist or specialist; none of the increased number of volunteers would undertake statutory work; but more of the professional workers' time would have to be devoted to enlisting and managing volunteers, as part of their broader 'social care planning' remit.

The case for developing community-based social work rests very much on the assumption that proximity will enhance effectiveness. None the less in both variants of the model many of the specialist social workers would be moved further away from the front-line area teams, despite the clear evidence from the Stevenson and Parsloe study, *Social Work Teams* (1978, p. 279 ff), that specialists or 'consultant' social workers who are not active members of area teams are seldom used effectively. In fact very few area team members were able to use them at all. As if in anticipation of this criticism, the Report prescribes that 'Both kinds of social workers, if they are to operate with a community orientation, must have knowledge of communities and how they function' (13.46). Again there is no indication of *how* they would acquire this knowledge. Presumably it would be up to the workers to study their locality while they were working in it; the specialists serving more than one locality would have to study very hard indeed.

The Report gives equal emphasis to the activities of social care planning and counselling in social work. However, the term 'social care planning' is misleadingly grandiose, although it accords with the model of community social work since it implies a range of responsibility beyond the competence and resources of social workers. If social care planning is intended to complement the task of counselling, which is primarily a one-to-one activity associated with individuals and families, the emphasis on the 'social' aspect is misleading. If it has broader implications, a social worker attempting to work at both disparate levels is unlikely to excel in either job.

None the less the claims and counter-claims that are likely to fall on the basic-grade worker in the community social work model are minimal in comparison with those reserved for the managers, or team leaders (13.51-53). The team leader would be a manager, an entrepreneur, a negotiator, a watchdog over various budgets and a planner. His responsibilities would encompass not only social workers, but a variety of other paid and unpaid workers. There is no serious discussion as to whether or not he would retain a case load. If so, it could well be the last straw; if not, the authority of his supervisory and supportive role in relation to junior colleagues would be seriously undermined.

It is very difficult to follow the Report's analysis of the relationship between social work and community work. The term 'social care planning' seems to subsume large elements of community work. We are told, for example, that 'Community work, in which social workers carry out activities overlapping, but not co-extensive, with those of community workers, includes direct work with local community groups' (10.21), and in the next paragraph the Report states that 'We do not find the distinctions made between casework, group work and community work as methods of social work particularly helpful' because 'these terms identify the client, without telling us anything clearly about social workers' activities or the settings in which they are undertaken' (10.22). In the community social work model all social workers will undertake social care planning and counselling and therefore all social workers will be involved in some aspects of community work.

The neighbourhood, or patch model does not bother with such fine distinctions. It would effectively convert nearly all the social workers into community workers with special responsibilities for the frail elderly and families with young, children. Within the patch teams, staff roles would be less narrowly defined than in the service delivery model, and counselling skills would have a less central place.

One of the most serious flaws in the Report is its neglect of specialised skills and knowledge and their role in social work practice. There are several paragraphs on specialisation in the Report which are intended to rebut the argument that the community social work model could not accommodate specialisation (10.34–37), but they are unconvincing for the following reasons. Within the community social work model all social workers would 'undertake social planning and counselling for any client group in a competent but basic way' (10.33), but, at the same time, 'Administrative structures may so relate the work and social workers together as to allocate most work of a particular kind to specially designated staff' (10.35). Specialists would be 'linked with' generalist teams (10.36), but in some cases, particularly where the volume of work is small, there would be centrally based specialist teams (10.37). The Report, however, goes on to insist that 'Whether or not an individual social worker is a specialist ... the "community dimension" of his practice must always be taken into account and applied by him in carrying out his work' (10.38).

The simplest test of the practicability of these proposals is to treat the list of skills and knowledge which the community social worker would be expected to acquire (10.23–29) as the broad outline of the 'community dimension' mentioned above, and then to ask the following questions. How could a general social worker maintain a basic level of competence as a social worker within the terms of such a broad remit? How could a specialist social worker remain a specialist whilst acquiring and applying more than a token knowledge of these 'community' skills? How would general social workers ever acquire specialist knowledge and expertise? The Report itself gives a partial answer to these questions by acknowledging albeit half-heartedly – that its recommendations would have profound implications for social work education if they were to be adopted (10.34). Most, if not all forms of specialist training in the CQSW courses would have to be abandoned to make room for more teaching about the 'community dimension'. The main responsibility for specialist training would, by default, devolve on post-qualifying courses. Generic social work training at CQSW level would become a form of generalist community social work training, and specialist training would be consigned to what is currently a very small and highly vulnerable part of social work education.

It should also be noted that any trend towards increasing generalism at the expense of specialism will run counter to present government policy, which is responding to the demand for more expertise. The Mental Health Bill before Parliament at the time of writing, for example, provides for the formal designation of approved mental health social workers and the restriction of this status to those who have followed an *additional* two-year course of training. If this principle is accepted in the field of mental health, it is arguable on grounds of natural justice alone that it should be extended to other highly vulnerable categories of need. It seems unlikely, for example, that the central government can long delay taking similar action with regard to children at risk who are under the age of 5. But the mentally ill and small children who are at risk are not the only special groups whose needs might well be neglected in a community-centred model.

The most vulnerable, disadvantaged and stigmatised clients will be at greatest risk in the community-based models of social work since they give greatest offence to local norms of behaviour and are often rejected by their local communities. The Report itself refers to the evidence submitted by the Family Service Unit (FSU), which revealed 'the great difficulty' with which certain families accept 'any notion of reliance on informal networks of family, friends or neighbours, their vivid fear of being victims of gossip and the importance they attach to confidentiality' (II.3 6). In addition the social worker's lack of special expertise is a recurring complaint from a variety of user groups, including a high proportion of physically handicapped people and ethnic minorities.

This is not to recommend reversion to a pre-Seebohm model in which social work is divided into isolated and narrow specialisms which, in turn, are separated from the other main social services. That is emphatically not the answer. Good social work practice depends on effective co-operation not only with other formal social services, but also with the informal networks of social care. The community social work model might well strengthen the links with the informal networks, but only at the expense of co-operation with the other formal social services and efficient discharge of statutory responsibilities.

The argument here rests on a number of considerations. First, a more precise definition of the role and tasks of social work is essential to the improvement of understanding and co-operation between social work and other social services. Secondly, the organisation of social work must make provision not only for an orderly internal division of labour based on generic team practice, but also for liaison with external services to be based on specialised expertise. Specialists within the area team should be the main co-ordinators of care when other services are involved. Thirdly, the Report admits that 'several points were made repeatedly in evidence from those whose work brings them into close and regular contact with social workers. Without exception they argued for specialisation by social workers in a particular range of work' (8.31). This point was made by the courts, the medical services and many voluntary agencies. The Report responds with the statement that 'We recognise its importance but are also acutely aware that ... we have not given this subject all the attention it requires. Others, however, have done so' (10.30).

Fourthly, the Report recognises that if a community social work model were to be adopted, new problems of co-operation with other social services would arise if they did not reorganise themselves on similar lines. The Report states that 'arrangements for collaboration need to be planned, and factors which affect relationships to be understood and not allowed to give rise to tensions ...in the relevant agencies' (Chapter 8, conclusion 4). The Report says nothing further about this issue, apart from suggesting that 'a new balance will be called for between the skills we have considered ... if social workers are to work in close partnership with other social services staff and with social networks, be these within local communities or within communities of interest which cross over geographical boundaries' (10.38). These are very vague recommendations from a committee that has been deliberating for over a year.

Co-operation and communication between social services departments and other social services are vital to the welfare of the most vulnerable clients. This was one of the issues which compelled Professor Stevenson to write a minority report to the Maria Colwell enquiry. In her covering letter she wrote that 'Time and again we have had to refer to failures in communication. However, as our comments section demonstrates, responsibility for effective communication in our welfare state is a two-way affair ... It is most disturbing to contemplate the amount of concern and anxiety about Maria which never reached Miss Lees' (the social worker who was in charge of the case) (Department of Health and Social Security, 1974, pp. 8, 88–115).

A model of social work which accentuates the organisational and operational differences between social work and other social services is unlikely to improve co-operation, and in all probability both community-based models would have that affect. The experience of the Maria Colwell enquiry and similar events since then must have contributed to Professor Stevenson's insistence that we get a sensible balance between genericism and specialism, and also uphold the specialist nature of liaison work with other social services. Clearly there is scope for improvement in the present system of liaison between social work and other social services, but it will not be achieved either by reducing the average size and increasing the number of area teams or by abolishing them altogether in the search for 'community'.

Specialism can be organised around particular activities such as adoption, fostering, welfare rights, and so on, around particular client groups such as the deaf and the blind, or around methods such as social casework, group work, community work and family therapy. The type of setting in which social workers are employed hardly seems to be a criterion of specialism in its own right, although it is sometimes the case that particular settings are developed on the assumption that special needs and skills are involved. Hospital-based social work is an obvious example. Similarly, residential work has specialist features partly because of the nature of its setting and partly because distinctions between its formal and informal aspects are neither possible nor desirable. Community work remains a vexed issue. It is one of the few specialisms which are definable largely in terms of method, although the method entails an orientation and focus differing markedly from those of social casework. Each different method of organising social work services will impose its own orientation and focus on all the workers involved.

In brief, the concept of specialism is a highly relative one, since it implies a variation from some understood norm of generic or general practice. Organisational change, if it is sufficiently radical, can therefore alter the whole frame of reference, and hence the meaning of the terms used.

Organising social work

To a very large extent the expectations that employers have of their social workers are directly determined by legislative imperatives. The 'autonomy of the employing bodies derives from the freedom with which they can organise their own social services not only to meet their mandatory duties, but also to provide for the permissive undertakings which they think are important.

For the past five years at least, the employers – local authorities in particular – have been discharging these responsibilities in conditions of intensifying disadvantage. The volume of legislation has grown steadily and it has outpaced the supply of resources required to meet newly recognised needs. Under such circumstances the inherent weaknesses in any system of organisation are bound to become more apparent, and even its best features will eventually be compromised. It is therefore a particularly difficult time for sorting out the intrinsic and the extrinsic causes of intra-organisational conflict. If there was adequate scope for specialisation as well as team work, social workers would be less likely to feel 'deskilled' and socially isolated, and more likely to cope effectively with the dilemmas of obligation and choice which characterise their job.

The questions facing us – what is social work and what should it be? – embrace the nature of the needs confronting social work, the kinds of resources required to meet these needs, and the modes of organisation best suited to service delivery within the framework of mandatory and permissive legislation.

Several themes recur throughout the mass of evidence received by the Working Party. First, with regard to the needs of social work clientele, there is little doubt that professional social workers are or ought to be mainly concerned with the welfare and interests of people who in general are rejected, vulnerable, disadvantaged and sometimes a danger to public safety. In addition to this minority of complex and difficult cases there are many other needs – largely material and advisory ones – which can be met fairly quickly and effectively by other professional, non-professional and untrained workers, with the help of volunteers – given the necessary resources.

The second theme is the issue of genericism and specialism in social work which, in principle, is far less contentious than might be supposed. It should no longer be seen as an 'either/or' issue, but as one of finding the best ways in practice of combining the two types of activity. Professor Stevenson's assertion that 'there is a common core of knowledge and skill which should be acquired on basic qualifying courses' (Stevenson, 1981, pp.13–28) is well supported by the evidence. None the less, in turning her attention to the relationship between the complex needs of a minority of difficult clients and more straightforward requests for help, Professor Stevenson goes on to recommend that 'ways are found of better utilising specialist expertise *outside* teams for the benefit of the team. But this does not dispose of the case for specialisms *within* teams [my italics].' She continues with the question, 'are people's diverse problems so straightforward that we do not need expertise in face-to-face dealings with them?' and she proposes that 'If social work is *only* about promoting, stimulating and supporting community networks, then some other occupational group will have to move in, or be invented, to offer service to those with specific and complex social and psychological difficulties' (p.26).

Expertise, however, develops through continuous experience on a basis of specialisation. Co-ordination and co-operation in social work depend on the development of a shared core of generic knowledge and skills. Where needs are complex, the tasks of co-ordination and co-operation extend from the social work team, in field or residential settings, to other social services. Whatever deficiencies there are in the current pattern of social work organisation in area teams, it seems improbable that an alternative system which is more geographically dispersed than present ones will improve levels of co-operation and efficiency in *both* the formal and the informal contexts of social care.

Thirdly, we know that traditional systems of organisation based on area teams have not always succeeded either in getting the best allocation between their generic and specialist workers or in harnessing the services of local communities. In part this is because the preventative, practical and community-orientated activities of social services departments do not give rise to the really intractable problems of organisation and resource deployment. It is the hard-core minority of families and individuals with longstanding and recurring problems that imposes a 'residual' status on the Departments and compels them to assume a reactive and contingent function which can never be justified on grounds of cost-efficiency alone.

In her impressive submission to the Committee and her related book, *Specialisation in Social Service Teams*, Professor Stevenson outlines a way of combining generalism and specialism. Her proposal is based on the so-called 'client–centred' model, with area teams and a formal, hierarchical system of administration. It also accepts and accommodates the need to improve liaison and co-operation between professional workers, volunteers and local communities. Professor Stevenson argues that 'every team should have within it a worker whose role is thus defined and whose remit is at once to sensitise the team to community need and to offer specific and concrete advice in relation to particular problems in a given locality. The links of such a worker with a range of voluntary and self-help groups would be invaluable' (26, cf. Stevenson, 1981, pp. 130–6).

But Professor Stevenson is insistent that this is only one part of the work of an area team, one specialism within a team of specialists, and her model shows how the total resources of the team can be divided and deployed not only by reference to the skills and resources of the team, but with regard to maintaining good working relations with *other* social services which may be needed by the clientele of the team. Her model also allocates to one of the team's six sub-units the primary responsibility for intake work and work with clients whose main problems are material and financial. All team members would serve the intake team on a rota basis, which would ensure that the most skilled and experienced staff played a part in this vitally important work and at the same time did not become over-specialised in their own work. There would also be close co-operation between the community-based sub-unit and the other sub-units.

The job of the team leader would still be an onerous one, but he would be working with a team of experienced specialists, and he would be able to concentrate on a finite number of tasks, including liaison with the team's social services department. This model was seriously considered by the Working Party and then rejected on the grounds that it gave insufficient emphasis to informal community networks of social care.

Social work values

As suggested earlier, it is unpopular and stigmatised people who are at greatest risk in a community-centred model of social work, and reference has already been made to the reluctance of FSU clients to accept help from informal local networks and their 'vivid fear' of gossip. The Report reassures us on this matter by declaring that 'Citizens are entitled to choose the person or people from whom help is most acceptable ... nothing we are recommending should be taken to imply that clients generally should have informal caring networks imposed upon them' (13.58). Yet the whole preventive rationale of community social work seems bound to lead to exactly this outcome. Scarcely any attention has been given to the ethical (as distinct from the economic) implications of preventive social work – or to its compatibility with the principles of respect for persons and confidentiality.

In localities where a community social work model was adopted it would be much more difficult to protect the privacy not only of clients, but of other citizens who have no intention of becoming clients. The dangers would be greatest in the case of the neighbourhood, or patch model whose advocates insist that their method of operation will greatly augment the flow of information about local needs into the local offices. At a time when profound public disquiet is being expressed about the indiscriminate and often *unreported* collection of information about ordinary citizens by public and private bodies, we are now invited to endorse the creation of a proliferation of local data banks based largely on hearsay, gossip and well-meaning but uninvited prying.

It is argued that in a patch system social work staff would be able to build up a detailed knowledge of the local patterns of informal care and that this knowledge will be augmented by fostering contacts with intermediaries or 'gatekeepers', including people such as publicans, corner shop-keepers, lollypop ladies, and so on, who often acquire roles as informal advisers. In some of the areas operating a patch system it appears that local commercial enterprises such as pubs and corner shops would become recognised as important sources of information.

Respect for persons must entail respect for people's privacy and, in turn, for their right to confidentiality. The idea of preventive social work on a local basis would seriously threaten the right to privacy, since it would licence strangers (including volunteers) to enquire into the personal circumstances of citizens who may neither have asked for help nor committed any offence. The best way of preventing breaches of confidentiality is to collect as little confidential information as possible, and to confine the collection of it to professional workers.

David Billis has pointed out that 'the preventive umbrella permits an unbounded variety of work to creep into the original sanctioned agency function. That body of issues for which the organisation was set up in the first place can be steadily increased'. He states that 'the abandonment of pseudo-prevention may be a step towards the clarification of departmental boundaries based on the analysis of problems rather than the attainment of ideal states. It may take us towards not only "workable limits to social work", but trimmer, more muscular, and defensible, social service departments' (Billis, 1981, p. 379). However, a move towards community-based social work would almost certainly take us in the opposite direction.

Is there any justification for the indiscriminate collection of information that would appear to be envisaged for the community-based system of social work? According to the Report, this information would help social workers to foster a general sense of community, and would also help them to detect needs at an early stage. Not to over-dramatise the issue, a system simultaneously governed by the concepts of community and prevention would be potentially lethal to our civil liberties. In totalitarian societies the imposition of community – in the form of a unified network of local loyalties which are subservient to the state – is one of the basic political aims of government. Democracies tolerate the coexistence of many different loyalties. It is important that some rapport exists between the formal and informal systems of social care. It is equally important that the state is not allowed to intrude too far into the private worlds of individuals, families and local communities.

The right to privacy in one's personal life is one of the hallmarks of a free society. Justification must always be made before that right is violated. Preventive social work is an insidious threat to privacy because it can always be 'justified' on grounds of social welfare. In this matter I am reminded of Lord Melbourne's remark made after he had listened to an evangelical sermon on the consequences of sin: 'Things have come to a pretty pass, when religion is allowed to invade the sphere of private life' (Russell, 1898, p. 79). The same could be said of today's secular welfare evangelicals, who wish to advertise their services in every pub, pulpit and private residence in the country.

In the case of the professional social worker there is an important difference between learning about a suspected case of child abuse, for example, in the ordinary course of his duties and intentionally helping to create an informal network of information. The difference is one of good manners and forbearance. There is already considerable disquiet about the existence of 'at risk' registers in our present system. Imagination quails at the thought of their possible scope in a community-based model of social work. The desire to locate and provide for unexpressed needs is not a defensible reason for jeopardising people's right to be left alone.

A general council and local welfare advisory Committees

The Report reviews all the main arguments on the subject of a general council. Some of the arguments against are serious ones, but none of them is conclusive. For example it is pointed out that the boundaries of social work are imprecise and that 'social work is concerned with social control as well as with caring for people' (12.8). It is not disputed that the boundaries of social work ought to be more clearly drawn; this minority report is submitted partly for the very reason that the implementation of community social work would undoubtedly add to their obscurity. On the question of social control, the same situation exists in other professions, including medicine and nursing, and it is precisely because social control is an element of most professions that antipathy to professionalism is generally expressed as part of a wider sociological critique of the allocation of power in society.

Again, the fact that 'the knowledge base [of social work] is not readily understood by the public at large' (12.8) is true of most forms of professional knowledge, and appears to be a reasonable argument *in favour of* according professional status to an occupation. Other factors have to be considered, but it is misleading to imply that the public accord high status only to knowledge and skills which they 'understand'. They do so not on the basis of understanding, but on the basis of trust, and trust becomes important when people's lack of certainty and knowledge makes them dependent on another person.

The argument that social workers are not entitled to professional status because the majority of them are employed in large-scale public bureaucracies and so few are engaged in private practice is also open to question. Are we to believe that architects in the employment of local authorities behave less professionally than their colleagues in private enterprise? And are we to assume that there has to be an extensive private market for a service before it can be professionalised? Paradoxically both arguments find support among collectivists, in spite of their belief in the moral superiority of the social market.

The Report correctly states that 'Bureaucratic development has also inevitably resulted in a division between management and worker which provides the basis for the influence of the Trade Unions. The move towards full professional status and the introduction of an intermediary in the shape of an independent professional body must constitute a threat to that influence' (12.10). This statement describes the crucial issue in the future status of social work. If it does not become a profession it will become fully unionised; it will certainly not retain its present ambiguous status.

The Report includes, 'without prejudging the issue', the argument that there is a tide of opinion in 'community action and community involvement' which is highly critical of professional authority and professional knowledge in most occupations (12.11–12). Social work, however, is in a singular position, since the greater part of its specialised knowledge and skills is focused on a minority of the public, most of whom are very poor and not very articulate. It therefore goes unchallenged when intellectuals and activists who are largely middle class condemn the elitist nature of professionalism, and debunk the status of 'esoteric' knowledge (in the pejorative sense of the term). If the characteristic patterns of risk and dependency confronting social workers were to spread to the majority of the population, the general public would very soon demand services of the highest quality from professional social workers of the highest calibre, the idea of applying egalitarian principles to standards of knowledge and skill would be laughed out of court.

The British Association of Social Workers is in no doubt that a general council would make a positive impact 'on the definition and actual performance of social work' (12.17). It would not be possible for a general council to be set up in the very near future, but the British Medical Association is right in implying that, without 'a properly structured profession', social work will never have the incentive to set its own house in order (12.22), and there is no reason why 'blanketing in' should be an insurmountable obstacle, as the Report acknowledges (12.26). The majority of field social workers are now qualified. The majority of residential workers are not qualified, but the position is beginning to improve with the changing state of the labour market and CCETSW's policy of encouraging courses to develop specialist options in residential care. Agreement on a suitable target date, say in three years, would give us a little time to reinforce what is best in social work and get rid of some of the most glaring anomalies.

In principle this note accepts the view advanced by BASW that a council should be set up to assume general responsibility for the regulation of professional conduct, licensing and accreditation. Whether or not the council would also be responsible for the regulation of education and training is another matter. There is a good case for the appointment of a small working party to advise the Secretary of State both on the advisability of having a general council of social work and on its relationship to CCETSW. The arguments for and against keeping the two organisations separate are fairly evenly balanced, and a decision at this stage would be premature. Madelaine Malherbe has already carried out a substantial amount of excellent work on the issues of accreditation, but there are other related matters which have still to be considered (Malherbe, 1979).

These include the problems of assigning personal responsibility in a profession which is predominantly a public service, and in which the law does not specify which duties have to be carried out by qualified workers (12.9); the problems which might arise in residential care, where as yet only a minority of staff are professionally qualified; the extent to which a general council would be concerned with the activities of non-social workers in the personal social services; and whether or not the probation and after care service would come under the aegis of a general council.

These are complex and highly sensitive issues requiring careful and impartial consideration. They are all related to two basic questions. The first concerns the extent to which local authority management structures can be made compatible with the degree of professional autonomy and accountability that would accompany the creation of a general council. The second concerns the present standing of BASW. The recent history of the Association has been troubled by a loss in membership and a serious financial crisis. Its policies have not always been consistent with those of a professional body. However, there are signs that BASW is beginning to put its house in order, and this is greatly to be welcomed.

Since the Working Party did not receive a substantial body of evidence to the effect that clients' rights are generally being put in jeopardy, it seems quite unnecessary to set up an expensive network of local welfare advisory committees. In many cases this would make it impossible in practice to distinguish between the responsibilities of local authorities and those of their social work employees – a point which is equally relevant to the case for having a general council. The introduction of advisory committees would be bound to encourage the growth of an 'adversarial' element in 'transactions between worker and client', and stimulate an increase in 'defensive practice' (12.69). It is difficult enough to administer speedy, efficient and cheap appeals systems in the field of income maintenance, where the distinction between mandatory and discretionary powers is relatively clear cut; it would be an impossible exercise in the field of local authority social services, where the distinction is harder to make.

The proposal for a system of local advisory committees and an inspectorate will only distract attention from the need to resolve the conflict between 'elitists' and ' egalitarians' in social work. If elitism means seeking to promote and maintain the best possible standards of public service, I am an elitist, and I see the eventual formation of a general council and the professionalisation of social work as useful means to that end.

Implications for social work education

The Committee is unduly confident – if vague – in its recommendations on the future of social work education. It accepts, for example, that 'social work training has concentrated too exclusively upon direct counselling-type support work with individuals and groups' (3.46). There were some assertions in the submitted evidence that this emphasis on counselling does dominate social work education, but not sufficient to justify such dogmatic endorsement by the Report. In fact the Working Party never looked at the curricula of social work courses, because education and training were not within its terms of reference. Nevertheless there is no lack of evidence to the effect that there is a *variety of* emphasis in the courses, and it could be argued that in some courses there is too little emphasis on basic social work skills such as counselling.

The Report, however, proceeds to invite CCETSW to 'consider how it can assist training courses to develop the social care planning aspect of social work, without detracting from the training needed by social workers to fill their other direct counselling role' (3.45). Yet our present curricula for social work education are already in danger of sinking under the weight of so many disparate training expectations.

Short of lengthening the duration of basic training for the CQSW or stripping the curricula of all contributory disciplines, the only practicable way of introducing additional community-orientated training would be to drop a considerable proportion of training in other methods. This would naturally benefit community social work, but it could not be done without damage to training for social casework and for duties which are directly connected with statutory work.

The Report also fails to explain how the qualified social worker would find time to undertake statutory duties and maintain a basic level of competence in community-based activity. Yet it is on the basis of these proposals that CCETSW and the Colleges are seriously asked to develop a drastically revised model of social work training.

This is not to imply that 'promoting community self-help' is unimportant, but social workers are not necessarily the best people to carry out this function, and it should certainly not be expected of all social workers. The Working Party's solution to this problem is to recommend a drastic change in the training of social workers, without asking whether or not the expensive end product would still be professional social workers.

If the Working Party's arguments are accepted at face value, there should be a powerful shift in emphasis, away from highly specialised, skill-intensive work to more generalised tasks with a high 'entrepreneurial' content. Differences between paid workers and unpaid helpers should be minimised in the interests of greater equality and more 'participation'. All but a minority of social work clients should be helped by unqualified volunteers.

There is a good case for reviewing the balance of social work training between courses leading to the CQSW and those leading to the CSS. CCETSW is currently seeking the advice of interested parties on this matter, including the Colleges and employers. The Working Party considered proposals that there should be opportunities for CSS-holders to convert their qualification into a CQSW, which would be sensible under the present system, but pointless if, in deference to egalitarianism, the roles, tasks and status of the two qualifications were to be made virtually identical. That is exactly the effect that community social work would have. It may already be true that over the whole range of the personal social services social casework occupies only a small proportion of the time of a minority of CQSW-qualified social workers in area teams. If so, a more explicit division of labour between social workers and social service workers would release a proportion of CQSW-holders for more specialised post-experience training. This already seems probable in the field of mental health, and it is a welcome and long overdue development. Its logical outcome under the present system of social work would be a stratified profession with a fairly circumscribed range of roles and tasks, a number of which would have legal status. The alternative paths of community social work and neighbourhood social work would lead to more diffusion and more equality all round, but also to the eventual disappearance of professional social work altogether.

Conclusion

Any general move towards a model of practice and organisation based on community-social work or neighbourhood-based, or patch social work will put the future of professional social work in jeopardy. There are at least two ways in which the community-based enterprise could go, because its two groups of advocates support it for totally incompatible reasons. First, there are those who believe that it would provide the ideal framework in which local communities could be mobilised into political pressure groups to obtain a massive increase in statutory resources. The danger here is that, if this expectation was not fulfilled, the consensual face of community would be transformed into one of open conflict between social workers as 'advocates' of 'community needs' and their employers.

Secondly, there are those who believe that the community model would generate a sufficient volume of informal care services to justify drastic cuts in statutory funding. This expectation is as questionable as the first, and equally liable to generate local conflict.

It would be foolish to make general predictions about anything as heterogeneous as local authority social services. None the less it is likely that in some local authorities, under the proposed new model, sustained efforts would be made by activists to put community social work to radical political use. Should this become widespread, the inevitable conflict would probably result in professional social work going the way of the ill-fated community development projects; then, by default, the gap left by the departing professionals would have to be filled by volunteers.

Lastly, there is the prospect of the neighbourhood, or patch version of community social work which I find most disturbing. It conjures up the vision of a captainless crew under a patchwork ensign stitched together from remnants of the Red Flag and the Jolly Roger – all with a licence and some with a disposition to mutiny heading in the gusty winds of populist rhetoric, with presumption as their figurehead and inexperience as their compass, straight for the reefs of public incredulity. Yet there is nothing fundamentally wrong with the ship in which we sail today, and certainly nothing that cannot be put right with common sense and cautious reform. It is not the present state of social work that gives cause for alarm, but the proposals for radical change in its nature and direction. I have submitted this note because I believe that the time for equivocation has passed.

Afterthought

The proliferation of risk registers in the early 1980s did little or nothing to check the escalation of child abuse and domestic violence scandals. The right to privacy is a fundamental human right – but it can seldom, if ever, be treated as an absolute right because it frequently comes into conflict with other fundamental rights as well as considerations of public interest.

In the 1980s, social workers lacked the specialised knowledge needed to make effective use of risk registers and resolve these conflicts on the basis of reliable evidence. There is, and always has been, a darker side to privacy and those private places in which dreadful things go on undetected for years behind closed doors. In cases involving minority groups, the dictates of political correctness may have discouraged some social workers from responding promptly and effectively to evidence of manifestly unacceptable practices.

SEVEN

The quest for community: From the Settlement Movement to the Griffiths Report: an historical perspective*

Robert Pinker

The history of British social welfare primarily concerns the interplay of formal welfare bureaucracy and informal networks of care based on families, neighbourhoods and communities and its effects on the relationship between the state and civil society. In order to appreciate the current vogue for welfare pluralism it is helpful to look back over this process as it unfolded. The record might have been very different, for example, if the British welfare state established before the First World War had been designed for individualist rather than collectivist purposes.

The quest for community – the desire to restore a vanishing way of life rooted in traditional loyalties and obligations and perpetuated by self-reliant citizens – has been one of the sustaining myths of politicians and social scientists since the beginning of the industrial revolution. Commitment to this ideal has not lessened as the proportion of the population living in complex industrial urban localities has grown larger. On the whole the quest for community has been conducted by middle-class social reformers on behalf of urban working-class people, regardless of whether these people have expressed any awareness of cultural deprivation, let alone a vanished heritage.

Rediscovery of the community ideal was the inspiration of the English Settlement Movement, which emerged in the 1880s. The sponsors of the movement included Samuel and Henrietta Barnett, Octavia Hill and Edward Denison and Oxford academics like Benjamin Jowett, T.H. Green and Arnold Toynbee. With varying degrees of intensity they held common objectives and shared the same anxiety about the growing powers of the state and they supported the new poor law principle of less eligibility and the workhouse test. Edward Denison was also a founder member of the Charity Organisation Society, which was subsequently taken over by the social reformers C.S. Loch and Bernard and Helen Bosanquet. The Society's pronouncements on the debilitating nature of state intervention in the relief of need are echoed today in the oratory of

---

* First presented as a plenary paper at a Social Service Inspectorate DHSS (NI) Conference at the Riverside Theatre, University of Ulster, Coleraine on 23 March 1988 and subsequently published in Pinker's *Social Work in an Enterprise Society* (1990: 96–121).

politicians like Lord Young and John Moore on the role of state welfare in the creation of a culture of dependency among the poor. These are arguments with more intellectual substance than the argument for using community services as an alternative to formal social services with which they are often associated.

In the case of the Settlement Movement, however, the quest for community embodied the ideal of social regeneration. Settlements like Toynbee Hall were established in the crowded, poverty-stricken slums of London and other big cities in order to 'preach not only the Gospel but also civilisation to the poor.'[1] Undergraduates from Oxford, Cambridge and other universities went to live and work in the slums, starting various social, cultural and educational programmes for the encouragement of self-help and community participation. Nevertheless, as Standish Meacham points out, moral leadership came from enlightened outsiders who chiefly relied on personal example and personal 'connection' to reverse the divisions of social class. 'Community, authority and hierarchy ... became the hallmark of the ethos espoused by the men of Toynbee Hall.'[2]

Meacham casts considerable doubt on the efficacy of the early Settlement Movement as an instrument for saving the 'helpable' poor from the demoralised 'residuum' of the unhelpable. He shows that at the end of the nineteenth century most of the active members of Toynbee Hall were respectable artisans, clerks and small shopkeepers and that only a minority of these activists even lived in the poverty-stricken locality of the Hall. Significantly it is clear from the available evidence that few of the sponsors of the Movement attempted to reach a better understanding of the ways of life which they hoped to change. They felt able to cross the divides of class and culture with their own preconceived ideas about the nature of the good life and the virtue of self-help. They were concerned not so much to identify themselves with the underprivileged as to persuade the underprivileged to adopt their moral frame of reference.

Toynbee Hall was a reflection in microcosm of the growing debate about social reform and the relief of poverty in Britain at the turn of the century. According to Meacham there were at least three schools of thought which went against the ethos of the Settlement Movement, beginning with the views of the Webbs and J.A. Hobson, whose advocacy of social reform in the interests of 'national efficiency' amounted to a new definition of a community as 'a complex network of agencies and institutions' – an entity which was virtually coexistent with the nation state and more in sympathy with the extension of formal social policies.[3] These writers stood for central government intervention and policy-making by experts, an approach which struck at the very core of the Settlement Movement's reliance on parish work, individual contact and networks of informal support organised by voluntary activists.

Second, in the eyes of radical Christian socialists like Scott Holland and Charles Gore, religious impartiality was a lesser weapon than the overt propagation of Anglican values in the struggle against deprivation. The Anglican movements had their equally zealous Catholic and nonconformist counterparts ranging from the Society of St Vincent de Paul to the Salvation Army. Third, the empirical research findings of the new discipline of positivist sociology laid stress on the environmental causes of poverty and the need for government intervention on a national scale. Empirical social research and positivist sociology subsequently provided the intellectual framework on which the discipline of social policy and administration has developed down to the present time. The title 'Social Policy and Administration' is itself significant: it is no coincidence that, in Britain at least, the academic study of social welfare – a term which ought properly to include the informal as well as the formal dimensions of welfare – has been defined in exclusively formal terms for so long.

Looking back over the history of British social welfare from the point of view of both scholarship and policy-making, we may wonder why the subject matter of informal welfare slipped down the scales of importance in British social science until its rediscovery in the 1950s and 1960s. Again in this respect Toynbee Hall represented in microcosm the cross-currents of ideology and interest which were to transform the relationship between the state and civil society in the formulation of British social welfare policies during the twentieth century.

In 1903 the young William Beveridge, already preoccupied by the problem of unemployment, became a sub-warden of Toynbee Hall, although his advocacy of labour exchanges, with their implication of increasing mobility of labour, was at odds with a localised notion of community. Beveridge's future brother-in-law R.H. Tawney joined Toynbee Hall at the same time. A committed Christian socialist he passionately rejected both hierarchy and impartiality. In his desire to 'awaken in working-class men and women a sense of the contribution they could make to the community of the nation'.[4] Tawney pioneered various tutorial educational programmes, but it is evident from Meacham's narrative that in the end 'Connection eluded the tutorial scheme as it had eluded Toynbee Hall.'[5]

Beveridge's and Tawney's views on the community were both dissimilar and incompatible with the Toynbee Hall ethos. Beveridge, who was to exert enormous influence on the future development of the British welfare state, recast the notion in terms of administrative procedure and expertise. Tawney's egalitarian and participatory approach remains a potent ideal for successive generations of well-intentioned communitarians who, unlike the founder members of Toynbee Hall, have been ready to identify themselves with the underprivileged. The founders attempted to reinterpret the concept of community in the likeness of their own values but they were also impelled by a fear of class conflict, which they hoped to avert by transmitting these values to the underprivileged. We know now which model of social welfare won the debate and shaped the future character of the British welfare state. The broad framework took its normative character from an administrative tradition which found institutional continuity and support in both governmental and academic circles across the divisions of party and ideology. The egalitarian, participatory approach based on enduring belief in the virtues of the family and the community managed to survive within this framework but the relationship between these administrative and communitarian traditions of welfare have more often been characterised by conflict than by consensus. The present vogue for welfare pluralism and a mixed economy of welfare has given a new twist to these old ideological conflicts. The advocates of community action and increasing reliance on informal welfare are vociferous across the political spectrum but their objectives differ from those of the past. Many collectivists now hope to shift the balance of power from the state to civil society in the regulation of welfare without cutting the level of statutory funding, but individualists, who are in the political ascendant, are working towards the transfer of power and financial responsibilities from the state to civil society. As the administrative framework of the post-war welfare state took shape during the late 1940s, the discipline of social policy and administration was mainly concerned with research centred on the formal welfare sector. The research carried out by sociologists and social anthropologists on kinship and community-based aspects of social care was scarcely acknowledged in the field of policy studies. In retrospect the pioneering community care initiatives of the late 1950s and early 1960s look like ill-conceived exercises in shifting vulnerable people out of the known miseries of long-term institutional care into a world of unknown contingencies where familial and neighbourhood structures of obligation and concern were assumed to exist, without benefit of evidence.

The recovery and cultivation of community

If the opponents of state welfare and expansion of the formal social services had won the political debate at the turn of the century, the discipline of social policy and administration would have found little institutional anchorage in British political life, and the cultural presumptions of the Charity Organisation Society, the Settlement Movement and the Poor Law Majority Report of 1909 would not have survived without modification. If the ideology of self-help and opposition to state welfare had become entrenched as the conventional wisdom of social welfare, the main thrust of applied social research might well have been directed towards informal community care rather than formal policy-making and administrative procedure. Instead of Sidney and Beatrice Webb, William Beveridge, A.L. Bowley and the Fabian Society, the founding fathers and mothers of welfare studies would have come from the great schools of late-nineteenth-century European anthropology. Scholars like Taylor, Evans-Pritchard and Malinowski, who followed the flags of empire to study the kinship and cultural habits of alien people, would have had their counterparts studying the culture and sub-cultures which make up the informal character of the British way of life.

Some of the earliest British social policy studies included work of this kind. The path-breaking enquiries of Charles Booth and Seebohm Rowntree in the 1880s and 1890s are packed with information about the way in which ordinary people lived, as distinct from how other people thought they lived.[6] The same can be said of the 1904 Report of the Select Committee on Physical Fitness, with its careful descriptions of child-rearing and caring practices among the urban poor.[7] This tradition of empirical enquiry and commentary on familial and neighbourhood patterns of mutual aid continued throughout the 1920s and 1930s, largely in the fields of urban planning and housing studies.

Nevertheless the major focus of enquiry in social policy and administration after the Second World War was the structure of formal welfare bureaucracy, which had become vastly extended in the wake of the Beveridge Report and the social reforms of the Attlee government. After that the collectivist bias in social policy studies was reinforced and exemplified in the work of Richard Titmuss. From the time of his inaugural lecture in 1951 until his death in 1972 Titmuss continued to study the 'structure and functions of the social services, the role of professionalism and the relations of economic resources to social priorities' and the impact of these processes on 'the informal patterns of family life and community life'.[8] Although he was one of the earliest advocates of community care, Titmuss was firmly committed to an institutional model of welfare in which statutory services performed the dominant role.

If he were alive today, it is probable that Titmuss would condemn the present trend towards welfare pluralism, or a mixed economy of welfare, as a more or less overt attempt to legitimate the shifting of welfare responsibility from the statutory sector to the voluntary, private and informal sectors of welfare. It is revealing to compare current models of welfare pluralism, which are based on the ideal of partnership, with the model set out in Titmuss's seminal essay 'The Social Division of Welfare', which was delivered in 1955.[9]

In Titmuss's division of welfare the various modes of provision are differentiated according to their aims and values. There are three institutional sectors, beginning with the statutory social services, which are directed towards egalitarian and redistributive ends and which embody the social market values of collectivist solidarity and mutual aid. This sector is compared with the growing sectors of occupational welfare based on industry and employment and fiscal welfare based on tax allowances and concessions. Titmuss regarded both occupational and fiscal welfare as having a divisive impact on society because they reflect and reinforce the inequalities of wealth, income and opportunity which statutory social services are intended to counteract. Titmuss describes the growth of these three welfare sectors as a manifestation of 'the play of powerful economic and social forces; the strength and tenacity of privilege; the continuing search for equity in a rapidly changing society'[10] – so much for partnership in the sense of welfare pluralism!

Both the informal and the formal voluntary sectors of care are noticeably absent from Titmuss's social division of welfare. In the predominantly collectivist climate of the time when he was writing, voluntary agencies were treated as junior partners in the enterprise of welfare, although they were rapidly coming to terms with a vastly extended statutory sector. Titmuss did occasionally refer, however, to the work of Willmott and Young on family and kinship in East London and that of Townsend on the family life of old people.[11] Michael Young and Peter Willmott established the Institute of Community Studies in 1954. Their book, *Family and Kinship,* and Townsend's *Family Life of Old People* were both published in 1957, and thereafter the Institute produced a series of major studies exploring various aspects of the impact of social change and social policies on informal kinship and neighbourhood networks.[12]

In contrast to the social reformers of the Settlement Movement the Institute's researchers came to their studies of working-class family life ready to learn and free from preconceptions as to the merits or otherwise of working-class culture. Using field research methods borrowed from sociology and social anthropology, they described various networks of informal social support which were all based on the extended family and sustained largely by (and at the expense of) women. These systems had functioned in conditions of economic adversity from generation to generation. Their boundaries were determined by the close geographical proximity of their indigenous populations, which were neither socially nor geographically mobile. These traditionally close-knit, working class communities were beginning to break up, however, under the impact of urban redevelopment policies, which were to scatter their members across the new estates of south-west Essex. Subsequent reports from the Institute showed that, without the benefit of geographical closeness, the ties of obligation and entitlement based on kinship became reconstituted in weakened and modified forms.[13]

The social reformers of the 1880s and 1890s had no hesitation in imposing their own cultural norms on those whom they considered to be less fortunate than themselves and they viewed with indifference bordering on contempt the ways of life which they had set out to change. Then, for almost half a century, community studies and comparative studies of formal and informal welfare lost their immediacy in policy studies. In other areas of intellectual life the revival of communities continued to be an important topic, as Martin Weiner so vividly demonstrates in *English Culture and the Decline of the Industrial Spirit. 1850-1980*. In novels, poetry, art and letters the 'real' England, as distinct from its despised urban and industrial realities, was continuously reinvented in different versions of traditional village communities populated by landed gentry, yeoman farmers and deferential labourers.[14]

The publications of the Institute for Community Studies mark a new stage in the academic quest for community. Given the fundamental hostility with which many collectivist social policy academics then regarded industrial society in general and capitalism in particular, it was probably inevitable and certainly predictable that the message of the Bethnal Green studies would be misconstrued. Nevertheless these publications reflect a change in the relationship between social reform and the community ideal. The respect with which the researchers approached their subject was tinged with regret over the rehousing policies which had broken up the old networks. Nevertheless it was acknowledged that these changes had created new opportunities for individual freedom and greater prosperity, for women in particular. Throughout the 1950s and 1960s there was a major revival of community research studies in rural as well as urban localities, the best of which have been summarised in the comparative analytical reviews published in Ronald Frankenberg's *Communities in Britain* and Jose Klein's two-volume study, *Samples from English Cultures.*[15]

It is ironic that the rediscovery of communities coincided with the moment when the traditional networks of kinship and neighbourhood described in these studies – along with the traditional structures of sexual inequality which sustained them – were undergoing fundamental social change. The old familial structures were already passing into history and losing their relevance to policy-making. Nevertheless successive governments and policy-makers missed the significance of this trend and based their plans for community care on the false assumption that the extended family and the urban village networks of mutual aid and social care had survived intact.

Early attempts to check the new enthusiasm, notably Margaret Stacey's essay, 'The Myth of Community Studies', published in 1969,[16] were no more successful than the later feminist exposés of the high degree of sexual inequality which formed the basis of community policy-making. A new bandwagon of community care was confidently rolling on its way over a carpet of green and white papers.

The current situation

The Seebohm Report, which appeared in 1968, gave considerable attention to the subject of community care but it did not fall into the trap of romanticising the notion of community. The authors of the Report made a point of stating: 'Our emphasis on the importance of community does not stem from a belief that the small closely-knit rural community of the past could be reproduced in the urban society of today and of the future.'[17] They did not equate the idea of community with geographical localities, pointing out that 'Members of a family may belong to different communities of interest as well as the same local neighbourhood.'[18] They gave high priority to the need to make better and more extensive use of volunteers and they were in no doubt that there was a large, untapped supply of such people.[19] They also noted that 'Basic descriptive data about the personal social services and the communities they serve are essential, though at the moment sadly lacking both centrally and locally.'[20]

The British social work establishment took its cue from the Report's endorsement of genericism and its ill-considered proposal that access to the personal social services should be universalised, and that they should be made available to all who needed them. The Central Council for Education and Training in Social Work (CCETSW) began its self-appointed task of transforming social work into a new hybrid form of multi-purpose social intervention, which was eventually formulated in the Barclay Report of 1982 as community social work.[21]

My reason for not signing the Barclay Report and for writing a minority statement was not hostility to the idea of community but scepticism about the Report's confident assertion about the universal strengths of communities and the feasibility of harnessing them to the ends and means of formal social policy. There was little evidence to support such enthusiasm for community social work. At the same time Philip Abrams' preliminary work on neighbourhoods and informal networks of care among other publications began to indicate that closer interlinkage between formal services and informal care might well lead to the formal sector 'colonising' the informal sector.

By the late 1970s and early 1980s there were other research findings which should have been taken into account by the Barclay Working Party, including the programme established by the Personal Social Services Research Unit at the University of Kent, G.C. Wenger s research in North Wales and some of the work of the Equal Opportunities Commission in Manchester. The first unrevised draft of Abrams's *Neighbours* could also have been made available but it was not called for. Social research on informal care and community networks had entered its fourth and current phase of meticulously planned national and local field studies which were conducted in a spirit of impartial enquiry unmarred by condescension or eulogy. Unfortunately, much of it went unheeded in the Barclay Report.[22]

Formal social services and informal care: some general issues

Government policy has been unpredictable with regard to the relative merits of genericism and specialism. For example, diffuse activities like social care planning have been encouraged in order to include more volunteers in social care and thereby contain or even cut statutory costs. At the same time, however, action has been taken to improve specialist skills in mental health, and a House of Commons Social Services Committee Report deplored the lack of expertise in child care, although it was concluded that increased specialisation would not 'fit into the present system of social work education'.[23] Nevertheless the main thrust of government policy has favoured social care planning and the enrolment of more volunteers. CCETSW's educational initiatives have reflected the same priorities.

At the Joint Social Services Annual Conference at Buxton in September 1984 Mr Norman Fowler stated that the cost of the social services was 'a major factor influencing the government's ability to achieve the economic recovery on which the future prosperity of the country depends'. In the effort to keep these costs down, he said, the government looked to the private and voluntary sectors to share part of the burden. With regard to the personal social services Mr Fowler suggested that in future the local authority social services should play a more active 'enabling' role so as to foster co-operation between the statutory, voluntary and private sectors and make more extensive use of unpaid volunteers.[24] In pursuit of these ends many local authorities have initiated experiments in the decentralisation of social services.

Cuts in local authority budgets have a significant effect on the formal voluntary sector because many voluntary agencies, especially those engaged in the personal social services, depend heavily on local authority funding. To a surprisingly large extent the formal system of voluntary social service in Britain is funded by public money. A few British voluntary agencies undertake statutory duties, and many carry out work contracted from statutory bodies.

The common assumption that there is still a large untapped reserve army of volunteers in modern Britain provides the incentive for strengthening the links between formal and informal providers of social care. There are some important differences, however, between a formal statutory system of social care and an informal one. Formal and statutory social services have greater scope for obligation and membership, eligibility for such services is determined not by personal relationships but by legal rules and administrative procedures, and their providers and users are normally strangers to each other.

Because an informal system of care based on membership of families and communities is governed by personal factors it is likely to be less enduring and less reliable in the long run than a formal system: members of a family may quarrel, move to a different locality or die, and there are people who have no family. The average size of families is smaller than it was, say, fifty years ago, and there is generally more geographical and social mobility so that people are less likely than they once were to live close enough to other members of their family to offer mutual support in times of adversity. Also in modern families it is common for both spouses to work outside the home so that fewer women are able to undertake long-term care for dependent relatives, without regular support from the social services. There is now a large number of families which would experience a sharp drop in living standards if they had to relinquish one of their two regular incomes. Similar uncertainties affect neighbourly services and local networks of mutual aid. Statutory services may be less personal but they offer more permanence and greater uniformity because they extend over a wider range of altruistic concern, which may also be tempered by self-interest, but is not so deeply felt.

Some useful findings have emerged from recent research.[25] First, of the one-and-a-quarter million 'carers' for dependent people in Britain the majority are women – usually daughters, daughters-in-law or spouses – the main beneficiaries being elderly relatives. Abrams estimated that there are about 300,000 people, or roughly 5 per cent of the population, who are actively engaged in organised voluntary work, which amounts to 'quite a serious resource committed to quite a serious project'.[26] Johnson and Cooper suggest that 'What shines unequivocally through the research is that families *do* care. Indeed it can safely be said that more people do more caring for relatives in major need than at any other point in recorded history.'[27] Nevertheless the bulk of the evidence suggests that volunteers are most numerous in well integrated and relatively affluent communities and least numerous in the relatively deprived ones. One of the features of seriously deprived communities is their lack of community spirit;–therefore policies based on the assumption that local volunteers will make up for the lack of statutory resources in these areas are unlikely to succeed. Put bluntly, the providers and the recipients of voluntary care in deprived communities tend to live in different localities, and there is no sign that high levels of mobility have contributed to increasing neighbourliness.

Second, there is a wealth of new evidence on the structure and culture of British family and community life, much of which has been reviewed in Bulmer's *The Social Basis of Community Care*.[28] Drawing on the work of Peter Willmott,

Bulmer points out that there is considerable variety in family structures and that only about one in eight of British families conforms to the traditional extended pattern based on three or more generations of people living in close physical proximity and permanently ready to provide each other with care or assistance. About half the population maintain contact by car and telephone and help each other in crises but their kinship networks are too geographically dispersed to allow support to be provided at more than weekly or fortnightly intervals.[29] Roughly one in three of the population belongs to a dispersed kinship network in which regular help and visiting are not possible, and about one in twenty has no mutual system of support.

Bulmer challenges the belief widely held by policy-makers that 'Because potentially, in principle, social ties can be formed ... they actually will be formed',[30] on the grounds that 'Many people value confidentiality as much as gregariousness, and characterise good neighbours as people who show a mutual respect for privacy'.[31]

Even in localities where the density of networks is high, as Willmott shows, it does not follow that there are high levels of support.[32] Bulmer concludes that 'It would be much more fruitful if applied network researchers could apply some of the insights of urban sociology, which has used network analysis to search for linkages and flow of resources, before tying them to particular spatial patterns.'[33] This, he points out, is precisely what the Barclay Report failed to do, preferring to categorise 'all informal ties as on a par with each other' and to treat 'any relationship in which an individual is involved as having a potential for becoming incorporated into a system of informal caring'.[34]

Third, there is a growing challenge to the conventional belief that volunteering and mutual aid are chiefly inspired by public spiritedness and unconditional altruism. Abrams suggested that a sense of duty or social obligation tempered by a prudential eye to the prospect of reciprocity in the future was a more important motive than simple altruism. He identified the phenomenon of 'new neighbourhoodism', defining it in instrumental terms. He argued that most people live in 'new' neighbourhoods and that 'Attempts to revive traditional local social networks are largely misguided'. In his view participation in neighbourly activities like mutual aid takes place after prudent consideration of the possible gains and losses involved.[35]

Abrams concluded that perhaps the only two features of traditional neighbourliness to have survived the impact of social change were 'mothers and gossip'[36] and that the effective basis of informal care had shifted from the constraints of kinship and locality to the more open but less predictable choices based on friendship. Research by Qureshi, Challis and Davies also confirms that in the absence of reciprocity the prospect of financial reward was 'a motivating factor' for as many as one-third of the volunteers whom they studied.[37] The Community Care scheme in Kent has developed successfully on this principle,[38] indicating that one way of extending and strengthening networks of care is to treat altruistic and pecuniary motives as complementary rather than conflicting factors. It will not surprise advocates of enlightened self-interest and competitive individualism that there is no evidence of a clear-cut division between egoism and altruism in human motivation, once the focus of interest is shifted from the workplace to the family and neighbourhood.

In addition, research has shown that, even when relatives provide continuous help without financial support, familial altruism is as likely to be sustained by duty and habit as it is by love. Offer, St Leger and Cecil's study of informal care in a small Ulster town (Garvagh) is particularly illuminating on this issue.[39] It begins with a brief review of policy trends in the personal social services since the publication of the Seebohm and Wolfenden reports and shows how they have led to a growth of interest in informal care. Informal care is defined as 'help given to individuals by nuclear and extended families, and by neighbours and friends'.[40] The authors note the Barclay Report's enthusiasm for 'flexible, decentralised patterns of organisation' which would encourage the growth of community social work.[41] They also draw attention to the general lack of knowledge about 'the cultural factors which shape carers' expectations', the need to analyse these caring relationships within the wider context of *social* relationships, and to better our understanding of the network of cultural meanings and ground rules which give structure and purpose to informal care activities.[42]

Garvagh, given the pseudonym of Glengow in the study, is a small Ulster town in a rural setting, with an impressive range of local community organisations, including churches, the British Legion, the Women's Institute and various clubs. It is a mixed community with a Protestant majority and a record of religious tolerance, although there is little intermarriage between Protestants and Catholics. The personal social services, which operate from another nearby larger town, are organised on fairly conventional lines, with an intake team and four specialist care teams. The level of unemployment is around 24 per cent, and there is evidence of real financial hardship among the people of Glengow.

In most respects Glengow is a traditional rural township. The authors describe its various household types and patterns of marriage and residence, drawing attention to the intensity of its familial loyalties and to the tendency for married women to settle in the locality of their husbands' extended families. Family relationships are characterised by a clear sexual division of labour, and women are defined by their familial roles, as men are not.[43]

After a description of four types of interactive family support the study concentrates on caring relationships. The evidence shows that caring 'is not a haphazard event, but is bound by recognised, yet unstated rules as to who cares for whom, and how'.[44] The typical pattern of care to emerge from these rules is unequivocal: the responsibility for caring falls mainly on women, and mainly on one woman in particular, with some support from other family members. Very few carers willingly assume these responsibilities, which are accepted from a sense of duty and obligation powerfully reinforced by cultural expectations. As the authors observe,

> The rules of care within the family arise directly from the structure of the family, and the value accorded to family life. Such values are held within the community, as well as shaping a number of policies within the statutory provision of social services and benefits.[45]

The force of custom and tradition is strong enough to trap some people in a cycle of caring for the better part of their lives, ministering to one dependent relative after another, and this role expectation is reinforced not only by kin but by statutory social service workers.

Fourth, recent research has drawn attention not only to the economic costs but to the emotional or 'psychic' costs of care. The psychological and physical costs of care are sometimes severe, and the provision of a certain level of statutory support in the form of home helps, occasional relief through day care, day-and night-sitters, incontinence laundry services and other aids to daily living is a requisite of good community care, especially in the case of carers who are near or over retirement age and not always in the best of health themselves.[46] These costs fall mainly on women and in families where women are faced with a combination of claims on their attention, the pressures can become intolerable.[47] The economic costs of both formal and informal care have been studied by the PSSRU at the University of Kent.[48] Knapp refers to two main schools of enquiry, the financial auditing approach, which is primarily concerned with 'value for money' and managerial efficiency, and the approach based either on cost-benefit analysis techniques or on a 'production of welfare' scale. Knapp points out that to date the best research has related mainly to the elderly. Other client groups have been relatively neglected 'in part because the *objectives* of care are often less clear, in part because studies of the *effectiveness* of care have been few and narrowly defined, and in part because, with few exceptions, the *costs* of care have been ignored.'[49]

Fifth, some researchers like Michael Bayley, Colin and Meg Ball and Roger Hadley believe that it is possible and desirable to 'inter-weave' the formal and informal systems of social care, but only after the decentralisation of local authority and other social services.[50] Others like Abrams and Pinker have argued that formal and informal systems of care are based on 'entirely discrete sets of paradigms' and that the gaps between them cannot be assumed to be bridgeable. In his posthumous study *Neighbours* Abrams appears to have qualified his earlier views on this relationship;[51] nevertheless, on the basis of his evidence, he held to his original view that, over time, increases in the provision of formal care tend to drive out informal care, as relatives and friends hand over their responsibilities to paid workers. He also argued that, although the involvement of formal social service workers in the informal sector increases efficiency and effectiveness, 'The very fact that incorporation works so well is what makes the ethical and political questions it poses so compelling'.[52] Unless the workers from the formal sector carry out their duties with sensitivity and circumspection, the probable outcome of closer liaison between the two sectors will be either colonisation or appropriation of the informal sector by its statutory supporters. This may be part of the cost of enlisting more 'paid' volunteers.

There are two main conclusions in Abrams' study, that in Britain the structural and cultural bases of 'natural' neighbourhood care are disappearing and that the motives behind community involvement are far from straightforward, including self-help, amenity society and pressure group interests, a very important religious interest, which inspired 60 per cent of the Good Neighbour schemes in the survey, and prudential self-interest. In commenting on Abrams' findings Bulmer observes that the traditional neighbourhood, with its 'relatively isolated, relatively closed and relatively threatened milieux with highly homogeneous populations', is becoming a thing of the past, and that few people would wish to recreate the economic circumstances which made it possible and necessary in the first instance. He concludes with the comment that 'Traditional informal networks are dying and should be allowed to die'.[53]

With regard to the largely untested assumptions underlying the recent promotion of community social work Bulmer emphasises 'the extent to which informal caring grows out of existing relationships'.[54] In his analysis such growth occurs within complex, idiosyncratic networks of 'beneficence, obligation and duty, and tradition' characterised by norms of reciprocity and social exchange which are quite different from those which characterise the provision of formal social services. Subtle cultural developments of this order, according to Bulmer, are 'not something to be "engineered" in a mechanical way, for example by "upholding" or "plugging in" to networks'.[55]

In place of such ill-considered initiatives in community social work Bulmer recommends that we become more specific in our statutory social policies for families, especially in relation to the needs of the poor; the burdens which fall on female carers; the problems facing previously long-term mentally ill or mentally handicapped hospital patients who have been returned to communities where they have no relatives, friends or neighbours; and the difficulties which are bound to arise in the 'interweaving' of formal and informal care.[56]

Decentralisation and specialisation: the Kent Project

Abrams's studies provided a mass of new information on the nature of informal care and they also present a challenging hypothesis concerning the relationship between formal and informal care. The other major British research initiative in this field of policy is a highly innovatory programme of community care designed and monitored by the PSSRU at the University of Kent, supported by the local authority and financed by the Department of Health and Social Security. The first major report on the project, *Community Care for the Frail Elderly*, was published in 1985.[57]

David Challis and Bleddyn Davies, the authors of the report, began their research in the late 1970s. The project was designed to provide a decentralised network of social work services for elderly people living in the community, in co-operation with other skilled staff such as home helps and occupational therapists. The first social workers to be recruited were not specialists in the care of the elderly, and within eight months it was found necessary to replace them with staff who had the qualifications and were sufficiently experienced to act as key workers.[58] However, it was not easy to find social workers who were skilled in 'case management, assessment, care planning, monitoring and family support',[59] although it was recognised from the start that decentralisation and delegation of responsibility to the field level would only be effective if the workers were suitably specialised, and that accountability could only be enforced if the workers' roles and responsibilities were clearly specified and understood.

The target group was restricted to 92 very frail elderly people, the aim being to enable them to live in their own homes for as long as possible, without prejudice to the quality of their lives, and there was a control group for comparative purposes. Each key worker was given a shadow budget and decision-taking powers over expenditure of up to two-thirds of the opportunity cost of a place in a residential home. One of the major purposes for which expenditure was authorised was the recruitment of paid volunteers. As the project developed, it became clear that specialisation was essential to both effective decentralisation and effective case management, and that it also had a direct bearing on the improvement of inter-agency co-operation and the production of integrated and economical 'packages' of care. In a comparison with the alternative 'patch' model of social care Challis and Davies unequivocally state that 'an important difference lies in the community care scheme focus upon a defined caseload of individuals within a particular client group providing the opportunity for closer inter-professional collaboration. Clearly specialisation is not incompatible with a sensitivity to the needs of informal carers and responding to local needs.'[60]

With regard to motivation for caring it was not found difficult to recruit helpers nearly all of whom were women. The fees were modest: the average payment for a one-to-two-hour visit was £1.75 at 1977 prices, or around £3.50 today.[61] Although formal training was not provided, support group meetings were arranged. In preparing formal contracts and determining fee levels the organisers of the project paid considerable attention to the specification of tasks and responsibilities. It was found that the best helpers, who stayed with the scheme, had had relevant experience in their occupational or familial roles, a high proportion of them having been nurses or nursing assistants. It is interesting that, although pecuniary motives were present, they did not prevent the development of friendships or 'care with an affective basis' between the paid helpers and the old people.[62]

With regard to the emotional and psychic costs of care the researchers found that, of the twenty-one relatives, friends and neighbours who were already primary carers, 'More than half experienced disruption of their social life and nearly half experienced strain and exhaustion ... whilst a high proportion suffered a degree of mental distress'.[63] The old people who had the benefit of informal carers were least likely to be receiving domiciliary services, and a key objective of the project was the provision of support for these informal carers, as well as additional care for the old people.[64] Challis and Davies' evidence does not support Abrams' hypothesis that formal care tends to undermine the motivation to provide informal care, but indicates that, with adequate complementary support, informal carers are likely to carry on, and the people whom they help are less likely to end up in residential care.[65]

These are significant findings with regard to the outcomes and costs of care. There were significantly lower rates of admission to residential care, fewer deaths and less deterioration in physical abilities among the experimental group than among the control group.[66] In addition the evidence from the subjective assessments of well-being indicates a generally high level of contentment and satisfaction with the quality of life among both the old people and their informal carers.

The researchers adopted an approach based on opportunity costs which took into account no fewer than nine separate interest groups, including the personal social services, housing, social security, the clients, and so on. They found that the scheme was 'a more cost-effective response for the frail elderly' than other available policy options, and that it was most cost-effective for the health services in both 'the lower and higher categories of dependency'.[67] They reserved judgement on whether in the longer run (more than one year) there would be an adverse effect on housing costs, but so far there is no evidence of that nature.

There are several general conclusions to be drawn from this study, first that the task-centred, case-review approach to long-term care can be successfully applied. Second, the study suggests that, if it is accompanied by a degree of specialisation, decentralisation and specification of tasks, formal care does not undermine informal networks of care, but on the contrary complements and strengthens them. Nevertheless this positive factor appears to be contingent on the delineation of boundaries between formal and informal care, and Abrams' reservations were largely connected with schemes which were based on the interweaving of formal and informal care. The Kent community care project was designed to encourage 'resource decentralisation to individual field workers specialising in work with elderly people, effectively balancing their greater autonomy through mechanisms enhancing their accountability', and it led to the conclusion that not only is there no unbridgeable gap between decentralisation and specialisation 'but rather that the presence of the latter complements the former'.[68]

Finally, it is clear that the approach adopted for the Kent project has potential relevance to other client groups like the young physically handicapped, children at risk and the mentally ill, all of which pose similar problems of co-ordination among different agencies and services over long periods of time.

The Kent researchers do not discuss the wider social implications for the occupational opportunities and future economic security of women, but it is women who constitute the great majority of the paid helpers not only in the Kent scheme but in other similar initiatives in community care. In the long term there is a risk that the type of recruitment policy adopted for the Kent project will create a new economic underclass of casual workers who are low-paid, hired on an hourly basis and denied the opportunity to optimise their own future social security entitlements. On the other hand, Qureshi and her co-authors present some evidence that this type of work is particularly attractive to certain groups of women – mothers wanting to re-enter the labour market after their children start school, the recently retired and the bereaved.[69]

One of the main achievements of the Kent project is that it succeeded in breaking out of the universalist tradition set by the Seebohm Report, with its emphasis on needs and its relative neglect of the resource implications of policy in the personal social services. In their most recent study, *Matching Resources to Needs in Community Care*,[70] Challis and Davies define their work as an attempt 'to improve equity and efficiency in long-term care by entrepreneurial case-management in an engineered environment of incentives'.[71]

Case-management as it is envisaged by the Kent research team is characterised by the precise formulation of ends and means, the continual review of performance and care planning, the improvement of management skills and the provision of incentives at all levels of intervention, with clearly delineated levels of accountability. With regard to the universalist content of the Seebohm and Barclay reports Challis and Davies comment that:

> If these broad generalisations are valid, we can understand why criteria about ends have not been made explicit and why efficiency in targeting has not been closely and explicitly monitored. They are the concerns of selectivist, not universalist argument. It is the selectivist critique of social policy which has focused on the efficient use of resources to attain ends which are defined clearly, on achieving benefits for those for whom the particular intervention is the most socially cost-effective, on the allocation of resources in conditions of assumed scarcity.[72]

They locate the origins of their own approach 'in the utilitarian assumptions of classical economics, which perceives collective provision as part of a range of substitutes and complements with streams of costs and benefits influencing the choices of clients as consumers'.[73]

This new interpretation of the personal social services will require some adjustment in the training of social workers since it goes against the universalist welfare tradition put forward not only in the Seebohm and Barclay reports but in the policies and publications of CCETSW and in much of the literature in social policy and social work during the 1970s and 1980s.

Social work and social control

If the chief objective of the Seebohm Report was to provide universal access to the personal social services for all who needed them, the chief implication of genericism was that social workers would become both agents of social change and 'advocates' in the sense that they would see to it that their clientele secured optimal access to all other social services in addition to social work. This clientele comprised almost entirely a residuum of the poor and the disadvantaged, who were heavily dependent on selectivist services such as supplementary benefit, public housing and housing benefit and school welfare services. Apart from marginal forms of cash support such as Section One and Section Twelve payments and other selective personal social services, all forms of support which social workers looked to for their clients came from the resources of other welfare agencies. In brief social workers were trained to think almost exclusively in terms of meeting needs at the expense of other agencies, not to relate the allocation of resources to their own budgetary constraints.

In addition to this ever-expanding range of indirect tasks social workers acquired increasingly onerous legal responsibilities throughout the 1970s and 1980s. Although they were not directly burdened with the practicalities and odium of exercising financial control over their clients, they did not escape the legal obligation to impose social control over them. However, they resented the notion that they were agents of social control rather than social change. For example, at the annual conference of the British Association of Social Workers in March 1988, Louis Blom-Cooper (the judge who had chaired the inquiry into the Jasmine Beckford child abuse case of 1985) suggested that 'The principles instilled in social work students of "client self-determination" and of "non-judgemental attitude" and of "going at the clients' pace" encouraged them in the belief that they were allies of the client in conflict with authority.' He added that the inculcation of such altitudes was having disastrous effects on the quality of supervision in child care and he argued that the legal component of social work had the highest importance and that social workers needed to accept 'the reality that the law is not an obstacle or a hindrance but a positive aid to sound professional practice'. The Conference received these words with the utmost hostility. David Jones, General Secretary of BASW, declared that Blom-Cooper had completely misunderstood the nature of social work, and the Chairman, Gwen Swire, expressed the opinion that 'If social workers were forced to take on the role of being agents of social control, everyone attending the lecture would quit the profession.'[74]

There has been much debate about the essential nature of social work apart from the direct tasks associated with social control and protection and the indirect tasks associated with assessing social care needs and procuring appropriate services from other agencies. From the late 1940s onwards the way in which the British personal social services developed increasingly withdrew social workers from direct involvement in the assessment of financial need, the provision of financial support and the purchase of other forms of social service. It was largely because British social workers were relieved of these responsibilities that the British social security system became more complex and overburdened with discretionary duties. The break was so complete that many social workers began to act as adversarial agents of welfare rights campaigning on behalf of their clients against the social security services. This development added an overtly political dimension to the social work role in community care.

As a result the profession of social work has become isolated from the rest of the political economy and woefully deficient in both entrepreneurial and managerial skills. It is not surprising that, in their isolation, social workers have taken to metaphysical speculation on their collective professional identity, their distinctive values and their relationships both with each other and with their clients. Their values are expressed as respect for persons and for client self-determination, and their relationships are developed through a variety of interventive techniques including social casework, group work and community work. Their search for intellectual coherence and a recognisable professional identity may explain the popularity of syncretic models of social work like genericism, systems theory and integrated methods, and these models have been given high priority in all British social work training programmes.

Law teaching, however, as CCETSW openly acknowledged, was seriously neglected in social work training.[75] This is largely attributable to the deep-seated reluctance of many social work educators to introduce changes in curriculum content which would add to the element of social control in social work, an attitude widely shared by members of BASW. For similar reasons the official representatives of the social work profession are hostile to the Social Fund: in their opinion giving advice to Social Fund officers concerning the financial priorities of the poor might be construed as a form of social control and hence a violation of social work values.

This reaction to the Social Fund accords with the communitarian values which so many social workers have adopted in recent years. The communitarian ethos contains an ideal of fraternity inspired by egalitarian and libertarian values which are as incompatible with the idea of social control as they are with the hierarchical and directive assumptions of the pioneers of the Settlement Movement.

Because of the dramatic increase in the range of tasks falling to social workers over the past twenty years CCETSW's campaign during the 1980s for a third year of professional training rested on the argument that it had become impossible in the existing two-year courses to fulfil all the teaching and practice requirements for both direct social work and indirect social work, with their various implications for social control, protection, prevention and treatment. This argument, however, is contingent on acceptance of a generic model of training in which all students are expected to follow a common basic course, with limited opportunities for specialisation. It is arguable that two-year programmes would be adequate if they were based on a division of specialist subjects and a reduction in the scope of common course elements. For example, the division of roles and tasks might be based on the separation of social care and social control, although such expedients are not acceptable to CCETSW or BASW or to most leading authorities on social work because they might lead to the fragmentation of what is a new and vulnerable profession, and to the identification of one part of the profession with social control. The fact that the tried and tested social workers known as probation officers have always been primarily concerned with social control and that their training is considerably specialised is seldom used as an exemplar for social work as a whole.

The Griffiths proposals

In addition to the problems associated with social control and financial welfare provision the whole organisation of local authority personal social services is faced with the challenge of the Griffiths proposals for community care.[76] The Griffiths Report was published soon after the reports of the Audit Commission and the National Audit Office, which both drew attention to the deficiencies in joint planning between health services and local authority social services and to the institutional impediments to the improvement of co-operation.[77]

Among the Griffiths proposals with a direct and immediate bearing on social work education and practice is the recommendation that local authority social services departments cease to be the main providers of care and concentrate first on assessing the needs of their localities and those of dependent individuals and their carers and secondly on designing, organising and purchasing 'packages of non-health care' from a mixed economy of public, voluntary and private sector agencies. The Report states that 'It is vital that social services authorities see themselves as the arrangers and purchasers of care services – not as monopolistic providers.'[78] These proposed changes are directed towards the improvement of consumer choice and the encouragement of innovation and efficiency.

In order to secure adequate resources for the proposed new system the Griffiths Report recommends the transfer of financial responsibility for community care to the local authorities from both social security and health authorities, including the community care element of the Social Fund. Social workers would then be required to advise on the allocation of grants to institutionalised patients who are resettled in the community, a process which is bound to involve the ordering of financial priorities. If BASW requested its members not to co-operate in such activities but to maintain their policy of determined advocacy, it would mean doing no more than presenting social work clients' own assessment of their needs while refusing to advise on priorities, and this would bring social workers following BASW's instruction into conflict with their employers, the local authorities.

It is clear from the Griffiths Report that many personal social service staff would require some form of training before they could assess the need for residential care or the financial means of clients who cannot afford residential care above a basic level. Other staff would also require training in care management and the maintenance of informal care; in the use of modern information systems and the monitoring of progress; and in joint planning with other social services. The Report goes so far as to recommend the creation of a new occupational group of 'community carers' who would work closely with relatives and neighbours who provide long-term care and support to elderly people. Activities of this nature could just as easily be undertaken by home-help organisers, community nurses or social administration graduates as by social workers.

Certain aspects of the Griffiths Report complement the proposals of the Barclay Working Party but there are important differences. The Barclay Working Party assumed that local authority departments would continue to be the main providers of care, whereas the Griffiths Report is committed to a mixed economy of welfare in which the job of public sector staff is to arrange suitable 'packages' of care. The Barclay Report did not diverge from the general pattern of training in social work values and skills for prospective social workers. Implementation of the Griffiths Report will depend on an injection of entrepreneurial and managerial values and skills into social work education. The Barclay Report was addressed to the whole range of welfare client groups; the Griffiths Report concentrates on community care for the elderly, the physically and the mentally handicapped and the mentally ill; children and young families at risk are not included.

Hunter and Judge even question whether traditional social work values and skills will be relevant to the Griffiths model of social care planning.[79] They suggest a possible case 'for advocating more specialisation within social services departments between child care and family services on the one hand and community care services on the other'.[80] If the Griffiths proposals were implemented along these lines, the division between social work training and social care training could be made more functionally relevant to the changing pattern of demand for personal social services. There would need to be a relatively small cadre of highly trained (or retrained) staff to work with children and families at risk and to undertake a range of legally specified protective, preventive and remedial tasks. Their curriculum would be built around an intensive training in child care and family law, although it might be sensible to transfer all cases of child abuse from the local authorities to the probation service. A larger number of students would be needed to train as social care workers in a mixed economy of welfare. They would concentrate on assessorial, managerial, entrepreneurial and legal skills related to the needs of the elderly, the mentally ill, the physically handicapped and the mentally handicapped.

Over the past twenty years much thought has been given to the analysis of social work by reference to various combinations of practice skills, including social casework, group work and community work, and to various syncretic models (some of dubious validity), but to little effect. The Griffiths proposals offer a decisive route out of this intellectual impasse, if only by creating greater scope for members of the public to identify what they want from social work and for social workers to specify what they can provide.

It has long been apparent that effective social work practice requires skills which are different from those associated with social care planning but that both types of service are due equal consideration in resource allocation as it affects the ordering of training priorities. In the absence of precise legal or managerial imperatives it has been difficult to assess these priorities because social workers have been unable or unwilling to adopt specific goals. Due to the deficiencies in social work law teaching there are some practitioners who are not even trained to carry out their duties within a legal framework. A clearer division of responsibilities between social control and social care might help to resolve these difficulties. We would have confirmation of this if, for example, ordinary users of social care services (in consultation with their informal carers) began to create a demand for social work skills as a component in their 'packages' of care, especially if they were paying or partly paying for the packages in question.

The value principles of self-determination and respect for persons inevitably came to the fore in services which were predominantly in the public sector, where the great majority of users manifestly lacked self-respect, the respect of others and the capacity to determine their daily lives. Adherence to these principles bolstered the self-esteem of social workers rather than the well-being of their clients. In a mixed economy of welfare social workers would deal increasingly with clients who are capable of running their own lives and are also in a position to exercise authentic choice. If such clients wanted a professional relationship with a social worker they would demand it, and social workers would probably find that consumer sovereignty is an excellent stimulus to effective practice, compared to formulae such as working in 'partnership' and 'going at the client's pace'. Social workers would retain their responsibilities for the underprivileged, and what they learned in keeping up with the demands of a more discriminating clientele would indirectly benefit their less fortunate clients.

The main weakness of the Griffiths Report lies in its explicit assumption that formal social services can be interwoven with informal networks of support, in conformity with entrepreneurial and managerial requirements. Although there is evidence that informal care is sustained as much by egoistic as by altruistic motives, it could still prove difficult to protect the distinctive character and integrity of informal care if it came under the regulation of professional social workers and formal care agencies. In addition there is no way of knowing how the incorporation of an entrepreneurial and managerial ethos will affect the values and practices associated with family and neighbourhood care. Of all the innovatory programmes in community care which have developed during the 1980s the markedly successful Kent project comes closest to the Griffiths model, giving grounds for cautious optimism over the Griffiths proposals. Every generation has its own way of renewing the quest for community and the Griffiths Report is a significant step in that direction. Progress will depend on the extent to which entrepreneurial and managerial objectives can be reconciled with the values and practices of family and neighbourhood life.

For the first time in a decade there are grounds for optimism about the future of the personal social services and the prospects for an effective policy of community care in Britain. The publication of the Griffiths Report signals a radical break with the policies which were endorsed in the Seebohm and Barclay reports and in the training programmes implemented by CCETSW since the early 1970s.

If the Griffiths proposals are implemented, more care managers and fewer professional social workers will be needed. Professional social work training will be concentrated on specialist programmes in child care, mental health and medical social work, with a view to improving the quality of practice and restoring public confidence. Since CCETSW has never shown any sympathy either to entrepreneurial and managerial values or to professional specialisation, it would be logical to disband it and substitute a smaller and more appropriately staffed training council with very specific terms of reference.

With regard to education in care management it would be premature to make institutional arrangements for training or for governing bodies until more is known about the range and variety of needs to be expected in a mixed economy of welfare. The establishment of an educational quango for care management would simply encourage a proliferation of planning blueprints and educational models, and such initiatives would almost certainly be incompatible with the ends and means of the Griffiths Report. The communitarian beliefs of the post-Seebohm period are as irrelevant to our present and foreseeable needs as were the doctrines of the Settlement Movement to the needs of the Victorian urban poor. Whereas the Settlement Movement lost its authority in social welfare as it lost its credibility, post-Seebohm communitarians have retained control of the personal social services despite their forfeiture of public confidence after a decade of monumental incompetence. In other words, when voluntary sector initiatives are tested and found wanting, they gradually fade away but, once erroneous doctrines become entrenched in the statutory sector, they are hard to remove. For this reason alone the mixed economy of welfare proposed in the Griffiths Report is preferable to state monopolies and unaccountable quangos.

Notes and references

[1] Meacham (1987), 2.

[2] *Ibid.*, 3.

[3] *Ibid.*, 94.

[4] *Ibid.*, 158.

[5] *Ibid.*, 187.

[6] Booth (1902); and Rowntree (1901).

[7] *Report of the Interdepartmental Committee on Physical Deterioration* (1904), Cd 2175, XXXII.

[8] Titmuss (1958b), 28.

[9] *Ibid.*, 34 *et passim*.

[10] *Ibid.*, 54.

[11] *Ibid.*, 93.

[12] Young and Willmott (1957/1968); and Townsend (1957).

[13] Young and Willmott (1960).

[14] Weiner (1985), esp. ch. 4, p. 41 *et passim*.

[15] Frankenberg (1966); and Klein (1965).

[16] Stacey (1969).

[17] *Report of the Committee on Local Authority and Allied Personal Social Services* (Seebohm Report (1968), para. 475.

[18] *Ibid.*, para. 476.

[19] *Ibid.*, para. 498.

[20] *Ibid.*, para. 460.

[21] *Social Workers: Their Role and Tasks* (Barclay Report, 1982).

[22] Wenger (1981); Bulmer (1986; 1987); Challis and Davies (1986a); Cecil, Offer and St Leger (1987). See also the special issue of *British Journal of Social Work* (1983) 13: 4.

[23] House of Commons (1984), see paras 276, 279 and 280.

[24] Fowler (1984).

[25] Johnson and Cooper (1984).

[26] Abrams (1985).

[27] Johnson and Cooper (1984), 108.

[28] Bulmer, *The Social Basis of Community Care* (1987).

[29] *Ibid.*, 73 *et passim.*

[30] *Ibid.*, 190.

[31] *Ibid.*, 93.

[32] Willmott (1987).

[33] Bulmer (1987), 138.

[34] *Ibid.*, 139.

[35] Abrams (1980).

[36] Abrams (1984a).

[37] See Qureshi, Challis, and Davies (1983).

[38] Challis and Davies (1981; 1986).

[39] Offer, St Leger and Cecil (1988).

[40] *Ibid.*, 5.

[41] *Ibid.*, 6.

[42] *Ibid.*, 8-10.

[43] *Ibid.*, 18.

[44] *Ibid.*, 21.

[45] *Ibid.*

[46] Johnson and Cooper (1984), 104.

[47] Finch and Groves (1983), 10.

[48] See Knapp (1984), 154-65.

[49] *Ibid.*, 166. The conceptual problems of defining policy objectives in relation to improving the 'quality of life' are usefully discussed in Robertson and Osborn (1984), see especially Robertson, (1984).

[50] See Bayley (1973; 1980); Ball and Ball (1982); Hadley (1981); and Appendix A of the Barclay Report (Brown, Hadley and White, 1982).

[51] Abrams (1978). See also Appendix B of the Barclay Report (Pinker 1982b; included as **Chapter Six** in this book); Abrams (1984b); Bulmer (1986); Bayley (1982).

[52] Abrams (1984a), 424-5.

[53] Bulmer (1985).

[54] Bulmer (1987).

[55] *Ibid.*, 171.

[56] *Ibid.*, 210-13.

[57] Challis and Davies (1985a); see also Challis and Davies (1985b).

[58] Challis and Davies (1985a), 46.

[59] *Ibid.*, 6.

[60] *Ibid.*, 87.

[61] *Ibid.*, 151 *et passim.*

[62] *Ibid.*, 187 *et passim.*

[63] *Ibid.*, 43.

64 *Ibid.*, 133.

65 *Ibid.*, 277.

66 *Ibid.*, 216.

67 *Ibid.*, 281.

68 *Ibid.*, 287.

69 Qureshi *et al.* (1983).

70 Challis and Davies (1986b).

71 *Ibid.*, xxvii.

72 *Ibid.*, 73.

73 *Ibid.*, 74.

74 'Anger at BASW conference over QC's view of social workers' role' (1988) *Community Care*, 31 March, 4.

75 Ball et al (1988).

76 Griffiths Report (1988).

77 Audit Commission (1986); National Audit Office (1987).

78 Griffiths Report (1988), para. 3.4.

79 Hunter and Judge (1988).

80 *Ibid.*, 14.

EIGHT

Citizenship, civil war and welfare: the making of modern Ireland[*]

Robert Pinker

Since the time of T.H. Marshall, the concept of citizenship has held a position of central significance in the study of social policy, notably with regard to the evolution of civil, political and social rights and duties. Less attention has been given to the association of citizenship with the growth of national consciousness and issues of national and cultural identity. Most social policy theories about the relationship between citizenship and welfare take the existence of a shared sense of national identity under conditions of peace for granted. The few social theorists who have written about the impact of war on the growth of civil, political and social rights have tended to concentrate on wars between sovereign states. Much less has been written about the significance of civil wars within sovereign states. Conflicts about land, sovereignty and national identity are the most frequent causes of these internal conflicts. This paper explores the extent to which the onset of civil war reverses the direction in which Marshall hypothesised that the civil, political and social rights of citizenship developed under conditions of peace, taking the examples of Ireland and Northern Ireland for illustrative purposes.

The Marshall perspective

Marshall developed a theory of citizenship and welfare that was explicitly pluralist in character and sympathetic to the roles of both competitive markets and a mixed economy of welfare. He defined citizenship as 'a status bestowed on those who are full members of a community. All who possess the status are equal with respect to the rights and duties with which the status is endowed' (Marshall and Bottomore, 1992: 18). Citizenship, in this broader and more general sense, becomes a basis for social solidarity. The pluralist character of Marshall's approach unfolds as he proceeds to identify three key elements in the status of citizenship. The first of these elements comprises our civil rights and obligations with regard to 'personal liberty, freedom of speech, thought and faith, the right to own property and to conclude valid contracts and the right to justice' (Marshall and Bottomore, 1992: 8). The second of these elements is 'the right to participate in the exercise of power' either as a voter or as a representative. In Britain this range

---

[*] Article originally published in *Twenty-first Century Society*, vol 1, no 1, pp 23–38 (2006).

of civil and political rights were all largely secured before the Second World War and the creation of a post-war universalist welfare state.

The third element in Marshall's model of citizenship encompasses our social rights 'to a modicum of economic welfare and security … and to live the life of a civilised being according to the standards prevailing in the society' (Marshall and Bottomore, 1992: 8). In summary, he goes back in time to locate the origins of civil rights in the 18th century. He traces the growth of political rights through the 19th century and beyond. He ends by equating the extension of social rights with the growth of the modern welfare state throughout the 20th century.

There is, however, substance in Bryan Turner's suggestion that Marshall took 'the existence of a British nation-state for granted' and consequently overlooked the processes by which it came into being (Turner, 1986: 46). Marshall, in fact, does address this issue but with reference to England rather than Great Britain when he draws attention to the institutional links between the growth of an English national identity and the major policy reforms that occurred during the 16th century.

Elizabethan England, he suggests, 'was a planned society, but of a conservative, not a revolutionary kind'. Throughout this period new economic and social policies were legislated on a national basis. They were designed to maintain and protect the political status quo 'by fixing both the wages of the workers and the relief of the poor' and the setting of pauper children to work (Marshall, 1981: 56–57).

Marshall goes on to assert that 16th century Elizabethan England 'witnessed the first expression of national patriotism, the first comprehensive national policy, and the first shift of interest from the revenues of princes to the wealth of nations' (Marshall, 1981: 56). These changes occurred against a background of military conflict, including a war with Spain, a botched invasion of Ireland and a failed Catholic rebellion against the Crown.

Military conflict was the catalyst through which England was transformed into the unitary sovereign-state of Britain. The Civil Wars of 1642–49 were, as Norman Davies describes them, fought over religion and 'opposing concepts of political liberty' but they also involved 'successful wars of subjugation against Ireland and Scotland'. It was not until the conclusion of these wars and the establishment of Cromwell's Protectorate in 1646 that 'for the first time in British history, England completely dominated the British Isles' (Davies, 2000: 498–503).

It was during this long period of civil wars and military conquest when a common national identity was being imposed on the people of the British Isles that the gradual evolution of English civil, political and social rights began gathering momentum. Turner makes a similar point when he suggests that the development of British citizenship through a process of internal colonisation was attended by a loss of political rights and regional autonomy in Ireland, Scotland and Wales. In his view, Marshall fails to explain how this expansion of social rights 'within a national core' came to be paralleled by 'the withdrawal of significant political rights at the periphery' (Turner, 1986: 46–47).

This seeming paradox might best be explained by the fact that both processes of change were fraught with conflict from the start. Wars of annexation and civil wars impose new national identities on victors and vanquished alike. They are less successful in creating the conditions that permit the subsequent evolution of an inclusive and egalitarian model of citizenship. Indeed, wars always leave a legacy of unresolved conflicts and inequalities in their wake.

This was the case with regard to Britain after the 1707 Act of Union that incorporated Scotland into England and the 1800 Act of Union that created the United Kingdom of Great Britain and Ireland. In England, Scotland and Wales, Catholics and Protestant Dissenters were not granted equal political rights until the late 1820s. Jews were not granted full parliamentary rights until 1860. It was not until the 'Fourth Reform Act' of 1918 that the right to vote was extended to all men over the age of 21 and all women over the age of 30, provided that the women were ratepayers or the wives of ratepayers. The full enfranchisement of women was not achieved until 1928. All these extensions of civil and political rights gave rise, at times, to episodes of civil unrest and conflict involving the use of armed force even in those parts of the country which were largely content to be members of a new British nation. The conflicts arose, however, among sections of the population who felt they were being unjustly denied their full rights as British citizens.

The subjugation of Ireland, however, left a uniquely bitter legacy of internal conflict and sporadic civil war. As the centuries of occupation, repression and mismanagement passed, even those Irish who initially wanted to secure their full rights as British citizens became disaffected and gave their support to what eventually became a popular movement for national independence. Both processes illustrate the ways in which civil wars can fundamentally change the relationship between the growth of national consciousness and the evolution of the civil, political and social rights of citizenship.

The origins of the conflict

The first English invasion of Ireland took place in 1171. Successive waves of English settlers colonised the best lands and drove out the Irish. They soon established a settlement around Dublin which became the seat of an Irish Parliament, dominated by a combination of Anglo–Norman and Irish landowners and subject to the authority of the British Crown (Smith, 2000: 2). The next stage in the colonisation of Ireland began with the establishment of plantations of loyal English settlers from the mid-1550s onwards. This policy was pursued with such rigour that the dispossessed Irish eventually rebelled in 1595. Soon after their defeat in 1598 the Gaelic nobility fled the country and 'the Tudor conquest was complete' (Beckett, 1971: 62).

New plantations of Scottish Protestants were settled in Ulster and the northern Gaelic-speaking Irish were evicted at the start of the 17th century. The Irish rebelled again in 1641 and the country remained in a state of armed conflict throughout the English Civil Wars. In 1649 Cromwell led a new invasion of Ireland. The Irish were defeated, most of the remaining Catholic landowners were dispossessed, the rebel leaders were executed or deported and the cultural institutions of Gaelic Ireland were suppressed.

The next Irish insurrection occurred in 1690 when the deposed King James II returned to Ireland and rallied the Irish Catholics to his cause. His defeat by William III's army marked the eclipse of Irish hope for independence. A new system of penal laws was subsequently imposed on the Irish Catholics. From 1728 onwards they were denied the right to vote, to pursue careers in the army, in government and in the learned professions. They were permitted to practice their religion but their children were not allowed to be educated abroad or to study at a university. The penal laws also placed severe restrictions on the rights of the few remaining Catholic land-owning gentry to buy, sell or increase their property holdings (Beckett, 1971: 95–99).

In summary, the Irish Catholic landed gentry had been deprived of their civil and political rights *before* the extension of these rights began to gather momentum on mainland Britain. The Protestant Ascendancy in Dublin was not greatly concerned about the mass of Irish peasantry. They had no rights to speak of and did not own their own land. The concept of welfare rights is a 20th century notion. The ownership of land, however, has always been a key determinant of status, wealth and the prospect of welfare. In 18th century Ireland it was also correctly viewed by the Protestant Ascendancy as 'the key to political power' which largely explains why they imposed such severe restraints on the property rights of Catholics (Beckett, 1971: 98).

In 1782 the British Government granted the Irish Parliament the right to make its own laws, subject to the continuance of British executive authority. Most of the penal laws against Catholics were removed, although they were still denied the right to vote. Some of the Irish patriotic reformers were content with these concessions. Another, more radical group of Protestants and Catholics, the United Irishmen, wanted still more fundamental reforms, including the right to vote for Catholics. Against the threatening background of the French Revolution this demand was conceded in 1793.

In the following year, a United Irish agent was arrested on his return from France and charged with plotting another Irish rebellion. The United Irishmen were officially suppressed, went underground and prepared for an armed insurrection. At the time they were led and supported by both Protestants and Catholics in Dublin and Belfast. The first lodge of the Orange Order was established in 1795 in response to the activities of another Ulster based Catholic movement, the Defenders.

The rebellion, when it came in 1798, was brutally put down. The British Government, now at war with France, acted swiftly to impose total control on the disaffected province. In 1800 the Irish and English Parliaments passed two identical statutes that merged Great Britain and Ireland into one United Kingdom. The Irish Parliament was abolished in 1801. Four centuries of military conflict and sporadic civil war had left the Irish stripped of the last vestiges of national independence. Henceforward they were to be citizens of the United Kingdom and any further extension of their civil, political and social rights would have to be won in the Parliament at Westminster to which they could now elect 100 members.

From Catholic emancipation to land reform

At the start of the 19th century, the right to vote and stand for Parliament was confined to a minority of landed property owners. A successful Catholic candidate would still be debarred from taking his seat in Parliament unless he was prepared to set aside his religious convictions and take an oath of supremacy acknowledging the English Crown in all temporal and spiritual matters.

In 1823 Daniel O'Connell formed a Catholic Association dedicated to achieving the goals of religious emancipation and national independence. In 1828 O'Connell won a by-election in County Clare. As a Catholic, he refused the Oath of Supremacy. The Irish countryside was in a state of turmoil. The British Government, knowing that it had to choose between conceding emancipation and a civil war, backed down. The passing of the Catholic Emancipation Act in 1829 granted equal political rights to all Catholics throughout the United Kingdom although 'the property franchise under which Irish MPs were elected was significantly reduced from 216,000 to 37,000' (O'Leary and McGarry, 1997: 84). Against the odds, backward Ireland had, nevertheless, won the extension of an important right of citizenship across the rest of the British Isles.

However, Ireland was already approaching a disaster that would have a devastating impact on its future economic and social well-being. By the 1840s, the Irish population had grown to over 8 million. Two-thirds of the Irish people were tenants exclusively dependent on their agricultural smallholdings. Their staple diet was the potato, and in 1845 the potato crop failed in many parts of the country. In the following year the crop failed again and the Great Famine began.

The Irish Poor Law was the only government agency in the country responsible for the relief of extreme destitution. In 1834 the old English Poor Law had been transformed into a system designed to deter all but the genuinely destitute. In 1838 this system had been imposed on Ireland despite the protests of an Irish Commission which had previously been appointed by the British Government to advise on the issue of poor relief (see McGauran and Offer, 2015).

As the famine intensified, it quickly became obvious that a deterrent poor law could not cope with such a tide of destitution. In 1847 the British Government reluctantly agreed to the provision of poor relief outside the workhouses under stringent conditions of eligibility. Within the year over 800,000 applicants were receiving outdoor relief (Burke, 1987: 136, 148). As a consequence of the famine, over 1 million died of hunger and disease, another 1 million were 'forced to emigrate within four years, and 3 million within three decades' (O'Leary and McGarry, 1997: 76–77; O'Connor, 1995: 169).

As Smith points out, the major cause 'of Ireland's rural impoverishment, her economic backwardness and her agricultural depression lay firmly with the evils of landlordism, which extracted wealth to London, evicted tenants at will and exercised a brutal, harsh regime across the Irish countryside' (Smith, 2000: 4). The historical origins of this regime grew out of the policies of land expropriation, eviction and resettlement that followed in the wake of military conquest. The Great Famine added the experience of mass emigration to the troubles of Ireland.

Ireland's next major nationalist movement began in the USA where a group of immigrants founded the Fenian Brotherhood in 1858. The Fenians were militant revolutionaries determined to win independence by violent means. In 1867 they launched terrorist raids on mainland Britain, including a series of bombings, murders and jail breaks. There were other Irish nationalists who opposed the use of physical force. Isaac Butt established a Home Rule Association in 1870 that became the Home Rule League in 1873. He led the Irish Home Rule MPs at Westminster but failed to win wider support for a limited form of self-government. Soon afterwards, he was replaced as leader by Charles Stewart Parnell.

The Prime Minister, William Gladstone, had long been preoccupied with the 'Irish Question'. His first response to the bombings was conciliatory. He persuaded Parliament to pass an Act disestablishing the Church of Ireland and thereby ended the ecclesiastical authority of the old Protestant Ascendancy. Two years later, in 1871, the passage of a Land Act gave greater security of tenure to Irish tenant farmers. The provisions of the Land Act of 1871, however, did not satisfy the Irish tenantry who wanted nothing less than perpetuity of tenure. Neither were they effective in stopping evictions. In the face of continuing rural unrest and violence a Coercion Act was passed and the ringleaders arrested.

In 1879 Michael Davitt and Charles Stewart Parnell formed an Irish Land League with the intention of using moral force to compel landowners to reduce rents by withholding payment if they refused to do so. More significantly, the League invented the stratagem of 'boycotting' evicting landowners. This stratagem took its name from a Captain Boycott who managed a large estate in the north-west of Ireland. When he evicted some of his tenants he was ostracised by the entire local community and threatened with crop burning.

In 1880 Gladstone's Liberal Party was returned to office and a year later passed a new Land Act guaranteeing Irish tenants their rights to a fair rent, free sale and fixity of tenure. For people who had traditionally associated their welfare with land this legislation marked, in modern terminology, a significant extension of their social rights. No such rights were granted to their English counterparts.

Irish home rule, British social reform and the First World War

Despite these reforms, the evictions continued. As violence in the countryside escalated, Parnell was arrested and his Land League called a rent strike. Parnell and the British Government reached a compromise. He agreed to use his influence in stopping the violence. The government agreed to give the tenants more protection and to end coercion. But Parnell was no longer able to control his extremists. Shortly after his release from prison, the Chief Secretary and Under-Secretary of Ireland were assassinated by a group of terrorists known as 'The Invincibles'. The atrocity was condemned on all sides. A new Coercion Act was passed and the violence went on.

Two new important laws were passed in 1884 and 1885. They extended the franchise throughout the United Kingdom in ways that greatly benefited the Irish parliamentary party. In the General Election of 1885, Parnell won enough seats to hold the balance of power at Westminster. Gladstone became Prime Minister and announced his conversion to Home Rule. Parnell supported Gladstone's Home Rule Bill but the Bill was defeated in the House of Lords, another General Election was called and Gladstone lost. Both the Liberal Party and Ireland were left deeply divided. In 1890, Parnell's political credibility was destroyed when he was cited as the co-respondent in a divorce case. As a consequence, he lost the support of both Gladstone and the Catholic Church in Ireland.

The victorious Conservatives were to remain in office from 1886 to 1905, apart from a brief interlude of Liberal Government. The Conservatives were implacably opposed to Home Rule. They were also convinced that policies of social reform, and in particular, the ending of landlordism, would persuade the Irish to accept their status as citizens of the United Kingdom. They introduced new legislation that gave financial incentives both to tenants who wanted to buy their land and to landlords who were prepared to sell. These policies were popular and strikingly successful. Their implementation was briefly interrupted in 1892 when Gladstone and the Liberals were returned to office. Undeterred by Ulster Unionist threats of armed insurrection, Gladstone introduced a second Home Rule Bill in 1893. For a second time the Bill was defeated in the House of Lords, the Liberals resigned and the Conservatives won the General Election with a large majority.

When the Liberals were eventually returned to office in 1905, they introduced a major social reform programme to be financed from the revenues of a People's Budget. After the House of Lords rejected this Budget in 1909, the Liberals called a General Election. They promised the Irish parliamentary party that, if they won, they would introduce a new Home Rule Bill. The Liberals were returned to office with a reduced majority, leaving them dependent on the Irish party in their struggle with the Lords. After much prevarication, the Lords conceded defeat and the People's Budget became law.

The Lords were also forced to approve a new Parliament Act. Under this Act, the House of Lords lost the power to veto any legislation initiated by the House of Commons. In the case of Bills involving money they could delay the legislation for only one month. They could also delay other legislation for two years which meant that they would not be able to veto the eventual passage of a Home Rule Bill as they had done in 1893. The Liberal Government's determination to extend the social or welfare rights of United Kingdom citizens consequently became the means by which the political rights of the Irish to a limited measure of self-government was conceded.

A Home Rule Bill was presented to Parliament in 1912. In the face of this renewed threat, the Ulster Protestant Unionists raised an armed militia of 100,000 volunteers prepared to fight either for complete independence or exclusion from the provisions of a Home Rule Bill. The Irish Catholic Nationalists were also prepared to fight if the Home Rule Bill was defeated. After twice being passed by the Commons and twice rejected by the Lords, the Bill was about to become law in the autumn of 1914 when all these events were overtaken by the outbreak of the First World War. The British Government, deeply concerned about the reliability of some sections of the army in the event of an Irish civil war, suspended the introduction of Home Rule until the ending of hostilities.

The Irish parliamentary party supported the war while a small group of militant nationalists, the Irish Republican Brotherhood, prepared for insurrection at home. In 1916 they seized buildings in the centre of Dublin and proclaimed an Irish Republic. The rising was put down and its leaders were court-martialled and shot. The brutality of the British reprisals alienated large sections of the Irish public.

In 1920 Lloyd George's post-war Coalition Government passed the Government of Ireland Act which partitioned Ireland and established separate Home Rule parliaments in the South and the North. A new Protestant province of Ulster was left with a large Catholic minority.

Sinn Fein rejected Home Rule and partition. Its elected MPs refused to take up their seats at Westminster and, in 1919, established their own provincial government in Dublin. Civil war broke out between the British armed forces and the Irish Republican Army. A cease-fire was agreed in 1921 and the Anglo-Irish Treaty of that year created an Irish Free State of 26 Southern counties with the status of a Dominion under the British Crown. Ulster opted to remain within the United Kingdom. The militant Irish republicans rejected the Treaty and another civil war began, this time between the Irish Free State Government forces and the IRA 'irregulars'. By 1923 the government had crushed the rebellion but the peace was to leave Ireland divided for decades afterwards.

The inter-war years and two kinds of post-war settlement

The scene had been set for another 70 years of sporadic and escalating terrorism. In Northern Ireland, the Unionist Government created its own police force with special internal security duties (Fraser, 2000: 6). It redrew all electoral boundaries in order to restrict the civil, political and social rights of its Catholic citizens. Throughout the inter-war years Northern Ireland became a semi-autonomous province within the United Kingdom, but it was a province divided on sharply sectarian lines and one which possessed all the coercive powers it required to enforce its inegalitarian policies.

In the Irish Free State, the momentum towards social reform was not sustained although, for a time, agriculture prospered under a free trade policy because almost all of its produce was sold in Britain (Fraser, 2000: 10). Throughout the 1930s the Irish farmers continued paying back the loans they had received from the British Government under the terms of the 1890–1903 land purchase Acts. The cost of repaying these annuities accounted for 18% of all government expenditure (Fraser, 2000: 18). De Valera, the Irish Prime Minister, suspended the payments and the British Government immediately imposed a 20% duty on all Irish exports. This dispute, which severely damaged the Irish economy, was not resolved until 1938. In 1937 the Irish Parliament adopted a new constitution which changed the country's name to Eire, affirmed the 'special position' of the Catholic Church in Ireland and categorically stated that 'the national territory consists of the whole of Ireland' (Fraser, 2000: 20). These actions heightened the anxieties and hardened the resolve of the Northern Ireland Unionists.

When the Second World War broke out in 1939 Ireland remained neutral and the IRA launched a number of terrorist attacks in Britain. After the British Labour Party won the 1945 General Election and started to implement Beveridge's proposals for a post-war welfare state, the Northern Ireland Government made sure that its citizens were included in this plan, partly to secure the welfare benefits it offered and partly to consolidate its political union with Britain.

In this way, the whole population of Northern Ireland formally secured a substantial extension of their social rights to welfare by virtue of being United Kingdom citizens. However, in reality the Catholic minority remained significantly disadvantaged. As O'Leary and McGarry point out, 'no religious discrimination could be made in the allocation of welfare benefits (as opposed to services) since entitlements were determined by Westminster and Whitehall'. In the field of local authority social service provision, however, the criteria of allocation were determined by the Stormont Government. The most important of these services were the provision of subsidised public housing according to need and access to secondary education (O'Leary and McGarry, 1997: 158).

The Stormont Government had no option but to press for Northern Ireland's inclusion in the provisions of the post-war British welfare state. It had to retain the political loyalty of its supporters across the whole constituency of the Nationalist movement. In doing so, however, it 'paved the way for Catholic demands for British rights in the late 1960s' and encouraged them to appeal 'to the metropole for their rights as British citizens' (O'Leary and McGarry, 1997: 157, 167).

In Marshall's theory of citizenship, the development of social rights followed the securing of political and civil rights. In the case of Northern Ireland, the campaign for equal social rights on the part of the Catholic minority was to take off in the late 1960s at a time when their other political and civil rights were far from equal. In many respects, the civil rights movement in Northern Ireland included all of the Marshallian components of citizenship in its agenda of political objectives.

The Irish Government did not launch a major programme of social reform in the late 1940s although some of its leading politicians wanted to follow the UK precedent. In 1950, the Health Minister, Noel Brown, introduced a Bill to provide free health services for pregnant mothers and post-natal care for nursing mothers and babies. The Catholic bishops and their clergy opposed the scheme on the grounds that state intervention of this kind was contrary to Catholic teaching on all matters relating to social welfare. It did not want the state to become more involved in any services affecting the institutions of family life, marriage and the upbringing of children. It was particularly concerned to defend its dominant role in education. The Irish Government, in the face of this opposition, quickly dropped the Bill.

The Catholic Church had checked the growth of social rights in Ireland far more effectively than the House of Lords had been able to frustrate the political aspirations of the Irish nationalists. The subsequent expansion of Irish statutory social services did not take off until the power and influence of the Church had declined and its own views on the role of government in welfare matters had begun to change. Ireland's admission to the EEC in 1973 proved to be an important turning point in this process.

From 'Bloody Sunday' to the Good Friday Agreement

From the 1960s onwards, Northern Ireland became the arena in which the unresolved historic conflicts about national identity, the partition and possession of land and citizenship rights were carried on with murderous intensity. Over the succeeding decades the violence went beyond the borders of Northern Ireland to mainland Britain and the Irish Republic. What was to become the most sustained and successful post-war challenge to the Unionist ascendancy in Northern Ireland started in the late 1960s in the form of a civil rights movement. It began with campaigns against discriminatory practices such as the allocation of public housing funds on sectarian lines designed both to segregate and minimise the voting power of Catholics.

The civil rights movement began as a reformist alternative to the more radical nationalist parties like Sinn Fein. Its members included organisations like the Campaign for Social Justice (CSJ), the Campaign for Democracy in Ulster (CDU) and the Northern Ireland Civil Rights Association (NICRA). Their primary objectives were the improvement of living standards, more open access to employment opportunities and political reform. NICRA's campaigning arena, for example, included 'universal suffrage at the local government level, anti-discrimination legislation covering public employment, subsidised public housing allocated according to need, repeal of the Special Powers Act' and the disbanding of the Ulster Special Constabulary (O'Leary and McGarry, 1997: 160, 167–168).

The first of the civil rights marches in 1968 were broken up with some violence by the police. Further clashes occurred between demonstrators and the police in Belfast and in August 1969 British troops were sent in to Derry (Londonderry). In 1971, the British Government agreed to the internment of suspected terrorists without trial. In 1972, it suspended the Northern Ireland Parliament at Stormont and introduced a policy of direct rule from Westminster. At the same time, more troops were sent in to strengthen the internal security role of the Royal Ulster Constabulary.

On the 30 January 1972, a civil rights march in Derry (Londonderry) against internment ended with the killing of 13 civilians by the British Army. The tragic events of what came to be known as 'Bloody Sunday' marked a turning point at which the violence escalated and many members of the civil rights movement began to question the possibility, or point, of social reform within the Northern Ireland status quo. As O'Leary and McGarry observe, it was the combination of internment without trial and 'the violent response to the civil rights movement which led many Catholics to return to a less complicated nationalism', dedicated to the ending of partition and the reunification of Ireland (O'Leary and McGarry, 1997: 168, 176).

From that time onwards, the sectarian divide in Northern Ireland grew wider and deeper. The civil rights movement became more radicalised and more disposed to sponsor acts of civil disobedience like rent and rates strikes. The main Northern Ireland political parties started to break up and realign into new groupings. The hard–line Unionists declared their opposition to any concessions and their nationalist counterparts refused to consider anything less than reunification. Each of these sectarian groupings had their own paramilitary organisations and recruited new members from their increasingly fearful and disaffected communities.

The British Government, for its part, strove to contain the growth of terrorism while it sought new ways of brokering some sort of truce or political compromise. It wanted to reach a peaceful settlement without conceding either a further partition of Ulster or a complete reunification of Ireland. To this end, it encouraged various power-sharing initiatives and carried through a fundamental reorganisation of the major welfare, housing and employment services in order to stamp out all forms of sectarian discrimination.

Throughout the succeeding years of violence, the British and Irish Governments worked together in their search for a constitutional solution. In 1984, they sponsored the appointment of a cross-national New Ireland Forum that published a report setting out various options for confederation or reunification. Once again, the peace process was thwarted when the IRA set off a bomb in a Brighton hotel where many Conservatives, including the Prime Minister, were staying in preparation for their Party Conference. Five people were killed and many others were badly injured.

For the next 10 years, Northern Ireland remained locked in a violent civil war. Sectarian terrorist factions fought each other, the army and the police. The death toll mounted as the violence escalated. The British and Irish Governments continued looking for constitutional ways to end the conflict. In 1985 they signed an Anglo-Irish Agreement which affirmed that any future change in the status of Northern Ireland would only come about with the consent of a majority of its people. The two Governments agreed to set up a new system of devolved administration in Northern Ireland, based on popular consent, power-sharing and equality of civil, political and social rights. In Northern Ireland, the

Agreement was denounced by the Unionists and Sinn Fein Nationalists (O'Leary and McGarry, 1997: 235–39). Shortly afterwards, Mrs Thatcher also rejected the Forum's proposals.

In 1992, John Major became Prime Minister and, after reviewing the situation, concluded that the paramilitary terrorists could be contained but not defeated. Secret talks were started with Sinn Fein and in 1994 the main paramilitary organisations on both sides agreed to a cease-fire. The British and Irish Prime Ministers published a 'Frameworks' proposal setting out an agenda for future discussions. In 1995, they invited an American Senator, George Mitchell, to chair an international committee on arms decommissioning. President Clinton endorsed this move. Shortly after Senator Mitchell published his report in 1996, a major business centre in central London was devastated by an IRA bomb outrage.

Nevertheless, progress towards a settlement continued. In 1997, the Labour Party won the General Election and reopened negotiations with all but two of the Unionist parties. On 10 April 1998, the Good Friday Agreement was brokered. The terms of the Agreement were drafted in such a way that Sinn Fein could see it as a 'transitory' stage in the progress towards Irish reunification and the Unionists could see it as a guarantee that their position was secure so long as it was endorsed by a majority of the Northern Irish people (Fraser, 2000: 79).

The Good Friday Agreement proposed an elected Assembly with nationalist and Unionist representation. Its elected members were required to pledge themselves to democratic and non-violent procedures. Other cross-border councils were established in Belfast, Dublin and London, with delegated representatives from the devolved Scottish Parliament and Welsh Assembly. It was agreed that convicted Republicans and Unionist terrorists would be released from prison.

The Agreement did not require a start to arms decommissioning as a precondition for peace but it did lay down a time scale for its implementation. Referenda in Ireland and Northern Ireland gave overwhelming support to the Agreement proposals. A few weeks later, a breakaway terrorist faction of the Real IRA exploded a bomb in a Northern Ireland town which killed 29 adults and children and two unborn babies. The scale of public outrage throughout Ireland and the United Kingdom in response to this atrocity was such that even this extremist group suspended its activities. The perpetrators have never been brought to justice.

The Agreement survived despite the slow progress of arms decommissioning which was only formally completed in 2005. The declining influence of the centre-ground parties has left the politics of Northern Ireland more sharply polarised than ever before. Dr Paisley and his Democratic Unionist Party remain deeply suspicious of the British Government's intentions and unconvinced that the IRA have finally decommissioned their forces. Sinn Fein, for its part, remains dedicated to the goal of eventual reunification. The great majority of Northern Irish people still support the Agreement and rest their hopes for a better future in its continuance, and there are grounds for such hopes. As Marc Mulholland observes, 'when it has operated, a wide-based devolved government in Northern Ireland has been surprisingly successful' (Mulholland, 2002: 188).

Conclusion

In *Citizenship and Social Class*, Marshall refers, only in passing, to the impact of conventional war on these two institutions. He makes no reference whatever to civil war and he focuses almost exclusively on historical developments in English society. The purpose of this paper has been to explore the relevance of his theory of citizenship to a country whose history has been inextricably linked with that of England's and shaped profoundly by the conventional and civil wars that preceded and followed its successive incorporation into Britain and the United Kingdom.

Marshall's theory of citizenship outlines an historical process in which civil, political and social rights evolved in a gradual and sequential way. However, he never claimed that the sequence of development he described was invariable. Neither did he rule out the possibility that, under certain circumstances, it might be reversed.

Marshall begins his analysis in feudal times when the three elements of citizenship 'were wound into a single thread. The rights', he suggests, 'were blended because the institutions were amalgamated' and there were no 'strict lines of demarcation between the various functions of the State' (Marshall and Bottomore, 1992: 8). Under these circumstances, there was no uniform collection of rights and duties based on a common status of citizenship. The only rights that ordinary people enjoyed were based on highly localised status relationships between those who held power and property and those who did not.

Marshall goes on to argue that it was the growth of national institutions in government and law which broke up this unity and set each element of citizenship on 'its separate way, travelling at its own speed under the direction of its own peculiar principles' (Marshall and Bottomore, 1992: 9). Under conditions of civil peace and a shared sense of national identity, these divergent processes of change eventually come together again under the unifying status of equal citizenship.

No such processes of gradual change occurred in Ireland. There was no shared sense of national identity between rulers and ruled and no unifying status of equal citizenship. There is ample historical evidence to support Turner's claim that the development of English citizenship was paralleled by a loss of comparable rights in Ireland. Nevertheless, the interactive character of the relationship between these two countries varied over time. It was political campaigning on the part of the Irish that eventually won Catholic emancipation for the rest of the United Kingdom in 1829. Without the support of the Irish MPs in Parliament, the Liberal Government might well have lost its battles with the House of Lords over the People's Budget in 1909 and the Parliament Act in 1911.

However, the Irish MPs did not support the Liberal Government because they wanted an extension of the people's rights to social welfare. They wanted Home Rule in return for their support. The land reforms of the 1880s and

1890s had failed to satisfy the growth of Irish aspirations for a measure of self-government. By the time that Home Rule was conceded, and was thereafter delayed for another five years, the impact of protracted civil war had transformed the conflict into a demand for complete independence. Marshall believed that, under conditions of civil peace, the rights of citizenship would compensate for inequalities of wealth and income, provided that these inequalities were not too extreme. The experience of Ireland demonstrates that no such compensatory mechanism operates under conditions of civil war over sovereignty. The right to self-governance is the most fundamental of all our political rights and it seems that ordinary people will forego all of their other rights in order to achieve it or defend it.

Between 1801 and 1921, the Irish people shared a common citizenship with the rest of the United Kingdom. The partition of Ireland began with the Government of Ireland Act of 1920, which provided for the establishment of two parliaments, one in Dublin and the other in Belfast and a continuance of Irish representation at Westminster. In 1921, under the terms of the Anglo–Irish Treaty, an Irish Free State with the status of a self-governing Dominion was established. (Complete independence was not achieved until 1949.) The six counties of Ulster with Protestant majorities were allowed to opt out and a self-governing province of Northern Ireland was also established in 1921.

The provisions of the new Irish Constitution of 1937 guaranteed the equal democratic rights of all Irish citizens. It also changed the name of the country to Ireland (Eire) and granted a special status to the Catholic Church. The change in nomenclature was especially significant since it clearly implied that the sovereignty of the new Constitution ought rightfully be extended to include the North.

As a constituent part of the United Kingdom, the citizens of Northern Ireland were also, in Marshallian terms, 'equal with respect to the rights and duties with which the status (of citizenship) is endowed' (Bottomore and Marshall, 1992: 18). In reality, they were far from equal. As Beckett observes, 'the government in Belfast administered Northern Ireland as if the whole population should conform to ... the patterns imposed by the protestant unionist majority' (Beckett, 1971: 177). It should also be noted that when Ireland finally became an independent republic in 1949 it was agreed between the Irish and British Governments that there could be no future change in the constitutional status of Northern Ireland without the consent of its own parliament.

The continuing partition of Ireland was totally unacceptable to the IRA. The great majority of Northern Ireland Catholics deeply resented being treated as second-class citizens by their Protestant government (Darby and Williamson, 1978: 10–11). The Protestant Unionists feared the loss of their own civil rights in the event of their being abandoned by the British Government. From the early 1950s onwards, the scene was set for the revival and continuance of civil war in Northern Ireland. Community relations were to remain polarised and Catholic mistrust of the civil and military authorities was to persist down to the present time (Gallagher, 1991: 59–86; Evans, 1996: 117–140; Mulholland, 2002: 48–54, 182–183).

When claims for national independence are denied and their denial leads to civil war, the focus of conflict shifts from the rights of citizenship to the rights of territorial possession. Competing claims to sovereignty over land are especially difficult to resolve, and notably so when issues of religious significance are also involved. Whether or not religion is a factor, the onset of civil war invariably reverses the processes by which the civil, political and social rights of citizenship gradually evolve with the passage of time under conditions of peace. As civil wars gather momentum they set in train complex counter-processes of *disenfranchisement*, *decivilisation* and *desocialisation*. As the three elements of citizenship break apart under the impact of violence, repression and counter-violence, they follow divergent and regressive paths until, once again, they are all subsumed into a singular and overriding preoccupation with the possession of land. When seemingly irreconcilable conflicts arise over its possession and ownership, land is swiftly transformed into a political symbol of competing claims to national sovereignty and all the other rights that make up the status of citizenship.

From the time of the early invasions onwards, the political and civil rights of the Irish were diminished by oppressive and discriminatory legislation. Catholic Emancipation in 1829 and the land reforms of the late 19th century did something to check and reverse these trends but they were not sufficient to weaken the growing demand for sovereign independence.

The desocialising consequences of protracted civil war are exemplified in the recent history of Northern Ireland. Trust in each other and in the integrity of our social institutions is the moral quality that holds societies together. It is not a quality that can be imposed by constitutions and due processes of law. It grows out of our personal experiences in the course of our daily lives and through the associations we form with other people. It is most likely to grow in societies where people live in the reasonable expectation that their rights will be respected because they know that the duties attached to these rights will be fulfilled. The relationship between authentic rights and duties is always reciprocal.

When people lose trust in the forces of law and order they set up their own vigilante associations to protect themselves which exacerbates the risk of further disorder. On both sides of the sectarian divide in Northern Ireland, it has always been difficult to draw clear distinctions between the activities of the paramilitary organisations, their associated vigilante groups and the criminal underworld. The decades of sectarian violence have left a legacy of organised crime centred round protection rackets and drug cartels. Beyond the world of organised crime, while sectarian killings and fire bombings continue, gangs of disaffected and unemployed young people add yet another dimension to the process of desocialisation that impoverishes the quality of daily life. Conventional wars may, for a time, strengthen the bonds of social solidarity. Civil wars always have the opposite effect.

Civil wars are not fought over the conventional issues of social welfare. Ordinary people are not prepared to kill or be killed in the cause of better social services. They are only prepared to do so once they are convinced that they will never become citizens on their own terms until they have won their national independence and the exclusive possession of whatever territories they associate with their ideal of nationhood. Since the land in question will always be the prime subject of dispute, neither side will ever enjoy the full benefits of freedom, welfare and peace until they are prepared to settle for some kind of territorial compromise.

Conventional theories of welfare fail to take these kinds of issue into account because they are based on conventional definitions of welfare that typically include essential goods and services like health care, social security, education and housing. The land on which these amenities stand is, more or less, taken for granted. When matters of national sovereignty are involved, however, land becomes a unique welfare good. It represents the beginning and end of all our welfare aspirations.

A nation state, faced with the threat of internal insurgency and secession, cannot be expected to concede part of its territory on terms which imperil its own future survival as a nation. At the same time, it cannot realistically expect to enjoy the full benefits of sovereignty as long as it has to live under conditions of continuous civil war. The Northern Irish Protestants have interests to defend as well as the Catholic Nationalists. The same dilemma confronts those who seek a sovereign independence of their own at the other's territorial expense.

Eventually, as the Irish experience demonstrates, the protagonists must choose between the options of permanent conflict and conciliation. Peace is the precondition of welfare but when all the rights of citizenship become contingent on the possession of disputed land, some kind of territorial compromise becomes the precondition for the recovery and growth of citizenship.

Marshall's theory of the growth of civil, political and social rights does provide a useful conceptual framework within which the regressive effects of civil war can be better explained and understood. It also provides, with other theories, some useful insights into how the drift to civil wars can be prevented. In this respect, however, the theories do not tell us much more than we know already. Peacemakers can impose the formalities of law and order and create the conditions under which a start can be made in repairing the physical and moral damage that civil wars inflict on civil societies. In the last analysis, however, only the protagonists themselves can make peace with each other.

Afterthought

Although 'ordinary people are not prepared to kill or be killed in the cause of better social services' (**p 185**), it remains the case that many might die for want of them.

INTRODUCTION TO PART THREE

On welfare pluralism

John Offer

One writer has described welfare pluralism as 'a vital, but relatively neglected, part of social policy' (Powell, 2007: 2). Pinker, however, did not neglect it. The third section explores some of the key arguments for pluralism in social policy in the UK which Pinker has highlighted since the 1980s. In this section in particular, space considerations have meant that it is a necessity that some of the many interesting essays by Pinker on pluralism have to be summarised here rather than reprinted.

Welfare pluralism certainly pre-dated the predominantly unitarist or state-centred approach to thinking about social policy adopted in the 1940s (among important historical studies are Johnson [1985], Lewis [1992] and Finlayson [1994]). But it was never entirely eclipsed in those years either in theory or practice, being embraced by Beveridge himself (in *Voluntary Action: A Report on Methods of Social Advance*, published in 1948). Pinker referred to this fact in his 'Making sense of the mixed economy of welfare', in *Social Policy and Administration* in 1992. Indeed, as we now know, the idea of pluralism in welfare policy lived on to be given new emphasis detectable from the late 1970s. In 1989, Martin Knapp wrote that 'Mrs Thatcher's governments of the 1980s brought about bigger changes to the mixed economy of welfare than there had been since the 1940s ... Dyed in the wool socialists would do well to recognise the undoubted successes within this huge social experiment. Blue-rinse Conservatives should acknowledge and seek to correct the failings. The prospects for Britain in the 1990s would be rosiest if research replaced rhetoric, and honest pragmatism replaced posturing' (1989: 252). Over 25 years later, all these judgements remain sound.

The first essay, **Chapter Nine**, 'Golden Ages and welfare alchemists', was first published in *Social Policy and Administration* in 1995 (Pinker, 1995b). It explores the idea of 'Golden Age' theories in social policy thought, and the 'welfare alchemists' whose visions these theories encapsulate. These are theories of the ideal society and how to realise it, whether drawn from the past or the future. Pinker argues that these grand theories are in reality ideologies. They can be collectivist or individualist in origin. But whatever their origins, they fail to address the need for the compromises between values which are reached in pluralist and democratic social contexts.

This need for a range of institutional compromises between the values of freedom and welfare shows through in the diverse and ever-mutating balances which characterise both national-level practical politics and the familial-level 'synthesis of custom and spontaneity' which expresses itself in informal care. Thus, for Pinker, welfare pluralist societies, not 'ideal' societies, whether collectivist ('institutional') or individualist ('residualist') in their inspiration, are likely to have the most agile and adaptable anticipations of responses to what he calls the 'subterranean currents of social change'. Pinker acknowledges the influences of culture to a greater extent than the 'welfare alchemists', perhaps again attributable to his sociological sensibility.

Pinker also, for much the same reason, at the same time distances himself from any claims which might amount to predicting the end of ideology: 'I see no reason why the institutions of *Gesellschaft* and *Gemeinschaft* and the traditions of collectivism and individualism should not continue to coexist in democratic societies' (**Chapter Nine, p 207**). On other occasions too in his work, Pinker introduces this pair of contrasting concepts, *Gemeinschaft* and *Gesellschaft*, to underline the contrast in the social relationships between, say, informal caring (tending to follow taken-for-granted, implicit 'customs') and formal caring (tending to follow explicitly discussed procedures and 'rules'). *Gemeinschaft* is commonly translated as 'community' and *Gesellschaft* as 'society', or sometimes 'association'. Today, our usage of course largely derives from that of the north German sociologist Ferdinand Tönnies, who in 1887 published his seminal book *Gemeinschaft und Gesellschaft* (Tönnies, 2001).

According to Pinker, the social and cultural reality of the institutions of *Gemeinschaft* and *Gesellschaft* must imply that it is a precondition of freedom that 'their coexistence should be marked as much by conflict as by consensus because, if either of these traditions overwhelms the other, democracy will be lost'. He also adds that it is 'a precondition of welfare that the distribution of life chances should be regulated by rational-legal and bureaucratic processes because, otherwise, there can be no guarantee that rights and obligations will be honoured'. Thus, in a self-understanding and hence consciously pluralistic society, all such arrangements will depend on the 'acceptance of an agreed set of values that underpin our notion of citizenship. It is entirely sufficient for most practical purposes if these values derive their legitimacy from the force of custom and convention'. For Pinker, one kind of marginal case in terms of the 'practical purposes' was investigated in 'Citizenship, civil war and welfare' (**Chapter Eight, in Part Two** of this book).

So, Pinker is committed to maintaining a balance between the guarantee that rights and obligations will be honoured and the practical outcomes of different versions of welfare pluralism. In this connection, Lund has argued that, with the interests of the public understood in this manner, and thus with the state responsible for rational-legal processes regarding rights and obligations, in certain circumstances in the absence of competition, the role of the state could become in essence no different 'from the state as provider' (2007: 55). On the other hand, it should be noted, that as a genuine welfare pluralist Pinker is not proscribing the state from being a provider.

Space precludes us from including Pinker's 'New liberalism and the middle way' (Pinker, 1999) here, but some of its chief ideas need to be mentioned.

Pinker shows how a long-term perspective on the changes of liberal thought in Britain reveals 'middle ways' of thinking about the aims of social policy. Idealist philosophical thought on social theory, between approximately 1880 and 1914, is particularly interesting (see Harris, 1992; den Otter, 1996; Offer, 1999a, 2006b). The Idealists, including Thomas Hill Green, Bernard Bosanquet and Henry Jones, were much concerned with 'duty'. They were reacting against the emphasis given to what they called 'atomic individualism' and the significance of the *consequences* of the actions by Jeremy Bentham and the Utilitarians (and also by Herbert Spencer, a favourite target who, in the 1890s, was completing his evolutionary theory, largely non-Darwinian in its structure, in his *Principles of Ethics* and *Principles of Sociology*).

Idealist social thought resonated with political life and social policy from 1906 to the First World War, when the policies of the Liberal government became known as 'New Liberalism'. New policies affecting children, education, old age pensions and, especially, health and unemployment insurance demonstrated innovative relationships and partnerships between the state, individuals and employers (Hennock, 1987). These were measures chiefly associated with David Lloyd George, Winston Churchill and Herbert Samuel.

Seebohm Rowntree's *Poverty: A Study of Town Life* (1901), dealing with the city of York, also became a challenge to complacency. Rowntree showed simply that much poverty, according to a definition of the word closely associated with the concept of subsistence, could not be attributable solely to the improvidence of the poor. The Old Age Pensions Act in 1908 and the National Insurance Act in 1911 opened the way for the old, the sick and the unemployed to recognise that they had an entitlement by right to assistance from the state. For Runciman, a principle had been accepted and a precedent set 'which thereafter differentiated the "new" Liberalism from the "old"; and after the First World War it was the "new" which came to dominate social policy despite the fact that some of the most influential carriers of its doctrines and practices operated outside of the Liberal Party itself' (1997: 53).

Pinker's position is similar, in that the degree of ideological shift in social policy assumptions over the same period which he adjudges to been have made were no less, but no more, far-reaching. In the closing pages of 'New liberalism and the middle way' (Pinker, 1999), he turns to what he regards as the vibrant enduring legacy of the 'New Liberalism', which was only temporarily displaced, and then only partially, by Titmussian welfare unitarism from the late 1940s to late 1970s. For Pinker, the legacy in its modern form owes much to T.H. Marshall, whose theories of welfare and citizenship were explicitly pluralist in nature. Pinker argues that welfare pluralism is more effective than unitarism in responding to the diversity of values and needs in modern societies because it embodies a matching diversity of formal and informal service providers, including a role for the state in regulation as well as in direct provision. This is the path pursued by the 'New' Liberals and their intellectual successors. Pinker adds though that to refer to it as the middle way is rather misleading. It is more a mosaic of intersecting paths pointing in roughly the same direction.

Unlike 'New liberalism and the middle way', which has just been discussed, we have actually included 'From gift relationships to quasi-markets: an odyssey along the policy paths of altruism and egoism' as **Chapter Ten** in this book. This essay was first published in its complete form in *Social Policy and Administration* in 2006 (vol 40, no 1, pp 10–25). The version included here is abridged to minimise any risk of undue overlap with 'Richard Titmuss and the making of British social policy studies after the Second World War', included earlier (as **Chapter Five** in **Part Two**).

Some of the themes here do echo ideas encountered in 'Richard Titmuss and the making of British social policy studies'; here, though, Pinker's discussion of the conditionality and 'mix' of altruism and egoism indubitably goes beyond providing support for his criticism of Titmuss's brand of welfare unitarism. It adds new depth to his case *in favour of* the adoption of forms of welfare pluralism. Pluralism rather than unitarism complements the capacity for social individuals to reach a diverse range of agile experiments and compromises in their decision-making, particularly over the balance between altruism and egoism in their actions. This is perhaps most evident when they are confronted with unexpected challenges. In many such cases, it is not easily to be settled whether one outcome is morally superior to another.

We are reminded that Pinker provides theoretical and rational rather than ideological or doctrinaire justifications for welfare pluralism. This is one of the reasons why his work continues to be important. The significance that Pinker's work gives to, first, understanding everyday ideas and informal caring practices concerning well-being, second, the flexibility which it finds that a mixed economy affords to the promotion of well-being in culturally diverse societies, and, third, the normative traps that it detects in Titmussian welfare unitarism, all coalesce into a formidable case in favour of versions of welfare pluralism.

Pinker's discussion moves from the 1960s to the contemporary scene. In 1968, the Institute of Economic Affairs (IEA) published the monograph *The Price of Blood* by Michael Cooper and A.J. Culyer. In their monograph, edited by Arthur Seldon, one of the Directors of the IEA, they reviewed the arguments for and against paying blood donors and developing a role for competitive markets in the sale and purchase of blood products. The IEA, as Pinker notes, 'was unequivocally committed to reducing the role of government in the provision of welfare and extending that of the private and voluntary sectors'. Titmuss passionately opposed these principles of the IEA in his *Commitment to Welfare* (1968) and *The Gift Relationship* (1970), both published around this time.

Pinker also reviews the evolution of his own ideas on the 'agency' of consumers and the 'motivations' of service providers. He then goes on to greet the publication of *Motivation, Agency, and Public Policy*, by Julian Le Grand (2003). Le Grand's own support for forms of welfare pluralism is welcomed. In the same manner as himself, says Pinker, Le Grand is arguing that 'altruism and egoism are not diametrically opposed forms of human motivation and that the values of the social and the economic markets do not have to be in permanent and irreconcilable conflict with each other' (see **Chapter Ten, p 219**. The first edition of Le Grand's book appeared in 2003, but later, in the 2006 edition, he generously acknowledged Pinker's contribution in the same area (Le Grand's comments on Pinker in 2006 were discussed earlier here in the **General Introduction**).

Perhaps the timing of our own publication is fortuitous, for there have been signs recently that the forces in favour of welfare unitarism are regrouping. For example, Beech and Page suggest, that having lost the 2015 general election to the Conservatives, the time is now right for Labour to adopt again a 'strong statist direction' in its policies and provisions for welfare services (2015: 342). Our book has brought back into focus (see **Chapters Six** and **Seven** in **Part Two**) the concerns of research studies from the 1970s onwards relating to informal carers and their problematic relationships with health and social care professionals. One further example of the concerns might be helpful here. An American research study, alert to the sociological nuances which resided in the sensitivities of everyday life, regarded professionals and informal caregivers as having to grapple with different assumptions and expectations about the meaning of 'support': 'In many ways, trying to combine the efforts of professional service providers with those of family members, concerned neighbours and devoted friends, is like trying to link two cultures in which very different beliefs, customs and norms of exchange prevail' (Froland et al, 1981: 260).

There is a risk that such 'misunderstandings' are likely to be exacerbated under a reversion to strong statist direction in policies and practices (a concern expressed by Johnson, 1999: 273). In situations where even in more propitious times professionals need 'a sophisticated sociological ear' (Howe, 1990: 76) there are no guidelines for how strong statist direction and 'the expressed needs of service users' (Beech and Page, 2015: 348–49) can reach mutually agreeable and meaningful accommodations. Reassurance would be needed that there are answers to the tensions and range of stigmas liable to be experienced by users and staff when statist direction sets cuts to budgets, or adopts particular priorities or performance targets. Since, for Beech and Page, welfare pluralism is 'attractive' only 'superficially' (2015: 351), another provider is unlikely to be found. In 2007, Holloway and Lymbery suggested that 'where, in the 1980s, informal carers were just beginning to make their voice known, their contribution to the mosaic of care is now established and assumed': the building of partnerships with carers is an important challenge for services which 'knit together "caring solutions" which are neither exploitative, neglectful nor dismissive of the user/carer's own way of doing things' (2007: 377; see also Bamford, 1990; Gray and Birrell, 2013: 129–42). Given the concerns with which we are now again familiar regarding a return to welfare unitarism, since they were originally of course raised by Pinker himself, the ball must remain in the court of Beech and Page, and others of a like-minded disposition. They need to show how their proposal can meet these concerns.[1]

Pinker's sustained interest in T.H. Marshall's sociology becomes the specific focus of the next two chapters in this Part. In his re-evaluation of the contributions of Marshall, he further develops his argument that Titmuss was a unitarist in relation to the means and ends of social policy, with an underlying collectivist social philosophy, by nature unsympathetic to any but state-controlled forms of welfare pluralism. The first of these chapters (**Chapter Eleven**) is 'The experience of citizenship: a generational perspective', which is based on the T.H. Marshall Memorial Lecture delivered at the University of Southampton on 30 April 1996.

It will, of course, have emerged already at several points in this book that Pinker holds the writing of Marshall in very high esteem. The two men were on cordial terms from 1972 and familiar with each other's thoughts, though they did not collaborate in writing papers. So, Pinker rightfully deserves to be accorded special respect as an interpreter of Marshall. This point is worth emphasising since, while references to Marshall on the concept of citizenship are common, the texture and nuances of his arguments which Pinker illuminates are often not very fully registered elsewhere.

In **Chapter Eleven**, Pinker introduces the three institutional features which have come to make up citizenship. They are: *civil rights*, such as liberty of the person and the right to justice; *political rights*, such as the right to participate in the exercise of power, as by voting or becoming a representative; and *social rights*, which cover the whole range from the right 'to a modicum of economic welfare and security to the rights to share to the full in the social heritage and to live the life of a civilised being according to the standards prevailing in the society' (see **Chapter Eleven, p 226**).

Pinker places his particular focus here on the 'largely unexplored' matter of how Marshall's concept of citizenship could be useful in understanding the everyday and subjective experience of citizenship at the level of ordinary life 'across the life cycle'. Pinker sees this topic as 'immanent' in all Marshall's work. For Pinker, Marshall's thought was not about pure abstractions but about giving shape to experiences. His theories of citizenship and welfare were pluralist in nature, and 'occupy the middle ground between the more extreme versions of individualist and collectivist theory' (**Chapter Eleven, p 226**). Thus, Pinker shows up the contrast between Marshall's own position and the more 'individualist' Hayek, together with the philosopher Michael Oakeshott, regarding their criticisms of social rights.

Later in the lecture, Pinker introduces the plurality of ways in which ordinary people secure their well-being and their welfare in everyday life, usually through means which include the market, social services, voluntary action and informal care. Pinker then makes the important observation that the concepts of 'citizenship' and 'welfare', are far from being coterminous. This arises because the boundaries of citizenship are drawn in terms of the coverage and content of formal rights grounded in the principles of either economic or substantive rationality. Beyond these boundaries, however, the allocation of welfare goods and services is determined more by the dictates of sentiment than reason. It is more accurate to talk in the language of felt obligations than of civil or social rights.

This insight allows us, by looking across the lived experiences of different generations, to build up a picture of the apparently inevitable 'trade-offs' that have occurred, especially because the substance of civil and social rights will have changed through time. Indeed, the raising of the level of taxation might extend the scope of our social rights and reduce the scope of our 'civil rights', or, rather more specifically, our liberty to meet our full *obligations* (Marshall's consistency on social rights is questioned by Rees [1995: 357–58]). As far as I can see, however, Pinker does not discuss how the felt experiences of people about such changes might feed through to their exercise of *political* rights.

The next contribution from Pinker on Marshall, 'The right to welfare' (**Chapter Twelve**), maintains a focus on Marshall's concern with welfare pluralism but it features more wide-ranging discussion of the context and structure of his thought. This chapter unites into one review the 'Introduction' which Pinker wrote for *T.H. Marshall: The Right to Welfare and Other Essays* published in 1981, and 'T.H Marshall', his contribution to George and Page's edited collection *Modern Thinkers on Welfare* (1995). The upshot is that we have made readily available again one of the genuinely indispensable sources for reappraising the contribution which Marshall made to illuminating the study of citizenship and welfare.

Marshall's interest in the idea of citizenship as a focus to adopt in the then relatively new subject of sociology was shared by Leonard Hobhouse, who was Professor of Sociology at the London School of Economics from 1907 to 1929 (Collini, 1979). He had studied and then taught philosophy at Oxford in the Idealist tradition of T.H. Green, and was familiar with the Idealist emphasis on the concept of citizenship as giving expression to the bonds between the individual on the one hand and the holistic society and the state on the other. But Hobhouse was also familiar with the evolutionary sociology of Herbert Spencer (Offer, 2010: 300–01). Spencer was at this time sometimes interpreted as a materialistic thinker, and many Idealists regarded his theory of evolution as one which undermined the precepts of Idealism. However, Hobhouse's book *Social Evolution and Political Thought* (1911) saw citizenship rights as a means to social improvement, and as 'the basis for a new and reconstructed liberalism' (Scott and Bromley, 2013: 22).

Now for the connection with Marshall. Marshall taught at the London School of Economics from the 1920s to 1956, and Marshall knew Hobhouse. Pinker tells us that Marshall regarded himself as teaching 'under the influence of Hobhouse', and making use of Hobhouse's 'threefold categorisation of kinship, authority and citizenship as the basic principles of social order'. Rees too has noted the link between Green, Hobhouse and Marshall (Rees, 1996: 3).

Chapter Twelve thus includes incisive and seminal discussions of some of the key reservations that have been raised over the years about aspects of Marshall's arguments. Note, however, that Marshall did not discuss how the impact of conventional or civil war might disrupt the securing of the three key elements in the status of citizenship. Pinker's own response to this particular lacuna is contained in 'Citizenship, civil war and welfare: the making of modern Ireland' (**Chapter Eight** in **Part Two** of this book).

Since Pinker first wrote, there has been a considerable enlargement of interest in Marshall on citizenship. Although foreshadowed by Pinker, links between

Marshall's formulation and the concept of agency have recently further enlarged upon 'a search for a new balance between the role attached to the welfare state and other actors, especially agency of the individual citizens' (Evers and Guillemard, 2012: 11). Similarly, it has been proposed that 'extending legal social rights and strengthening citizenship are two different issues': only with a 'healthy civic culture and political life' in the division of responsibilities in the 'welfare mix' will the two coincide (Evers and Guillemard, 2012: 28). On the other hand, as Ruth Lister has maintained, it still seems to be the case that the concept of citizenship is not well rooted in academic discourse in the UK; the term lacks the constitutional 'resonance' it has in France, for example (2012: 123; see also Ashford, 1986).

In the course of working on this book with Bob Pinker, it has been brought home to me that two other writers on social policy hold the keys to what he has been trying to achieve. They are of course Marshall and Titmuss. In both cases, the issues at stake were essentially sociological in nature, but different in substance. Pinker did not have deep qualms about Marshall's sociology. Here, he found a springboard in Marshall's treatment of citizenship, and the associated concepts of civil, political and social rights, which led him to develop a sociologically and philosophically justified underpinning for welfare pluralism.[2]

By contrast, in Pinker's view, Titmuss lacked a deep enough appreciation of what may be called the sociology of everyday life. When it came to normative concerns Titmuss retained the patrician touch. Instead of asking people themselves what they thought their needs might be – the starting point for sociology (in principle, if not always in practice) – his instinct was to tell them what those needs should be – the voice of moral 'authority'. It is said often enough that Titmuss 'was first and foremost a moralist' (Deacon, 2002: 197). But it is also true that he persisted in favouring the pursuit of his specific moral ideals at the expense of learning from the sociological research regarding the conditional nature of altruism available during his lifetime (for example Tunstall, 1966; Mayer and Timms, 1970). Indeed, it seems to me that Pinker remains as doubtful as he was in 1993 of Titmuss's assumption that the statutory social services 'could act both as institutional exemplars of social solidarity and shared moral purpose and as agents of radical redistribution'. 'This hypothesis', Pinker adds, 'was implausible even in his time, when there was economic growth, but under the ensuing conditions of stagnation and decline it became unsustainable' (Pinker, 1993: 70). The difficulty once more was the problem of the practicable limits of altruism in everyday life.

So in our selection Pinker now turns to review the likely development of welfare pluralism in the UK, in the context of the present uncommon turbulence in political affairs which it is experiencing at home and abroad. The essays involved are 'The Prospects for Social Policy in the United Kingdom after the 2015 General Election' (covering the period up to March 2016) (**Chapter Thirteen**), and an **Afterthought**, 'On the Post-Brexit Prospects for Social Policy in the UK'. These essays were expressly prepared for inclusion in this book.

In **Chapter Thirteen** Pinker considers the implications of the largely unexpected outcome to the 2015 General Election which meant the termination of the Conservative and Liberal Democrat coalition and the return of single party government by Conservatives (with a majority of 12) for the first time since 1992. He also charts the rising fortunes of the Scottish Nationalist Party at Westminster which accompanied the slump in the vote for Labour and the Liberal Democrats. Pinker fears that Westminster has been left without a major party actually being committed as a matter of ideology to the 'middle way' of making social policy. If One Nation Tories are losing out to the welfare residualists in the Conservative Party, then Jeremy Corbyn might lead Labour to renewed schemes of public ownership and the imposition of 'a unitary model of social welfare in which the state is the main or monopolistic social provider' (**Chapter Thirteen, p 290**).

One theme pursued in both of the essays is devolution, divergence and nationhood, which concerns comparisons between the changing experiences of welfare pluralism and citizenship within the UK, in the light of devolved administrations in Northern Ireland, Scotland and Wales.

Pinker possesses a distinguished track record of elucidating how welfare pluralism has had an unique history within the UK, in Northern Ireland in particular. Evidence of his commitment to understanding the hows and whys of the variety of 'welfare' within the areas of the UK goes back to the 1970s. For example, as Series Editor of the landmark series of books 'Studies in Social Policy and Welfare' for Heinemann he was instrumental in publishing *Violence and the Social Services in Northern Ireland*, edited by John Darby and Arthur Williamson in 1978, and *Health and Welfare States of Britain: An Inter-country Comparison*, edited by Williamson and Graham Room, in 1983. Indeed, we have already illustrated the point by the inclusion in **Part Two** of one of his essays which displays an aspect of his own publications relevant to Northern Ireland (**Chapter Eight**, 'Citizenship, civil war and welfare: the making of modern Ireland'). His concern with comparisons within areas of the UK was to find relevant answers to crucial questions about social policy, not to record differences for their own sake.[3]

If the referendum in Scotland on leaving the UK did not in the end presage the break-up of the UK, the subsequent referendum in the UK on EU membership in 2016 may yet do so. In fact the outcome of the Scottish Referendum in September 2014 stands out as the SNP's only significant electoral setback in recent years. Nearly 85 per cent of the electorate turned out on the day. Fifty-five per cent of them voted against leaving the UK and 45 per cent voted in favour of leaving. By contrast, in the 2015 General Election the SNP won 50 per cent of all votes cast and increased their number of MPs from 6 to 56. However, in the EU referendum held on 23 June 2016, it is important to note that while 78 per cent of the UK electorate turned out to vote (with an overall vote of 52 per cent to 48 per cent in favour of exiting the EU, or 'Brexit'), in England the vote was 53 per cent to 47 per cent and in Wales 52 per cent to 48 per cent for Brexit, whereas by contrast Scotland voted to remain in the EC by a massive 62 per cent to 38 per cent and Northern Ireland did likewise by 56 per cent to 44 per cent.

The SNP and the Scottish Parliament wished Scotland to remain in the EU and were now at loggerheads with the Westminster UK Parliament which was embarking on the complex process of leaving the EU. Meanwhile Northern Ireland apparently had a divided Assembly, an electorate that had voted to remain, with the UK Parliament set on Brexit and the unique challenge of sharing a land border and extensive trading with the Republic of Ireland, whose continued membership of the EU was, of course, not in question. As a consequence, the future of UK as a political entity is now under threat from two fronts.

Pinker's writing about social policy has always emphasised the practical and comparative dimensions of the experiences in everyday life of our capacity for agile agency in changing circumstances. This in turn shapes our ideas of citizenship, altruism (and discrimination), welfare pluralism, and nationhood. It was natural in this past year that Pinker should have seized the opportunity to understand about the range of consequences likely to befall the regions of the UK following the momentous outcome of the UK's referendum on continued membership of the EU. So this book concludes with his new essay 'Afterthought on the Post-Brexit Prospects for Social Policy in the UK'.

Notes

[1]   A short note on informal care, social care services, and 'personalisation' will be helpful here. 'Personalisation' is a recent and contested concept within social care services. In 2012, in *Caring for our Future,* the government stated: 'Personalisation is about giving people choice and control over their lives, and ensuring that care and support responds to people's needs and what they want to achieve. It is central to enabling people to lead active, independent and connected lives' (Department of Health, 2012: 54). It is also specifically connected 'with the devolution of budgets down to the individual or a nominated budget-holder' (Needham, 2015: 357). Glasby has remarked that some see personalisation 'as a civil rights struggle, promoting greater citizenship for disabled people', while others see this 'as a neoliberal agenda designed to undermine traditional public sector services and values, transfer responsibility from the state to the individual and "dress up" unfair and draconian cuts as a more positive policy' (2015: 85).

In the event, therefore, the vogue for 'personalisation' (and users as 'co-producers') is producing divergent estimations of its significance in welfare policy, from the positive of enhancing subjective well-being to the negative of viewing people as 'atomised subjects of an inexorable neoliberal capitalism' (Williams, 2015: 104).

However, it should be stressed that there is no *necessary* association between these 'negative' forms of 'personalisation', sometimes, as we can see, linked to a 'neoliberal' agenda, and roles for informal care and social care services in welfare pluralism (Larkin and Mitchell, 2016).

[2]   For some aspects of Marshall's own pluralistic and political outlook with socialism, see Evan Durbin (1940) and Elizabeth Durbin (1940).

[3]   From the 1970s onwards Pinker also took keen interest in the teaching and examining of social policy at undergraduate and postgraduate levels in the newly established New University of Ulster, and then in the enlarged institution which superseded it in 1984, the University of Ulster (acknowledged when Ulster awarded Pinker an honorary doctorate in June 2016).

NINE

Golden Ages and welfare alchemists*

Robert Pinker

The art, or science, of alchemy probably originated among the Alexandrian Greeks in the early Christian era, and eventually became a reputable field of study throughout medieval Europe. Although alchemy was concerned with the conversion of base metals into gold or silver, in another sense it expressed a search for a philosophical principle that would explain the nature of the material world – a *prima materia* commonly described as the philosopher's stone and sought after by alchemists, who believed that it would reveal the essential unity of all things, animate and inanimate. Once discovered, the philosopher's stone would serve as a catalyst through which base metals would be transmuted into precious ones (Holmyard, 1957).

It was not until the mid-eighteenth century that alchemy was consigned to the realms of occult speculation. In some branches of the social sciences, however – notably in those directly concerned with the enhancement of human welfare – the quest for a universal explanatory principle or theory – an economic, political or social counterpart to the philosopher's stone – has gone on ever since. Such a theory, it is hoped, will explain how the base metals of imperfect humans and their social institutions can be transformed into nobler beings inhabiting a more perfect social order.

Concepts of this kind go back to antiquity, sometimes looking back to a visionary Golden Age, sometimes anticipating a Utopia of the future. They take religious forms like the Garden of Eden or the Heavenly City, and there are countless secular equivalents. The Golden Age is invariably seen as an ideal society in which poverty, sickness, oppression and war are banished, giving way to plenty, health, justice, order and liberty. The Age of Enlightenment – itself looked back on as a Golden Age of sorts by many scholars – produced numerous theories of progress based on a belief in the possibility of personal and collective development towards an ideal state of society (Berlin, 1990, chs 1 & 2; Goodwin and Taylor, 1982).

---

* Article first published in (1995) *Social Policy and Administration*, vol 29, no 2, pp 78–90.

Classical political economy and the New Right

Turgot, Condorcet and Ferguson were typical of the great Enlightenment scholars who strove to discover a unifying principle that would explain the dynamics of social progress and show how such progress could be achieved (Bierstedt, 1979; Gay, 1973; Berlin, 1980; Porter, 1992). Both Turgot and Ferguson had an influence on the work of Adam Smith, although Smith, like Ferguson, did not so much elaborate a unilinear theory of progress or vision of a perfect society as put forward a set of interrelated principles and a body of economic theory whose practical application would produce a happier and more prosperous society (Ferguson, 1966: xiv; Heilbroner, 1986: 8; Smith, 1976a; Smith, 1976b). Smith argued that leaving the economic market to the workings of the 'invisible hand' of supply and demand would result in a natural reconciliation of individual and collective interests and the best possible allocation of resources under an 'obvious and simple system of natural liberty'.

The other two founding-fathers of political economy, Robert Malthus and David Ricardo, took a more pessimistic view of the future. For somewhat different reasons both men thought that in the long run Smith's 'progress of improvement' would slow down, giving way to a stationary state of wealth and capital in which wages would sink to the level of subsistence (Malthus, 1970; Ricardo, 1929).

Smith was an optimist, but never a Golden Age theorist. He looked neither backwards nor forwards to ideal models of society and he never claimed that the rational pursuit of profit was the be-all and end-all of social behaviour. The gradual impoverishment of classical political economy, both morally and politically, began with Ricardo and Malthus. Thereafter, as Karl Polanyi describes it, economics became increasingly preoccupied with market determinants of profit and efficiency, with conditions of Pareto-optimality and the refinement of cost–benefit analysis. The institutional diversity of social life was reduced to the concept of an all-pervasive market economy and a market society dominated by a narrow doctrine of competitive individualism (Polanyi, 1977: 5–7).

In the same way, the popular versions of classical political economy exemplified in the laissez-faire doctrines of the Manchester School played down Smith's emphasis on the role of sympathy and civic responsibility as well as his positive assertion that the state had a vital role to play in the provision of poor relief, public education, the administration of justice and the sponsoring of public works.

In our own time the policy analysts of the New Right have looked to Adam Smith and the theories of classical political economy for inspiration but they have been just as selective in their use of his work. It is in their only too visible hands that the idea of perfect competition has been invested with all the miraculous properties of a philosopher's stone. In addition they have looked back to Smith's own time and the subsequent heyday of early Victorian England and reinvented it as a Golden Age of rugged individualism, unparalleled economic growth, innovation, burgeoning prosperity and exemplary 'family values' (Green, 1993;

Murray, 1990; Bulpitt, 1986; Kavanagh, 1990; Riddell, 1991; Skidelsky, 1989; Gilmour, 1993).

Although Britain was blessed with these attributes in the early nineteenth century, it had negative features as well. There was much destitution and avoidable suffering and, ironically, a poor law whose chief deterrent was the threat of family break-up. These problems are acknowledged by New Right theorists but they are seen as no more than transitional difficulties. Nevertheless the Victorian era is treated as the dawn of a Golden Age rather than the full, confident morning itself. So what went wrong? Put simply, the promise of laissez-faire was thwarted by the insidious progress of collectivism and statutory welfare.

During the 1980s Mrs Thatcher and her ministers enthusiastically adopted the slogan of 'Victorian values' to promote the virtues of self-help, thrift, stable family life, hard work and patriotism. It seems to be the fate of politicians who caricature the present that they will end by caricaturing the past. The idea that something called 'Victorian' society was held together by 'a single set of moral notions' over a sixty-year period is, as James Walvin observes, a 'banal and historically dubious proposition' (Walvin, 1987: 4). Nevertheless Mr Major has recently added a variation to this theme, with his urge to 'get back' to what he describes as 'basic values', and his list of virtues goes beyond Mrs Thatcher's to include law and order, basic educational skills, 'decency, courtesy, neighbourliness and respect for others' (*Evening Standard*, 6 January 1994, p. 1).

Similar concerns have been addressed by the New Right. David Green, for example, argues that the 'hard-boiled rationalism' of the Thatcher years has 'diverted our gaze from the deeper questions facing any civilization'. He concludes that Thatcherism 'suffered from a missing ingredient', giving too little importance to the 'civic virtues' of 'self-sacrifice, duty, solidarity and service to others'.

Green maintains that these virtues have always found their best and most effective expression not in public sector services but in the non-governmental agencies and institutions of civil society, notably in provident associations and voluntary bodies and in mutual aid between neighbours (Green, 1993: ix). Green also acknowledges that the classical economists were influenced too much by Ricardo's teaching and too little by Smith's observations on the beneficent influence of moral sentiment in civil society (Green, 1993: 14).

In my view this argument exaggerates the civic virtues of private enterprise and voluntary service at the expense of the public sector in exactly the same way that Titmuss used to exaggerate to the opposite effect. Both of these disparaging comparisons are misleading and unnecessary (Titmuss, 1974; Pinker, 1993). The civic virtues are not a monopoly of the private sector or of the business community, but are equally inherent in the long tradition of public service and statutory welfare provision that has its modern origins in nineteenth-century Britain.

Victorian Britain was a society of dazzling cultural diversity in which economic life was transformed by generations of innovative and energetic entrepreneurs. Our Victorian forebears also had the prescience to recognize the limitations of competitive markets and they laid down the institutional foundations of our major public services, a municipal health service and a framework of elementary education. These initiatives in the public sector did not spring out of a moral vacuum; they were as characteristic of the political culture of Victorian society as were laissez-faire and commercial enterprise. Political ideologies that treat the public sector as if it were intrinsically inferior to the private and commercial sectors in its aims and achievements oversimplify the diversity of human values and purposes that shaped Victorian society, and continue to shape our own.

The social policies pursued by successive Conservative governments since 1979 have manifestly been influenced by New Right thinking. In ideal terms these policies are directed towards raising the quality and efficiency of service provision and extending consumer choice while holding down the overall level of social expenditure. Latterly, these objectives have been set out in a general Citizens' Charter, its derivative manifestos, and the government White Paper, *Competing for Quality* (Prime Minister's Office, 1991; Department of Education, 1992; Department of Health, 1992; and Treasury, 1991).

There is, however, a paradox at the heart of all these policies of market testing, competitive tendering, privatization and the universal adoption of business enterprise managerial practices. The government's intention is to create a more pluralist welfare system but, if current trends persist, it will find that it has replaced what always was a relatively pluralist welfare state with a new kind of unitary model dominated throughout by the values and practices of the competitive market.

Socialism

Socialism is the second great repository of Golden Age theorizing. If private property, profit maximization and production and distribution carried out through the market mechanisms of competitive capitalism made up the philosopher's stone of classical political economy, under socialism the catalysts of change were equality, common ownership of the means of production and distribution on the basis of need and fraternal co-operation. Both paradigms shared the goals of enhancing human freedom and welfare, while differing fundamentally over the means by which these goals could be achieved.

Early British socialists like Robert Owen, William Godwin, William Thompson, Thomas Hodgskin and John Gray viewed capitalism as an essentially exploitative and oppressive system that would prevent the poor from enjoying the products of their own labour and con trolling their own lives. These men argued that human nature was shaped by its environment and that social conditions could be changed in ways that fostered co-operative altruism instead of competitive egoism. Some of these early socialists – notably Godwin – were profoundly suspicious of government as a trustworthy agent of social reform. As for the anarchists, who subsequently developed their own theories of socialism, the very idea of a welfare state would have been a contradiction in terms (Godwin, 1976; Owen, 1991; Hodgskin, 1922; Gray, 1931; Thompson, 1968; Bray, 1931; Beales, 1933; Stafford, 1987).

Yet there was another dimension of early socialist thought that was explicitly statist. Saint-Simon, for example, was a precursor of Fabianism and modern corporatism, in attributing a leading role to intellectuals, experts and bureaucrats in the creation of a planned, dirigiste alternative to laissez-faire. He looked forward to the dawn of an efficiently administered Golden Age of peace and prosperity within the framework of a unified socialist state of Europe (Saint-Simon, 1956).

Some of these early socialists and anarchists believed that capitalism could be overthrown by peaceful persuasion and democratic processes. Others believed that direct action and revolution were the only way. Karl Marx and Friederich Engels denounced them all as 'critical-utopian socialists' and dreamers of 'duodecimo editions of the New Jerusalem', and they were equally contemptuous of the emerging democratic socialist parties in Germany and elsewhere (Marx and Engels, 1959: 83, 87; Marx, 1972). The anarchists, in their opinion, were wrong in believing that the transition from capitalism to communism could be achieved without taking over the agencies of the state, and the democratic socialists were wrong in believing that capitalist governments could be converted to socialism by peaceful persuasion backed up by the ballot box.

Marxism emerged from these doctrinal conflicts as the most influential political critique of twentieth-century capitalism, with its theory of class struggle in which the overthrow of capitalism would be followed by the dictatorship of the proletariat, the transition to socialism and eventually the coming of a new, classless society, where the processes of production and distribution would be governed not by private property, the division of labour and the profit motive but by the principle of 'from each according to his abilities; to each according to his needs'.

Time and events have left these revolutionary hopes in ruin. Marx wrote little about the kinds of life that people would live under communism, apart from some pastoral intimations of hunting, fishing, livestock-farming and after-dinner discourse (Bottomore and Rubel, 1963: 111). On its revolutionary way to this Golden Age, Marxism went off course and spawned a multitude of political dystopias. So what went wrong? Once again there was allegedly nothing intrinsically deficient in the theory; the promise of communism was thwarted by human fallibility and the insidious corruption of absolute power.

Of the more democratic versions of the socialist tradition that gathered support in the capitalist societies of western Europe, some retained their statist and dirigiste outlook and others turned back to the participatory, communitarian ideals of the early socialists, while continuing the struggle for gradual and incremental progress towards a more just and equal society. Some of this collectivist idealism was incorporated into the policies of both liberal and conservative reformers, who were concerned not with the transformation of capitalism but with its salvation.

In their study of *English Ethical Socialism* Norman Dennis and A.H. Halsey illustrate the continuities of thought linking the utopian visions of Sir Thomas More and the populist writings of William Cobbett to those of much later thinkers like L.T. Hobhouse, George Orwell, T.H. Marshall and R.H. Tawney, and we might add for good measure the names of Evan Durbin, Barbara Wootton,

C.R. Crosland and Richard Titmuss, under whose influence the policies of post-war socialist governments were directed towards reducing inequalities and strengthening the bonds of social solidarity (Dennis and Halsey, 1988).

The fact is, nevertheless, that the resurgence of economic liberalism in Europe and North America during the 1980s owed as much to the failure of democratic socialist governments in the 1970s as it did to inspiration from the New Right. In Britain memories of our winter of discontent, when the economy was blighted with industrial strikes, soaring inflation, falling production and a balance of payments crisis, still haunt the public consciousness. Today's democratic socialists in Britain confront a majority of voters who prefer competitive markets to planned economies. These voters may not want to go all the way with privatization but they have no interest in renationalizing the commanding heights of the economy. Democratic socialists may have rejected the Marxist theory of class struggle but socialism *as a theory* is still committed to the nationalization of the means of production, the redistribution of wealth and income by reference to social rather than economic criteria and therefore the extension of the powers of government. If democratic socialism is to survive as an electoral force, it will have to be radically revised on lines that will make it relevant to the world today and not to some future Golden Age. At the time of writing, it remains to be seen whether or not the British Labour Party moves in this direction of relevance, with regard to modifying or abandoning Clause Four of its Constitution.

Pluralism

We may never reach the 'end of ideology' in political thought but there are ample signs that the two great unitary ideologies that have dominated welfare theory for the past two centuries are at the end of their useful lives. We cannot pursue the philosopher's stone of market individualism without unravelling the delicate strands of interdependency that hold civil societies together. Nor can we give unqualified support to the collectivist ideologies of equality, fraternity and co-operation. If we neglect the imperatives of wealth creation, we will end with equal shares in poverty.

Ideologies, like material goods and services, are subject to a law of diminishing returns. As with material goods, so with the doctrines of individualism and collectivism – and for the same reason – no single political ideology can encompass or reconcile the diversity of human principles and desires that find expression in the institutions of a free society.

Isaiah Berlin put the case for pluralism in social theory and social life with exemplary force in pointing out that the great despotic visions of left and right are based on the belief that there is a fundamental unity underlying all phenomena, deriving from a single universal purpose. All of these visions, whether they are conservative, liberal or socialist, are essentially determinist in character (Berlin, 1980: 150). And I would add that such visions are all infused with intimations of a Golden Age located either in times past or in the future.

The case for welfare pluralism rests on the belief that the quality of life is improved if we encourage choice and diversity in the provision of social services. However, authentic choice in welfare depends on two things, the first being the preservation of the distinctive features of the statutory, voluntary and private sectors of welfare and the second, authentic equality of access to the non-statutory services. This depends on our willingness to guarantee a base-level of effective demand, in other words, the ability to pay for such services. As far as the poorest service users are concerned, effective demand is contingent on the redistribution of income either in the form of direct cash transfers or in the form of indirect statutory payments to the non-statutory agencies. It is through the redistribution of income that the notion of a mixed economy of welfare ceases to be merely a synonym for diversity and becomes a mechanism that gives authenticity and balance to the plurality of choices.

This issue of redistribution continues to separate individuals and collectivists, and the old models of residual and institutional statutory provision have reappeared in the context of welfare pluralism. Indeed some policy makers and analysts regard welfare pluralism as simply a transitional phase in the process of moving towards one or other of these extreme models rather than as a commendable position in its own right.

Yet there is a powerful case to be made for welfare pluralism at both the macro- and micro-levels of policy-making. It is often argued in macro-terms that the social costs of statutory welfare place western democracies at a disadvantage in their competition with free-market rivals like Japan, Taiwan, Singapore, Hong Kong and South Korea, although none of these nations have ever been replicas of western models of capitalism. Japanese levels of social expenditure have been on the increase for the past two decades and there are also indications that, as the other fast-growth economies of the Pacific rim have become more prosperous and more democratic, the popular demand for statutory welfare provision has increased. As William Keegan reminds us, the most successful western economies of the past two decades have built their success on "a policy mix of the invisible hand of the market and the visible hands of public institutions" (Keegan, 1993: 104).

Welfare pluralism is an essential ingredient in this 'policy mix' because it is within the context of a nation's welfare institutions that political, economic and social imperatives come to terms with each other, or else the bonds that hold the nation together in prosperity or adversity will fall apart. Peter Baldwin reaches a similar conclusion in his study of European welfare states. He suggests that 'Social solidarity is justice defined in terms of need' (Baldwin, 1990: 31) and acknowledges that solidarity has less in common with altruism than with 'a generalized and reciprocal self-interest. Not ethics but politics explains it' (Baldwin, 1990: 299). And it is the task of politics to reconcile the egoism of the economic market with the altruism of the social market.

Given the critical nature of this challenge, it is clearly not good enough to leave the meeting of essential needs to the uncertainties of administrative or charitable discretion. A commitment of this magnitude must rest on a concept of citizenship embodying mutually supportive principles of entitlement and obligation.

At the micro-level of everyday life successive public attitude surveys in the United Kingdom confirm that the majority of voters are neither radically individualist nor collectivist in outlook. They accept the need for a degree of redistribution, and are willing to pay more in taxes, if it is the only way to preserve high standards in public services. There is a ground swell of electoral support across all the social classes and political parties for retaining the British welfare state in its present form, including a measure of welfare pluralism. Only a minority of voters are in favour of limiting statutory social services to the poor, or cutting back the non-statutory sector (Pinker, 1992).

The eclecticism of these beliefs owes more to an awareness of financial realities than to welfare theory or political ideology. The present trend towards pluralization and privatization has sharpened people's awareness of the comparative merits of statutory and non-statutory social services. A British married couple with two dependent children on an average income do not have to be professional accountants to work it out that they would be significantly worse off if the welfare state were dismantled, leaving only a few residual services for the poorest minority. The value of this couple's tax rebates would fall far short of the cost of the services that they would then have to buy in the private market.

Our average-income family might be able to maintain their customary standard of living if both parents worked, but a substantial minority of families with below-average incomes would not be able to cover the costs of their basic welfare and educational needs. Helping even a proportion of the latter families through state agencies would correspondingly reduce the scope for tax reductions for average- and above-average-income families. In addition there would still be a number of risks — notably long-term unemployment and chronic sickness and disability — that the private sector would not cover.

At the same time there are many non-statutory services that our average income family is happy to use because they enhance its quality of life. Access to these services would be lost if policies of wholesale collectivization replaced wholesale privatization, as they would be swept away. Only a tenured academic looking forward to an index-linked pension (there are still some such around) could contemplate either of these scenarios with enthusiasm. Only a politician equally divorced from the experiences of everyday life could want to make a reality of them.

Community

One endearing fact about welfare pluralism is that neither intellectuals nor politicians invented it; they only discovered it and, as with the equally elusive concept of 'community', they have struggled ever since to understand and systematize it. Welfare pluralism evolved over time in the multitude of domestic economies that characterize complex industrial societies. Millions of ordinary people learned pragmatically how to reconcile the diversity of their principles, desires and interests. They did so not by espousing the methods of unitary system-builders or rational-choice theorists but by relying on a mixture of reason, sentiment and habit and the lessons of experience. Similarly, in that indefinable context known as 'community', the customary practices of home-making, child-rearing and mutual aid have developed mostly without the benefit of external expert advice or the imperatives of either statutory or market forms of rationality.

Nevertheless this is a time when experts from every field have become increasingly interested in the dynamics of familial and community-based forms of mutual aid. Governments with tight budgets regard the informal sector as the last great Eldorado of unexploited altruism to be quarried and rendered more cost-effective. With this end in mind, the New Right theorists have pinned their hopes on a renewal of family values and informal caring as a path towards expenditure cuts. On the left, radical feminists, grass-roots activists and political correctionists challenge the unjust structures of gender inequalities which they believe to be intrinsic to the modern nuclear family and the networks of community care. Denied much access or influence in political and industrial life, they have turned their attention to the private worlds of reproduction and domestic politics. Excluded from policy-making and political influence, they seek to re-shape our personal domains of thought, speech and informal relationships.

There is always trouble in store for the ordinary run of people when doctrines of moral improvement rise too high on the political agenda. From the individualist point of view, only total exposure to the disciplines of the competitive market will improve people's characters. The collectivist premise is that only the discipline of statutory altruism will have this effect. Each of these prospective Golden Ages has its drawbacks. In the individualist utopia we will quake with anticipatory guilt at the prospect of becoming dependent on anyone other than our kith or kin. In its collectivist counterpart we will be riven with anxiety lest any state of dependency, real or imagined, is left uncovered, undefined or unmet.

In one sense at least, most social scientists are children of the Enlightenment, being educated to believe that, through the exercise of reason and obedience to the moral injunctions of experts, a social solution can be found for every social problem. Yet the evidence suggests that, even in the context of formal welfare policy, the processes of supposedly rational decision-taking are shaped as much by passion and prejudice as by the exercise of reason. Moreover, where formal and informal welfare practices overlap, the interplay of interests and motives becomes even more complicated.

Policies adopted in response to the rising incidence of births outside marriage will illustrate the point that I am making. Deterrent policies are usually based on the assumption that young people's sexual behaviour is a matter of rational choice or that it can be made so. In the United Kingdom unmarried mothers are not given priority on housing lists, as they were until recently, because it was increasingly alleged that some women deliberately became pregnant in order to get to the top of the list. Yet it is quite likely that some young women – especially those least qualified to find jobs at a time of high unemployment – might believe that becoming a mother – even an unmarried one – will bring them more personal fulfilment than any other course of action open to them. The same might also be said of their mothers, who would rather help them to keep their babies than put them out for adoption. Social workers, counsellors and teachers who have direct contact with these matters tend to be more sensitive to the complexity of the motives involved than are policy-makers intent on tightening up the rules of eligibility for income, housing and other social services.

With regard to informal care in the case of elderly relatives, if considerations of rational choice and reciprocity were the primary determinants of the willingness to care, the networks of mutual aid would unravel overnight. And which of us, when our time comes, will lie on our sickbed calculating whether we are ending our days on earth as net givers or receivers of care, and whether we should feel guilty or grateful, short-changed or satisfied? I, for one, do not want to end my days reflecting on some theory of patterned justice. In the dynamics of community care the accounting books of inter-generational exchange are never closed – nor are they ever entirely open to rational analysis. At the heart of every welfare theory is the enigma of why we care for each other at all. What I fear most is that some future Newton or Einstein of the social sciences will solve this riddle and illuminate the last mystery of social policy with the light of reason and rational planning.

Unless we are extremely circumspect, the implementation of policies designed to re-shape the networks of informal care in the images of market efficiency or collectivist bureaucracy or communitarian fraternity will ultimately destroy the unique synthesis of custom and spontaneity that only the gentle currents of cultural change flowing through countless generations can create.

The best relationship between freedom and welfare is found in societies where the institutional fault-lines are just flexible enough to give with the subterranean currents of social change. When tremors strike a pluralist society – as they are bound to do from time to time – some institutional parts may totter and even crumble, but the rest will remain standing. In a unitary society every tremor has the potential impact of an earthquake. Therefore it is essential that the various forms of institutional life making up the components of welfare pluralism should never converge, never unite and never be allowed to achieve any sort of quasi-Hegelian synthesis.

Conclusion

Some of my arguments concerning the limits of rationality as a guide to policy-making, the breakdown of unitary value systems and the deficiencies of large-scale theories of social progress may seem to be post-modernist. I have certainly emphasized the regulatory potential of the welfare bureaucracies of the modern state and I have argued the case for limiting their powers. I also agree with Lyotard and other post-modernists that what they call the *grandes narratives* of theory have failed. Nevertheless I do not deny the need for planning in social policy and I do not accept that, in the absence of some grand, overarching theory of progress, we are left in a state of relativist chaos, deafened by a plurality of competing interest groups (Lyotard, 1984; Walzer, 1983).

I see no reason why the institutions of *Gesellschaft* and *Gemeinschaft* and the traditions of collectivism and individualism should not continue to coexist in democratic societies. It is a precondition of freedom, however, that their coexistence should be marked as much by conflict as by consensus because, if either of these traditions overwhelms the other, democracy will be lost. It is also a precondition of welfare that the distribution of life chances should be regulated by rational–legal and bureaucratic processes because, otherwise, there can be no guarantee that rights and obligations will be honoured. All such arrangements depend on acceptance of an agreed set of values that underpin our notion of citizenship. It is entirely sufficient for most practical purposes if these values derive their legitimacy from the force of custom and convention. In free societies all the great systems of patterned justice based on theories of a social contract or theories of human progress must eventually come to terms with the dictates of custom and 'the devices and desires of our own hearts'. As David Hume observed, 'Custom, then, is the great guide of human life ... that principle, alone which renders our experience useful to us' and teaches us 'how to adjust means to ends' (Hume, [1748] 1955: 58–9).

Nevertheless custom does not provide us with consistent guidance, and experience shows that, in certain aspects of our lives – not least with regard to social policy – there is a place for reason and regulation. It also shows that, in a good society, there are places where government does not intervene. In the words of Michael Oakeshott, 'The silence of the law will brood over large tracts of the subject's life, and where there is silence there is liberty, the liberty of being not subject to unnecessary laws' (Oakeshott, 1946: xliii).

Policies based on so-called laws of history and theories of progress are the ones that do most damage to liberty, welfare and human happiness. They are the schemes and blueprints designed to re-shape and improve the totality of our lives and social activities in the image of some future Golden Age. This is not in any way to argue against change, but to see change as the outcome of chance rather than necessity.

It is hard to think of two great novelists who differ as much in temperament and choice of subject-matter as Leo Tolstoy and George Eliot. Nevertheless they appear to have been in virtual agreement on the merits of unhistorical persons. They were both keenly aware of the fact that most ordinary people wish for nothing more than that history will pass them by, and that they will live out their lives in a decent but comfortable obscurity.

In reflecting on the momentous events of 1812 Tolstoy observed that 'The majority of the people of that time paid no attention to the broad trend of the nation's affairs, and were only influenced by their private concerns. And it was these very people who played the most useful part in the history of the day'. The heroes, the altruists and the 'amateur dialecticians' speculating on the significance of great events proved to be 'the most useless members of society' (Tolstoy, 1957: 1116). George Eliot reflects this sentiment in concluding her domestic chronicle of *Middlemarch*, with the opinion that 'The growing good of the world is partly dependent on unhistoric acts; and that things are not so ill with you and me as they might have been, is half owing to the number who lived faithfully a hidden life, and rest in unvisited tombs' (Eliot, 1959: 364).

In any event we do not have to choose between base and noble metals. Polish hard enough, and, beneath the counterfeit surface of every Golden Age theory, we will find some good family silver in the form of the social institutions that we already possess – which is only to say that, if there is an alchemy that shapes our ends, it works through the changing sentiments of custom in ways that cannot be reduced to a single principle or formula by theoreticians or system-builders.

From gift relationships to quasi-markets: an odyssey along the policy paths of altruism and egoism[*]

Robert Pinker

Introduction

The first issue of *Social Policy & Administration* appeared in 1967 under the title *Social and Economic Administration* – the same year in which the Social Administration Association was established. Richard Titmuss, in company with other leading social policy scholars, was a prime mover in this latter initiative. In the following year, Michael Cooper and A.J. Culyer published their monograph on *The Price of Blood*. Cooper was the first editor of this journal and A.J. Culyer was one of his two assistant editors. In their monograph they reviewed the arguments for and against paying blood donors and developing a role for competitive markets in the sale and purchase of blood products.

They concluded that there was a positive case to be made and that it should be tested further, by setting up an experimental market-based scheme for a trial period. Their monograph was edited by Arthur Seldon and it appeared under the imprint of the Institute of Economic Affairs. The Institute, Arthur Seldon (who was one of its directors) and the monograph were all anathema to Richard Titmuss.

The Institute had been established in 1955 as a policy think tank, specializing in the study of markets and pricing systems. Reappraising the effectiveness of the postwar British welfare state, and the potential role of competitive markets in the provision of social services were both subjects that stood high on the Institute's research agenda.

The Institute was not a conventional 'right wing' think tank. It was as critical of the social policies of the Conservative Party as it was of Harold Wilson's Labour government, which had taken office in 1964 after thirteen years of Conservative rule. Throughout the 1950s and early 1960s the Conservatives had done nothing to challenge the collectivist, universalist and redistributive principles on which the postwar British welfare state was based and to which Titmuss was so passionately committed.

---

[*] Article originally published in (2006) *Social Policy & Administration*, vol 40, no 1, pp 10–25.

In this respect, it is worth noting that, from time to time, Titmuss had served as a policy consultant to Conservative governments, notably with regard to the research he undertook with Brian Abel-Smith into the cost of the National Health Service (Abel-Smith and Titmuss, 1956). The Institute, however, was unequivocally committed to reducing the role of government in the provision of welfare and extending that of the private and voluntary sectors. It is inconceivable that Titmuss would ever have served as a policy consultant to any government that wanted to residualize the statutory social services, as advocated by 'the founders and followers of the Institute of Economic Affairs' (Titmuss, 1974: 31).

By the late 1960s, the Institute had become a prime mover in exposing the failures of the statutory social services, in advocating market-based alternatives, and in placing greater reliance on neo-liberal theories of economic and social policy across the institutional spectrum. What it lacked was any significant constituency of support within the higher echelons of the Conservative Party. To all intents and purposes, the collective consensus about the future of the welfare state seemed to have become a permanent feature of the British political landscape. Few, if any, social policy scholars believed that the policies advocated by the Institute posed a serious threat to the welfare consensus. Titmuss was the exception, and subsequent events proved him right. After Margaret Thatcher became leader of the Conservatives in 1976, 'the tide of influential opinion in the party' was to turn 'sharply against all forms of collectivism and the neo-liberal theories of the "new right" moved into their ascendancy' (Pinker, 2003: 82).

Titmuss published his second collection of essays entitled *Commitment to Welfare* in 1968. The opening essay on 'The Subject of Social Administration' was based on the lecture he had given at the first meeting of the Social Administration Association in the previous year. On the purposes of the new Association, he suggested that 'we are not here to found a branch of the Conservative, Labour or Liberal Parties' or to advance 'any particular political ideology. Our first duty and our last duty is to the truth ... and to expose more clearly the value choices that confront societies in the arena of social welfare' (1968: 14).

Titmuss went on to define the discipline of social administration as 'the study of a range of social needs and functioning, in conditions of scarcity, of human organizations, traditionally called social services or social welfare systems, to meet those needs. This complex area of social life lies outside or on the fringes of the so-called free market, the mechanisms of price and tests of profitability'. It therefore followed that social administration was concerned 'with different types of moral transactions, embodying notions of gift exchange, of reciprocal obligations, which have developed in modern societies in institutional forms to bring about and maintain social and community relations' (1968: 20–1).

The logical relationship between these statements is difficult to unravel. Having distanced both the Association and the discipline from any ideology, and having committed both of them to the pursuit of truth and to the 'exposure of value choices', Titmuss then proceeded to define the study of social needs as an intellectual enterprise that was normatively autonomous and institutionally divorced from the values and activities of competitive markets. It would seem, therefore, that in the making of value choices between public sector and private sector policy options in the meeting of needs, further debate was unnecessary.

In July 1968, Arthur Seldon published a highly critical review of *Commitment to Welfare* in *Social and Economic Administration*. He acknowledged Titmuss as 'the doyen of postwar academic social administrators' and noted, in passing, 'his increasing displeasure with the Institute of Economic Affairs'. He then went on to suggest that Titmuss simply did not understand how markets worked or the indispensable role they played in the efficient allocation of resources, the extension of choice and the enhancement of welfare. In Seldon's view, 'the difficulty of conducting a debate with Professor Titmuss is that he makes his adversary feel not only wrong but also wicked. His Achilles heel is that he knows (or, more accurately, feels) he is right' (Seldon, 1968).

We do not know if Titmuss had read this review before he came to Nottingham to chair the second annual conference of the Association. We do know that, prior to the conference, there had been extensive consultation across the membership as to whether the Association should start its own journal or develop closer links with *Social and Economic Administration*. It was well known at the time that Titmuss wanted the Association to have its own journal, and he made a proposal to that effect at its Annual General Meeting.

In the course of the ensuing discussion, Cooper put forward a counter-proposal: namely, that the membership should adopt *Social and Economic Administration* as their own journal. To that end, his colleagues were willing to change the journal's title, increase the editorial board membership and make any other changes deemed necessary. Bob Leaper also spoke in Cooper's support, arguing that the research output of the discipline was insufficient to provide enough good articles for two journals. The Association voted almost unanimously in favour of setting up its own journal. Two years later the first issue of the *Journal of Social Policy* appeared under the editorship of Garth Plowman and the imprint of Cambridge University Press. Both journals went on to establish themselves as leading publications in the field of social policy with one important difference – unlike *Social and Economic Administration*, the *Journal of Social Policy* enjoyed the benefit of a guaranteed list of subscribers from the Association's members.

The outcome of the vote at the Annual General Meeting might have been different if Titmuss had been in favour of adopting *Social and Economic Administration* as the Association's journal. He was certainly held in great esteem and affection by the membership. It is also possible that the publication of Cooper and Culyer's monograph under the Institute's imprint, and Seldon's highly critical review of *Commitment to Welfare*, led Titmuss to conclude that *Social and Economic Administration* had become too closely associated with the Institute to serve as the academic flagship of the Association.

To the best of my knowledge, there is no evidence to support this interpretation of events. Titmuss felt no animosity towards the journal as such. I still remember how pleased he was when I told him Cooper had offered to publish the plenary paper I gave at the second annual conference. And it should also be noted that the membership of the journal's editorial and advisory boards reflected a wide spectrum of academic and political interests, albeit including some 'liberal' economists with Institute affiliations.

Neither, therefore, is there any evidence to support the view that *Social and Economic Administration* was associated with any particular ideological perspective. The first five issues included articles by Odin Anderson, Bleddyn Davies, David Donnison and Clare Ungerson, Frank Honigsbaum and François Lafitte, all of whom were either friends or colleagues of Titmuss. As for Seldon's critical review, from what I can remember of Titmuss from my time as a former student and research assistant in his department, I suspect that he would have looked on it as a kind of battle honour in the progress of the remorseless campaign he waged against the Institute of Economic Affairs. In my view, Titmuss wanted the Association to have its own journal because he thought it ought to have total control of all editorial and board appointments from the start. His preliminary soundings may also have confirmed that this was what the majority of Association members wanted.

Reappraising *The Gift Relationship*

The Price of Blood has long been out of print but its publication was swiftly followed by Titmuss's rejoinder, *The Gift Relationship*, which subsequently became an established classic in the literature of social policy. It gave rise to a debate which, in its intensity, had as much to do with the drawing as with the donation of blood. The subject of the book is the role of altruism in modern society, taking the example of voluntary blood donorship as one of the ultimate tests of where the 'social' begins and the 'economic' ends in order to demonstrate the potential scope for 'providing and extending opportunities for altruism in opposition to the possessive egoism of the market place' (Titmuss 1970: 13). It is also a passionate indictment of the corrupting influence of competitive markets across the whole field of social policy.

The empirical sections of *The Gift Relationship* consist of a detailed and illuminating survey of blood transfusion services and donors in England and Wales, the USSR, the USA, South Africa, Japan and other countries. From these data, Titmuss constructs an eight-point typology of blood donors, in which he explores the causal relationships between their personal motivations to give and the dominant political and moral values of the societies in which they live.

On the basis of this comparative study, he concludes that blood supply systems based on an altruistic ethic of voluntary donorship are administratively more efficient, clinically safer and morally superior to those based on the egoistic values of competitive markets. From this conclusion, he proceeds to a sweeping moral indictment of all forms of private sector service provision. Market forces coerce the poor, corrupt the rich and exacerbate class conflict. By contrast, collectively provided social services foster the values of altruism, social integration and fellowship.

There are a number of reasons why I found Titmuss's analysis of the moral qualities that underpin exchange relationships deeply unconvincing. In the first instance, as I wrote at the time, he uses the terms 'altruism' and 'egoism' in such a way as to describe a polarity of antipathetic sentiments and motives which, in the real world, are more likely to be interactive and conditional. In their extreme forms, altruism and egoism are marginal phenomena.

As I suggested in *The Idea of Welfare*, 'for the egoist social life is meaningless, and for the altruist it is impossible. The egoist could be likened to a black hole in the social universe, devouring everything which comes within its range, while the altruist may be compared to a brightly burning star, ineffectually striving to illuminate and warm a dark and limitless universe' (1979: 10).

As for the welfare claims of Titmuss's 'universal stranger', I can think of no reason why we should treat them as being self-evidently more morally deserving of our attention than those of our closest relatives and friends. There is no master principle by which the claims of one social group may be measured against the claims of others, once we abandon the crude utilitarian principle of seeking the greatest good for the greatest number. This is not to deny that the claims of Titmuss's universal stranger merit our consideration but only to point out that they are a part of a highly complex network of claims and obligations.

Even if we were to make unconditional altruism the crowning glory of our moral sentiments, it would still be as well to remember that crowns are reserved for special occasions, and that most good deeds are done in the fustian of a more homespun philosophy. Titmuss invests his concepts of the 'unnamed' stranger, the 'universal' stranger and 'stranger' relationships with immense moral significance. Giving to strangers and, in particular, the 'universal' stranger is his ultimate touchstone of altruism and the good society. It is as if the virtue intrinsic to the act of giving grows exponentially as the recipients become more anonymous, more scattered and more distant from the giver. Yet it remains the case that none of the donors interviewed in his survey were 'purely altruistic' in their actions because they were well aware that they might also, at some time, need a blood transfusion and, therefore, stood to benefit from the altruism of 'future unknown strangers' (1970: 238–9).

Secondly, the example of blood donorship fails to bring out the full complexity of the phenomenon of altruism. The fact that blood is a gift which costs the donor nothing is more important than the fact that giving blood can be profitable. A more searching test of the scope and limits of altruism would be the giving of bodily organs, the loss of which will place the donor's life or health in jeopardy. Most adults would unhesitatingly donate a kidney to a needful spouse or child. Nevertheless, such prospective donors would have to consider very carefully the extent to which they are morally justified in placing at risk the future welfare and security of their own families in order to save the life of a total stranger. Blood donorship poses no such dilemma and it is, therefore, by no means self-evident that other kinds of altruistic acts on behalf of strangers are morally superior to altruistic acts on behalf of one's immediate kin.

Thirdly, Titmuss's concepts of altruism and egoism so elevate the institutions of the social market and debase those of the economic market as to give the impression that the main effects of competition and entrepreneurial activity have been the infliction on humanity of diseconomies, diswelfares, social disintegration and alienation. Much of Titmuss's published work can be read as a continuous indictment of the values of private enterprise and the profit motive. It is, therefore, easier for us to form an impression of the kind of economic system which he would have eschewed than the one he would have preferred.

We are left in ignorance about the system of values and means by which wealth is to be created and goods and services are to be produced. Competitive markets are demonstrably more effective in the continuous creation of wealth than any other known system of economic organization. Globalization may well have inflicted 'diseconomies' on the poorest nations of the Third World but these failures are open to remedy. It remains the case that without the wealth-creating capability of competitive markets, the whole structure of international aid, both statutory and voluntary, would swiftly collapse and the needs of countless 'universal strangers' would go unmet (Pinker, 1977: vii–xvi).

Fourthly, we come to the philosophical implications of Titmuss's views on the respective roles of freedom and compulsion in public policy-making. He categorically rejected Cooper and Culyer's modest proposal that, for a limited trial period, the voluntary system of blood donorship should be supplemented by a fee-paid market scheme so that their respective performances could be evaluated. Titmuss dismissed this proposal because its authors were doing nothing less than 'making an economic case *against* a monopoly of altruism in blood and other human tissues. They wish to set people free from the conscience of obligation' (1970: 159).

It is difficult to understand why a social scientist would reject outright a proposal for a limited control study of this kind on moral grounds. Part of the explanation lies in Titmuss's highly determinist account of the interrelationships between types of society, human nature and the respective opportunities for altruism and egoism that these societies provide. Titmuss was convinced that the statutory social services, in general, and the voluntary giving of blood, in particular, fostered social integration and encouraged the growth of altruism more effectively than any other system of welfare provision. Having compared the different blood transfusion services of six very different countries, he concluded that a free service was not only morally superior but administratively and economically more efficient than its private market alternatives. The quality of freely given blood was also safer because it was less likely to carry dangerous infective diseases. The offer of payment attracted donors who tended to be very poor and, therefore, more prone to such diseases. (With the benefit of hindsight, of course, we now know that statutory services relying exclusively on voluntary donors can also inadvertently collect and provide contaminated blood to patients with tragic consequences for them.)

Titmuss, however, was adamantly opposed to the suggestion that patients, as consumers, should have any choice in the matter. In the interests of freedom, altruism and public safety, he thought that the buying and selling of blood should be prohibited by law and that the resolution of this matter 'has to be a policy decision; in other words it is a moral and political decision for society as a whole' (1970: 242). He justifies this conclusion on the grounds that, 'in a positive sense ... policy and processes should enable men to be free to choose to give to unnamed strangers. They should not be coerced or constrained by the market. In the interests of the freedom of all men they should not, however, be free to sell their blood or decide on the specific destination of the gift' (1970: 242).

It would seem, therefore, that Titmuss wanted to prohibit people from making the 'wrong' choices so that they could be 'free' to make the right choices. The alternative was to leave them at the mercy of the 'atomistic private market' which 'freed' men from 'any sense of obligation to or for other men regardless of the consequences to others' (1970: 239). People's opportunities for altruism are ultimately determined by the type of society in which they live. They become more altruistic only in societies where needs are met primarily by reference to the collectivist values of the social market. They inevitably become more egoistic in societies where the individualist values of the economic market prevail.

Rather than leaving people to make their own decisions as to where the path of duty lies, Titmuss wanted to compel them to be moral. He does not seem to recognize that acts of duty are only moral acts if they are voluntarily undertaken. Throughout *The Gift Relationship* he frequently refers to the problem of alienation in capitalist societies. Marx's remedy for this state of mind was the abolition of private property, social classes and the division of labour. Titmuss's remedy appears to be the creation of a unitary welfare state and a drastic reduction in the range of consumer choice in the use of social services. All these considerations led me to the conclusion that the philosophy of *The Gift Relationship* is based on a double oxymoron – namely, that, in policy terms, we are 'free' to choose between compulsory altruism in the social market and compulsory egoism in the economic market.

Reappraising *Social Theory and Social Policy* and *The Idea of Welfare*

In 1973, shortly after Titmuss's death, T.H. Marshall published 'An Appreciation' of his achievements in the *British Journal of Sociology*. He generously acknowledges Titmuss's masterly skills as an assembler and classifier of factual data and his idealistic commitment to social reform. He also suggests that whenever he stepped outside 'the confines of his official subject of social administration into regions where sociologists fear to tread ... a gap appeared between his factual evidence and the conclusions he helped to derive from them, a gap which could not be effectively bridged without the help of a more elaborate conceptual and theoretical apparatus than he had needed hitherto' (1973a: 138–9). On the theory underpinning *The Gift Relationship*, Marshall concludes that 'the facts illuminated an arresting concept, that of the free, altruistic gift to the stranger ... But they were too specialized and a-typical to provide a basis for generalizations about the possible role of altruism as a cohesive force in a whole society. For this one must re-examine the concept of altruism' (1973a: 139).

This was exactly what I set out to do in the 1970s when I wrote *Social Theory and Social Policy* (1971) and *The Idea of Welfare* (1979). It was largely thanks to the encouragement of Marshall that I did so. In *Social Theory and Social Policy*, I set out a model of social welfare as a system of exchange relationships between providers and recipients of social services. Shortly after the book appeared, Marshall advised me to develop my model of exchange relationships in a second book, giving greater attention to the value systems that underpinned them. The moral dynamics of welfare institutions and the respective roles of egoism and altruism became the two main themes of enquiry that I explored in *The Idea of Welfare*.

At the time when I wrote *Social Theory and Social Policy*, I was becoming increasingly disenchanted with Titmuss's unitary model of social welfare or, to use his own terminology, 'the institutional Redistributive model of Social Policy'. In this model, Titmuss conceptualized social welfare 'as a major integrated institution in society, providing universalist services outside the market on the principle of need' (Titmuss, 1974: 31). It is important to note that concepts like 'unitary' and 'pluralist' models of welfare were not generally used by social administrators in the 1970s. In terms of his ideology and interests, however, Titmuss was undoubtedly a unitarist. He wrote very little about the voluntary sector and it is scarcely mentioned in his benchmark essay on 'The Social Division of Welfare'. The occupational and fiscal welfare sectors are subjected to much closer scrutiny, but they are conceptualized in largely negative terms – as institutional obstacles to the creation of a more unified and egalitarian welfare state (Titmuss, 1958b: 34–55).

In *Social Theory and Social Policy*, I paid particular attention to the impact of universalist and selectivist modes of social service on the status of citizenship and the implications for that status of being dependent on different kinds of service provision. On reflection, I think that I ought to have given more prominence to the two main forms of social service organization – unitarism and pluralism – in developing my model of social welfare. If I were to undertake a revision of *Social Theory and Social Policy*, I would reformulate my thesis on the following pluralist lines in order to make their intellectual continuities more explicit.

The problem with the unitary model of social welfare is that it cannot respond with sufficient sensitivity to the diversity of human aspirations and needs and this will be the case, irrespective of whether the sole providers of services are statutory, voluntary or private sector agencies. Most significantly, the risks of total dependency are maximized when there is only one provider of social services and support.

By contrast, a pluralist system of welfare is less likely to generate stigma and undermine the authenticity of citizenship than a unitary system – irrespective of the relationship that holds between universality and selectivity. Not all universalist services enhance the status of citizenship. Not all selectivist services debase it.

Too much universality can leave the residual means-tested minority profoundly stigmatized. Too much selectivity can residualize the welfare state altogether. The ideal compromise is a pluralist model in which the state is both a direct provider and purchaser of non-statutory social services, and selectivity operates within a broadly universalist structure. At times, dependency is an inescapable fact of life but partial dependency is preferable to total dependency. For most people complete independence is an unattainable and unattractive condition. The same may be said of complete dependency.

Good social policies ought, therefore, to be designed to complement and reinforce the qualities of interdependence and reciprocity. These are the ideals by which most people try to order their social relationships. Welfare pluralism optimizes opportunities for interdependence and reduces the risks of total dependency. The greatest risks of stigma arise when the dependency is total and only one set of welfare agencies – public or private, formal or informal – has a monopoly or near-monopoly of service provision. In a pluralist mixed economy of welfare there is a diversity of service providers which greatly reduces the risk of total dependency and, of course, the risk of total system failure.

Given the diversity of human values and aspirations it is, therefore, essential that the component rights and duties that make up the concept of citizenship are grounded in a similar diversity of social institutions and personal experiences and sentiments. Unitary models of welfare, whether they are ideologically driven by individualist market values or collectivist welfare values, ignore this diversity, increase the risks of total dependency and thereby impoverish the status of citizenship.

The theoretical models outlined in *The Idea of Welfare* were developed within this pluralist tradition of social policy analysis. It was my interest in the relationship between modes of service delivery, dependence and the status of citizenship that led me on to explore the moral dynamics of welfare institutions and, more specifically, the respective roles of egoism and altruism in shaping our notions of entitlement and obligation. All of our normative models of welfare ends and means rest on certain assumptions about the moral qualities of human nature. On the basis of the relevant empirical evidence, I rejected those models which drew sharp distinctions between our propensities for egoism and altruism. I argued that if people were predominantly altruistic, compulsory forms of social services would not be necessary. Conversely, if people were exclusively self-regarding, such compulsion would be impossible.

Egoism is often equated with self-interest but it is also associated with the positive qualities of self-help and a willingness to accept restraints on our more selfish dispositions and to show consideration for other people. Familial altruism is the first and most natural way in which we express our concern for other people's welfare.

Familial altruism may be a limited form of altruism, restricted to those we know and love, but it is the mainspring from which all our other moral concerns for other people's welfare flow. As we mature and become citizens of a wider community, our notions of obligation and entitlement also grow more extensive and take on the formal character of social rights and duties. As I extended my institutional field of enquiry in *The Idea of Welfare*, I subsumed the concept of familial altruism under the broader category of conditional altruism (1979: 39).

Once again, this extension in the range of our awareness is driven by a combination of egoistic and altruistic motives. We learn from personal experience that familial altruism alone cannot guarantee our welfare in an uncertain world. We learn that collective forms of social provision – statutory and voluntary – are sensible ways of pooling risks and helping each other in times of need. The compassion we feel for those less fortunate than ourselves is also an important factor but, as I suggested in *Social Theory and Social Policy*, the welfare institutions of a society can best be understood in terms of 'an unstable compromise between compassion and indifference, between altruism and self-interest' (1971: 211).

The continuities of familial altruism both complement and conflict with the formal redistributive ends of statutory social policies. Through acts of voluntary saving, we give substance to the hope of leaving wealth to those we know and love. Through the processes of redistributive taxation, we make provision for the welfare of total strangers who lack the means to help themselves. All governments have to live with the difficult task of striking the right balance between the conflicting claims of familial and collective altruism.

Although conflicts of interest frequently arise between these institutional elements, they are, in the last analysis, dependent upon each other. The welfare of many individuals and families would be jeopardized if statutory social services were to disappear. Conversely, the statutory social services could not compensate or provide adequate substitutes if the structures of familial altruism ceased functioning.

In summary, I rejected the idea of a unitary model of welfare on the grounds that it took insufficient account of the diversity of human preferences and needs and increased rather than reduced the risks of people experiencing conditions of stigmatizing dependency. I also concluded that a model of human motivation based on a sharply drawn distinction between the qualities of egoism and altruism bore little or no relationship to what we know about human nature and the realities of the world in which we live. By contrast, pluralist approaches which conceptualized social policies in terms of a mixed economy of welfare are more likely to generate useful explanatory theories and the provision of better-quality social services.

Appraising *Motivation, Agency and Public Policy*

I now recognize – with the benefit of hindsight – that, in my preoccupation with the issues of citizenship, status, stigma and dependency, I failed to give sufficient attention to those of motivation and agency which Le Grand explores with such insight and authority in *Motivation, Agency and Public Policy* (2003). Had I been familiar with Le Grand's illuminating variations on the game of chess, I would have described users of non-statutory social services as 'queens' endowed with independence and freedom of choice, in contrast with the 'pawns' dependent on the statutory services. 'As we grow up,' I suggested, 'the most authentic rights we acquire and exercise are those we use in the roles of buyers and sellers in the market-place. We do not have to be persuaded that we have rights to what we buy.' By contrast, 'the idea of paying through taxes or holding authentic claims by virtue of citizenship remains largely an intellectual conceit of the social scientist and the socialist ... Consequently most applicants for [statutory] social services remain paupers at heart' (Pinker, 1971: 141–2).

Le Grand convincingly demonstrates how, in the pluralist mixed economy of quasi-markets, the likelihood of more social service users becoming 'queens' rather than 'pawns' (or paupers) can be greatly enhanced. As for the service providers, Titmuss would have categorically rejected his suggestion that public administrators could ever behave like 'knaves', or that private sector managers could ever be motivated by 'knightly' sentiments. Least of all would he have accepted the possibility that by providing the right kinds of incentive at the agency levels of service provision their qualities of altruism and egoism could both be directed towards enhancing public welfare.

Like Titmuss, Le Grand recognizes that the ways in which social policies are designed and implemented have a profound influence on people's disposition to behave altruistically or egoistically in their roles as service providers and users. Unlike Titmuss, he argues that the most effective social policies are those which complement and encourage the positive qualities of both of these moral dispositions. Drawing on a wide range of empirical evidence, he argues that altruism and egoism are not diametrically opposed forms of human motivation and that the values of the social and the economic markets do not have to be in permanent and irreconcilable conflict with each other.

Le Grand starts by exploring the ways in which the growth of quasi-markets has beneficially influenced 'the balance of knightly and knavish behaviour in the individuals affected' (Le Grand 2003: 50). Most public service providers, he argues, derive great personal satisfaction from helping other people. In this respect, they behave like 'act-relevant' knights who are directly involved in helping needful people. At the same time, their motivation to act altruistically 'also seems to depend positively upon *the degree of personal sacrifice associated with the act*' (2003: 51; Le Grand's emphasis).

Le Grand describes personal sacrifice in terms of its 'opportunity cost', that is, 'the cost to the individual concerned of other opportunities for personal benefit that have had to be forgone because he or she has chosen to undertake that act' (2003: 51). If, however, the personal (or opportunity) costs involved are too great or too little, the motivation of the service provider to act altruistically will be weakened.

Intelligently designed incentive structures can, however, be used to achieve more effective 'trade-offs' between the altruistic and egoistic motivations of service providers. Le Grand argues that such outcomes may 'lead to the provision of more public services, which, other things being equal, would be morally desirable' and also less exploitative of the altruism of service providers 'which again would be desirable on moral grounds' (2003: 66). Le Grand's theory of public service motivation rests on the premise that *both* altruism and egoism have positive moral properties, and he goes on to conclude that 'it is impossible to say that, in all circumstances, the morality of altruism should always be in the ascendant over that of positive service outcomes' (2003: 66–7).

We can summarize the essential difference between Le Grand's and Titmuss's approach to this issue in the following terms. Le Grand believes that positive service outcomes are more likely to be optimized when social policies work with the grain of human nature and take account of the duality of our moral sentiments. Titmuss believed that social policies should be directed towards changing human nature and should give unequivocal priority to the moral claims of statutory altruism.

Le Grand's theory of public service motivation is complemented by a second theory about the role of welfare agencies and the status of social service users in the public sector. He describes this approach as a 'theory of pawns and queens' and he starts by asking what 'a successful system for delivering a public service would look like'. His answer is that 'it would be one that treats the users of the service as queens not pawns: that is, it would have user power at its base'. Such a system would have to be able to prevent the over-usage or over-provision of the service concerned, or the 'use of the service in such a way that damages either the user himself or herself or the wider society'. It would have to include appropriate incentives for service providers which took account of both their altruism and egoism. It would also have 'to do all this in as efficient a manner as possible, and in a way that did not violate equity or other social objectives that society might have with respect to the service' (2003: 84).

Le Grand goes on to illustrate the various ways in which some of these objectives have already been partially achieved in the policy fields of health care and education by providing 'robust incentives' to medical and other professional workers, more choice for patients, more autonomy for primary care budget-holders, hospital consultants and headteachers, and more choice and information for the parents of schoolchildren.

Throughout his review of these policy trends, Le Grand contends that we cannot 'rely solely upon purely knightly motivations – upon the public service ethos – to deliver public services to the level of quality and quantity that we require'. What matters most is that 'knavish and knightly incentive structures' should complement each other and 'be aligned in a "robust" fashion'. As for the service users, they are most likely to behave like 'queens' rather than 'pawns' when social services are provided through 'a system of quasi-market competition with independent providers run by public sector professionals and with users or their agents having fixed budgets' (2003: 118).

From this retrospective review, Le Grand proceeds to set out his own policy proposals for further change. His most radical proposal is for the provision of a universal capital grant of £10,000 to all young people on reaching the age of eighteen. Such a scheme would be financed from the proceeds of a reformed inheritance tax. Le Grand describes the scheme as a policy of 'asset-based egalitarianism'. It is asset-based insofar as the capital grants would be invested and managed by public trustees. Withdrawals of cash would be subject to trustees' approval and might be restricted to such purposes as payment of educational fees, down-payments on house purchases, the start-up costs of small businesses or investment in a personal or stakeholder pension. It is egalitarian insofar as the scheme would redistribute from rich to poor and enable more people to become asset-owners in their own right.

Le Grand suggests that such a scheme would have widespread appeal across the political spectrum. From the perspective of the right, it extends the ownership of assets and encourages self-help. From the left, it reduces inequality and increases equality of opportunity and outcome (2003: 124). More than anything else, it gives people more power, more independence and more choice in making their own welfare decisions (2003: 125).

What would Titmuss have made of such a proposal? In terms of its redistributive implications, the whole idea of a universal capital grant can be seen as a revamped version of *The Gift Relationship*, designed to function on a much broader institutional scale than the voluntary giving of blood. Nevertheless, it seems likely that Titmuss would have rejected such a scheme on both political and moral grounds.

On all matters relating to the political ends and means of social policy, as had been noted, Titmuss was an uncompromising unitarist. The idea of a universal capital grant could only be effectively implemented within the pluralist framework of a mixed economy of welfare and quasi-markets providing more scope for competition and consumer choice. On all matters relating to choice in welfare, Titmuss believed that it was more important that people should make the right choice than that they should be free to choose for themselves. Most importantly, he argued, 'for the vast majority of workers covered by ... private schemes, there is no choice' (1968: 144). And he would have found the whole idea of providing opportunities and incentives for *both* altruism and egoism a morally objectionable proposition. For similar reasons, Titmuss would probably have rejected Le Grand's other proposals regarding the hypothecation of health taxes, partnership saving schemes and long-term care provision.

Nevertheless, Le Grand's pluralist model of welfare still leaves a substantial role for the statutory social services. While making provision for the extension of personal choice, it also leaves ample scope for compulsion, notably with regard to people's obligations to plan and pay for their long-term needs. In particular, he accepts that governments and welfare agencies must retain sufficient powers to prevent service users from acting in ways that damage 'either the user himself or herself or the wider society' (2003: 84).

Among the various reasons why people should not be left entirely free to choose for themselves, Le Grand cites those cases in which individuals lack the willpower to make the right choices. They include people who damage their own health through overeating, smoking and other forms of self-damaging personal behaviour. In these respects, it is worth noting that governments are becoming increasingly active in seeking to change people's personal behaviour by exhortation, education and regulating what they may or may not do in public places. In these respects, private insurance companies are able to be more actively interventionist and regulatory than governments. Their policies include both incentives to adopt healthy styles of living and penalties for not doing so. So far, governments have not found it possible to adopt similar policies without infringing more general social and political rights to welfare. They cannot exclude or penalize people who make themselves 'bad risks' because of their self-indulgent lifestyles.

Conclusion

The Gift Relationship and *Motivation, Agency and Public Policy* are both benchmark texts in the literature of social policy. *Social Theory and Social Policy* and *The Idea of Welfare* are both out of print, although *Social Theory* is still cited as a 'key text' in Blackwells *Student's Companion to Social Policy* (Alcock et al, 2003: 468). Taken all together these publications illustrate the ways in which the normative debate about the ends and means of social policy has changed, as has its entire institutional framework. Titmuss's approach is charged throughout with the intensity of his moral commitment to a vision of collectivist social progress. As I wrote nearly two decades ago, it is really a book about the possibility for human redemption and its message, like that of John Bunyan's *Pilgrim's Progress*, is advanced in the form of an allegory.

Apart from both being Bedfordshire men, Bunyan and Titmuss shared the same unmistakably English quality of moral earnestness in the pursuit of self-improvement. Bunyan was driven by religious and Titmuss by secular convictions, but both were sustained by a distinctive vision of salvation. Bunyan's pilgrim, Christian, confronts the 'foul fiend, Apollyon' and scorns the material temptations of Vanity Fair (Bunyan, 1965: 90, 124). Titmuss confronts the menace of predatory competitive markets and exposes the falsity of the promises that they can deliver greater freedom of choice. Christian sets out for a heavenly Celestial City. Titmuss tells us what kind of social institutions we must establish in order to build a more just and compassionate society here on earth. And it is this visionary quality that explains why *The Gift Relationship* is still read while better works of scholarship have slipped into obscurity (Pinker, 1987: 60).

Both *Social Theory and Social Policy* and *The Idea of Welfare* were written largely as critiques of Titmuss's analysis of the moral dynamics of welfare institutions, the uncompromising distinction he drew between egoism and altruism, and the unitary model of social policy on which his analysis was based. I thought that his ideal of social welfare as 'a major integrated institution' – were it ever to be realized – would impose nothing less than an intellectual and normative straitjacket on the diversity of policy ends and means that ought to characterize a free society. I preferred the idea of a pluralist mixed economy of welfare which took more account of the realities of human nature and gave more opportunities for us all to pursue what *The Book of Common Prayer* describes as 'the devices and desires of our own hearts'. Titmuss, in his preoccupation with 'opportunities for altruism', would undoubtedly have endorsed the whole of this quotation, which penitentially confesses that 'we have followed too much the devices and desires of our own hearts'.

Like *The Gift Relationship*, *Motivation, Agency and Public Policy* also conveys its message in the form of an allegory, but its similes are drawn from the chessboard where games are won, not by passionate commitment, but by the cunning of reason and the insights of imaginative calculation about other people's intentions. Nevertheless, Le Grand does succeed in demonstrating that 'market systems can encourage mutuality of respect and indeed even other virtues such as equity or altruism'. At the same time, the fact that public service providers are often driven by altruistic motives 'does not necessarily imply a respect' for the people whom they are serving. Some providers will always feel they are 'in a superior position to the beneficiary' and 'feelings of superiority are difficult to reconcile with mutuality of respect' (2003: 166–7). As Le Grand concludes, 'it is not necessary to turn knights into knaves for pawns to become queens. What is needed is well-designed public policies, ones that employ market-type mechanisms but that do not allow unfettered self-interest to dominate altruistic motivations' (2003: 168).

Reading these texts, separated as they are by forty years of continuous policy changes, we are left with a choice between two very different normative models of welfare, service providers and service users. We can opt for Titmuss's dichotomous and confrontational model of chivalrous public sector knights and self-interested private sector knaves. Alternatively, we can settle for Le Grand's more equivocal portrayal of knightly knaves and knavish knights whose motivations are as complex as those of the people they serve and as diverse as the pluralist economies of welfare in which they work.

I agree with Le Grand's conclusion that, in the real world, it is preferable that the relationship between knights and knaves should be symbiotic rather than confrontational. They need each other in the same way that those two great archetypal figures of chivalric romance, Don Quixote and Sancho Panza, needed each other. At one level, Cervantes often seems to be juxtaposing the visionary idealism of the knightly Don Quixote and the pragmatic realism of his squire, the knavish Sancho Panza. But as the story unfolds, it becomes clear that these companions survive the vicissitudes of their perilous expeditions because, in their differences, they complement each other so perfectly. And that, in essence, is what Le Grand seems to be telling us about the conjunction of moral attributes that are most likely to bring success in the more prosaic enterprises of social policy.

ELEVEN

The experience of citizenship: a generational perspective[*]

Robert Pinker

Introduction

All the preceding contributors to this distinguished series of memorial lectures bear witness to the enduring significance of Marshall's intellectual legacy. Some of them have drawn attention to aspects of citizenship which, in their opinion, Marshall overlooked or neglected. Others have explored issues that have only come to the forefront of academic and political debate since his death. These oversights and later developments are cogently reviewed in Anthony Rees's introductory essay to *Citizenship Today* and in the concluding essay that he wrote with Martin Bulmer (Bulmer and Rees, 1996: 1–23 and 269–83).

In choosing my subject for this lecture I decided to discuss Marshall's concept of citizenship from a generational perspective as it might be viewed from different vantage points in the life cycle. I chose this approach because I have long been of the opinion that there is a largely unexplored and potentially useful dimension to Marshall's model relating to the informal and subjective experience of citizenship at the level of everyday life.

In his account of the growth of citizenship and its component parts, Marshall focuses on changes that occurred at the level of formal institutions and across a broad continuum of historical development spanning three centuries. The tenor, style and content of his synthesis bears the qualities of a patrician detachment. Rees and Bulmer are, surely, correct when they describe Marshall's model of citizenship as a kind of Weberian 'ideal type', the purpose of which is to develop a 'one-sided accentuation of reality in order to understand at an abstract level what are the properties of a class of events or processes and their workings' (Bulmer and Rees, 1996: 270).

In this lecture, however, I want to bring out another aspect of Marshall's 'ideal type' of citizenship that he never developed but which, I believe, is immanent in all his work. I will start with the premise that Marshall's models of citizenship and, for that matter, 'democratic welfare capitalism', are much less one-sided

---

[*] Based on T.H. Marshall Memorial Lecture delivered at the University of Southampton on 30 April 1996, not previously published.

'ideal types' than the more extreme individualist and collectivist welfare models on offer. In particular, his account of the relationship between citizenship and welfare expresses a range of beliefs and values that are shared by a very wide constituency of ordinary people. Marshall charts the development of these beliefs about political, civil and social rights in historical and formal terms. Ordinary people are more likely to develop their beliefs about citizenship within the terms of their subjective experiences over the course of their everyday lives. They do so, not in the seven-league boots of history but shod in the sandals, shoes and slippers of their own autobiographies and the limited compass of their generational relationships.

In brief, I want to add a populist theme to Marshall's patrician view of the growth of citizenship which makes more explicit the interactive processes that link the formal and the informal dimensions of welfare and the objective and subjective ways in which we conceptualize policy change. In this approach we may deepen our understanding of how these changes come about. As Rudolf Klein and Jane Miller observe – 'understanding how people make their welfare choices requires analysis of the interactions between the beliefs and attitudes of people and the structures of the systems which they face'. And they go on to point out that, 'These interactions are not simply one-way. Just as the structure of welfare provisions help create the context in which people behave, so their behaviour and their attitudes help create the context for what is possible in policy' (Klein and Miller, 1995: 311).

Marshall on citizenship

Marshall's theories of citizenship and welfare occupy the middle ground between the more extreme versions of individualist and collectivist theory. He locates the origins of the civil rights of citizenship in the eighteenth century when the 'rights necessary for individual freedom – liberty of the person, freedom of speech, thought and faith, the right to own property and to conclude valid contracts, and the right to justice' – became established institutional features of British society (Marshall and Bottomore, 1992: 8.) He defines the political element of citizenship as 'the right to participate in the exercise of power' either as a representative or voter and he traces the extension of these rights for the adult male population through the passage of the nineteenth century and beyond. He describes the social element as comprising 'the whole range from the right to a modicum of economic welfare and security to the rights to share to the full in the social heritage and to live the life of a civilised being according to the standards prevailing in the society'. Marshall equates the extension of these social rights with the rise of the modern welfare state which he sees as a largely twentieth-century phenomenon (Marshall and Bottomore, 1992: 8-10).

Within this analytical framework, 'Citizenship is a status bestowed on those who are full members of a community. All who become members are equal with respect to the rights and duties with which the status is endowed' (Marshall and

Bottomore, 1992: 18). He describes civil and political rights as preconditions of the extension of social rights, which, once universalized, ensure that such extension will take place. He thus presents us with 'a conflict of principles' which are intrinsic to the institutional character of 'democratic-welfare-capitalism'. In this kind of society the rights of citizenship – and, more specifically, the social rights of citizenship – inhibit the inegalitarian tendencies of the free economic market, but the market and some degree of economic inequality remain functionally necessary to the production of wealth and the preservation of both civil and political rights (discussed further in **Chapter Twelve** of this book).

Marshall's conceptualisation of citizenship describes a set of institutional arrangements, or contradictions, that stand between the extremes of individualism and collectivism. His approach, as Rees observes, 'is humanitarian, mildly ironic, favouring liberal consensus and the middle way'. Yet his position in the political spectrum between left and right is sufficiently right-wing for some moderate individualists and liberals to claim him as a Whig and sufficiently left-wing for some moderate collectivists to claim him as a socialist (Bulmer and Rees, 1996: 21–2).

No such temporising is allowed at the two extremes of the political and ideological continuum because radical collectivists and individualists disagree fundamentally over the extent to which statutory social services should function as agents of redistribution from richer to poorer citizens. Collectivists favour compulsion through statutory welfare in order to give the poor a wider and more authentic range of social rights which they also see as preconditions for the enjoyment of political and civil rights. Individualists argue that the extension of statutory controls over what people earn with the aim of enhancing social rights results in the diminution of everybody's political and civil rights. They dismiss the claim that guaranteeing basic social rights helps the poor to become more independent and more able to look after themselves. Individualists argue to the contrary, that more state welfare and more social rights demoralise the poor and create a culture of dependency. This is why Hayek, for example, rejects all adjectival definition of justice, liberty and rights. These principles are unequivocally and simply legal and civil in character and meaning (Hayek, 1982: 62–100).

Oakeshott on the state

The whole analytical and normative tenor of Marshall's approach to the relationship between state and civil society and the independent nature of human rights is antipathetic to Hayek's uncompromising liberal individualism. The extent to which his approach is unequivocally collectivist shows more clearly when we compare his views on the growth of statutory powers and the extension of social rights with those of Michael Oakeshott, another philosopher, sometimes described as a liberal, sometimes as a conservative, but never, to my knowledge, as a collectivist. Neither Parry nor Rees persuade me that Marshall and Oakeshott were 'perhaps ... fellow liberals under the skin, of a sceptical, patrician kind' (Bulmer and Rees, 1996: 23; see also Parry, 1991).

Oakeshott starts with the proposition that 'hidden in human character, there are two powerful and contrary dispositions, neither strong enough to defeat or put to flight the other'. The first of these, he goes on to suggest, is a disposition to be 'self-employed' and the second is a disposition to 'identify oneself as a partner with others in a common enterprise and as a sharer in a common stock of resources and a common stock of talents with which to exploit it. The enterprise may be described in various terms: the search for Truth, the pursuit of the Common Good .... it is a cooperative undertaking ... in terms of managerial decisions about performances; and there is a notional "one best way" of conducting it' (Oakeshott, 1975: 323–4).

Oakeshott leads us on to a choice between an individualist or residual model of social policy and its collectivist or institutional alternative. But for Oakeshott these alternatives are embedded in two fundamentally different kinds of society. The residualist model is associated with the idea of a minimal state (or societas) as a civil association based solely on a system of rules, or covenant, under which citizens go about their own business while recognising a common authority. In this kind of state there is no place for economic or social policies concerned with the ends of distributive justice and the satisfaction of substantive wants because the state has nothing to distribute.

This notion of the state, Oakeshott suggests, has been steadily eroded by 'progressive beliefs that the powers of government ought to be extended and used to achieve various collective ends'. He attributes the genesis of these ideas to the 'audacious imagination of Francis Bacon' and the subsequent growth in influence of the rationalist theories of social progress that characterised Enlightenment thought (Oakeshott, 1975: 287).

Explicitly collectivist and proto-socialist ideologies also contributed to the transformation of the state as a civil association into the state as an enterprise association. This new version of the state pursues general objectives like the 'common good' and educating its citizens in the ways of virtuous and enlightened conduct. Increasingly driven by the imperatives of rationality and productivity, the state inevitably assumes special responsibilities for the problem of poverty. The poor are redefined as a 'wantonly wasted asset' – subjects in need of moral regeneration. Oakeshott, 1975: 304). They become a reproach to themselves and to the principles of enlightened estate management.

Even in the heyday of competitive market capitalism the administrative responsibilities of the state had to expand to keep pace with these new responsibilities. Under the combined influences of classical political economy and utilitarianism, the traditional forms of poor relief were transformed into more rational systems of deterrent support and 'scientific' charity that made political disenfranchisement a condition of assistance. Under collectivist and socialist regimes, the social rights of the poor were extended and their status as independent citizens diminished.

Oakeshott offers a less than complementary definition of the outcome of this process – the modem welfare state. It is, he says, a state to be understood as 'an association of invalids, all victims of the same disease ... and the office of government as ... the directors of sanitoria from which no patient may discharge himself by a choice of his own' (Oakeshott, 1975: 308).

The state as an enterprise association does not restrict its concerns to matters of formal policy. The aims of collective welfare and the common good acknowledge no such boundaries and to these ends the modern welfare state becomes the major agency in 'the quest for community' and in strengthening the bonds of 'social solidarity'. The informal private lives of citizens also become legitimate concerns of government. As Oakeshott remarks, 'every prospectus for a state as association in pursuit of a common purpose has recognised the importance of such an apparatus: Utopia has no lawyers but it bristles with inspectors and overseers' (Oakeshott, 1975: 321 and 268).

In Oakeshott's preferred model of the state as a civil association, statutory welfare and social rights have no more than a residual role to play and 'the silence of the law will brood over large tracts of the subjects' life; and wherever there is silence there is liberty, the liberty of being not subject to unnecessary laws' (Oakeshott, 1946: xliii).

By contrast, under the government of the state as an enterprise association those 'large tracts of the subject's life over which the law broods in silence' are reduced to small allotments.

Oakeshott's views on the growth of citizenship are manifestly antipathetic to those of Marshall and most other social policy theorists. His description of civil society as 'a negative gift, merely making not impossible that which is desirable' would scarcely serve as a clarion call to collectivists, communitarians and other advocates of social rights (Oakeshott, 1946: lxvi).

Weber on rationality

Nevertheless, Marshall and Oakeshott share one common disposition – they both tend to exaggerate the extent to which the imperatives of rationality and purposive social planning have transformed the economic and social institutions of Western capitalism. In this respect, they have something in common with Max Weber. Here, however, the similarities end. Marshall viewed the whole process with relative equanimity. Oakeshott viewed it with distaste and, true to form, Weber equivocated between regret and resignation. Rationalisation, for him, was the inescapable concomitant of economic and social progress. It became one of the key ideal types that he developed in order to make explicit what he thought was one of the most important forms of meaningful social action in the new world of industrial capitalism.

Rational social action was, for Weber, action in which the choice of both ends and means is made with one overriding consideration in mind – the maximization of efficiency. He thought that 'The fate of our times is characterised by rationalisation and intellectualisation and, above all, by the "disenchantment of the world". Precisely the ultimate and most sublime values have retreated from public life ... into the brotherliness of direct and personal relationships'(Gerth and Mills, 1961: 155).

Weber, however, draws an important distinction between what he calls 'formal' and 'substantive' rationality. By formal rationality he means the rational pursuit of profit in freely competitive markets, where needs are met through the mechanisms of effective demand and supply. At the same time he also notes that there are other social needs which cannot be met in this way. In these instances appeal must be made to standards of what he calls substantive rationality (Weber, 1964: 184–6).

Weber recognised that a case could be made in favour of a 'planned economy' on grounds of substantive rationality. Planning of any kind, however, meant that new forms of bureaucratic administration would have to develop in the pursuit of optimal efficiency in the conduct of government. Taken together, the systematic pursuit of profit in competitive economic life and the systematic pursuit of bureaucratic efficiency in an expanding public sector would lead to greater prosperity but also a more secularised and disenchanted society. The traditional loyalties and values of the family, religion and local communities would, in time, lose their pre-eminence as the arbiters and transmitters of culture (Weber, 1964: 213).

Weber predicted, that the satisfaction of wants through a planned economy would undermine the work ethic and the incentive to labour. (Weber, 1964: 214). Planned economies are more dependent on altruism than on appeals to self-interest. In this respect 'substantive and formal rationality are inevitably largely opposed. This fundamental and ... unavoidable element of irrationality in economic systems is one of the most important sources of all the problems of social policy, above all, the problem of socialism'. Weber, in essence, anticipates with apprehension the same contradictions of democratic welfare-capitalism that Marshall accepts with equanimity (Weber, 1964: 215).

Rationality and sentiment

Developmental models of citizenship and welfare that over emphasise the formal dimensions of social change also tend to exaggerate the role of economic and substantive rationality in our daily lives. When the concept of citizenship is too formally defined it encompasses a world of strangers but excludes the more bounded habitations of kith and kin.

In formal terms the association of goods and services in competitive economic markets is determined by the rational and efficient pursuit of profit and the criteria of merit or desert. All of these activities are closely associated with the values of self help and independence. Marshall had this connection in mind when he linked the acquisition and extension of civil rights with the rise of competitive market economies under early capitalism. 'Civil rights', he observed, 'were indispensable to a competitive market economy. They gave to each man, as part of his individual status, the power to engage as an independent unit in the economic struggle, and made it possible to deny to him social protection on the ground that he was equipped with the means to protect himself' (Marshall and Bottomore, 1992: 20-1).

Yet the rational pursuit of profit and economic independence is manifestly not an end in itself for the great majority of the working population. On the contrary, it can be argued that most people work and save as hard as they do for the sake of their families and, in particular, their children. They are motivated for the greater part, not by economic rationality for its own sake but by the loyalties and sentiments of familial and generational altruism. The formal world of economic activity is complemented by another informal world in which sentiment rather than rationality is the dominant motive.

In formal terms the allocation of goods and services in statutory welfare systems is determined by reference to various patterned models of social justice and notions of equity which emphasise the criterion of need rather than desert. As Marshall put it, the subsequent incorporation of rights to social protection into the status of citizenship created 'a universal right to real income which is not proportionate to the market value of the claimant' (Marshall and Bottomore, 1992: 28). These social rights, however, could only be extended by reducing the autonomy of some civil rights, or at least, their economic element.

But, again, the dynamics of formal social policy and planning cannot be explained exclusively by reference to the imperatives of substantive rationality. In the context of social welfare, the bounded principle of Pareto optimality, which is so central to the economic element of civil rights, gives way to a collectively driven notion of opportunity costs and a potentially open–ended extension of social rights.

It is difficult enough to define the boundaries of familial altruism, given the informal and subjective criteria by which we define our kith and kin. It is even harder to answer the question 'Who is my neighbour?' within the wider contexts of citizenship and community. In this broader world of extra–familial altruism the scope of legitimated obligations and entitlements can be extended to whoever has paid their taxes and welfare contributions, whoever is a member of the same society and even to Richard Titmuss's ideal type of 'universal stranger'. Indeed, there are currently a large number of academic papers commending the internationalisation of social rights, at least with regard to Europe.

There is also a third world of extra–familial altruism that overlaps and interacts with the others. I refer, of course, to the formal voluntary sector and the various kinds of informal volunteer service. Although formal voluntary agencies are increasingly run on rational management principles and increasingly dependent on statutory funding much of their revenue still comes from the wellsprings of charitable sentiment.

Individualists and collectivists agree on the value and importance of the voluntary sector. They disagree on what should be its future role. Some individualists would like to reduce the roles of the statutory sector as both funders and providers of social services and place greater reliance on charitable provision. One of the main collectivist objections to such proposals is that they would, if implemented, reduce the social rights of citizens to welfare and increase their dependence on the sentiments of charitable discretion.

Civil rights and social rights

In summary, we can see that the pursuit of welfare takes many forms and is driven as much by sentiment as rationality. There is a natural continuum between the work we do in the economic market and our worlds of familial altruism. Along this continuum the determinants of well-being are economic – employment and income, job security and occupational welfare. They come within Marshall's definition of civil rights and Oakeshott's definition of society as a civil association.

In the context of the statutory social services we find a mixture of principles and practices defining the boundaries of obligation and entitlement. The insurance principle combines elements of economic and substantive rationality but the principle of redistribution extends the boundaries of entitlement into a different sphere of collectivist altruism. The services provided come within Marshall's definition of social rights and Oakeshott's definition of society as an enterprise association. And then there is the voluntary sector that is characterised by a distinctive combination of formal and informal, and rational and altruistic, qualities.

When we take all of these institutional features into account, we can see that the worlds of citizenship and welfare are far from being coterminous. The boundaries of citizenship are drawn in terms of the coverage and content of formal rights grounded in either the principles of economic or substantive rationality. Beyond these boundaries the allocation of welfare goods and services is determined more by the dictates of sentiment than reason. It is more accurate to talk in the language of felt obligations than of civil or social rights.

There is, however, a degree of functional overlap and interdependence between Marshall's definitions of civil and social rights. Job security and social security are interdependent statuses linking the worlds of work and welfare. Trends in labour market deregulation and unemployment levels affect the aggregate demand for social security.

When we take a generational perspective we can see how conflicts arise between the claims on limited resources from these different welfare sectors both here and now and over time. The cross-generational transfer of wealth and income takes place through the institutions of familial altruism and the extra-familial altruism of statutory welfare. Insofar as families have only one source of wealth, as do nations in aggregate, conflicts are bound to arise between the claims of these two kinds of altruism. Whatever is taken from families by redistributive taxation in the enhancement of social rights leaves less for family members to distribute at their own discretion within the domain of their civil rights. Raising taxes extends the scope of our social rights and reduces those of our civil rights. Cutting taxes has the opposite effect. The nature of the balance of the 'mix' determines which of our needs have to be met from our own efforts, from family members and from statutory and voluntary welfare provision.

Towards a generational perspective

At a time when all public institutions, including the social services, are subject to continuous audit by experts of one kind or another, it is easy to overlook the fact that, in an autobiographical sense, we are also auditors of the impact of social and policy change on our own lives.

When we undertake these audits we reflect on our past experience, make judgements about our present circumstances and speculate on what the future might hold for us. The older we are, the more the nature of our past experience will influence our future hopes and expectations. The younger we are, the less we have on which to reflect. The older we are, the less we have to anticipate. As Francis Bacon once observed, hope is a good breakfast in our youth but a poor supper in old age. Nevertheless, if we have children or younger kin, our hopes for the future can still run beyond the limits of our own mortality. In reflecting on these generational continuities, Edmund Burke once described society as 'a partnership not only between those who are living, but between those who are living, those who are dead, and those who are to be born' (Burke, 1982: 194–5).

Burke did not see this partnership in terms of the big battalions and grand alliances of policy making. Although he accepted that there was a role for government and for the exercise of reason in public affairs, he believed, however, that for the greater and better part, men were motivated not by reason, but by sentiment and attachment to the established conventions of society. He also described the sentiments which create the moral framework of a nation in developmental terms: 'to be attached to the sub-division, to love the little platoon we belong to in society, is the first principle (the germ, as it were) of public affections. It is the first link in the series by which we proceed towards a love of our country and to mankind' (Burke, 1982: 135).

There are echoes in this passage of Burke of Marshall's developmental model of the growth of citizenship although Burke rejected the idea that society was based on either the abstract natural rights of individuals or notional and hypothetical social contracts. Although he acknowledges the existence of 'ancient rights' he measures the quality of social progress in terms of the development of precedent and custom, not of political, civil and social rights in the abstract.

The range of our expectations extends beyond our personal interests to encompass the obligations of familial altruism and beyond. It is not only wealth that trickles down from one generation to the next, but the continuity of our affections and concerns. These continuities both complement and conflict with the distributive concerns of collectivist social policies. In a pluralist society there are many different ways by which we give substance to the hope that the ruins of our own mortality will build mansions in perpetuity for our children and grandchildren.

In recent years the structure of family life has been changing in several significant ways. The increasing incidence of family breakdown and family reconstitution and in the number of one-parent families is certain to have profound implications for these patterns of inheritance and transfer. We can only speculate on what their impact will be. The networks of felt obligation and entitlement are likely to become more complex and characterised as much by animosity as affection. And some are bound to find that there is little or nothing to transfer or inherit. The imperatives of sentiment can play just as much havoc with our future expectations as the dictates of rationality in social welfare.

There seems to me to be a number of compelling reasons for giving more attention to the generational dimensions of citizenship. The formal symmetry of historical accounts tells us what policy analysis and other scholars think were the determinants of change in the development of citizenship. The informal symmetries of autobiographical accounts tell us what ordinary people think these determinants were at an experiential and subjective level.

This is not to equate a generational approach with those tasks of disaggregation so beloved by post-modernists. There is little or nothing to be gained by reducing Marshall's structured synthesis to an anarchic babble of competing discourses. The two enterprises are best seen as complementary to each other. In any event, as Marshall himself has suggested, both the formal and the informal dimensions of social life are highly structured. These structures, or institutions, possess both objective and subjective qualities which are shaped as much by the imperatives of human sentiment as that of rationality. Similarly, history imposes its own structures on biography insofar as people of the same age living in the same place experience similar historical events subject to the variables of class, gender and race.

Our necessarily brief descriptions will serve to illustrate the diversities of experience implicit in the concept of citizenship at a subjective level. For a ninety-year-old living today in 1996, their recollections of the impact of social policy change go back to the First World War. The welfare services they used as children were established before 1914, and in early adulthood they would have lived through the beginnings of contributory pension schemes for widows, orphans and the elderly. Between the wars, they would have escaped or suffered periods of unemployment, being on poor relief, public assistance or the dole.

The Beveridge Report and the creation of the post-war welfare state would have fundamentally changed their future expectations in middle age, and the last two decades of their working lives would have coincided with the years of full-employment, a regulated labour market, stagflation and widespread consensus about the future of the welfare state. On retirement at 60 or 65 they would have missed the benefit of SERPS [the State Earnings Related Pension Scheme] and, in default of an occupational pension, become dependent on social security, their personal savings and the equity of their home if they owned one.

By their mid-eighties they would have been catapulted into a new world of welfare pluralism in which they faced the prospect of having to exchange some of their housing equity for domiciliary or residential care. In summary our ninety-year-olds would have lived through the transition from a minimal social service state to a unitary welfare state and onwards into a further period of radical policy change. Whether or not they saw themselves as net beneficiaries or losers at the end of their lives, and the extent to which they were left in a position to pass on any wealth to their children and grandchildren would depend on such variables as their past patterns and levels of earning and spending. We would also have to take into account their gender, their race and, most unpredictable of all, the nature and constancy of their political convictions. And in Marshallian terms, much would depend on the relative importance they attached to the changes in the scope of their civil and social rights. In this respect whether or not they had anything to leave to their children would depend greatly on what they had left from their housing equity after paying for their own terminal care.

If we compare the life experiences of a sixty-year-old, a forty-year-old and a twenty-year-old with those of our own ninety-year-old, the most important variations would relate to the differences in the relative significance of their past experiences and future expectations and the nature of the policy events through which they had lived.

Linking the formal and the informal

Is it possible to incorporate these informal generational and autobiographical variables into a formal model of citizenship without losing the clarity in the detail? In my view we are more likely to succeed in such a task when the coverage of the model in question is national rather than international and its normative content has some manifest affinities with the dominant welfare beliefs and practices of that nation. Marshall's concept of citizenship meets both of these conditions. It has, indeed, been widely criticised for its intrinsic Englishness on the grounds that its ethnocentral qualities make it 'misleading' when it is 'applied to other countries' (Bulmer and Rees, 1996: 14).

Marshall, of course, never claimed that his model could be universalised. On the contrary, he disclaimed any such ambitions in his inaugural lecture, 'Sociology at the Crossroads', which he delivered in 1946. In this essay he argued that sociology, at that time, was faced with a choice of paths. One path led towards the search for universal laws and ultimate values. 'We might call it', he suggested, 'the way to the stars and, although few at any time can profitably follow it, it should never be barred'. The other path, he thought, might be called 'the way into the sands'. It leads to the expenditure of great energy 'on the collection of a multitude of facts with sometimes an inadequate sense of the purpose for which they are being collected' (Marshall, 1963: 13, 15; 1981: 3).

Marshall, rejected both of these paths, choosing what he calls 'a middle way which runs over firm ground'. 'It leads', he says, 'into a country whose features are neither Gargantuan nor Lilliputian, where sociology can choose units of study of a manageable size – not society, progress, morals and Civilisation, but specific social structures in which the basic processes and functions have determined meanings' (Marshall, 1963: 21-2). And he went on to include the informal dimensions of social life in presenting his case for setting limits to the boundaries of sociological theorising. He recognised that there were many aspects of society that, on the surface, did not seem to be systemic where we exercise free choice in our personal behaviour and in our relations with other people. Nevertheless, closer investigation would show that these reciprocal activities were also governed by rules and normative expectations insofar as they make orderly and purposive behaviour possible in social life and ensure a measure of continuity of action and identity during social change.

At these informal levels of social life the plans we make for the future are shaped by the values and meanings we have developed on the basis of our past and present experience. What we expect from our own efforts, from our family members and friends, and from the provisions of social policy are salient elements in these plans. They are not greatly informed by theory. They are profoundly influenced by practical experience. Consequently, the more general and comparative our approach, the more difficult it becomes to take these informal dimensions into account. Welfare theorists who seek the comparative 'way to the stars' will never escape into the firmament of cold abstractions while they are weighed down by the multitudinous sands of autobiographical and cultural detail.

This is exactly what happens in much of what passes for comparative welfare theorising. As the details of the really interesting cultural and subjective variables are jettisoned, the models become so abstract and formal that they amount to little more than collections of institutional platitudes. Any reasonably competent social scientist should be able to produce up to ten different models of 'welfare state regimes' in as many minutes. Unfortunately, they do.

The really challenging and difficult task is not to identify the similarities in different welfare states, but to explore the nature and causes of their dissimilarities. And this is a task that requires analysis of their informal as well as their formal properties. Marshall's model of citizenship is sufficiently ethnocentric to accommodate such an approach.

Too much history is just as self-defeating an approach as too much comparison. The more we reach back into the past, the more likely we are to encounter the methodological problems identified by John Goldthorpe in his earlier Marshall lecture on 'The Uses of History in Sociology' (Bulmer and Rees, 1996: 101–24). The problem, as he puts it, is that 'the relics of history are finite and incomplete'. The sociological way to the stars can therefore be seen to offer a choice of two trajectories – upwards and outwards into a boundless comparative firmament. Fortunately there is a more modest middle way by which we can link the present to the recent and still living past through what I have called a generational approach that draws on the spoken and written evidence of autobiographical experience.

The methods of oral history alone will not suffice in this undertaking because the evidence collected needs to inform our social theories and concepts of the middle range. Again, it can be argued that Marshall's models of citizenship, welfare, and social change are normatively better suited to this task than the more extreme, competing and divergent models of individualism and collectivism. These models tells us more about the beliefs and values of academics and politicians than those of ordinary citizens.

Marshall's models, by contrast, have fairly close affinities with the mixed economies of welfare that are typical of many Western industrial societies and especially the United Kingdom. The affinities between the ideological tenets of neo–liberalism and dirigiste social planning and the welfare beliefs and practices of ordinary citizens are more tenuous. Their prescriptions for radical social change are continuously being subverted and undermined by the stratagems of countless families in the daily management of their own domestic economies.

As I wrote in a recent article on 'Golden Ages and welfare alchemists' [Pinker, 1995b; see **Chapter Nine, p 204**], the doggedness of popular resistance to radical change 'owes more to an awareness of financial realities than to welfare theory or political ideology. The present trend towards pluralisation and privatisation has sharpened people's awareness of the comparative merits of statutory and non-statutory social services. A British married couple with two dependent children on an average income do not have to be professional accountants to work it out that they would be significantly worse off if the welfare state were dismantled, leaving only a few residual services for the poorest minority. The value of this couple's tax rebates would fall far short of the cost of the services that they would then have to buy in the private market.'

Social policy and administration

There is evidence to suggest that neither the radical version of welfare individualism nor that of welfare collectivism enjoy much support among British voters. Even in 1988 when the present government was more popular than it is today there was no groundswell of support either for residualising the welfare state or greatly extending its coverage. At that time the British Social Attitudes research and other surveys found that the largest single group of voters – ranging from just over 40 per cent to over 50 per cent, depending on the surveys used – supported a modestly institutionalised version of welfare pluralism that has much in common with Marshall's model of 'democratic-welfare-capitalism'.

Most survey respondents wanted to keep the existing welfare state system, with more scope for the private and voluntary sectors. The great majority opposed any further run–down in state services, and they wanted more services rather than more tax cuts and privatisation. The clear message was that 'Neither Socialist planning nor free enterprise enjoys majority support' among British voters. The largest single group of voters seemed to favour a pluralist model of welfare in which the state continued to play a major role. (Lipsey, Shaw and Willman, 1989; Heath and Evans, 1988).

More recent Social and Community Planning (SCPR) surveys on the same issues suggest that, if anything, popular support for statutory social services has grown stronger over the last six years. On the other hand the most recent survey found that, although the great majority of respondents equated poverty with living below a subsistence level, only 25 per cent of them agreed that it should be measured by reference to other people's living standards. (Taylor-Gooby, 1995: 7–9).

Conclusion

There are some encouraging precedents in the field of generational and cross-generational studies of the experience of poverty. Rowntree's study of the life cycle of poor families was, of course, the pioneering work. More recent initiatives include the publications of the Panel Study of Income Dynamics in the USA, such as Corcoran, Duncan and Hill's (1984) article 'The economic fortunes of children: Lessons from the Panel Study of Income Dynamics'; Walker and Ashworth's comparative analysis of poverty dynamics (1994), Leisering and Leibfried's *Zeit der Armut. Lebensläufe im Sozialstaat* (1995, later also published in 1999 as *Time and Poverty in Western Welfare States: United Germany in Perspective*), and Leisering and Walker's (1998) *The Dynamics of Modern Society: Poverty, Policy and Welfare*. Research of this kind that spans the life cycle across generations and the spectrum of living standards from poverty to wealth has much to contribute to our understanding of citizenship as an experiential and subjective phenomenon.

When the variables of class, gender and ethnicity, as well as age, are taken into account we may gain a better understanding of the dynamics of both citizenship and welfare. And when we have added a more explicit subjective dimension to Marshall's more objective and formal approach we will be able to make a balanced assessment of the respective contributions of rationality and sentiment to the enhancement of social welfare. In my own populist approach this evening I have, perhaps, shown too much sympathy with David Hume's famous dictum that 'reason is, and ought only to be, the slave of the passions' (Hume, [1739] 1996: 127). But that is because I also agree with his less well-known observation about our human nature, namely, that is 'some particle of the dove, kneaded into our frame, together with the elements of the wolf and the serpent' (Hume, [1751] 1998: 74).

TWELVE

The right to welfare[*]

Robert Pinker

Introduction

I

Marshall's first collection of essays was published in 1950 under the title *Citizenship and Social Class*, and these essays were subsequently reprinted in a larger collection, *Sociology at the Crossroads*, which was published in 1963.[1] In Britain at that time the dramatic growth of sociology as an academic discipline was only just beginning, and the subject of social policy and administration was still being taught mainly as an option within other social science degrees or in the context of post-graduate diplomas, usually as a prologue to social work training. Very few practising sociologists had read the subject for a first degree; Marshall himself did not become a member of a sociology department until he was in his late thirties. As an undergraduate he read history at Cambridge, and, after spending the First World War interned as a civilian prisoner in Germany, he was elected in 1919 to a fellowship at Trinity College, Cambridge. He was appointed to the London School of Economics in 1925 as a tutor in social work – a subject about which he says that he 'knew nothing'. He claims that when he joined Morris Ginsberg's department in 1929 and began teaching comparative social institutions, he was 'quite ignorant of sociology in the professional sense', although he had developed during his internment 'a sociological curiosity and had acquired, in my historical studies, some skills in the analysis of social systems and the interpretation of social change'.[2]

In paying tribute to Marshall's contribution to the development of social policy and administration one must first honour his achievement as a sociologist. He became a sociologist when he was teaching at the London School of Economics, 'very naturally, almost totally under the influence of Hobhouse, as interpreted by Ginsberg'.[3] Marshall has referred to his 'use of Hobhouse's threefold categorisation of kinship, authority and citizenship as the basic principles of social order' and

---

[*] The first six parts of this chapter were taken from Robert Pinker's Introduction to Marshall's *The Right to Welfare and Other Essays* (Pinker, 1981). Parts VII and VIII were taken from Pinker's essay, 'T.H. Marshall', which was published in George and Page's *Modern Thinkers on Welfare*. (Pinker, 1995c).

his study of the works of Max Weber, Emile Durkheim and Karl Mannheim, which formed the basis of his sociological education and can be discerned in his own work. These were the beginnings from which he went on to make his own distinctive and original contribution to the subject.

In the title essay of his second collection, *Sociology at the Crossroads*, which was first presented as an inaugural lecture in 1946, sociology is described as a 'partner' and not a 'pirate' in the enterprise of the social sciences. While he acknowledges its analytical tasks, Marshall emphasises its vitally important role as a synthesising discipline in relation to other disciplines such as economics, psychology and education. To illustrate the practical uses of sociology he chose the problems of social planning, educational opportunity, poverty and policies for improving the quality of family life, all of which, significantly, fit equally well into the remit of social policy and administration.

Sociology, as Marshall saw it in the 1940s, stood at a crossroads, uncertain of direction and faced with a choice of paths. One path led towards the search for 'universal laws and ultimate values'. 'We might call it', he suggested, 'the way to the stars and, although few at any one time can profitably follow it, it should never be barred'.[4] The other path, he thought, might be called 'the way into the sands'. It leads to the expenditure of great energy 'on the collection of a multitude of facts with sometimes an inadequate sense of the purpose for which they are being collected'.[5]

Marshall rejects both of these paths, choosing what he calls 'a middle way which runs over firm ground'. 'It leads', he says, 'into a country whose features are neither Gargantuan nor Lilliputian, where sociology can choose units of study of a manageable size – not society, progress, morals, and civilisation, but specific social structures in which the basic processes and functions have determined meanings'. Durkheim's 'social types or species', Weber's device of the 'ideal type', Hobhouse's concepts of structure and function, and Karl Mannheim's notion of 'middle principles' exemplify 'the stepping stones in the middle distance'.[6]

This approach is further developed in the essay, 'Sociology: The Road Ahead',[7] in which Marshall defines as 'the central concern of sociology … the analytical and explanatory study of social systems', a term which he takes to cover both general social phenomena such as nations and states and different kinds of polity, on the one hand, and more specialised phenomena at an institutional level, on the other. He acknowledges that there are many features of social life which do not wear a systematic appearance, but he observes that 'If society were not systematic there could be no social science … that if the fundamental elements of which social systems are made were not essentially the same in all societies (though differently combined), and if the possible ways of using these fundamental elements were not limited in number, the social sciences, so called, would be devoid of all general theory.'[8]

The distinguishing features of a social system are described as 'a set of interrelated and reciprocal activities' which permit orderly and purposive behaviour in social life and ensure continuity of action and identity during change. Marshall does not equate the idea of a social system with total functional interdependence. In all societies, he suggests, we can observe 'non-system' elements, activities which are not relevant to 'the system as such' and which constitute areas of free choice. There are also 'pro-system' areas of relatively free choice in the forms of social activity which are 'not strictly repetitive but nevertheless have room made for them within the system, and in fact help to make it work'. Finally, there are 'anti-system' elements of conflict or deviance which are not compatible with the orderly operation of the social system.[9]

Marshall's model of society therefore postulates a high degree of 'predictable, repetitive and co-operative' behaviour, but it does not preclude the reality of conflict, the possibility that conflicts may eventually improve or destroy a social system, or that there are many aspects of social life which are unsystematic. Marshall argues that the task of sociology is 'to explore the interplay of these elements and to find the clue to their relationships. And it undertakes this task by studying both social institutions and individual behaviour'.[10] There is a very important place for the study of social policy within Marshall's sociological framework, which could, for example, encompass both the formal and the informal dimensions of social welfare and which has direct implications for the individualistic concerns of social work as well as the collective concerns of social administration.

Marshall's work in social policy and administration developed from his enduring commitment to sociology as an intellectual discipline. He suggests that 'The core of this alleged discipline does not reside within a general theory of society', nor upon 'the exclusive possession of a methodology', but in the cultivation of a disciplined approach to the study of social phenomena.[11] He goes on to describe this approach as a 'disciplined command of a body of knowledge and concepts, a style of thought and an accumulation of experience in their use [which] is, like the diagnostic skill of the physician and the forensic skill of the lawyer, both individual and at the same time collegial'.[12]

Marshall has always asserted that attachment to a particular discipline is vitally necessary to the scholar working in an applied field of the social sciences if he is to maintain a balance between the claims of knowledge for its own sake and knowledge for use. This belief, as I have mentioned, was the central theme of his major essay, 'Sociology at the Crossroads', in which he draws a sociological distinction in order to set out his own path of sociological enquiry into 'specific social structures in which the basic processes and functions have determined meanings'.[13] At the same time, however, he observes that 'Sociology need not be ashamed of wishing to be useful', adding the proviso that it ought to be concerned not only with the failures but also with the successes of social life.[14] Sociologists ought to respond to calls for help 'in the preparation of plans for action', although they should also be careful in doing so 'not to prostitute their service'.[15]

The uses of sociology in these practical endeavours are expounded in a more recent essay published in 1973, 'A British Sociological Career',[16] in which Marshall acknowledges the 'great progress' which has been made in the application of sociology to social policy studies. It is an acknowledgement attended by a warning, as he also maintains that one outcome of the closer association between sociology and social policy is that sociology 'is in perpetual danger of being over-dominated by social ideals and political purpose, and the only defence against this is a body of scientific hypotheses in process of development towards a working system of relevant sociological theory. In other words what both extremes need is a sociology which is truly a discipline, strong enough to draw together the unquestionably valuable contributions of the fashionable schools of thought and give scientific stability to the remarkably vigorous exploration of the real facts of contemporary life, especially its ills and their treatment.'[17] Apart from this shift in emphasis from normality to pathology, Marshall's view has stayed remarkably constant over a period of 20 years.

Marshall has never claimed that sociology ought to have a 'special relationship' with social policy or, for that matter, with any other subject. His aim has been to preserve the integrity of his own subject, not to launch it on enterprises of academic imperialism. The content and perspective of his writing have remained distinctively sociological, but he rarely, if ever, uses the sort of recondite terminology which bogs down communication with other social scientists. Consequently his work exemplifies a rare form of academic achievement. It stands as an original and authoritative contribution in two fields of social science; sociologists read his works as sociology, and social policy scholars read them as social policy. Marshall has also played a vital part in establishing the academic identity and disciplinary status of social policy and administration, a field of knowledge which was once categorised almost exclusively on the basis on commonly shared 'social ideals and political purpose', in other words, it was subject to the same kind of domination which he saw as a threat to the integrity of sociology.

II

Much of Marshall's best work on social policy has been written during his retirement, without the benefit of a teaching base or any direct and regular access to students. His earlier contribution to the development of social administration and social work at the London School of Economics is a matter of history. The Department there was already a major centre of teaching in social policy and social work when Marshall was succeeded by Titmuss in 1950. The Titmussian view of social administration dominated the field of welfare studies from the mid-1950s to the mid-1970s to the extent that it came to represent an orthodox academic consensus, strongly collectivist in value orientation and characterised by a moral rather than a theoretical identity, which was exclusive rather than inclusive in nature. Those who entered the field outside this consensus were welcomed on something less than equal moral terms. The most important of these intruders were the economists of the Institute of Economic Affairs and, later on, a few Marxists and quasi-Marxists from a variety of disciplines, including sociology, economics and political science.

In retrospect I do not think that this state of affairs was created intentionally, but that it came into being partly because the subject was not widely offered before the mid-1950s and partly because it took nearly two decades for the new generation of scholars and for new schools of social administration to become established. We are referring here to a period of remarkable growth and innovation in the subject fields of both sociology and social policy and administration. During the 1960s and 1970s there was a quickening of interest among sociologists in the study of welfare institutions and practices.

In the case of social policy and administration the two decades were a period not only of innovation but of consolidation, and these were, in effect, complementary processes. The development of new theoretical and conceptual approaches to the study of social policy drew on a number of social sciences, including sociology. This heightening of theoretical interest was crucial to the search for some unifying identity for a subject which would repay study both for its own sake and because of its practical use in the resolution of various social problems and its value in social work education and other vocational courses. In 1967 the Social Administration Association was established, and it soon attracted members from a wide range of social science disciplines. Four years later the Association brought out the *Journal of Social Policy*, and since then the discipline has been strong enough to sustain not only the journal of the Association but two other major academic quarterlies.

Marshall was not directly involved in these developments, which began several years after his retirement in 1956. It is interesting, however, to note that he was invited to contribute to the first issue of the *Journal of Social Policy*. The essay published on that occasion, 'Value Problems of Welfare-Capitalism',[18] has since become recognised as a seminal essay in the field of social policy. The continuing strength of Marshall's influence in the field is recognised by John Baker in his article, 'Social Conscience and Social Policy'. Baker refers to a survey carried out in January 1976 by the Joint University Council for Public and Social Administration on the content of the 'first and most elementary reading lists for social administration' prepared by all its member institutions. Two-thirds of the colleges replied, so the listing is 'fairly secure but not definitive'. Baker notes that the 'Most notable was the range of books recommended – over 200 in all – of which only a third were on two or more lists'. Three books were mentioned by half or more of the institutions – T.H. Marshall, *Social Policy in the Twentieth Century*, R.M. Titmuss, *Essays on the Welfare State* and R.M. Titmuss, *Social Policy: An Introduction* – and Marshall is later described as 'the author of the most frequently recommended textbook'.[19]

Among students of social administration Marshall's books and essays are probably more widely read than those of any other authority apart from Titmuss. His introductory text, *Social Policy in the Twentieth Century*, is now in its fourth edition.[20] Yet there has never been a Marshallian 'school' of social administrators of the kind that Titmuss gathered together during his lifetime. This is surprising, considering the sustainedly high quality of Marshall's work, its analytic range and depth and its stylistic elegance. Few authorities have sought as consistently and as successfully to locate the study of social welfare within a broader context of institutional change. At the same time his work does not fit readily into any of the major groupings or schools of thought which have come to characterise the subject field of social policy and administration.

In this respect we should note the quality of detachment that pervades Marshall's writings. This is not to imply that he either ignores the key value issues in social welfare or fails to make his own values explicit, but he approaches questions of value in a spirit of scholarship rather than partisanship. His conclusions tend to stand against the currents of fashionable opinion. He is explicitly in favour of the middle way between the extremes of individualist and collectivist ideologies. He poses the truly awkward questions about the nature of welfare and the relationships between its political, economic and social components, often without having to hand an answer which will be immediately comforting to social administrators. Finally, his distinguished record of public service is not of a kind to have placed him in the centre of the domestic political debates. Marshall's reputation rests, therefore, on his record on scholarly achievement, and owes little or nothing to his record as a protagonist of worthy causes.

Baker observes that the dominant perspective in the literature recommended to students of social administration presented 'a distorted view of the state in society and indeed of social processes as a whole.... Very few students were asked to read items which questioned the present role of the state in any fundamental way. Among the handful of critical items, Marxist or socialist texts predominated. Right-wing or free-enterprise commentaries were virtually non–existent.'[21] I think that Baker was a little less than fair to both Titmuss and Marshall in this respect. Titmuss's 'The Irresponsible Society'[22] still stands as one of the most sustained and impassioned critiques of the misuse of power and influence in capitalist societies, and there is sufficient evidence in essays by Marshall to show that Marshall's attitude to state activity was always critical and discriminating. Nonetheless, on the whole, Baker's thesis stands up; the subject has suffered until very recently from a surfeit of consensus in basic assumptions about the relationship between state activity and social welfare. It was not until the mid-1970s that the fundamental debate began to open out.

Despite the growth of theoretical interests to which I have referred, the character of this debate is still taking its shape and momentum from the normative and political imperatives which are, perhaps, inevitable features of all forms of theorising in the applied social sciences. A major advance has been made, however, in that the subject is ceasing to be dominated by any one school of thought. In this intellectual climate it becomes more likely that the relationship between explanatory and normative theory which I have described above will be reversed, so that our political beliefs will sometimes be modified as a result of academic enquiry.

Three major positions were being advanced and defended in the debate about social welfare during the 1970s. First, there was the argument that only a greater reliance on the freely competitive economic market could preserve and increase individual and collective welfare. Secondly, there was the argument that only through the abolition of capitalism as a form of social organisation could we begin to realise our collective potential for the enhancement of welfare. Thirdly, there was the argument of the broadly Fabian-socialist school of Titmussian social administrators who rejected capitalism on moral grounds, believing that the creation of a socialist society could be effected by a process of social reform through the institutions of parliamentary democracy.

III

Marshall has been almost the only major contributor to social policy studies to have held to the view that a modified form of capitalist enterprise is not incompatible with civilised forms of collectivist social policies. Indeed, it appears to be a central part of his thesis that a free economic market is a necessary condition for the creation and enhancement of welfare. For the exposition of this thesis we most turn to his major essay, 'Citizenship and Social Class',[23] the development of which is as much historical as it is sociological.

Marshall takes as his starting-point the question posed by the economist, Alfred Marshall – will it eventually prove possible through economic and social progress to make every man 'by occupation at least' a gentlemen?[24] Alfred Marshall hoped that through reduced incidence of soul-destroying manual labour and extended educational and cultural opportunities, the divisive effects of class would give way to new forms of social consensus and co-operation within a society still characterised by a free market economy. T.H. Marshall begins his answer by replacing the term 'gentlemen' with the term 'civilised', since, as he observes, it is clear that Alfred Marshall 'was taking as the standard of civilised life the conditions regarded by his generation as appropriate to a gentleman'.[25]

He then proceeds to reinterpret the question in order to explore the relationship between the evident inequalities of class and the prospective equality of citizenship. He identifies three elements in the concept of citizenship. The civil element concerns the 'rights necessary for individual freedom – liberty of the person, freedom of speech, thought and faith, the right to own property and to conclude valid contracts and the right to justice'.[26] Marshall locates the origin of these rights in the eighteenth century, but notes also their embodiment in seventeenth-century statutes such as the Habeas Corpus Act and the Toleration Act, as well as 'Catholic Emancipation, the repeal of the Combination Acts, and the successful end of the battle for the freedom of the press…. It could then be more accurately, but less briefly, described as the period between the Revolution and the first Reform Act.'[27] The political element of citizenship is 'the right to participate in the exercise of power', either as a representative or as a voter, and the social element comprises 'the whole range from the right to a modicum of economic welfare and security to the right to share to the full in the social heritage and to live the life of a civilised being according to the standards prevailing in the society'.[28]

Marshall observes that the most significant extension of political rights occurred in the nineteenth century, though not for women, and that it was an extension of rights already enjoyed by a minority to the majority of the adult male population. The more universal enjoyment of social rights he sees as a feature of our own century, pointing out that the relationship between social rights and their exercise was not always direct and positive, because the processes of institutional differentiation gradually separated the societal bases of their legitimacy. He also draws our attention to the significance of the change in emphasis from local rights and obligations based on small communities to those based on the rise of national institutions. With these changes, a national dimension was added to the idea of citizenship, so that 'When freedom became universal, citizenship grew from a local into a national institution.'[29]

In order to set this central point of his argument in historical context Marshall goes back to feudal society, in which the three elements of citizenship 'were wound into a single thread. The rights were blended because the institutions were amalgamated'. The rights which people enjoyed then were not, however, comparable with those of modern citizenship, because in feudal society 'status was the hallmark of class and the measure of inequality. There was no uniform collection of rights and duties with which all … were endowed by virtue of their membership of society. There was, in this sense, no principle of the equality of citizens to set against the principle of the inequality of classes.' Only in the towns were a few examples 'of genuine and equal citizenship to be found, but these were local phenomena'.[30]

It was the growth of national institutions in government and law which broke up this unity and set each element of citizenship on 'its separate way, travelling at its own speed under the direction of its own peculiar principles'.[31] The example of the New Poor Law can be taken to illustrate the conflicts of interests and rights which attended these changes. The New Poor Law required that the enjoyment of a social 'right' to poor relief should be contingent on the surrender of political rights. As Marshall points out elsewhere, 'The pauper was a person deprived of rights, not invested with them'.[32] Similarly, the special claims of women and children to protection under the Factory Acts came to be recognised because neither women nor children enjoyed political rights. They were fit subjects for protection because they were dependent. Thus, Marshall reminds us, after 1834 'The tentative move towards the concept of social security was reversed. But more than that the minimal social rights that remained were detached from the status of citizenship'.[33] Nonetheless, while it was 'appropriate that nineteenth-century capitalist society should treat political rights as a secondary product of civil rights', it was 'equally appropriate that the twentieth century should abandon this position and attach political rights directly and independently to citizenship as such'.[34]

Marshall defines citizenship as 'a status bestowed on those who are full members of a community. All who possess the status are equal with respect to the rights and duties with which the status is endowed'.[35] Within his analytical framework, citizenship becomes a basis for social solidarity and a measure of consensus; civil and political rights become a pre-condition of the extension of social rights, and, once universalised, ensure that such extension will take place. But Marshall includes within his model of equality and fraternity on the basis of citizenship the seeming paradox that the egalitarian extension of rights coincided with the development of capitalism precisely because capitalism is a system based on economic inequality. In Marshall's opinion these trends are complementary and not incompatible: 'Differential status, associated with class, function and family was replaced by the single, uniform status of citizenship, which provided the foundation of equality on which the structure of inequality could be built.'[36]

Marshall maintains that the enjoyment of social rights in the form of social and educational services contributed more to the equalisation of statuses than to the equalisation of incomes, but that the proper and necessary purpose of social services is the abolition of poverty and not the abolition of inequality. Finally, he discusses 'the combined effects of three factors. First, the compression, at both ends, of the scale of income distribution. Second, the great extension of the area of common culture and common experience. And third, the enrichment of the universal status of citizenship, combined with the recognition and stabilisation of certain status differences chiefly through the linked systems of education and occupation. The first two have made the third possible'.[37] The rights of citizenship inhibit the inegalitarian tendencies of the free economic market, but the market and some degree of economic inequality remain functionally necessary to the production of wealth and the preservation of political rights.

Marshall recognises that a 'conflict of principles' springs from the very roots of our type of society, but he concludes that these 'apparent inconsistencies are in fact a source of stability, achieved through a compromise which is not dictated by logic', although he suggests that 'This phase will not continue indefinitely'.[38]

In writing about the ends of social policy Marshall separates the abolition of poverty from the abolition of inequality, suggesting that 'Poverty is a tumour which should be cut out, and theoretically could be; inequality is a vital organ which is functioning badly',[39] and he states unequivocally that 'The task of banishing poverty from our "ideal type" society must be undertaken jointly by welfare and capitalism; there is no other way'.[40] The alternative is 'something more totalitarian and bureaucratic, and that is not at all what the more novel and significant elements in the movement of protest are seeking'.[41] Marshall's central theme is that collectivist social services contribute to the maintenance and enhancement of social welfare so long as such interventions do not subvert the operation of the system of competitive markets.

If we accept the basic premises of Marshall's argument set out in 'Value Problems of Welfare-Capitalism', then our chief commitment in welfare will be to resolve the persisting incompatibility of three separate sets of values and aims: that of the social market, that of the economic market and that implicit in democratic political processes. Marshall suggests that we have so far failed to devise a formula for social justice which would enable us to equate 'a man's value in the market (capitalist value), his value as a citizen (democratic value) and his value for himself (welfare value)'. We will also have to take account of the continuing conflict between the welfare ethic, which stresses 'the equality of persons', and the democratic ethic, 'which *also* stresses equality of opportunity'.[42] In Marshall's view these issues constitute 'a structural problem' to which 'there is no purely structural solution', and his conclusion is that 'It is futile to imagine that differentials can be made acceptable simply by scaling them down, however necessary this may be. It can be done only by changing the attitude towards them'.[43]

Marshall's position is both interesting and unusual, since he writes as one who believes that broadly collectivist ends can be realised in a society which accepts it as a matter of principle that all its members are equal as citizens, although they may be unequal in other respects. He argues that the claims of equality and those of inequality can be reconciled within a mixed economy, and, further, that such reconciliation would offer all of us the surest way to the enhancement of welfare. Although Marshall used the hyphenated term 'democratic-welfare-capitalism', to describe this kind of society, he appears to be advocating a more positive relationship not so much between welfare and capitalism, but between welfare markets and competitive markets. The competitive market is seen as a central element in a mixed economy in which the pursuit of private interest and profit is encouraged, and a measure of inequality in income and wealth accepted – though not beyond the point at which they become excessive and thereby undermine the authentic and equal rights of citizenship on which the general enhancement of public welfare depends.

In describing Marshall's position we can identify some of the salient principles of the social democratic tradition in political thought. It is a position which leaves several important issues open to debate at the same time as it lends itself to certain conclusions. One fundamental question turns on the extent to which competitive markets can be rendered accountable to the imperatives of public welfare and those of capitalist enterprise at the same time. Although there is no definitive answer, we have the living evidence of various contemporary societies which are very similar to the type which Marshall has outlined. We can use these societies as the basis of evaluations, comparisons and predictions about development and future change in society. We do not have to speculate about possible kinds of society which have not yet come into existence.

A democratic-welfare-capitalist society may have closer affinities with socialism than with capitalism, or vice versa, but it may be labelled 'socialist' by one school of thought, and 'capitalist' by another. Some Marxists might argue that so long as a competitive market operates to the extent proposed by Marshall, then the society in question will remain quintessentially a capitalist one. Classical economists might content, on the other hand, that when the competitive market has been restricted to the extent proposed by Marshall, then it will effectively have ceased to be competitive in a truly capitalist sense, and that it can be classed as a subordinate feature of a socialist command economy. A third conclusion can, however, be found in Marshall's analysis: 'The substitute of the mixed economy for capitalism marks the passage from arguments about values to attempts to analyse a specific historical social system – the one which evolved in Britain and most of Western Europe in the first 20 years or so after the war, and still survives in a recognisable though, at least in Britain, a rather battered condition'. Marshall allows that 'It is perfectly legitimate to assign this system to the broad category of capitalism (some call it neo-capitalism), but it is a type of capitalism of which a distinguishing feature is the presence of a mixed economy'.[44]

Marshall does not go beyond this point; indeed, it is hard to tell whether or not we have witnessed the emergence of a new and specific type of social system in democratic-welfare-capitalism, if only because the processes of transition have been so gradual and so relatively peaceful. Where societal change is more sudden or violent, it is easier to be persuaded that a fundamentally new type of society has emerged, although we have only to read the work of certain critical Marxists to be reminded that a change is not always what it (initially) seemed to be, and that the end results are not always those that were desired.

Marshall is never in any doubt that if we wish to protect and extend our individual freedoms and the institutions of representative democracy then some kind of balance must be preserved between the productive capacities and claims of the economic market and the redistributive capacities and claims of the social market. The best balance is one which will permit marginal shifts and adjustments to take place over time, but will stop well short of changes which are likely to lead to a serious diminution of political freedom – without which welfare in its fullest sense cannot be said to exist at all. The idea of welfare in its broadest sense rests on this balance between the claims of different kinds of right and the satisfaction of different kinds of need. Economic, political and social rights all express different dimensions of welfare. We cannot continue to extend any one of these rights at the expense of the others without crossing the critical threshold at which the relationship between freedom and security becomes one of diminishing marginal utility.

These are the issues to which Marshall returns in his 'afterthought' on 'Value Problems of Welfare-Capitalism'. He looks again at this 'hyphenated' phenomenon to remind us that 'The hyphen links two (or it can be three) different and contrasting elements together to create a new entity whose character is a product of the combination, but not the fusion of the components, whose separate identities are preserved intact and are of equal and contributory status'. It is this emphasis on combination and equality which distinguishes Marshall from the Titmussian tradition, which has always implied that in a better-ordered society the values of the social market would, as it were, take over and dominate those of the economic market. Titmuss's ideal of social welfare was based on a normatively unitary model of a good society, but, according to Marshall, the differences between these institutional elements 'strengthen the structure because they are complementary rather than divisive'.[45]

Titmuss started from the protective institutions of social policy and worked outwards to the broader social structure. Welfare is at the centre of his universe. Marshall started, as a sociologist, with the total society, and he locates social policy among its several institutional parts. The quality of 'hyphenation' in democratic-welfare-capitalism, he suggests, exists because all of its component institutional parts 'enjoy a measure of autonomy derived from the power inherent in their axial principles'. To illustrate this separateness Marshall points out that 'The welfare principle cannot be derived from the principle of majority rule; its duty is to provide not what the majority want but what minorities need – which [had] once led to the question: should welfare recipients have votes?'.[46] Similarly he draws our attention to the problem of reconciling the claims of democracy, socialism and welfare in a free society, and reminds us of the policy boundaries which in practice have come to be drawn around the seemingly unitary and universalist idea of a welfare state: 'The part did duty for the whole and claimed for itself the authority, and the autonomy to which the whole would have been entitled. And that is where the hyphen came in. For authority inherent in, not bestowed upon, a part of a whole provides a basis for the hyphenated relationship of autonomic interdependence. With the emergence, not of a socialist, but of a mixed economy, the tripartite pattern was complete. The golden calf of democratic socialism had been translated into a troika of sacred cows'.[47]

In Marshall's analysis there is more than a hint of Weber's conceptualisation of society as 'a delicate balance of opposing forces', although Marshall is convinced that such oppositions can be productive rather than destructive. He touched briefly on the same theme when he was writing about India in the 'afterthought' to his essay, 'Freedom as a Factor in Social Development'. Although the institutional and cultural components are different from those of Western societies, the problems of balance and potential conflict are very similar. India is described as a different type of hyphenated society, a 'parliamentary democracy uncomfortably linked with a mixed economy, with, as a third partner, the Hindu Brahmanic tradition'. In India, in fact, the economy comprises not only a public and a private sector but a growing sector of capital-intensive industry and a large productive sector based on labour-intensive craftsmanship.[48] Marshall's approach to the study of social policies is consistent with and highly derivative from his approach to the study of sociology. It is based on a model of social welfare which takes account of the structural and cultural determinants of needs and the policy responses to them. It is alive to the multidimensional nature of welfare, including the connections between wealth and poverty and the exercise of freedom and power. The Marshallian approach can help us to construct a path linking the broader institutional issues to specific issues of policy and administration, so that the 'stepping-stones of the middle distance' will lead us into the wider ranges of comparative enquiry and the more restricted but equally important study of national concerns. This approach can also help us to relate our enquiries to the generic issues of sociological and moral theory. In the remaining sections I will examine Marshall's exploration of some of the key issues in British social policy, I will ask how his approach might be employed in further comparative studies and, finally, I will look at some of the theoretical implications.

IV

Marshall returns on several occasions to review the changing relationship between universalist and selectivist policies and the problem of poverty. In *Social Policy in the Twentieth Century* he focuses on three things – what he terms 'the dilemma of the gap' between the levels of benefit granted under social insurance and those granted selectively as supplementary benefits; the anomaly of the 'poverty trap'; and the 'discrepancies between economic and welfare values' manifested in the 'wage stop'. He concludes that 'Perhaps we are getting the worst of both worlds' – an inefficient and anomaly-creating network of selectivist policies and universalist services which are inadequate if they are economical but could only become adequate if they were also extravagant. His search for remedies is pragmatic: 'how to devise a scheme of general application which operates selectively, and how to unify the systems of income taxation and income maintenance'.[49] Child endowment, negative income tax, the social dividend scheme and tax credits are reviewed in turn. At the end of his analysis Marshall concludes that the variability and idiosyncratic nature of human needs is such that there will always be an essential role for discretion and selectivity. What matters is that they should be exercised within a Titmussian type of universalist infrastructure[50] and that the necessary discrimination should not entail humiliation.

The first essay in *The Right to Welfare and Other Essays*, 'Changing Ideas about Poverty', illustrates Marshall's ability to set issues in their broader historical context. He traces through mediaeval and Elizabethan England the changing state of law and public opinion relating to the nature of rights and welfare needs, from the notion of poverty as a normal and natural state 'with a natural remedy', to the notion of 'functional poverty' – ideas which, with the catalyst of Malthusian teachings, were converted into the full rigours of the New Poor Law, supported by the fashionable theories of social Darwinists.[51] Marshall finds 'something peculiarly unpleasant about the idea of "functional poverty"', and suggests that fear of unemployment is more likely to act as a brake on productivity than as an incentive to it.[52] At the same time he insists on his distinction between the concept and problem of poverty and the concept and problem of inequality.

In the essay 'The Right to Welfare', Marshall returns to the linked issues of universality and selectivity by examining the association between rights and discretion. He argues that 'There can be no legal right in the fullest sense to a benefit the award of which is subject to discretion',[53] but he asks why discretionary assistance should be accorded a lower status. He points out that means tests can be administered in the spirit of a needs test, and that 'It would be nearer the truth to say that this notion of discretion as positive, personal and beneficent can only be realised in the "welfare society", that is to say, a society that recognises its collective responsibility to seek to achieve welfare, and not only to relieve destitution or eradicate penury'.[54]

Marshall attributes our reluctance to adopt this view to the influence of Beveridge, who, in placing such emphasis on the superiority of benefits based on insurance rights in comparison to those deriving from the exercise of discretion, reinforced beliefs which had long been dominant in British social policy. In Marshall's view the existence of discretion can be taken as evidence of a felt obligation on the part of society to meet need irrespective of legal rights. It is the status of citizenship which makes this kind of 'right' an authentic one. What the courts cannot do, he adds as an 'afterthought', is to 'convert discretion into rights in cases where the law has left an area free for discretionary judgements'.[55]

His concern that social policies should have the discretionary capacity to respond to the idiosyncrasies of human need is also reflected in the essay, 'Welfare in the Context of Social Development'. In this short piece Marshall succinctly draws to our attention what he calls two dimensions, or axes, 'along which welfare moves': one of these is defined in terms of wealth to happiness, which 'marks the boundaries of the territory in which welfare dwells'; and the other moves between individualist and collectivist dimensions, which must both be encompassed in welfare policies if they are to have regard for the whole person.[56] This essay is complemented by 'Welfare in the Context of Social Policy', which demonstrates how civilised social policies become expressions of 'mutual aid on the basis of common citizenship', when they bring together the formal provisions of statutory services and the informal services of the family and the neighbourhood. This process of enlargement is the best protection against the intrusion of services which would divide and humiliate the needful. The danger of stigmatising the needful exists because discretion is necessary and because some needs can only be diagnosed and met on a one-to-one basis. Welfare, we are reminded, has both a collective and an individual dimension. Where, then, asks Marshall, should we 'put the emphasis in all human situations which are *psycho-social*?' His answer is 'bang in the middle, on the hyphen', because 'At that point of perfect balance the social worker can exercise an expertise which is not that of the psychiatrist, a systematised procedure which is not that of the bureaucrat and a personal influence which is not that of a moral censor'.[57]

Once again Marshall returns to his concern that social welfare should have regard for the whole person – or that at least some agency or individual within the social welfare context should have that regard. This commitment finds expression in basic principles of social work practice such as respect for persons and self-determination, although, as Marshall reminds us, these principles require us to respect the individual's right to make wrong choices as well as right ones. As he suggests in 'Freedom as a Factor in Social Development', the 'essence of freedom consists in the right and power to choose and act according to one's choice. And the right to choose, if it is to have real substance, must include the right to choose wrongly and to take the consequences'.[58]

We find that Marshall's concept of citizenship, like his concept of welfare, has both an individual dimension and a collective dimension, and this is entirely consistent with the distinction which he draws elsewhere between 'personal' and 'positional' status, when he is discussing the nature of professionalism.[59] Thus it becomes apparent that the preservation of self-respect in conditions of dependency is a task of social work and other personal service occupations which parallels and complements the task of building positive associations between the positional status of citizenship and social policies. Indeed, the principles of respect for persons as persons and respect for persons as citizens are indivisible. When sharp discrepancies arise between a person's civil, political and social statuses, as they tend to do in a welfare crisis, these principles represent a moral imperative to redress the discrepancies whenever that is possible, but still to act with due regard for the person's self-esteem when it is not.

It is therefore vitally important that statutory social services retain a distinct moral identity, in spite of the contingent nature of this identity: it is not entirely autonomous, nor is it sacrosanct. The principles of citizenship and universality are essential elements of that identity, and together they represent the best protection of the status of citizens who lack a full sense of civic identification, whose rights are consequently at greatest risk and whose sense of self-esteem may be poorly developed or seriously damaged. A large proportion of the clientele of social workers consists of such people. The principle of universality ensures, as far as anything can, that some of the services which they use are a part of everyone's experience. The principle of selectivity ensures, as far as anything can, that their particular needs are met in a flexible way.

Within the bounds of our post-war social policies, the principle of universality found its fullest expression in health and educational services. The distinctive identity of the statutory social services, Marshall suggests, is now in danger of erosion as social insurance becomes 'a part of incomes policy', as selective means-tested services assume a more critically important role in the relief of poverty, and as the growth of union militancy within the social services gives a new harshness to the contours of their 'welfare image'.[60] Mounting evidence of tax avoidance suggests in addition a weakening of the sense of collective obligation which is essential to a welfare society.

In the last section of the 'afterthought' on 'Value Problems of Welfare-Capitalism', Marshall stresses the essential complementarity as well as the difference between welfare institutions and market institutions, and he points to the increasing degree of overlapping: we have reached a stage, he suggest, at which we are beginning to make excessive use of our social services simply to make up for the inability of the economy to meet its social obligations, and the end result will be 'the gradual degradation of the welfare principle'.[61]

Here Marshall's approach reminds us that because the claims of the economic and social markets are legitimated by reference to different principles, there are limits to the extent to which the one set of institutions can compensate for the deficiencies of the other, and that because their claims are, in another sense, complementary, there are political limits to the extent to which the one can pursue its objectives at the expense of the other.

V

Is Marshall's approach to the study of social welfare any more successful in reconciling the claims of 'social ideals and political purpose' with the canons of scholarly impartiality than approaches which advance more radical views? It is no defence in this respect to say that he espouses a value position in the middle ground of the debate. The vital difference, in my opinion, is that Marshall's approach is grounded in a theoretical tradition – in his case derived from the discipline of sociology – and this is what makes it amenable to theoretical analysis and criticism, as part of an open constituency of intellectual discourse. Marshall's value position is the outcome of a process of reasoning in which credible connections have been established between means and ends. One can disagree with the values without dismissing the argument simply because it is about something more than making moral choices or proving that one viewpoint is more moral than another. A theoretical approach which locates social welfare within a broader institutional context is one which also sustains the development of comparative research.

With the exception of India, Marshall has written mainly about the democratic-welfare-capitalist societies of the Western world, but his approach could very usefully be applied to the study of welfare institutions in socialist societies, which, as Mishra reminds us, are committed to becoming 'welfare societies *tout court*'.[62] Mishra and others have noted, for example, the insignificant role of fiscal and occupational benefits, the absence of effective pressure groups, the relatively low status of welfare professionals, the absence of a private market, and the persistence of poverty in Russia and other socialist societies. The Soviet system, however, rests on a remarkably polarised principle of citizenship, quite unlike that pertaining to the democratic-welfare-capitalist societies discussed by Marshall.

Soviet society is characterised, on the one hand, by a highly developed welfare system which discriminates positively in favour of a majority of its citizens and, on the other hand, by an equally well developed anti-welfare system which discriminates negatively against certain of its minorities. This hierarchy of reward is ordered by reference to various political criteria of desert, on the basis of which a sub-class of political undesirables was formed as the new social order developed. Indeed, the segregation and control of this under-class was functionally necessary to the creation of the new society. Its existence poses a fundamental question to all socialists – if, as it appears, a truly socialist society cannot be created by the processes of representative democracy, how can it be created through revolution without ending in repression?

Marshall's concept of citizenship would be particularly relevant to an understanding of the functional connections between positive discrimination and negative discrimination. His account of the growth of citizenship describes a sequence in which the growth of civil and political rights precedes the extension of social rights. The acquisition of political rights provides citizens with the means to claim social rights; they are, then, not merely passive recipients. This does not occur in a totalitarian society characterised by a command economy, without the consent of the ruling elite. It is in this sort of environment that, as Mishra observes, 'the quest for equality and fraternity can lead to oppression'.[63] The fact is that all welfare institutions can be used to diminish liberty, but liberty can be enhanced only by welfare institutions to which it has itself given rise, as the services provided by any other sort of welfare institution are enjoyed as concessions rather than rights. Welfare institutions are least likely to curtail freedom when they reflect the ambivalence of people's loyalties and expectations, and most likely to do so when they are used as instruments of radical change.

Once again we are faced with the perennial problem of finding a sensible balance between the respective claims of freedom and security. Social administrators are prone to fits of moral passion which expose them too readily to the imperatives of security, because they are so frequently concerned with the victims of insecurity. This is one of the weaknesses of the discipline. Social administration has developed as a field of academic study mainly in democratic capitalist societies, where economic forces undoubtedly impose disservices on some citizens. It has therefore been all too easy for social administrators to assume the role of public guardians against the immoralities of the economic market and to overlook the fact that in the opinion of some citizens, the social market is equally responsible for injustice.

The strength of social policy and administration lies in its direct involvement with human need and in its acknowledgement that all processes of social change, both political and economic, create losers as well as beneficiaries. It is this kind of awareness which impels social administrators to go on asking 'concrete questions about specific policies and services rather than to generalise broadly about "social policy" in the abstract'.[64] Such enquiries become increasingly insistent as we accumulate the evidence of our failures in social policy. Wilding observes that, within the Titmussian tradition, we have continued to look for 'a social policy-social service-centred explanation for the failure. There is little discussion, for example, of the relevance of the distribution of power in society … and there is little analysis of dominant social values and the nature of the relationship between the ethic of capitalism and the ethic of welfare.'[65] In a more broadly based discipline which employs comparative methods we would automatically ask questions about the ethics of other social systems. Nonetheless it is encouraging that the generation of writers such as George, Mishra, Sinfield and Wilding is not only posing structural questions but availing itself of sociological theory, in an attempt to extend the range of the debate.

There is, however, a danger that this process will leave the old value consensus of social policy and administration at the mercy of the normative orthodoxies currently dominating certain politically and morally inspired areas of sociology. Social administration must not abandon its well-worn path into the sands of empirical fact-gathering only to set foot on a detour through the stars of the sociological firmament. The discipline needs sociology, but it needs, more than that, an open-minded association with a variety of social sciences. A more positive relationship with economics, for example, would diminish the present tendency to use exclusively moralistic terms in the differentiation of economic and social policy objectives. The academic constituency of social administration has always included scholars of political science, statistics, philosophy and history, and it cannot do without this variety of other intellectual associations for two main reasons: first, the idea of welfare is multi-dimensional in Marshall's sense. Its constituent elements are political, social and economic. Secondly, the study of social welfare is singularly evocative of emotional responses, and while social administrators have tended until recently to be so affected by the immediacies of human suffering that they have neglected the strategies of reform in favour of the tactics, now the increasing influence of sociology is beginning to steer some of them towards grand theories of strategic change, regardless of the short-term consequences. They should remember that life is short not only in relation to art but in relation to history; the enjoyment of welfare ought not to be simply a prospect for posterity.

VI

The preservation and development of a broad range of academic associations will help to hold in check and to harness the various currents of idealism which will always characterise social policy and administration. The task of the discipline in future will be one of synthesis, but it will be even more formidable than the task of synthesis which Marshall commended to sociologists. Given the nature of the subject matter, synthesis in social policy and administration will require in addition to contributions from other social sciences a more productive relationship between practice and theory. Like social work, social policy and administration is very closely bound up with the lives and expectations of ordinary people. It inhabits the frontier between thought and action, an area of contradictions and compromise, in which theories of all kinds are tested – usually to destruction. We work in a subject in which the application of bad theory or the misapplication of good theory can have disastrous consequences for real people. This, I think, is one of the reasons why Titmuss was so suspicious of theory.

Marshall and Titmuss did not base their approaches on the same assumptions about the relationship between society and social policy, but their views about the relationship between the means and ends of social policy are similar. Both authors bear witness to the belief that if the means we choose are not morally defensible, then the end results will be immoral; both uphold the political morality of representative democracy.

The liberal schools of thought which assert the overriding importance of self-help and competitive individualism in the pursuit of welfare came to pre-eminence in societies which were in the process of becoming representative democracies. It is doubtful, however, whether such an approach to social welfare would coexist for very long with an established representative democracy. We need look no further than the Poor Law system to see what happens when social policies are made to serve exclusively economic ends – in the case of the Poor Law an approach to welfare underpinned by popularised versions of classical economic theory which were based on a highly simplified model of 'economic' man. Titmuss's reiterated distinction between the morality of the economic market and that of the social market can perhaps be understood as an informed and compassionate reaction against such inhumane doctrines. Although there is always the danger that this sort of reaction might lead to the adoption of an alternative but equally simplified model of 'social' man, this would at least be a model which treated people as ends in themselves and not as means to broader and more abstract ends.

Marx indicted capitalism as an inhumane and dehumanising type of social organisation for very similar reasons. Capitalism, he argued, is based on exploitation and ruthless pursuit of profit. It denies individuals all hope of realising their full potential as human beings. It has also been a central tenet of Marxist theory that the dominant forms of economic activity and the relations of production under capitalism inevitably determine every other aspect of social life, but that capitalism can be destroyed through the heightening of class conflict, and be replaced by socialism. Under socialism the residual economic, social and political contradictions of capitalism will eventually be resolved.

Marx did not rule out the possibility of a peaceful transition from capitalism to socialism through the processes of parliamentary democracy, but he thought it was extremely unlikely to occur. Nor did he have much respect for the institutions of bourgeois democracy, which he saw largely as a device for the maintenance of class domination.

In one respect Marx has been proved correct; there are no societies which have changed peacefully on the basis of a democratic mandate from capitalism to socialism. It is, however, equally true that the operation of revolutionary socialism in various countries has imposed massive dis-welfares on the citizens of those countries. Marshall and Titmuss agree that political freedom and individual rights are essential elements of welfare, but Marshall differs significantly when he insists that, whether the process of change to socialism is democratic and peaceful or undemocratic and violent, material welfare is likely to be diminished, and political liberty placed in serious jeopardy, if the end result is the disappearance or marked diminution of a free and competitive economic market system.

Our only historical or contemporary examples of societies characterised by a 'command' economy happen to be left-wing or right-wing totalitarian societies. Although this does not rule out the possibility that the democratic socialists might eventually be proved right, it leaves us for the moment with a world in which the only socialist societies happen to be non-democratic politically, relatively inefficient in economic performance and not at all superior in social welfare provision. We have yet to see whether socialism can realise its welfare promise.

In its institutional range and balance Marshall's model of welfare provides a framework for analysis and synthesis which sustains enquiry at various levels of social life and organisation. Like every major contribution to the study of social welfare, it also expresses a distinctive value position. The intellectual climate within which useful concepts and theories are most likely to flourish is one in which the different normative divisions of a subject are made explicit, not so that one value position will be reinforced at the expense of others but so that all will be exposed to a greater measure of objective scrutiny.

Charles Taylor touches on this issue when he refers to the traditional liberal argument put forward by J.S. Mill that 'Truth can be approached only when different beliefs, different theories, different manners of seeking truth are allowed to dispute with each other'. Taylor discusses the possibility that 'The necessity for intellectual polarisation is fundamental and inescapable so that even where one is sure that one theory or approach is superior to its rival, one nevertheless loses by prohibiting this rival because the acuity and depth of one's perception of that truth declines when it is no longer forced to define itself against rivals'.[66] We are concerned here simply with the old-fashioned academic virtue of impartiality, which Broady rightly defines as 'a moral property, a disposition to attend scrupulously and open-mindedly to all sides of the case'.[67]

VII

That Marshall's work is highly relevant to the study of social policy is perhaps more widely recognised now than it was in his lifetime. Marshall's enduring commitment to sociology as a synthesising discipline provided the intellectual grounding for his model of social welfare, which made allowance for the structural and cultural determinants of needs and for the way in which policies might also take account of these factors. His model encompassed both the formal and the informal dimensions of welfare and its multidimensional institutional aspects, including the connections between wealth and poverty and the exercise of freedom and power. The Marshallian approach is uniquely well suited to showing how specific issues of policy such as the exercise of discretion are related to the broader institutional issues of citizenship, class and welfare typologies. Marshall's guidance over the 'stepping-stones of the middle distance' prepares the ambitious student for bolder excursions into the wider ranges of national and comparative analysis.

Marshall argued that the essence of a sociological approach to the study of social policy resides in 'a disciplined command of a body of knowledge and concepts, a style of thought and an accumulation of experience in their use [which] is, like the diagnostic skill of the physician and the forensic skill of the lawyer, both individual and, at the same time, collegial'.[68]

His writings exemplify a rare form of academic achievement. They stand as an original and authoritative contribution in two fields of social science, and they can be read both as social policy and as sociology. Marshall played a vital part in establishing the academic identity of a field of knowledge previously categorised almost exclusively by common 'social ideals and political purpose'. Many students are drawn to a subject like social policy in the hope of being confirmed in their beliefs or of finding a basic theory or model capable of providing answers to the dilemmas of social welfare. Reading Marshall reminds us that the first task of students is to get rid of their prejudices. Far from offering unitary explanations, the logic of Marshall's analysis shows that the dynamics of social policy stems from a set of institutional dilemmas which are by their very nature unresolvable.

Marshall is seen by George and Wilding as a 'Fabian socialist',[69] and by Dennis and Halsey as one of their six exemplars of English ethical socialism.[70] While it is true that Marshall's views on welfare are socialist rather than collectivist, they are none the less part of a broader political analysis which readily accepts competitive market capitalism as the best available guarantee of economic prosperity and social welfare. Halsey saw Marshall as 'the outstanding interpreter and advocate of the central development of an alternative social solidarity – the welfare state' (1996: 100). However, in today's context, Marshall's dictum that 'The task of banishing poverty ... must be undertaken jointly by welfare and capitalism' would not pass for a socialist sentiment.[71]

Marshall's conceptualisation of citizenship and his account of its evolution in modern times are perpetuated in current debates about social change and the nature of social rights, responsibilities and needs. Baker[72] and Giddens[73] have criticised Marshall for expounding an evolutionary, even a Whiggishly optimistic, theory of the growth of citizenship. More recently, Hirschman has called for 'a corrective of Marshall's optimism', and a greater awareness of the 'dilemmas and conflicts' which he overlooked would be worth cultivating – if Marshall had indeed overlooked them in the first place.[74]

Other commentators like Turner and myself are more interested in the importance given to institutional conflicts and value contradictions in his analysis. Citizenship may play a balancing role between the moral claims of the economic and social markets, but the balance is never more than precarious. Marshall was as alive to the possibility of regress as to that of progress in social change, and he did not claim that the rights of citizenship developed in immutable order. As Turner[75] observes, Marshall's account of citizenship 'does not *necessarily* entail some commitment to an immanent logic in capital; on the contrary, his view of citizenship appears to rest on a contingent view of historical development'.[76] The development of social welfare is determined by fortuitous changes of circumstance rather than by forces of historical necessity.

Marshall's sense of historical contingency was complemented by his understanding of normative relativism and ethical relativity. It may be, as Jayasuriya observes, that Marshall's approach to citizenship was 'framed primarily within a liberal, individualist tradition' of philosophical thought.[77] Nevertheless, in his analysis only a pluralist model of welfare was capable of encompassing the variety of principles and aspirations that demand expression in complex industrial societies. With regard to the problem of choosing between equally desirable but potentially conflicting ends in policy making, Marshall's approach inclined towards the relativities of compromise rather than the absolutes of economic freedom or state-regulated security. As Marshall himself remarked, 'This kind of ethical relativity has been a feature of very nearly every society since civilization began'.[78]

At the present time, when the whole institutional basis and rationale of the British welfare state is the subject of radical reappraisal from all points of the political compass, students will find Marshall's position in the middle ground a useful starting point for their own reading and reflection. The value issues addressed by Marshall are still at the heart of the debate about the nature of welfare rights and obligations that has been gathering momentum since the early 1980s. Plant, Lesser and Taylor-Gooby's *Political Philosophy and Social Welfare*[79] links this debate to the seminal works of Rawls[80] and Nozick[81], and Barry[82] on justice and brings it up to date.

Rieger comments on the historically specific and individualist nature of Marshall's conceptualisation of the rights of citizenship, which is far removed, in his opinion, from what he describes as 'the modern view' of these rights, which accords them the status of 'natural rights'.[83] Like other collectivists, Rieger draws attention to the undeveloped communitarian possibilities contained in Marshall's approach. Like Jayasuriya and Turner, he argues that only by encouraging more active forms of political participation can citizenship become an authentic framework for social solidarity and integration.[84] Turner goes further, in arguing that Marshall's approach to citizenship 'can be used as the basic definition of modernization' and as a 'universalist criterion on social development which is not ethnocentric, teleological or idealist'.[85]

Other writers, like Walzer, have interpreted and broadened the concept of citizenship to include multiple 'spheres of justice' encompassing a variety of social goals.[86] Among Marshall's critics, Barbalet has linked his concepts to a wide range of social movements committed to advancing the civic claims of women, ethnic groups and environmental issues.[87]

Marshall wrote little on women's issues, and the main focus of his writings was on citizenship as a feature of sovereign independent states. Williams, however, is wide of the mark in claiming that Marshall does not face the 'fundamental contradiction that although women developed their political rights as individuals, a woman's eligibility to many social rights through welfare policies is as a dependant of her husband or the man with whom she lives'.[88] Marshall did in fact address this issue in *Citizenship and Social Class* in order to emphasise a different but closely related point – that protection (under the early Factory Acts) was confined to women because they were not considered to be full citizens and, as he remarked, the 'champions of women's rights were quick to detect the implied insult'.[89]

Marshall attached as much importance to fulfilling obligations as to the assertion of right, recognising the symbiotic nature of their relationship in free societies. Here his approach has much in common with that of Janowitz,[90] Glendon[91] and Mead.[92] When the debate loses contact with legal, economic and other institutional realities, it degenerates into the 'rights-babble' of political activism.

On the question of citizenship defined within the terms of nationality, it has been pointed out by Bottomore and others that since Marshall's death, two divergent trends have emerged in the relationship between citizenship and national identity. The first is the dramatic growth in the number and variety of separatist movements throughout the world, a phenomenon apparent in places as different and as far apart as Canada, Spain, Northern Ireland, Italy and the former Soviet

Union and Yugoslavia. These movements are largely driven by powerful cultural ideologies in which issues concerning civil rights are given enormous importance. Where autonomy is achieved, we see the formation of smaller nation-states with a strong sense of their own distinctive and exclusive rights and obligations.

The second trend embraces powerful political movements driven by ideological, economic and technological imperatives, and committed to unifying existing states within new international entities. Islam is one such force, the European Community another. Throughout Europe we can observe both centrifugal and centripetal forces at work. Massive post-war migrations have also diversified the cultural and ethnic characteristics of many Western nation-states. In the case of the European Community, the trend is towards creating a shared framework of legally sanctioned civil, economic and social rights. Rieger, however, points out that, while the Social Chapter may be seen as an incipient form of European citizenship, it reflects in reality 'a community of quite limited liability' with regard to the status of migrant workers and the largely symbolic nature of its general provisions.[93]

The continuing friction between the UK and other member states over the principle of subsidiarity suggests that these provisions will remain largely symbolic for some time to come. In a recent essay, Spicker[94] utilises the universalist elements in Marshall's concept of citizenship to support the idea of an authentically European framework, noting that 'The challenge to universalist social policy goes beyond a simple clash of values', but adding that 'As the community develops, services will become progressively more comprehensive in their scope'. He acknowledges that 'The kind of model this is consistent with is the argument for "citizenship" put, for example, by T.H. Marshall or more recently by Ruth Lister'.[95]

The principle of citizenship underlies the concept of 'democratic-welfare-capitalism' as a distinctive form of mixed economy and a specific, historical social system in its own right. Marshall stands out as the intellectual precursor of our current analysts of mixed economies of welfare and welfare pluralism, his ideas forming a recurring point of reference for advocates and critics alike. He saw the competitive market as a central element in a mixed economy, in which the pursuit of private interests was to be encouraged, and a measure of inequality in income and wealth accepted – although not beyond the point at which they might undermine the equal rights of citizenship on which the general enhancement of welfare ultimately depends. At times he could be taken to be advocating a more positive relationship, not so much between welfare and capitalism, but between welfare markets and competitive markets.

This distinction has exposed him to justifiable criticism from different quarters. Some Marxists have argued that, so long as a competitive market operates to the extent proposed by Marshall, the society in question will remain quintessentially capitalist. On the New Right, the theory is that when a competitive market is restricted to the extent proposed by Marshall it ceases to be truly competitive and becomes a subordinate feature of a collectivist command economy.

There is a third interpretation to be found, however, in Marshall's own analysis, in his 'afterthought' on 'Value Problems of Welfare-Capitalism'. Here he observed that:

> The substitution of the mixed economy for capitalism marks the passage from arguments about values to attempts to analyse a specific historical social system – the one which evolved in Britain and most of Western Europe in the first twenty years or so after the war, and still survives in a recognizable though, at least in Britain, a rather battered condition.

However, he allowed that 'It is perfectly legitimate to assign this system to the broad category of capitalism (some call it neo-capitalism), but it is a type of capitalism of which a distinguishing feature is the presence of a mixed economy'.[96] Marshall did not live to see the full extent of the battering that was still to fall on the British welfare state – or the extent to which the concept of a mixed economy could be stretched to accommodate divergent models of pluralism.[97]

He believed that the best balance was one permitting marginal shifts and adjustments to take place over time, but stopping well short of changes which would be likely to lead to a serious diminution of political freedom – without which welfare in its fullest sense cannot be said to exist at all. His idea of welfare rested on this balance between the claims of different kinds of right and the satisfaction of different kinds of need. He considered that economic, political and social rights all expressed different dimensions of welfare, and that it was not possible to go on extending any one of these rights at the expense of the others without crossing the critical threshold at which the relationship between freedom and security becomes one of diminishing marginal utility.

VIII

I take the term 'classical sociologist' to refer to someone whose work displays a deep understanding of the structure of major social institutions, of the processes which cause these institutions to survive and change, and of the ways in which they affect the lives of ordinary people. Marshall chose social policy as the institutional context for his explorations, but it is the clarity and originality of his sociological understanding that give his work enduring relevance. His sociological influence can be seen in Turner's *Citizenship and Capitalism*,[98] Harris's *Justifying State Welfare*[99] and Miller's *Market, State and Community*,[100] books concerned with the development of new institutional frameworks for the analysis of social policy issues. In them, the normative balances are made to shift between different versions of 'democratic welfare-capitalism' and 'democratic-market socialism', and this adds to our understanding, as old ideological stereotypes are broken down.[101]

In his comparative study of the politics of social solidarity, Peter Baldwin states the premise that solidaristic policies 'have become accepted, legitimate and uncontroversial only to the extent that they are regarded as a right rather than as charity or altruism', adding that this was 'the point of Marshall's trinity of rights and the concept of social citizenship'.[102] Pierson, in an equally informative reappraisal of welfare states, links Marshall's work to theories of modernisation and the extension of political rights.[103] Describing Marshall as a 'new liberal' – which strikes me as more accurate than labelling him a socialist – Pierson draws parallels between Marshall and Rawls relating to their social democratic values, and in his conclusion he suggests that Marshall, like his 'new liberal forerunners', failed to show 'how citizens are to exercise effective control over a state from which their capacities as citizens derive'.[104] Failure in this respect, however, may be seen as characteristic of all the other social and political theorists who go beyond the idea of a minimalist state. They, in turn, have to ask how the rights of the poorest citizens are to be protected without a measure of statutory intervention and provision.

It is revealing to compare Marshall's essays in *The Right to Welfare* with Esping-Andersen's *Three Worlds of Welfare Capitalism*. Esping-Andersen makes much of the concept of 'de-commodification' in delineating and justifying the processes by which citizens are emancipated from dependence on market forces for the meeting of certain basic needs through the extension of statutory social services. What he does not show is why dependency on the state is any more liberating than dependency on the market. He agrees with Marshall's proposition 'that social citizenship constitutes the core idea of a welfare state', but insists that the concept must be 'fleshed out'[105] by taking fuller account of the status of individuals *vis-à-vis* the market and commodification, the system of stratification, and the family's role in social provision.

Marshall, however, was acutely sensitive to the effect of market forces on the status of individuals. He did not use the term 'de-commodification', but he was well aware of the process which it describes and, with characteristic succinctness, he gave an interpretation of the liberating and disabling propensities of market capitalism that was rather different to Esping-Andersen's. He observed that 'Socialists have maintained that capitalism treats labour as a *commodity*. Of course it does, and this is its contribution to freedom, for the alternative was to go on treating the *labourer* as a commodity, and that meant slavery and serfdom'.[106]

To turn to a very important part of the subject-matter of social policy, relating to more substantive and specific issues such as the links between needs, rights and discretion, and the causal connection between poverty and inequality, if, as seems likely, the government dismantles what is left of the universalist framework of the British welfare state, there can be no guarantee that a future Labour government would have the will, the resources or the political mandate to put it together again. Unlike Beveridge, Marshall did not place unequivocal emphasis on the superiority of benefits based on insurance rights, rather than those deriving from the exercise of discretion as the expression of a felt obligation on the part of society to meet need irrespective of legal rights. In his view, it was the status of citizenship which made this kind of 'right' an authentic one. Troubled in his last years by the policy trends and rising incidence of unemployment which were beginning to drive more and more people into states of welfare dependency, Marshall deplored the economy's increasing inability to meet its social obligations, and he feared that the end result would be 'the gradual degradation of the welfare principle'.[107]

The combination of recession, high levels of unemployment, welfare retrenchment and demographic pressures is testing the conceptual and institutional credentials not only of democratic-welfare-capitalism, but of other hybrids like 'democratic-market socialism'. This state of crisis across the Western world is partly due to intermittent failures of capitalist markets as a system of wealth creation, and partly due to the more comprehensive failure of the various forms of socialism, both democratic and *dirigiste*, to meet welfare expectations. If, as a result of these problems, statutory social service provision becomes residual, and universal welfare gives way to selective welfare, the Marshallian concept of social citizenship will be able to survive only if the rights which it embodies are given some form of constitutional status. Without such reinforcement, the institutional links between the concept of universal citizenship and the right to welfare – at however modest a level – will be broken.

Finally, there is Marshall's contribution to the textual legacy of social policy and administration. In the face of ever-lengthening reading lists, students will find one special cause for gratitude to Marshall. He always used his remarkable talent for conceptualisation and synthesis in the interests of clarity and brevity. Perhaps the most impressive tribute paid to his scholarship over the years is to be found in Michael Oakeshott's review of *Citizenship and Social Class* in 1951, shortly after its publication: 'Professor Marshall', he remarked, 'is not a voluminous writer, but when he gives us something of this quality we can resign ourselves to his long periods of silence'.[108] Oakeshott thought that Marshall's treatment of social rights was too narrow, neglecting as it did some of their legal and religious dimensions. Nevertheless, he acknowledged Marshall's 'subtlety and reflectiveness' and the non-partisan quality of his writing, and he observed that 'Nobody can read him without enlightenment and the pleasure that comes from a sincere and cogent argument'.[109] At a superficial political level, Marshall and Oakeshott had little in common, but they had the same distaste for zealotry and the same devotion to the pursuit of knowledge for its own sake.

Notes

[1]   Marshall (1950; 1963).
[2]   Marshall (1973b), pp. 90-1.
[3]   *Ibid.*, p. 95.
[4]   Marshall (1963), p. 13.
[5]   *Ibid.*, p. 15.
[6]   *Ibid.*, pp. 21-2.
[7]   *Ibid.*, pp. 25-43.
[8]   *Ibid.*, p. 27.
[9]   *Ibid.*, pp. 28-9.

[10]   *Ibid.*, p. 31.
[11]   Marshall (1973b), pp. 97-8.
[12]   *Ibid.*, p. 98.
[13]   Marshall (1963), p. 21.
[14]   *Ibid.*, p. 22-3.
[15]   *Ibid.*, p. 16.
[16]   Marshall (1973b), p. 97.
[17]   *Ibid.*
[18]   Marshall (1972), reprinted in Marshall (1981), with a substantial 'afterthought'.
[19]   Baker (1979).
[20]   Marshall (1965).
[21]   Baker (1979), p. 181.
[22]   Titmuss (1976b), pp. 215-43.
[23]   Marshall (1963), pp. 68 *et seq.*
[24]   The paper in question was read by Alfred Marshall 'to the Cambridge Reform Club in 1873 on "The Future of the Working Classes"', and it was republished in A.C. Pigou (ed.), *Memorials of Alfred Marshall*: see Marshall (1963), p. 69.
[25]   Marshall (1963), pp. 71-2.
[26]   *Ibid.*, p. 74.
[27]   *Ibid.*, p. 77.
[28]   *Ibid.*, p. 74.
[29]   *Ibid.*, p. 79.
[30]   *Ibid.*, pp. 74-75.
[31]   *Ibid.*, p. 75.
[32]   Marshall (1970), p. 84.
[33]   Marshall (1963), p. 83.
[34]   *Ibid.*, p. 81.
[35]   *Ibid.*, p. 87.
[36]   *Ibid.*, p. 91.
[37]   *Ibid.*, p. 121.
[38]   *Ibid.*, p. 127.
[39]   Marshall (1972), p. 30; (1981, p. 119).
[40]   *Ibid.*, p. 28 (117).
[41]   *Ibid.*, p. 32 (121).
[42]   *Ibid.*, p. 30 (119).
[43]   *Ibid.*, p. 31 (119).
[44]   Marshall (1981), 'Afterthought', p. 123.
[45]   *Ibid.*, pp.124-25.
[46]   *Ibid.*, p. 126.
[47]   *Ibid.*, p. 129. Compare Halsey, 1996.
[48]   Marshall (1965b), 'Afterthought', pp. 174-5.
[49]   Marshall (1970) p. 195.
[50]   *Ibid.*, p. 198.
[51]   T.H. Marshall, 'Changing Ideas about Poverty', paper presented at a conference on 'Poverty and Stratification' organised by the American Academy of Arts and Sciences (conference papers never published). First published in Marshall (1981), with Afterthought, pp. 50–2.
[52]   Marshall (1981), p. 51.
[53]   Marshall (1965c), p. 264; (1981, p. 86).

54 *Ibid.*, p. 266 (88).
55 Marshall (1981), 'Afterthought', p. 98.
56 Marshall (1966a), p. 27; (1981, p. 55).
57 Marshall (1966b), p. 58 (1981, p. 81).
58 Marshall (1965b), p. 2 (1981, p. 157).
59 Marshall (1963), pp. 154-7 and 188.
60 Afterthought on 'Value Problems of Welfare-Capitalism', in Marshall (1981), pp. 131-2.
61 *Ibid.*, p. 135.
62 Mishra(1977), p. 124.
63 *Ibid.*
64 Titmuss (1974), p. 49, quoted in Wilding (1976), p. 146.
65 Wilding (1976), p. 163.
66 Taylor (1975), p. 133.
67 Broady (1972), p. 21.
68 Marshall (1973b), p. 95.
69 George and Wilding (1976), pp. 62-84.
70 Dennis and Halsey (1988), pp. 122-48.
71 Marshall (1981), p. 119.
72 Baker (1979).
73 Giddens (1982).
74 Hirschman (1991).
75 Turner (1986).
76 See also Pinker (1981).
77 Jayasuriya (1992), pp. 22-3.
78 Marshall (1981), p. 129.
79 Plant et al (1980).
80 Rawls (1981).
81 Nozick (1974).
82 Barry (1973), p. 19.
83 Rieger (1992), pp. 28-33.
84 *Ibid.*
85 Turner (1986), p. 59.
86 Walzer (1983).
87 Barbalet (1988).
88 Williams (1989), p. 129.
89 Marshall and Bottomore (1992), p. 15.
90 Janowitz (1976).
91 Glendon (1991).
92 Mead (1986).
93 Rieger (1992).
94 Spicker (1993).
95 Lister (1990).
96 Marshall (1981), p. 123.
97 Pinker (1991).
98 Turner (1986).
99 Harris (1987).
100 Miller (1989).
101 Reisman (1984).

[102] Baldwin (1990), p. 29.
[103] Pierson (1991), pp. 22-25.
[104] *Ibid.*, p. 202.
[105] Esping-Andersen (1990), p. 21.
[106] Marshall (1981), p. 163.
[107] *Ibid.*, p. 135.
[108] Oakeshott (1951).
[109] *Ibid.*, pp. 629-30.

THIRTEEN

The prospects for social policy in the UK after the 2015 General Election*

Robert Pinker

Introduction

This essay begins with a brief overview of the two main traditions of ideological thought that have shaped the ends and means of social policy in the UK over the past century. I go on to review the social policy proposals set out in the Conservative and Labour Party 2015 election manifestos. I follow this review with an appraisal of the way in which the government clarified its post-election policy intentions in three keynote speeches as it prepared the ground for the Chancellor's presentation of his July Budget.

The focus then shifts to the Chancellor's presentation of his Budget, Labour's response to his budget proposals, the concurrent progress of its leadership election campaign and its eventual outcome. In the concluding part of this essay, I speculate on the diversity of ways in which these events, and their ideological implications, might shape the prospects for social policy in the UK over the next five years.

Comparing the ideological options

I started watching the declaration of results on election night 7 May 2015 hoping that the outcome would be another hung Parliament and a continuation of some form of coalition government. As a traditional middle-of-the-road 'One Nation' Conservative, my preference was for a renewed partnership with the Liberal Democrats. As a middle-of-the-road welfare pluralist, the prospect of either the Conservatives or Labour gaining a secure working majority in Parliament filled me with apprehension.

As a welfare pluralist, I share William Keegan's view that the most successful democratic Western economies have built their achievements on 'a policy mix of the invisible hand of the market and the visible hands of public institutions'.[1] In the context of this 'policy mix', welfare pluralism takes the form of a mixed economy of statutory and non-statutory private and voluntary sectors in which agreement on the relative importance to be attached to each of these sectors

---

* Written in March 2016 for publication in this collection.

is reached through a process of pragmatic compromises between a plurality of interest groups of different ideological persuasions.

Middle-of-the-road compromises of this kind are more likely to be achieved in coalition governments where it is difficult for any one of the collaborating parties to dominate the policy making process. My main concern on election night was that either the Conservatives or Labour would be elected to office with a substantial working majority that freed them from the ideological constraints that coalition government imposes.

Governments with working majorities rediscover the courage of their ideological convictions and escape from these pluralistic restraints. They can abandon the middle way of policy making and return to what they believe is the true way back to one or other of the two great unitary ideologies of individualism and collectivism that have dominated welfare theorising and shifted the directions of change in social policy back and forth across the left–right political spectrum over the past century.

As I said in my essay 'Golden Ages and welfare alchemists', on the right of the political spectrum, the individualist ideology still holds the trust and imaginations of some of the world's most powerful politicians and policy makers.[2]

On the left of the political spectrum, the collectivist ideology of a benevolent, rationally planned and radically egalitarian society remains the 'ideal type' benchmark by which all other models of social science provision are measured and judged.

I set out the reasons why I became and remain a welfare pluralist in a paper which was published 20 years ago in 1995. In 'Golden Ages and welfare alchemists' (reproduced here as **Chapter Nine**), I came to the conclusion that these two great ideologies, individualism and collectivism, are reaching the end of their useful lives as *exclusive* guides towards the creation of better and more equitable societies, although they still have much to contribute when used in conjunction with each other.

Comparing the manifestos

Throughout the campaigning months leading up to polling day, politicians, policy makers and media commentators rarely, if ever, used terms like 'individualism', 'pluralism' and 'collectivism' when debating and defining the ideological differences between the competing parties. They drew a more sharply focussed distinction between those parties that espoused and those who opposed policies of fiscal austerity. The advocates of fiscal austerity gave over-riding priority to cutting the budget deficit as quickly as possible, largely by cutting public expenditure. The anti-austerity parties were committed to reducing the deficit more gradually, largely by raising more taxes at the expense of the better-off in ways that gave as much protection as possible to the poorest and most vulnerable members of society. The more radical left-wing Scottish Nationalist and Green parties believed that the budget deficit could be managed without inflicting any austerity policies on the poor.

During their term of office, the Conservatives in coalition with the Liberal Democrats clearly prioritised policies of fiscal austerity. Nevertheless, the restraints imposed on these policies by pluralist One Nation Conservatives as well as the Liberal Democrats ensured that, in general terms, a 'policy mix of the invisible hand of the market and the visible hands of public institutions' survived and the cuts in public expenditure were less draconian than they might otherwise have been.

In their election manifesto the Conservatives were able to claim that although the government's target dates for reducing the budget deficit had not been achieved, the deficit had been cut from 10% of GDP to 5%. This measure of success had 'helped restore confidence to the economy' and 'keep mortgage rates lower than they would otherwise be'. The economy was now growing at a faster rate than any of Europe's other major advanced economies and had already created more jobs since 2010, 'than the rest of the European Union combined'. Inflation was at a record low and living standards were set 'to grow strongly every year for the rest of the decade with the average family £900 better off'.[3]

The manifesto also served notice that if the Conservatives were returned to office' there would be 'a further £30 billion in fiscal consolidation over the next two years' which would include a further £12 billion of cuts in welfare spending in order 'to ensure that debt keeps falling as a share of GDP and to deliver a balanced structural current budget in 2017–18'. Having balanced the current budget, the government would maintain the momentum of its fiscal policies by moving into a surplus in order to reduce the UK's overall level of debts and the scale of its annual interest repayments. The authors of the manifesto went on to say that, after the surplus had been achieved, 'a new fundamental principle of fiscal policy monitored by the independent Office of Budget Responsibility will ensure that in normal economic times, when the economy is growing, the government will always run a surplus in order to reduce our national debt and keep our economy secure'. There would be 'no increases in VAT, Income Tax or National Insurance' while these policies were being implemented.[4]

On 23 April, the Institute for Fiscal Studies (IFS) published a report on the manifestos of all the main political parties.[5] It noted that, for the first time, 'the Conservatives, Labour and the Liberal Democrats were all promising to "balance the books"'. They drew attention, however, to 'potentially large differences in their fiscal plans'. The versions of fiscal austerity proposed by Labour and the Liberal Democrats allowed them to borrow for investment spending. The Conservatives were the only party aiming to achieve an overall budget surplus.

Labour's fiscal targets were viewed as being less austere than those of the Conservatives and they might give rise to higher levels of debt in the longer run. Comparisons, however, were difficult because Labour was not willing to say what it would consider an appropriate level of borrowing to be and 'without knowing how much deficit reduction Labour [was] aiming for, one cannot say exactly what their plans mean for spending on public services'.

As for the Conservatives, they had said very little in their manifesto about where they would find the large cuts to spending that their plans implied. While the National Health Service (NHS), education and international aid budgets were protected against cuts, those of the unprotected departments had already been cut by 'around a fifth' and it would therefore be 'surprising if there were many efficiency savings' left. The Conservative manifesto provided little or no detail as to on whom the cuts in welfare spending would fall and there was a general lack of information as to how more revenue should be raised. The authors of the IFS report concluded that, although all three main parties had outlined their plans for 'cracking down on tax avoidance', in their view, 'they were unlikely to raise anywhere near the billions of pounds they are hoping for'.[6]

On 26 May 2015, the IFS published a second report in which it reviewed the policy options which the Conservative government might pursue in seeking to cut welfare spending by £12 billion.[7] The party manifesto had already confirmed that, if re-elected, the Conservatives would freeze most working-age benefits and tax credits for two years, reduce the benefits cap from £26,000 to £23,000 and remove housing benefit entitlement from 18- to 21-year-old jobseekers. In aggregate, these cuts would yield around £1.5 billion pounds in savings. A more radical option would be 'to abolish child benefits' while increasing 'the child element of child tax credit', (and Universal Credit, when it is fully implemented). Low-income families would still be able to claim their means-tested benefits.

The IFS authors acknowledged that cuts of this kind would inflict more 'potential hassle and stigma' on these claimants and that 'the majority of families with children would lose at least £1,000 per year'. Welfare expenditure, however, would be cut by 'around £5 billion'. A similar amount would be saved by cutting tax credits, which would reduce entitlements for 3.7 million families 'by an average of £1,400 per year'. Up to £2.5 million would be saved by cutting child benefits for the first children in families. The IFS report also considered the option of cutting expenditure on housing benefits. The most draconian of these cuts would be to withdraw housing benefit altogether from claimants under the age of 25 who are on jobseeker's allowance. A cut of this magnitude would adversely affect around 300,000 claimants by an average of around £5,000 per year. Lastly, the government could means-test disability living allowances (and their replacement – personal independence payments) as well as the pensioner's attendance allowance and thereby save another £1.5 billion.

The second IFS report draws attention to the difficult balancing act involved in making welfare cuts of this magnitude. It points out that 'saving money while only affecting better-off claimants will tend to weaken work incentives. Saving money while protecting or strengthening work incentives tends to mean hitting some of the poorest in society and hence increasing poverty'.

Preparing the ground for the July Budget

The Queen's Speech: one nation or two?

On 8 May, we all knew that the prospects for social policy in the UK over the next five years would be determined and configured by a Conservative government with a working majority. We did not yet know for certain what kind of Conservative government it would prove to be. Would its policies of fiscal austerity eventually residualise the statutory social services or would they prove to be compatible with maintaining a pluralist One Nation policy mix of the invisible hand of the market and the visible hands of public institutions?

On 27 May 2015, Conservative Central Office issued a bulletin in which it said 'we have a golden opportunity ... to renew the promise to those least fortunate that they will have the opportunity for a brighter future, and to renew the ties that bind every part of our United Kingdom. We now have the mandate to deliver that renewal. And it starts with today's Queen's Speech: a clear programme for working people; social justice and bringing our country together – put simply, a One Nation Queen's Speech from a One Nation Government'.[8]

In other words, it seemed that the Conservatives would find ways of making its fiscal policies compatible with a pluralist mix of social policies and service providers designed to steer a middle way between the ideological extremes of individualism and collectivism. Just a week earlier, Tim Montgomerie – a high-profile Conservative Party activist and co-founder of the Centre for Social Justice – published a short but swingeing critique of his own party's manifesto pledges and policy proposals. He questioned the extent to which these policies were One Nation Tory in character and went so far as to entitle his critique 'This so-called one-nation Toryism stinks'.[9]

Montgomerie contended that the party manifesto's tax cutting agenda would disproportionately benefit the better-off and that 'a genuinely one-nation tax policy would raise the threshold for paying national insurance, increase work incentives offered by the Universal Credit benefit or reduce some of the consumption taxes that fall most heavily on the lowest paid'. In his view, a genuinely One Nation tax policy 'would not discriminate so strongly in favour of the over-65s and better off and against poorer people in work with young families'.

Montgomerie argued that 'Mr Osborne's lopsided tax cutting agenda would be controversial enough if it wasn't also scheduled to coincide with £12 billion of welfare cuts'. In any event, there was 'no good reason to cut benefits to fund tax cuts for people inheriting £1 million homes'. In his conclusion, Montgomerie said, 'I'll put this simply: the middle classes shouldn't be getting tax cuts while those in tough, poorly paid jobs ... are getting their benefits cut. That's not one-nation conservatism; it's two-nations conservatism.'

Montgomerie also acknowledged that his party's social welfare agenda included policies that were essentially 'One Nation Tory' in character. He cited the manifesto's promises to raise 'the minimum wage above and beyond the rate of inflation', to 'invest record amounts in apprenticeships', to raise educational standards in underperforming schools located in poor neighbourhoods and to reform the UK's immigration policy 'so that it protects people who suffer most from large influxes of unskilled foreign labour'.

The main thrust of Montgomerie's critique, however, was that the new Conservative government was already planning to cut taxes in order to help the better-off while leaving the working poor to shoulder the burden. Such policies were clearly at odds with the manifesto's claims that the Conservatives are 'the party of hard working people' and that 'we're all in this together'. He also noted that 'the only age group that voted decisively for the Conservatives two weeks ago was the over-65s. It ill became them to restyle the party as a "workers' party" after they had won an overall majority only because of the votes of those who've largely left paid employment behind'.

Montgomerie's response to the policy proposals outlined in the Queen's Speech was a timely reminder that, since the early 1950s, the British Conservative Party has been a coalition of individualist economic Liberals and more collectively minded One Nation Tories, some of whom had serious reservations about the ideological direction in which the government's plans for social policy were moving.

The Chancellor's Mansion House Speech

In his Mansion House Speech of 10 June, Chancellor George Osborne formally confirmed that his government intended to legislate for a permanent budget surplus. He explained that the time had come to reach a 'new settlement in the way we manage our national finances'. He reminded his audience that 'we have a budget deficit that remains at just shy of 5% of national income, one of the highest in the developed world'. In addition, the UK's 'national debt stands at over 80% of GDP'.

The Chancellor went on to say that the new settlement would ensure that 'in normal times, governments of the left as well as the right should run a budget surplus to bear down on debt and prepare for an uncertain future'. In the forthcoming Budget of 8 July, with these considerations in mind, he would 'bring forward a new fiscal framework to entrench this permanent commitment to that surplus'.[10]

As has already been noted, in the run-up to the general election, there were some signs that a degree of convergence was taking place between the Conservatives, Labour and the Liberal Democrats regarding the need to cut the structural deficit. They differed on the time it would take to balance the books, on whether they would rely mainly on cutting expenditure or raising taxes in doing so and – in the case of Labour – how much they would hope to borrow over the lifetime of the next Parliament.

The key difference between these parties, however, was whether it would be sufficient to balance the books or whether it was essential for the government to go further by moving towards a budget surplus that would be maintained in 'normal times' and that this obligation should be made permanently binding in law on future governments.

The Prime Minister's Runcorn Speech

A third keynote post-election speech was delivered by the Prime Minister in the town of Runcorn on 22 June. He left his audience in no doubt that most of the £12 billion cuts in social welfare expenditure would fall on tax credits and housing benefit. Mr Cameron said that he wanted to see the UK move on from being 'a low wage, high tax, high welfare society to a high wage, low tax, low welfare society' over the next two years.

He wanted to end the 'ridiculous merry-go-round' of taxing low earners and then handing the money back in benefits. (Pensioners and child benefits would remain protected from cuts.) The 'right track' in social policy for Cameron would be to recognise and remedy 'the causes of stalled social mobility and economic opportunity. It was time to stop dealing with the symptoms of the problem – topping up low pay rather than extending the drivers of opportunity – helping to create well-paid jobs in the first place'.[11]

There was a mixed but largely negative response to David Cameron's speech from politicians, policy analysts and media commentators. In an anticipatory response to his proposals, which was published in *The Guardian* on 17 June, Owen Jones had already pointed out that 'At least half of Britons in poverty are in work: so much for making work pay. And so the state shells out perhaps £11 billion a year on poverty pay, effectively subsidising major businesses'. With regard to housing benefits, Jones went on to say that 'Billions of pounds are wasted subsidising private landlords' in contrast with housing policy in the 1950s when Conservatives competed with the Labour Party over who could build more council housing, ensuring money was spent on bricks, not benefits.[12]

Harriet Harman contended that cutting tax credits would inflict indefensible hardships on those working families whose wages were so low that they would not be able to make ends meet without these credits.[13] In *The Guardian*, Rowena Mason noted that the Prime Minister had 'made no commitments to asking companies to introduce the Living Wage, simply pointing out the minimum wage was predicted to rise to £8 by 2020'. She concluded that he was 'unlikely to force companies to pay the living wage but has not yet set out how he would encourage employers to agree higher salaries to offset lost tax credits beyond modest increases in the living wage'.[14]

It could be argued that, in recent years, tax credits have been transformed into a more generous version of the Speenhamland system that underpinned the Old Poor Law and subsidised the low wages paid by employers who were well aware that the low wages would be topped up by the local Poor Law Guardians. Critics of the government's plans for the reform of the tax credit system may also argue that there is more than a touch of the New Poor Law's 'less eligibility' principle in these plans and the impact they will have on the lives of the poorest and most vulnerable social service recipients.

There are, however, justifiable reasons for trying to end the current 'ridiculous merry-go-round' of taxing low earners and then handing the money back in benefit. Nevertheless, it was generally agreed that the plans outlined in the Prime Minister's Runcorn speech were unlikely to succeed without imposing unacceptable hardships on the poor, unless the government could be persuaded to compel employers to pay a living wage.

The Chancellor's Budget, July 2015

The centrepiece of the Chancellor's Budget proved to be his surprise announcement that, as from April 2016, the National Minimum Wage for workers over the age of 25 would be raised from £6.50 to £7.20 an hour and, thereafter, rise incrementally to £9.00 an hour in 2020. This new version of the Living Wage would be legally enforceable on all employers. Workers under the age of 25 would continue being paid at the current lower rate. As matters stand, employees working 40 hours a week on the current Living Wage of £6.50 receive an annual income of £13,520. With the terms of the new compulsory scheme, they will receive just under £15,000, rising in annual increments to about £18,720 by 2020.

Under the terms of the new Welfare Bill, however, working-age benefits (including tax credits but excluding disability benefits and maternity pay) will be frozen for the next four years. Child tax credit benefits will be restricted to the first two children only. Young people aged between 18 and 21 will lose their automatic right to housing benefit. University maintenance grants for students from low-income families will be abolished and replaced by loans. The household benefit cap will be cut from £26,000 to £23,000 in London and £20,000 elsewhere. As from April 2017, these cuts in welfare and social security benefits will be phased in over a period of four years instead of two. As a consequence of this policy change, the target date for achieving the intended budget deficit has been moved on from 2018–19 to 2019–20. It remains to be seen whether the income enhancements in the new National Living Wage will be sufficient to compensate for these substantial cuts in benefit entitlement.

The Times newspaper's political editor, Francis Elliott, described these proposals as a Budget 'packed with policies raided from the manifestos of the Tories' defeated opponents'. In Elliott's view, they have 'helped Mr Osborne to spread austerity more evenly and forced businesses to accept some of the pain, while robbing Labour of a totemic policy' insofar as he has topped its own election pledge to introduce a compulsory Living Wage rising to £8.00 an hour by 2020. It now remained for the Labour Party 'distracted by a leadership contest to … decide within days which benefit cuts to oppose and why'.[15]

In the course of his Budget speech, the Chancellor also confirmed that the government would be raising the inheritance tax (IHT) threshold over the next five years. As from April 2017, a 'family home allowance' would be added to the present £325,000 tax-free allowance. This 'family home allowance' would initially be worth £100,000 in 2017–18 and thereafter rise incrementally to £175,000 by 2020–21. This new scheme would allow individuals to leave their assets (including their family home) to one or more of their direct relatives up to the value of £500,000 without paying any IHT. Couples and civil partners would be able to pass on a total of £1 million.[16]

In his 'morning after' analysis of the Chancellor's Budget, Larry Elliott described him in *The Guardian* as 'Osborne the pragmatist, Osborne the political magpie not averse to stealing policies from his opponents, Osborne the Chancellor who sees himself as the latest in a long line of one nation Tories'. He went on to say: 'This was a budget that included measures Ed Balls might have introduced had Labour won the election: the crackdown on non-doms; a training levy for big companies; making the tax breaks for buy-to-let landlords less generous. There was extra money for the NHS and most significantly, the announcement of a compulsory national living wage from next April'. What the Chancellor offered 'was not an ideological package, but a dish of Conservative and Labour ingredients seasoned with the promise of economic competence'.[17]

Labour responds to the Budget and elects a new leader

The Chancellor's offer was directed – with deadly intent – at a Labour Party still reeling from a catastrophic defeat which had been immediately followed by Ed Miliband's resignation and Harriet Harman replacing him as acting leader. She swiftly set in train the process for electing a new leader. While the Government was able to focus exclusively on preparing the ground for the Second Reading of the Welfare Reform and Work Bill on 20 July, Labour was faced with the additional challenge of electing a new leader in which the candidates were very likely to have conflicting views on how the party should respond to the Budget proposals.

Under the party's procedural rules, candidates had to be nominated by a quorum of at least 15% of the Parliamentary Labour Party, which constituted 35 MPs. All fully paid-up party members, registered and affiliated supporters were eligible to take part on a 'one member one vote' basis under the terms of an alternative vote (instant run-off) system.

As the closing date for nominations drew closer, only three MPs – Andy Burnham, Yvette Cooper and Liz Kendall – had gained sufficient support from the centre-left of the party to proceed as candidates. Burnham had become the leading contender but, under the alternative voting system, Cooper would remain in contention if he failed to win outright on the first count. Kendall, the 'Blairite' candidate, was the least strongly supported of the three contenders. Jeremy Corbyn – the only radical left-wing candidate – was left trailing in fourth place behind the other contenders, with 18 sponsors. The campaign itself was failing to engage the interest of the general public and the media. It was chuntering towards an outcome without ever really taking off.

A last-minute decision was taken on 15 June to 'broaden the terms' of the political debate by rescuing Corbyn's candidature. Eight more Labour MPs were persuaded to nominate him in order to ensure that the case for a radically left-wing response to the Budget was put to the voters. Most of Corbyn's new sponsors went on record to say that they had no intention of voting for him.

Two days later, the *Daily Telegraph* columnist, Toby Young, drew its readers' attention to Labour's newly revised electoral rules under which members of the public could become registered party members eligible to vote in the leadership election on payment of a £3 fee and confirmation that they supported its 'core values'and had no other political allegiances. He went on to advise his Conservative readers to join the Labour Party – under false pretences – so that they could vote for Corbyn and thereby eventually 'consign Labour to electoral oblivion' in 2020.[18]

This was the state of play in the leadership contest when Harriet Harman addressed a meeting of the Parliamentary Labour Party on 13 July.[19] She urged her colleagues not to vote against the Welfare Reform and Work Bill at its Second Reading on 20 July. The time had come to acknowledge that the public had lost confidence in the party's capacity to manage the economy. There were cuts in welfare spending that the party ought to oppose but 'a blanket opposition' to the Budget proposals would be widely construed as a 'campaign against the public'. With these considerations in mind, the party should abstain when Parliament voted on the Bill at its Second Reading.

On the day of the Second Reading, the party's response to the Budget turned out to be a compromise designed to go some way towards satisfying those MPs who were unequivocally opposed to its proposals and those who believed that such a response would be both untimely and counter-productive. It took the form of a three-line whip ordering Labour MPs to support a 'reasoned amendment' rejecting the Bill. If this amendment failed to pass, the party would then abstain on the Bill's Second Reading. The amendment proposed that 'This House declines to give a Second Reading to the Welfare Reform and Work Bill because the Bill will prevent the Government from continuing to pursue an ambition to reduce poverty in both absolute and relative terms ...'. The amendment failed to pass by 208 votes to 308 votes. The party then abstained on the Bill's Second Reading but 48 of its MPs, including Jeremy Corbyn, defied the three-line whip and voted against the Bill.

The day after the Bill's Second Reading, *The Times* published the results of a YouGov poll based on a sample of Labour Party members, registered supporters and Trade Union supporters. It indicated that Corbyn had already established a 17-point lead over the other three candidates, with 43% of the first preference votes. The poll also predicted that, in a run-off against Burnham, Corbyn would win 53% of the vote.[20]

The party's problems were compounded when Kendall and Cooper announced that, if Corbyn was elected leader, they would not serve as members of his Shadow Cabinet. Burnham subsequently confirmed that, in the interests of party unity, he would be willing to do so. Meanwhile, throughout July and August, a number of high-profile Labour politicians – including Tony Blair, Gordon Brown, Neil Kinnock, Peter Mandelson and Jack Straw – came out of political retirement to warn party members that it would be electoral folly to vote for Corbyn. Tony Blair went so far as to tell those who were intent on doing so – for reasons of the heart – that they 'should get a transplant'.[21]

Corbyn was transformed from being a rank outsider into a runaway favourite because he was seen as the only candidate who stood out as an unequivocally authentic socialist. The publication of two YouGov polls on 11 August confirmed that Corbyn was so far ahead of Burnham that he might win outright on the first vote. Neither Cooper nor Kendall were willing to stand down so that Burnham could pick up some of their transferable votes.

Labour elects its new leader

On 12 September, Jeremy Corbyn was elected leader of the Labour Party. Sixty per cent of its members had voted for him in the confident expectation that, under his leadership, Labour would be transformed into a radically left-wing socialist party and, thereafter, go on to win the 2020 General Election.

A new grass-roots movement calling itself 'Momentum' had played a key role in mobilising support for Jeremy Corbyn. Shortly after his election, they declared that their next objective was 'to build on the energy and enthusiasm from the Jeremy Corbyn for Labour Leader campaign'.[22] Some of Labour's moderate centre-left MPs described Momentum's members as covert hard-line Trotskyists intent on securing the deselection of any Labour MPs who opposed their radical policies. Momentum insisted that their overriding aim was the restoration of party unity.

At the start of his leadership campaign, Corbyn stood out as the one candidate who was unequivocally opposed to the Conservative government's fiscal austerity policies. He let it be known that, if Labour won the 2020 election under his leadership, priority would be given to stimulating economic growth, increasing social expenditure *and* reducing the budget deficit.[23] These policies would be funded through a new programme of 'people's quantitative easing' under which the Bank of England would be mandated to print new money for investment in the transport, energy and digital industries. The railway and energy companies would be gradually renationalised as their franchises expired. The Royal Bank of Scotland would also be renationalised.

In the field of social policy, most of the provisions of the Welfare Reform and Work Act would be repealed, the gradual privatisation of health services would cease and a fully funded NHS would be integrated with the social care services. A Corbyn-led government would also explore the possibilities of setting up a new fund designed to purchase debts incurred by the NHS and relieve the Trusts of the high financial burdens they had incurred with the Private Finance Initiatives. The commissioning of services by general practitioners would also cease.

In the field of housing policy, a Corbyn-led government would set a building target of 250,000 new houses each year, of which at least a half would be built by local authorities. Council tenants would lose their 'right to buy' in localities where acute housing shortages prevailed. In the private sector, however, the new Labour government would explore the possibility of giving the tenants of large-scale landlords 'a right to buy' and linking rents to local average incomes. Corbyn's 10-point leadership election manifesto also included a promise to reintroduce rent controls.

In the field of education policy, a Corbyn-led government would abolish university tuition fees, restore student maintenance grants and reappraise the role and status of free schools and academies with a view to bringing them back under local authority control.

The implementation of these new policies would be funded by shifting more of the tax burden on to the shoulders of the better-off. The top rate of tax would be raised to 50%. Other possible sources of revenue would be found by cutting back on corporate tax reliefs and subsidies, by increasing the level of corporation tax and also by raising the National Insurance contributions paid by people earning more than £50,000 a year.

Corbyn claimed that Her Majesty's Revenue and Customs (HMRC) were currently losing around £120 billion every year as a result of tax evasion and avoidance as well as taxes left uncollected. Most of this lost revenue could be recovered by increasing the number of HMRC staff and a more rigorous enforcement of existing tax regulations. The Treasury questioned the credibility of these estimates and claimed that, even with staff increases, the most likely amount of additional recoverable taxes would be in the region of £35 billion a year. During the course of his leadership election campaign, Corbyn also went on record to reaffirm his lifelong commitment to unilateral nuclear disarmament.

It remained the case, however, that just over 90% of the Parliamentary Labour Party had not voted for Corbyn in the leadership election and were implacably opposed to most of his policy proposals. Many middle-of-the-road Labour MPs were mindful of the catastrophic defeat their party had suffered under Michael Foot's leadership in the 1983 General Election.

On that occasion, the policy proposals in the party's election manifesto included substantial uncosted increases in social expenditure, the renationalisation of recently privatised industries and public utilities, withdrawal from what was then known as the European Economic Community, abolition of the House of Lords and unilateral nuclear disarmament. In retrospect, Gerald Kaufman memorably described this manifesto as 'the longest suicide note in history'.[24] A substantial number of Labour MPs were already fearful that this record would be superseded if Corbyn was still their party leader in 2020.

The Chancellor's U-turn on tax credits

By mid–September it was becoming evident that, in the aftermath of the General Election, a victorious Conservative Party was moving towards the ideological right and a defeated Labour Party with new leadership was about to move at greater speed in the opposite direction. With the demise of the Liberal Democrats, the middle ground of policy making and welfare pluralism was being abandoned and left effectively unrepresented in the Westminster Parliament.

Serious concerns, however, were being raised by some One Nation Conservatives as well as the opposition parties and independent research centres regarding the likely impact of the cuts. The independent IFS had already gone on record in claiming that the Chancellor's arithmetic simply did not add up and that three million families would lose at lease £1,000 a year in benefits if the cuts were implemented.

In early October, the Resolution Foundation published a working party report chaired by David Willetts (a leading One Nation Tory) which claimed that the cuts would drive at least 200,000 working households into poverty under the terms of the official definition that the government was already in the process of abolishing. This definition has been based on measurements of the number of children living in families with an income lower than 60% of median household income.[25]

These unfortunate families, however, would not be the only casualties if the Chancellor went ahead with the envisaged cuts. Shortly before a Labour opposition debate scheduled for 20 October, *Labour Press* published a brief report claiming that in 71 marginal Tory seats, the incumbent MPs had majorities that were smaller than the number of families who would be adversely affected by the cuts. This report went on to cite a House of Commons Library estimate that '3.2 million families who depend on tax credits to make ends meet will be on average £1,300 a year worse off – with some losing up to £3,000 from their family income – if the tax credit cuts are not reversed'.[26]

This was the context of concern and dissent in which the provisions of the Welfare Reform and Work Bill came before the House of Lords on 26 October. To the government's great consternation the Bill was blocked by two delaying amendments. The first of these amendments was put forward by Lady Meacher, a crossbencher, who wanted to give the Conservatives time to think again and come up with a reform package that would be less draconian in its impact on the families affected. Lady Hollis's amendment, on behalf of the Labour Party, was also designed to require the government to review the Bill's provisions and phase in the changes over a longer period of time. Both amendments were passed – by a majority of 307 to 277 votes.

The successful passage of the two delaying motions constituted a challenge to the 'financial primacy' of the elected House of Commons insofar as the unelected House of Lords is traditionally not expected to frustrate the passage of financial legislation. In his response to this setback, the Chancellor said that he would listen to the concerns raised in the Lords and take them into account in preparing his Autumn Statement.

When George Osborne rose to make his Autumn Statement in the House of Commons on 26 November he sprang yet another surprise on his friends and foes alike. He announced that the Office for Budget Responsibility had advised him that there had recently been a marked improvement in the prospects for the public finances to the tune of £27 billion over the next five years. The economy was now expected to grow at a rate of 2.4% every year to 2020 and the volume of tax receipts would grow accordingly. It was therefore possible for the government to abandon its plan to impose yearly tax credits cuts of over £4 billion for the next five years.

At the same time, the Chancellor predicted that it would still be possible to achieve a £10 billion budget surplus by 2020. He would be raising an additional £28.5 billion over the next five years by means of three major tax changes. A new apprenticeship levy on the bigger businesses would yield an extra £3 billion a year. Local authorities would be empowered to raise an additional £2 billion a year in council taxes, which would be ring-fenced for social care purposes. A further £1 billion a year would be raised from higher stamp duties in the purchase of buy-to-let properties and second homes.[27]

The Resolution Foundation, in company with other think-tanks and commentators, was quick to point out that the Chancellor's U-turn on tax credits constituted a delay rather than a departure from his ongoing intentions. Tax credits were already scheduled to be replaced by the Universal Credit scheme and the cuts would, in all probability, be imposed incrementally over a longer period of time as this transfer was effected.

The Foundation estimated that 'a single parent with one child, working part-time on the National Living Wage, making a new claim [was] set to lose £2,800 by 2020'. The effect of these cuts would be felt much sooner by the 140,000 people already receiving Universal Credit – 'a working single parent with two children [would] be £2,600 worse off' when the new regulations took effect in April 2016.[28]

As the transition from tax credits to Universal Credit gathers momentum it seems likely that lone parents and disabled people will be among the hardest-hit claimants. A small number of families with children will be better off under Universal Credit in exceptional cases where both parents are working full time and are being paid the National Living Wage. For the time being, however, the Chancellor's axe will not fall on the host of tax credit beneficiaries but – as matters stand – we have no means of knowing whether or when they will be left worse off as they are taken into the Universal Credit scheme.

The prospects for health and social care

In the broader policy context, however, it remains to be seen whether this Government will prove to be a One Nation or a Two Nation Tory government.

It is difficult to see how its often repeated claims to be a One Nation government can ever be reconciled or rendered compatible with its unequivocal commitment to transforming the UK's 'low wage, high welfare economy' into a 'low welfare, high wage economy' while achieving a budget surplus of £10 billion and reducing the role of the state to 36% of GDP by 2020.

In his spending review, the Chancellor gave a £3.8 billion boost to the beleaguered NHS but it was provided by 'frontloading' some of the extra £8 billion already promised in his July Budget. The chief economist at The King's Fund, Professor John Appleby, considered this to be 'a good settlement' at a time when so many other public sector services were being cut back. He went on to say, however, that it fell 'a long way short' of what was required 'to place the NHS and social care on a sustainable footing for the future'. In Appleby's view, much of the extra £8 billion would 'be absorbed by additional pension costs and dealing with provider [hospital] deficits leaving little breathing space to invest in new services and unlock productivity improvements'.

At the same time, Appleby and other health policy experts were greatly concerned that unprotected public health budgets were being drastically cut back. The publicly funded bursary scheme for student nurses and midwives was to be phased out and replaced by a loan scheme at a time when NHS hospitals were having to hire expensive agency nursing staff on a temporary basis because of the shortfall in applications for permanent posts. In more general terms, it was also noted that 'the share of UK GDP devoted to publicly funded health care will fall from an internationally low 7.3% in 2015–16 to just 6.7% of GDP in 2020–21'.[29]

Most significantly, in his Autumn Review the Chancellor reiterated his call for the NHS to make a further £22 billion-worth of 'efficiency savings' by 2020–21. Philip Inman questions whether much more can be 'saved' in NHS budgets other than in the form of further 'relentless cutbacks in administrative costs'.[30]

In the context of public expenditure on health care, it can be argued that budget cuts can only be described as 'efficient' in their outcomes when they are made without adversely affecting prevailing standards of treatment and care. It seems highly questionable that £22 billion-worth of 'efficiency savings' can be made in the case of the NHS without lowering standards. It is equally questionable whether the government's plans for reducing the role of the state to 36% of GDP can be realised without imposing cuts of this magnitude. The NHS budget may enjoy a 'protected' status, but as matters stand, it is not protected from having to impose its own cuts in the form of efficiency savings. Neither can it protect its patients from the adverse effects of the draconian cuts that are currently being imposed on the unprotected local authority social care services.

Improving the quality and quantity of residential and community-based social care services would, in its own right, constitute a significant efficiency saving for the NHS – and the taxpayer. It costs roughly three times as much to care for elderly and infirm patients in hospital as it does to care for them in residential settings or their own homes. Many of these patients 'block' hospital beds because the necessary social care services in non-hospital settings are not available. In his

Autumn Statement, the Chancellor made provision for local authorities to raise council taxes by up to 2% a year in the form of a designated 'social care precept'.

Unfortunately, as Janet Morrison of Independent Age points out, even if every council in England levied the full 2% they would 'raise only £500m a year (in 2015–16), just a fraction of the £2.9bn annual shortfall in adult social care budgets predicted by 2020'. As matters stand, however, central government grants to local councils are being cut by 56% and, in order to meet their commitments, many councils will have to sell off more of their remaining land and buildings assets.

Thirty-seven per cent of the 425,000 people currently living in residential homes are wholly dependent for coverage of their care costs on their local councils. Councils, for their part, find it increasingly difficult to keep up with the rising costs of residential care. Fifteen of the main providers of residential care services warned the Chancellor just before he delivered his Autumn Statement that, if current trends continue and the funding gap reaches £2.9 billion by 2020, 'up to half of Britain's care homes could close'. Closures on this scale would have a cataclysmic impact on the cost-effectiveness of the NHS and the quality of care provided to 'very infirm and vulnerable old people'.[31]

How could it be otherwise? The ideological *leitmotif* that gave momentum and direction to policy making after the 2015 General Election was orchestrated by a radically neo-liberal Conservative government firmly committed to rolling back the frontiers of the state to 36% of GDP. Given the magnitude of the cuts envisaged, their main target had to be the public sector social services and the strategically significant role they have traditionally played in the UK's pluralist mixed economy of welfare.

The contemporary policy packages designed to ease the effect of these budget cuts and efficiency savings can best be seen as muted One Nation Tory counterpoints to the dominant neo-liberal *leitmotif* that currently calls the tune in the making of Conservative social policy. It has all turned out much as Tim Montgomerie predicted in his rejoinder to the Queen's Speech on 27 May.

I have focused on our health and social care services in this essay because they are currently facing financial meltdown. As proved to be the case with regard to tax credit cuts, the government's arithmetic simply did not add up. The hospitals in financial crisis are currently being told to shed frontline staff, which is bound to affect standards of care, patient safety and staff morale. As Richard Murray, The King's Fund's Director of Policy, points out: 'Three years on from Robert Francis's report into Mid-Staffs which emphasises that safe staffing was the key to maintaining quality of care, the financial meltdown in the NHS now means that the policy is being abandoned for hospitals that have run out of money'.[32] At a more general level, in February 2016, The King's Fund published the findings of a survey of levels of patients' satisfaction with hospital, general practitioner and social care services. This work was undertaken by British Social Attitudes on behalf of the Fund. It was based on interviews with 2,000 patients in July and October 2015.[33]

The key findings were that: 'Overall, NHS satisfaction, which peaked at 70 per cent in 2010, fell from 65 per cent in 2014 to 60 per cent' in 2015. Almost one in four respondents said they were 'actively dissatisfied'. Overall, general practitioner services peaked at 69%, which was 'the lowest since the survey began' in 1983 and 'constituted a 10 per cent drop since 2009'. Satisfaction levels with the social care services were the lowest of all. They had fallen by 5% to 26% in 2015. Only one in four social care users were satisfied with the services they received.

The main causes of dissatisfaction were waiting times for appointments with hospital staff and general practitioners, followed by patients' 'perceptions of underfunding and staff shortages'. The report concluded that by, mid-2015, NHS underfunding was already having a deleterious effect on levels of patient satisfaction. The estimated cost to the NHS of the shortfall in social care services was in the region of £900,000 per year.

Labour in opposition

The Conservatives won the 2015 General Election because they were able to convince enough voters that – unlike the Labour Party – they could be trusted to manage the economy. In 2020, after a decade of austerity-driven policies, the Conservatives will also be judged on how effectively they managed the statutory social services and the extent to which the cuts and economies imposed have adversely affected the quality of those services.

In Andrew Rawnsley's view, as matters stood, Jeremy Corbyn's approval ratings in the opinion polls were 'dismal', with Labour 'even less trusted with the economy than it was under its previous management'.[34] Writing a few days prior to the Autumn Statement, Will Hutton had already concluded that 'the Leadership of the Labour Party offers no substantive intellectual or political opposition, nor represents a potential governing coalition, nor, wedded to a bankrupt, simplistic top-down statism, understands the complexities of these new times. Rarely has the principal opposition party been so irrelevant at a time of national need'.[35]

Under Corbyn's leadership, Labour was becoming a party that was increasingly seen by the general public as an unpatriotic party. Corbyn and his supporters want Britain to enter into 'reasonable' discussions with Argentina regarding the future of the Falkland Islands and, at a time of heightened international insecurity, to leave the North Atlantic Treaty Organisation (NATO) and unilaterally give up its nuclear weapons. On two previous occasions – in 1983 and 1987 – Labour made unilateral nuclear disarmament a centrepiece in its General Election campaigns and went down to humiliating defeat. It looks very much as if Labour is set to do so again in 2020.

As Rawnsley suggested, it is already the case that 'everyone suspects there are no circumstances in which [Corbyn] would ever want to protect its citizens and assist its allies'. When asked if 'there were any circumstances in which he would deploy military forces', he was on record as saying, 'I'm sure there are some but I can't think of them at the moment'. The great majority of British voters were well aware that, in an increasingly dangerous world, making adequate provision for our defence and national security is a matter of paramount importance in policy making. In the world of *realpolitik*, political parties that lack credibility in such matters simply render themselves unelectable, no matter now credible their economic and social policies appear to be.

Devolution, divergence and nationhood

The devolution of legislative powers to our home countries has diversified the way in which social policies are made in the UK. Most of the powers devolved to the governments of Scotland, Wales and Northern Ireland have related to matters of social policy. Writing in 2009, Derek Birrell describes how the Scottish National Party and Plaid Cymru were already well on the way towards developing their own distinctive policies within the terms of these devolved powers.

Birrell goes on to suggest that these policies were distinctive insofar as they were based on the values of 'social solidarity and collectivism rather than individualism'. In Scotland and Wales, however, these values were also closely linked to the task of nation-building which 'contributed to a deepening sense of national identity in each country'. In Northern Ireland, however, devolution 'has not [had] so much of a relationship to national identity' because national identity itself has remained a 'divided and contested' concept.[36]

Since 2009, the SNP has been much more successful than Plaid Cymru in developing social policies that are both collectivist and nationalist and presented in ways that appeal to a broad constituency of voters. The SNP's salient message to its electorate has always been that they will only enjoy the full benefits of being social citizens in a truly universalist welfare society when Scotland becomes an independent nation state. In 2011, the SNP was returned to office in the Scottish Parliament with its first working majority. Under the provisions of the Scotland and Welfare Act, more policy-making powers will be devolved and with these powers more scope for making them distinctively Scottish.

Birrell draws attention to Vernon Bogdanor's concern that devolution will eventually create a state of affairs in which different standards of welfare entitlement prevail in different parts of the UK. In his view, such divergencies will undermine the uniformity of citizens' rights to welfare on which the social services of the UK were originally based. In Birrell's view, however, 'the contributions of UK and devolved Governments to social citizenship can be complementary and coexist. Ultimately devolution must result in some significant social policy divergence, and consequently some unbalance in social citizenship and that is the inevitable and desirable outcome of devolution'.[37]

The outcome of the Scottish Referendum in September 2014 stands out as the SNP's only significant electoral setback in recent years. Nearly 85% of the electorate turned out on the day; 55% of them voted against leaving the UK and 45% voted in favour of leaving. By contrast, in the 2015 General Election the SNP won 50% of all votes cast and increased their number of MPs from 6 to 56. The Scottish Conservative, Labour and Liberal Democrat parties were left in Westminster with one MP apiece. The Liberal Democrats, traditionally typecast as the quintessential party of the middle ground, lost 49 of their 57 seats.

The SNP replaced the Liberal Democrats as the third-largest party in the Commons but they did so as a party whose anti-austerity policies were, in many respects, more radically left-wing than those of Labour. In their election manifesto the SNP promised that it 'would oppose further spending cuts and propose modest spending increases – of 0.5 per cent above inflation – in each year of the next Parliament'.[38] These additional expenditures would be paid for by a new package of revenue-raising measures including the reintroduction of the 50% top tax rate.

Most significantly, the SNP also promised that if there was an anti–Tory majority in the House of Commons, they would 'vote in a motion of confidence against a Tory Government getting off the ground'.[39] In most other respects, the SNP's interpretation of the English votes for English laws (EVEL) principle left relatively few policy issues on the political agenda that were deemed to be of exclusive concern to the English.

Unlike the British Labour Party, the SNP appeared to be united in its commitment to unilateral nuclear disarmament and, in this respect, it is noteworthy that the Scottish Labour Party has decided to oppose the renewal of Trident.

The SNP is united in its opposition to the government's decision to renegotiate the terms of the UK's membership of the European Union and to have a referendum on the outcome of these negotiations. In its election manifesto, the party claimed that 'being part of Europe is good for business and it supports jobs in Scotland and across the UK'. The SNP also served notice on the government that 'if an in/out referendum does go ahead, we will seek to amend the legislation to ensure that no constituent part of the UK can be taken out of the EU against its will'. This amendment would take the form of a 'double majority rule – meaning that unless England, Scotland, Wales and Northern Ireland each vote to leave the EU, the UK would remain a member state'.[40]

The former Labour Prime Minister Gordon Brown has described this proposal as 'the championing of a dubious constitutional principle' that, if it were to be adopted, would subordinate 'the interests of the UK as a whole to the sectional interests of one nation, not just Scotland, but Wales, England and Northern Ireland', who could exercise 'a veto that frustrates the rest of the UK's will'.[41]

Nevertheless, it remains possible that if an EU referendum yielded a result in which the majority of UK citizens voted in favour of leaving the EU and a majority of Scottish citizens voted to stay in, such an outcome might provide credible grounds on which the SNP could secure a second referendum on Scottish independence. It remains the case that, if the future progress of devolution goes well for the UK, new dimensions of welfare pluralism will be added to the political geography of its four home countries. If devolution goes badly, it will all end with the break-up of the UK and the dissolution of its own distinctive national identity.

If a majority of the UK electorate vote for Brexit, the SNP will undoubtedly press hard for a second referendum on Scottish independence. Accommodating divergent and distinctive social policies within a devolved constitutional framework that falls short of independence can be achieved when there is forbearance and a willingness to compromise on all sides. It is harder to achieve with regard to economic policies but not impossible to do so. In all matters relating to defence policies and EU membership compromises of this kind are not possible. Only sovereign nation states can make their own defence policies and apply to join or decide to leave other sovereign federal entities like the EU. If the UK were to vote for Brexit and Scotland voted to leave the UK, it would have to reapply for EU membership in its new status as a sovereign nation state.

Conclusion

The Conservative Party has always been a coalition of individualist neo-liberals and more collectivistically minded One Nation Tories. Since the party was returned to office with a working majority in 2015, however, the neo-liberals have dominated the government's policy making process. Their long-term strategic goal is the transformation of the UK from 'a low wage, high tax, high welfare society' into 'a high wage, low tax, low welfare society'.

In pursuit of this objective, the role of the state will be reduced to 36% of GDP by 2020. In the context of the UK's pluralist mixed economy of welfare, the government is committed to rolling back the frontiers of the statutory social services and extending those of the non-statutory sectors. The concept of 'a low welfare state' is a euphemistic synonym for what can otherwise be described as a residualised welfare state. Full or (near-full) privatisation is one way of achieving that end.

Julian Le Grand reminds us that, although Mrs Thatcher's first neo-liberal Conservative government 'flirted briefly with full privatisation of public services, it rapidly realised that there were both political and economic reasons why that would not be possible in the British context. These included the adverse consequences of private markets for equity: no British government could allow the distribution of, for instance, education and health to be left to be determined by the distribution of income'. Rather than opting for privatisation, the first Thatcher government adopted the mechanism of the 'quasi-market' in which 'the state retains control of financing the service. This divorces the distribution of the service concerned from the distribution of income and this contributes to a more egalitarian distribution of the service'. In the context of quasi-markets, 'the state allows provision to be undertaken by independent providers competing with one another for custom'.[42]

Although quasi-markets fell out of political favour in the late 1990s, some key elements of competitive market forces survived and were given greater salience after the coalition Conservative-led government took office in 2010. In my view, however, health care could never be fully privatised in the UK or in any other democratic society. Some kind of residualised means-tested public health service would have to be provided for the poorest individuals and families.

Nevertheless, it might be argued that the subsequent proliferation of private sector providers would constitute a reinvigorating individualist version of welfare pluralism that was more efficient and offered more choice than any collectivist model of welfare pluralism. In my view, however, the distinctive feature of an authentically pluralist model is to be found not in the number of its service providers, but in the number of people who are able to access and use its services. In this respect, the NHS is optimally pluralist in its coverage simply because access to its services is determined solely by clinical need and provided free of charge at the point of usage.

The 2012 Health and Social Services Act included procedures for extending the role of state-funded provision by private sector providers on exactly the same universalist terms. Nevertheless, significant suspicions persist regarding the government's longer-term intention.

As Carrier and Kendall remind us in their recently updated authoritative history of the NHS, towards the end of the 2012 Act's stormy passage through Parliament, 'there remained continuing and serious misgivings amongst health and social care professionals and managers that the provisions of the Bill will irreparably undermine the most important and admirable principles of the National Health Service'. Such was the persistence of these misgivings that, shortly after the passing of the Act, the then Health Secretary, Andrew Lansley went on record to insist that there was 'nothing in the Act 'that "permits or promotes privatisation" or that will lead to the fragmentation of the NHS'.[43]

It is, indeed, the case that Section 1 of the Act reaffirms the Secretary of State's duty to promote a comprehensive health service. When a new version of the NHS Constitution was published in March 2013, it included further reassurances that the 'purpose, principles and values of the Service were enshrined in law'. One of these guiding principles was that the NHS would be a comprehensive service 'free at the point of need with the highest standards ... in partnership with other organizations'.[44]

Whatever is 'enshrined' in law, however, can be revoked by Parliament or undermined by stealthy incremental changes that do not require further legislation. In February 2016, a group of trade unions representing half a million health service staff published a joint statement in which they claimed that the rate of privatisation in the NHS was gathering momentum. Since April 2013, 'more than a third of the total value of contracts put out to tender had been won by private companies'. They went on to claim that if this trend continued there was 'a real danger ... we could end up with a repeat of the American experience where income, rather than need, dictates the level of care a patient can expect'. The Department of Health's response to these claims was that 'only 6.3 per cent of the NHS budget was spent on private providers'.[45]

Over the next four years, the prospects for the NHS and all our other key social services will depend on whether our government is able and willing to reconcile the imperatives embodied in its commitment to creating a 'high wage, low tax, low welfare society' with the principles of universality, adequate provision and authentic choice.

The prospect of sustained economic growth and higher wages cannot be taken for granted in an increasingly volatile global market. Even in good times these benefits do not automatically trickle down to the poorest breadwinners and their families. In a truly 'low tax' society, only the higher wage earners will be able to afford high quality social services. Nevertheless, the possibility that the government will privatise more parts of the NHS and other key social services cannot be ruled out. If that were to happen, Labour under the leadership of Jeremy Corbyn might win in 2020 and impose a unitary model of social welfare in which the state is the main or monopolistic service provider.

There remains, however, a pluralist middle way between these two ideological extremes in which the claims of social justice and universality can coexist with authentic opportunities to choose between alternative kinds of service provider as befits a free society. Since May 2015, however, the Westminster Parliament has been left without a major party committed to the middle way of making social policies. The Conservative government's shift towards the radical right has been complemented by Labour's shift in the opposite direction. The SNP has replaced the Liberal Democrats as the UK's third-largest party. Its social policy proposals are as radically left-wing as those of Labour.

Throughout their first year in office with a working majority, the Conservatives have spoken with two voices regarding their policy intentions. As William Keegan notes, the Prime Minister occasionally makes reassuring One Nation Tory speeches which purport to show that he wishes his 'domestic legacy to be one of a decent, harmonious Britain'. At the same time, 'the entire thrust of the Chancellor's policies points the other way, aggravating the plight of those who are already finding it difficult to make ends meet'.[46]

There are already signs that some One Nation Tories are becoming disillusioned with their party's austerity-driven policies. Writing in *The Times* in February 2016, Tim Montgomerie told his readers that he was 'quitting the Conservative Party after 28 years of membership'. He went on to say that his 'greatest disappointment will be that we failed to build the socially just Conservatism that an extended period in power provides the space for'.[47]

Montgomerie singled out 'Michael Gove's school reforms, Iain Duncan-Smith's universal credit and Osborne's living wage' as 'considerable achievements'. In his view, however, 'the overall direction of housing, tax, pensions, immigration and family policy has been to intensify inequality between the propertied and the unpropertied, between the old and young and those with children and those without'. He also condemned the government for recommending that we should vote to remain in the European Union. He was in no doubt that its austerity-driven policies had proved to be 'the greatest source of social misery on the continent'.

I am not a member of the Conservative Party but, as a One Nation Tory by political disposition, I will vote to remain in the EU because my overriding concern is that opting for Brexit would imperil the territorial and constitutional integrity of the UK. If Scotland voted to remain in the EU and the rest of the UK voted to leave, the SNP might well call for a second Scottish referendum because eventual independence is its political raison d'être. Only the UK Parliament is empowered to authorise a referendum but, if it refused to do so, the UK would swiftly become a seriously disunited kingdom. While it remains open to question whether Northern Ireland will vote to remain in the EU, in all probability Scotland and Wales will do so by substantial majorities.

There is always the possibility that the SNP will lose a second referendum at a time when the price of North Sea oil has fallen from $110 to $30 per barrel. In the event of an SNP victory, there would be several years of political and economic uncertainty as the UK began negotiating its way out of the EU and Scotland waited to become a sovereign state empowered to negotiate its way out of the UK. A 'leap in the dark' would become a leap into the 'dark backward and abysm of time'.

In my view, David Cameron negotiated just enough concessions to protect the UK from 'ever closer political union with the EU', the operations of the single currency and being required to give EU immigrants unconditional and immediate rights to welfare benefits. He also negotiated the introduction of a 'red card' system which would allow the parliaments of member states to block unwanted EU laws.

As a conditional altruist, I had hoped that we would have recovered more control over our own borders. Unconditional altruists tend to overlook the additional hardships that fall on the poorest citizens when the volume of immigration is insufficiently regulated and social service budgets cannot cope with the rising level of demand for services. An acrimonious Brexit from the EU, however, could end with our Channel border being moved back from Calais to Dover.

If the UK votes to remain in the EU it will be well placed to engage the support of other member states in negotiating further reforms of an order that require significant treaty changes. It is generally agreed that the EU is afflicted with a chronic 'democratic deficit' and that the relationship between its national courts and the European Courts is in urgent need of review.

I agree with David Cameron that 'Britain will be safer, stronger and better off by remaining in a reformed European Union'.[48] I am also persuaded that in the context of a faltering global market with China's economy moving into recession, the prospect of Britain leaving the EU constitutes 'the biggest risk' to our 'domestic financial stability'.[49]

Britain already confronts the prospect of political instability in the aftermath of the EU referendum and the June local elections. Both the Conservative and Labour parties are riven with internecine conflicts that could trigger the breakaway of dissident factions. The Conservatives are polarising into two warring camps as the debate about leaving or remaining in the EU becomes more openly acrimonious. It could become still more belligerent if the electorate vote for Brexit and triumphant Tory Eurosceptics mount a challenge for the party leadership.

In the Westminster Parliament the two main parties have become more ideologically polarised as generally happens in first-past-the-post voting systems. Under these systems, most electors assume, for good reason, that voting for one of the smaller parties will prove to be a 'wasted vote'. Consequently, they are left with a choice between two major parties that will leave them in thrall to the dictates of one or other of the two great unitary ideologies of individualism and collectivism.

It is most unlikely that the Westminster Parliament will ever adopt any of the versions of proportional representation that devolution has brought to Scotland, Wales and Northern Ireland. Consequently, it becomes even more unlikely that any middle-of-the-road One Nation Tory, Liberal Democrat and Labour MPs will break away from their parties and form a new political movement.

Such a movement would be based on the best values and principles that guide both the 'invisible hand of the market and the visible hands of public institutions'. Its social policies would take the form of a pluralist mixed economy of statutory and non-statutory private and voluntary sectors in which agreement on the relative importance of each sector takes account of the needs of the whole nation in ways which equitably reconcile the imperatives of wealth creation with those of social justice. Neither of the two unitary ideologies of individualism and collectivism will ever be able to encompass or reconcile the diversity of principles and values that might find expression in a genuinely pluralist and democratic society.

Notes

[1] Keegan (1993), p 104.
[2] Pinker (1995b), reproduced here as **Chapter Nine**.
[3] *The Conservative Party Manifesto 2015*, p 7.
[4] *Ibid.*, pp 7-8.
[5] Crawford et al (2015).
[6] Soumaya Keynes, 'Expert economy commentary: Institute of Fiscal Studies', 3 May 2015, https://fullfact.org/economy/expert-economy-commentary-institute-fiscal-studies/
[7] Joyce (2015).
[8] Bulletin issued by the Press Office, Prime Minister's Office, 10 Downing Street, 27 May 2015.
[9] Montgomerie (2015).
[10] Osborne (2015).
[11] Cameron (2015).
[12] Jones (2015).
[13] See http://www.bbc.co.uk/news/uk-politics-33221966
[14] Mason (2015).
[15] Elliot, F. (2015).
[16] See https://www.gov.uk/government/speeches/chancellor-george-osbornes-summer-budget-2015-speech

[17] Elliott, L. (2015).

[18] Young, T. (2015).

[19] See http://www.theguardian.com/politics/2015/jul/13/harriet-harman-struggles-to-hold-labour-together-over-welfare-changes

[20] Kellner (2015).

[21] See: http://www.telegraph.co.uk/news/politics/tony-blair/11755234/Tony-Blair-if-your-heart-is-with-Corbyn-get-a-transplant.html

[22] See: http://www.peoplesmomentum.com

[23] See: http://www.theguardian.com/politics/2015/sep/12/what-does-jeremy-corbyn-think.

[24] On Kaufman's own view of this description see: http://www.spectator.co.uk/2009/11/how-my-party-was-betrayed-by-kgb-bootlickers/

[25] Finch (2015).

[26] *Labour Press*, 18 October 2015.

[27] Wintour and Elliott (2015).

[28] *Ibid*.

[29] See Campbell (2015).

[30] Inman (2015), pp 6-7.

[31] See Ruddick (2015), p 3.

[32] Campbell (2016), p 1.

[33] Donnelly (2016); see also: http://www.kingsfund.org.uk/projects/public-satisfaction-nhs/bsa-survey-2015.

[34] Rawnsley (2015).

[35] Hutton (2015).

[36] Birrell (2009), pp 147 and 153-4.

[37] *Ibid.*, pp 190-1.

[38] SNP (2015), p 7.

[39] *Ibid.*, p 11.

[40] *Ibid.*, p 9.

[41] Brown (2015).

[42] Le Grand (2006), pp 9-10.

[43] Carrier and Kendall (2016), pp 237 and 253.

[44] *Ibid.*, p 261.

[45] See Taylor (2016), p 8.

[46] Keegan (2016).

[47] Montgomerie (2016).

[48] Cameron (2016), p 6.

[49] The view of Mark Carney, governor of the Bank of England, 8 March 2016: http://www.bbc.co.uk/news/business-35751919

AFTERTHOUGHT

On the post-Brexit prospects for social policy in the UK*

Robert Pinker

In **Chapter Thirteen**, I reviewed some of the key trends in UK social policy between May 2015 and the end of March 2016. By the time the page proofs were returned to us in August, however, the UK electorate had already voted to leave the EU (for 'Brexit') by a narrow but decisive majority on 23 June 2016. The implications of this vote were momentous, reaching far beyond the prospects for social policy to encompass every kind of policy making, including what needed to be done to ensure the survival of the United Kingdom itself as a united political entity.

The EU Referendum and its outcome

In the run-up to polling day, both the 'Remainers' and the 'Leavers' resorted to negative forms of campaigning and the publication of misleading and inaccurate news. The 'Remainers' ran what was widely considered to be a campaign designed to evoke widespread fear of the appalling consequences that would immediately follow a vote to leave the EU. The 'Leavers' misleadingly claimed that all of the £350 million currently paid every week to the EU could be redirected to increase the budget of the NHS immediately after Brexit was achieved. The 'Leavers' also launched a fear campaign of their own regarding countries which were in the process of seeking accession to the EU. They claimed that if Britain did not regain control over its own borders it would eventually be overwhelmed by thousands of Turkish, Macedonian, Montenegrin, Serbian and Albanian immigrants. It was this perceived need for stricter border controls, rather than the state of the economy that became the key concern of many voters during the last two weeks of the campaign.

And so it came about that on 23 June, 78 per cent of the UK electorate went to the polls and voted 52 per cent to 48 per cent for Brexit. England voted 53 per cent to 47 per cent for Brexit, along with Wales, which voted 52 per cent to 48 per cent. Scotland voted to remain by a massive 62 per cent to 38 per cent and Northern Ireland did likewise by 56 per cent to 44 per cent.

On the following morning, David Cameron announced that he would resign as Prime Minister and Party Leader as soon as his successor was appointed. Theresa

---

* This Afterword was completed on 27 July 2017 for publication in this collection.

May became the Party's new Leader and the UK's new Prime Minister. Thus, it transpired that a formerly high-profile Cabinet Minister who was generally considered to have played little more than a low-profile role in support of the Remain campaign found herself leading a new government firmly committed to leaving the EU.

What kind of Brexit?

The process of leaving would start immediately after the UK Government declared its intention to leave by triggering Article 50 of the Lisbon Treaty. This decision would be followed by a two-year period in which the UK and the EU negotiated the terms on which the UK would leave. If necessary, this period could be extended by mutual consent. The wording of the Referendum required voters to make an unqualified choice between 'Remain' or 'Leave'. Throughout and after the Referendum campaign, however, it became increasingly clear that those who wanted to leave the EU were sharply divided with regard to the kind of Brexit they wanted – a 'hard' or a 'soft' one.

Opting for a 'hard' Brexit would, in all probability, mean giving up full access to the single market and the customs union, as well as membership of the EU itself. Thereafter, the UK would rely on World Trade Organization rules in its dealings with the EU. It would, however, be free to make its own laws, negotiate its own trade deals and, of key significance to most Brexiteers, regain full control over its own borders. Advocates of a 'hard' Brexit contended that proceeding in this way would obviate the need for prolonged negotiations. All the necessary institutional changes could be swiftly implemented which would shorten the period of economic uncertainty to everyone's benefit.

Critics of the 'hard Brexit' option frequently pointed out that the EU happens to be the UK's closest and biggest trading partner. Building new trading relations with more distant nations would almost certainly prove to be a more complex and lengthy process than many Brexiteers were willing to admit. Denied free access to the EU's single market and customs union, many banks and businesses would be strongly tempted to relocate their financial services elsewhere and thereby deal a crippling blow to London's status as an international financial hub.

In August 2016, the Institute for Fiscal Studies (IFS) estimated that the cost of leaving the EU without first negotiating sufficient replacement trade deals could prove to be the equivalent of 4 per cent of the UK's GDP. Advocates of a 'soft Brexit' wanted the negotiations between the UK and the EU to end with an agreement on terms that resembled existing arrangements as closely as possible. Without continuing access to the single market and the customs union on preferential terms, the movement of British goods and services would become subject to tariffs of up to 10 per cent as well as long and costly delays affecting goods in transit through ports and airports. The IFS concluded that full membership of the single market reduces the 'costs of trade' and 'other non-tariff barriers' in a way that no other option does. It went on to claim, however, that obtaining membership without accepting EU regulations, the free movement of EU citizens across the borders of other member states and contributing to the EU's budget 'would be unprecedented'.

The IFS review also reminded us that the services sector accounts for about 80 per cent of the UK's economy and that the EU, with its 550 million people, is 'by far the largest market for UK service exports', accounting, as it does, for nearly 40 per cent of that market.[1] Roughly 50 per cent of all the UK's exports go to the EU. The European Commission, the European Parliament and all of the other 27 EU member states repeatedly warned the UK that if it wants to retain access to the single market after Brexit, it must accept and uphold all of the EU's 'Four Freedoms' regarding the movement of people, goods, services and capital. In particular, the rights of EU citizens to move freely across the borders of any other member state in order to live and work there would not be open to any kind of negotiation.

In June 2016, however, we had yet to be told how Theresa May and her new Government would respond to this particular challenge, whether they would opt for a 'hard' or 'soft' Brexit and whether, in doing so, they would be able to preserve the territorial integrity of the UK. Our future economic and social policy and constitutional prospects would all be contingent on the Government finding the right answers to these complex problems.

Theresa May delivered her first speech as Prime Minister on the 13 July, outside Number 10 Downing Street. She began by reminding the public that David Cameron had 'led a One Nation Government' and she promised it would be 'in that spirit' that she also planned to lead. May went on to say that 'the full title of my party is the Conservative and Unionist Party'. She believed 'in the union, the precious, precious bond between England, Scotland, Wales and Northern Ireland', including the 'union between all of our citizens … wherever we are and wherever we come from'. The Prime Minister affirmed that her Government's economic and social policies would be grounded in the principles of social as well as economic justice. It would be her 'mission to make Britain a country that works for everyone', including those families who are hard-pressed and 'just about managing'.

At that point, a new acronym referring to those 'just about managing' – JAMs – had entered the vocabulary of our everyday political discourse. It had originally, and fittingly, been invented by the Resolution Foundation, a social policy think-tank chaired by David Willetts, a One Nation Tory and former Minister for Universities and Science. It was, therefore, entirely fitting that Theresa May should end her first speech as Prime Minister with a ringing endorsement of One Nation Tory values and policy objectives. She promised that, 'As we leave the European Union … we will make Britain a country that works, not for the privileged few, but for every one of us'.[2]

A few days later, the publication of a list of new government and ministerial appointments revealed that Boris Johnson was the new Foreign Secretary, David Davis had been made Secretary of State for exiting the European Union, and

Liam Fox was made Secretary of State for International Trade. Three of the key Cabinet Ministers who were to play leading roles in navigating the UK's route out of the EU were totally committed to achieving a 'hard Brexit' as swiftly as possible.

Preparing the way for Brexit

In the Prime Minister's opening speech on 2 October 2016 to the Conservative Party's annual conference there were some clear indications that she was thinking along the same lines. She began by outlining her plans for restoring the supremacy of UK law over European law. A new 'Great Repeal Bill' would be introduced as a first step on the way towards taking the UK out of the European Union.

At the same time, the European Communities Act 1972, which gives direct effect to all European law, would also be repealed. Parliament would then write those parts of EU law it wishes to keep into UK law and discard those parts it did not want to keep. Assurances were given that all of the key employment and other welfare rights which are currently embodied in European law would be retained. This tranche of new legislation would be introduced in the next Parliamentary session in March 2017 in readiness for immediate implementation on the day in March 2019 when the UK leaves the EU.

May told the party that, under her leadership, the UK would not be 'leaving the EU only to give up control of immigration again. And we are not leaving only to return to the jurisdiction of the European Court of Justice'. She went on to say that the people who wanted to do everything possible that would allow them to stay in the single market were looking at Brexit 'the wrong way' by drawing misleadingly sharp distinctions between supposedly 'hard' and 'soft options'.

In the Prime Minister's view we were on our way to becoming a 'truly Global Britain', in which our future relationship with the EU was not going to be based on a 'Norway model' or a 'Switzerland model', it was 'going to be an agreement between an independent sovereign United Kingdom and the European Union'. It was, however, still the case that she wanted 'to give British companies the maximum freedom to trade with and operate within the Single Market – and let European businesses do the same'.

Shortly after Theresa May became Prime Minister it became clear that, in order to maintain momentum in the Brexit stakes, she was planning to trigger Article 50 without the prior approval of Parliament. The legality of this stratagem for fast-tracking Brexit was about to be challenged in the High Court in London. Seven private actions had been grouped together as a single legal challenge with Gina Miller, an investment expert and philanthropist, acting as the lead complainant.

The Prime Minister now gave notice in her conference speech that her government would resist 'these people' who were intent on arguing in court 'that Article 50 can only be triggered after agreement in both Houses of Parliament'. In her view, they were 'not standing up for democracy, they're trying to subvert it' and, at the same time, trying to 'kill' Brexit by 'delaying it'.[3] The Attorney

General would be representing the Government when the case was heard in early November.

No reference was made to legal challenges that were being brought to the High Court in Belfast by Roger McCord, a private citizen whose son was murdered during 'The Troubles' and representatives from Sinn Fein, the Social Democratic and Labour Party (SDLP), the Alliance and the Green Parties. The action rested on the claim that Brexit would breach the terms of the Good Friday Agreement by reinstating a 'hard border' with the Republic of Ireland and undermining the 1998 peace deal.

Legal challenges to a fast-track Brexit

On 28 November 2016, the Northern Ireland legal challenge against Brexit was rejected in the Belfast High Court. The judge noted that there was nothing in the 1998 Good Friday Agreement preventing the UK Government from triggering Article 50. The legal challenge brought in London with Gina Miller as the lead complainant was upheld in the High Court on 3 November. The three judges ruled that the Prime Minister could not trigger Article 50 without the prior approval of both Houses of Parliament. The Government gave notice that the High Court's ruling would be challenged in the Supreme Court. The hearing would take place in early January 2017.

The pro–Brexit press was outraged by the High Court's ruling. The reporters from *The Sun* wrote: 'A motley handful of EU–based campaigners led by a foreign-born multi-millionaire threw Theresa May's Brexit plans into chaos yesterday'.[4] They warned that the ruling could delay Brexit for several years. The *Daily Mail* published a front page article with pictures of the three judges above a headline describing them as 'Enemies of the People'. In its Leader Comment, the Mail described their ruling as 'a betrayal of common sense, the people and democracy by forcing the Government to declare its negotiating hand before the talks even begin'.[5] The *Daily Express* described 3 November as 'the day democracy died' in Britain and went on to insist that 'the royal prerogative can be used 'to hasten its exit from the EU'.[6]

However, Polly Toynbee's *Guardian* article carried the headline, 'The court's ruling is a chance for MPs to put the national interest first and halt Brexit before it wreaks any more havoc'. The meaning of the 'momentous decision' was that 'Theresa May cannot tear up our right to be EU citizens without the authority of Parliament'.[7] The *Daily Mirror* had also backed the 'Remain' campaign. In its Leader of 4 November it described the High Court ruling as 'a great victory for democracy … that MPs will determine our future, rather than Downing Street's struggling tenant'.[8]

The Prime Minister's Lord Mayor's Banquet Speech and the Chancellor's Autumn Statement 2017

On 14 November, the Prime Minister gave a keynote speech at the Lord Mayor's Banquet in the Guildhall of the City of London. In this presentation, she extolled the 'forces of liberalism and globalisation' which had 'delivered unprecedented levels of wealth and opportunity' by lifting 'millions out of poverty around the world'. At the same time, the Prime Minister acknowledged that these forces of change had 'left too many people behind' with their jobs 'outsourced and wages undercut'. She was determined that her government would adopt 'a new approach to managing the forces of globalisation so that they work for all'. This would be done by ensuring that 'the prosperity they provide is shared by all'.[9]

Although there was much in the Prime Minister's speech to gladden the hearts of One Nation Tories, she said nothing about the kinds of policy that would be needed to deliver fair shares for all. At the time it was generally assumed that this matter would be addressed by the Chancellor of the Exchequer when he delivered his Autumn Statement on 23 November. Throughout the summer months there had been mounting concern in Parliament and across the country regarding the funding crisis in the NHS and social care services and the extent to which cuts in social expenditure were falling disproportionately on the very poor as well as those families who were 'just about managing'. In presenting his Autumn Statement, however, the Chancellor, Philip Hammond, made no reference whatever to what a growing number of policy analysts perceived as a looming catastrophe in health and social care service provision. With the onset of winter approaching, these services remained in the grip of a worsening financial crisis, underfunded, understaffed and overwhelmed by rising demand.

In reality, the vote for Brexit had left the government little or no scope for increasing social expenditure even if it had wanted to do so. Despite the decision to reduce the taper on Universal Credit as earnings increased, many recipients would still be left worse off than they would otherwise have been. There was to be no significant easement in the government's future plans for continuing financial austerity. It was still poised to impose a further £12 billion of welfare cuts in April 2017. Indeed, the prospects for social policy in the United Kingdom were looking bleak before the Brexit vote, as one would expect them to be under a government committed to transforming Britain from being 'a low wage, high tax, high welfare society [into] a high wage, low tax, low welfare society'. The Chancellor told Parliament that, in pursuit of this end, the government would borrow £23 billion to invest in a National Productivity Fund focused on developing economic infrastructure, the digital economy and new house building starts. By focusing on raising productivity in this way it would be possible to create more jobs and raise living standards throughout the country with more people sharing in the UK's prosperity and an economy that 'works for everyone'.[10]

This new strategic plan, however, was going to be implemented over a period of five years and, as such, it was unlikely to yield any immediate benefits to the general public. MPs of all parties had come to the House with the crisis in the NHS and social care services uppermost in their minds and their concern was widely shared by their grassroot constituency members. For this reason, the timing of the Chancellor's announcement was singularly inept and his failure to say anything about the health and social care crisis was singularly insensitive.

The initial impact of the Brexit vote had undoubtedly compounded the welfare funding problems confronting the government. In its leader column of 24 November, the *Guardian* claimed that as a result of 'the self-inflicted wound of Brexit … the nation's income will be 2.4% smaller than previously expected over the next five years. The referendum vote will add £59 billion in additional borrowing over the same period, contributing to the extra £122 billion the Office for Budget Responsibility calculates will be needed 'over the next five years'.[11]

The Chancellor based his estimates on research material provided by the Office for Budget Responsibility (OBR) and the Institute for Fiscal Studies.[12] Their generally gloomy forecasts claimed that the government was no longer on course to balance the budget by 2020. They predicted that future economic growth was likely to be sluggish. The OBR forecast was that, after Brexit, there would be a sharp decline in economic growth and tax revenues while rising inflation would inflict new hardships on low-income families.

The reliability of these 'doom-mongering' predictions was, however, quickly called into question by pro-Brexit newspapers and other commentators. In the *Mail Online*, Daniel Martin asked who were the IFS 'trying to kid' when they claimed that 'families faced the biggest squeeze in living standards since the 1920s 'and that workers would still be earning less in real terms in 2021 than they were in 2008 before the financial crash'. Downing Street and 'furious Tory MPs' had also 'lined up to dismiss' the IFS and the OBR's 'dire predictions' regarding the UK's post-Brexit prospects.[13]

Mark Littlewood, Director-General of the Institute for Economic Affairs, offered a more even-handed review of the IFS and the OBR's forecasts. Writing for the *Mail on Sunday*, he suggested that, during the referendum campaign, 'all sorts of extravagant, elaborate and precise claims were being made by both sides about the merits of remaining in or leaving' the EU. While some 'Remainers' made 'apocalyptic predictions' about what would follow after a Brexit vote, there were also 'Leavers' who were 'overly euphoric' about what would happen next. In Littlewood's view, both the IFS and the OBR were trying to make 'genuinely independent assessments about how the British economy will fare during the coming years'. They were, however, confronted by 'so many imponderables and so many unknowns' and the relevant precedents to which they could refer. As a Brexiteer himself, Littlewood thought there would be 'some short-term pain' in exiting the EU but in the longer term this would prove to be 'a price worth paying'.[14]

The funding crisis in health and social care services

While the debate about the likely impact of Brexit on the UK economy continued, the debate about the immediate funding crisis in the health and social care services was becoming more openly confrontational. In the first week of December 2016, Mike Adamson, the Chief Executive Officer of the Red Cross went on record to describe it as a 'humanitarian crisis' in which the safety of patients was being put at risk and could no longer be guaranteed. Two patients had died at the Worcester Royal Hospital after long waits for attention and care in the corridor of the Accident and Emergency Department. Dr Mark Holland, President of the Society for Acute Medicine, warned the public that 'the NHS is now broken'.[15] Professor Keith Willett, Director of Acute Care for NHS England, questioned the accuracy of these claims, as did the Prime Minister and the Health Secretary, Jeremy Hunt, who thought they were 'irresponsible and overblown'.

When Simon Stevens, Chief Executive of NHS England, appeared before the Public Accounts Committee a few days later, he told them he thought the Prime Minister's claim that the NHS 'was getting more than it asked for was not true'. He contended that it was 'a matter of fact that … we got less than we asked for [in the spending review] so it would be stretching it to say that the NHS got more'.[16] There were further reports that, as a result of these funding shortfalls, 'nearly two dozen hospitals in England have had to declare a black alert … after becoming so overcrowded that they could no longer guarantee patient safety and provide their full range of normal services'. At a time when the government was planning to make further cuts in the number of hospital beds, more hospitals were finding it impossible to accommodate the increasing number of patients urgently needing treatment and care.[17]

In the same week that the Prime Minister was dismissing claims that the NHS was in a state of 'humanitarian crisis', she was telling *Sunday Telegraph* readers that her government would use the opportunity provided by Brexit 'to build the shared society by embracing genuine and wide-ranging social reform'.[18] The Prime Minister singled out mental health as the field of care in most urgent need of reform and extra resources. Nevertheless, she declined to answer Jeremy Corbyn when he asked her why the government had recently cut the number of professional mental health staff by 6,000 nurses and 400 doctors.[19]

There is, however, nothing that should surprise us in these seeming disjunctions between the ends and means of Conservative social policy making. As I suggested in **Chapter Thirteen**, once the ascendant neo-liberals of the party had broken free from the restraints of working in coalition with the Liberal Democrats after the 2015 General Election, they publicly committed their government to rolling back the frontiers of the state. In making this commitment, however, allowance had to be made for the fact that the Conservative Party itself was a long-standing coalition of individualist neo-liberals and collectivistically minded One Nation Tories who were ideologically opposed to residualising almost the entire public sector including the statutory social services. And there was no other acceptable way in which cuts of this magnitude could be achieved. I went on to suggest that the government's sporadic U-turn attempts at easing the immediate effects of its budget cuts and efficiency-saving directives 'could best be seen as muted One Nation Tory counterpoints to the dominant *leitmotif* that currently calls the tune in the making of Conservative social policy' (**Chapter Thirteen, p 284**).

Some of the proposed budget cuts were postponed by George Osborne in response to pressure from One Nation Conservatives and opposition parties. These cuts will shortly be re-imposed and when this happens they will fall disproportionately on some of the most vulnerable and needy groups in the UK. The long-standing shortfalls in social provision are manifest not only in the crises besetting our health and social care services but in the phenomenon of child poverty. On 26 January 2017, the Royal College of Paediatricians and Child Health published a report which claims that one in five of our children are living in poverty to the detriment of their health and life chances. The report claims that the UK 'has the 15th highest mortality rate for babies under the age of one year out of 19 European countries' and 'one of the highest rates for older children and young people'. The Child Poverty Action Group, in its response to these findings, warns that 'in the face of a projected 50% increase in child poverty of 2020, this report should sound alarms'. This projection will have been based on estimates of the negative impact that future planned-for budget cuts will have on the living standards of poor and 'just-managing' families.[20]

It would be prudent to assume, as Mark Littlewood suggests, that there will be at least 'some short term pain' to be expected and lived through. Much will depend on what sort of Brexit results from the negotiations. In this respect it should be noted that most of the Conservative advocates of a 'hard Brexit' are neo-liberals who are equally enthusiastic about residualising the statutory social services. With those considerations in mind, there will be no need to speculate on whom the pain will be inflicted, only on how long it will last.

In democratic pluralist societies, statutory social services are designed not only to enhance general living standards, but to act as a safety net for the casualties of political, economic and social change. It is, perhaps, ironic that many of the electorate who voted for Brexit did so because they were already casualties of change and had been so for a very long time. And some of them would not have known the difference between a hard and a soft Brexit. In such uncertain times, a socially responsible government would be reinforcing rather than residualising its welfare safety net. The Brexit vote, however, has concentrated more power in the hands of a clique of ideologically driven neo-liberal Conservatives and thereby increased the momentum with which Britain's safety net is being dismantled.

The morning after Donald Trump was invested with the Presidency of the United States, he was issuing an executive order rolling back the remit of Obamacare. If the crisis in our National Health Service intensifies, it is just possible that the government will speed up the rate at which it is currently being privatised.

When Sir John Major was touring the country during the EU referendum in support of the 'Remain' campaign he claimed that among the leading Brexiteers,

Sir Iain Duncan-Smith wanted to fund the NHS through a new contributory social insurance scheme, Boris Johnson wanted to charge patients at the point of need and Michael Gove simply wanted to privatise the service. Sir John predicted that if these three high-profile politicians 'rose to power following Brexit', the NHS would be 'about as safe with them as a pet hamster would be with a hungry python'.[21] The three key figures in the Brexit negotiating team are now David Davis, Liam Fox and the Foreign Secretary, Boris Johnson.

The Government's 12-point Brexit Plan

On 6 December 2016, the Government accepted a Labour amendment asking it to publish its plan for leaving the EU before it triggered Article 50. The plan, which the Government published on 17 January 2017, set out 12 negotiating objectives for leaving the European Union. These objectives included the UK recovering control of its own laws by bringing an end to the jurisdiction of the European Court of Justice and taking back control of its own borders.

The plan's key message was that this kind of Brexit 'cannot mean membership of the EU Single Market because such membership would require compliance with European Court of Justice rulings, free movement and all other EU rules and regulations without having a vote on what those rules and regulations are'.[22] Full customs union membership would also prevent Britain from becoming a 'global trading nation, striking trade agreements around the world'.

The Prime Minister and her negotiating team would have been well aware that, given the sheer volume of UK–EU trade, not having access to either the single market or the customs union would be seen by many people as a very 'hard' and risky kind of Brexit. Nevertheless, a 'softer' Brexit which secured the UK's access but left it excluded from voting on vitally important regulatory matters would have satisfied neither the Brexiteers nor the Remainers.

It was for this reason that the 'priority' objective in the Government's plan was to 'pursue a bold and ambitious Free Trade Agreement with the European Union', which would allow for 'the freest possible trade in goods and services between Britain and EU member states'. At the same time it would be preparing to negotiate 'new trade agreements with other non-EU countries' throughout the world. Although full customs union membership prevents members from making their own agreements, the Government still wanted 'to have a customs agreement with the EU' and it had an 'open mind on how we would achieve this end'.

In its statement of objectives, the Government's plan also gave assurances that it would 'put the final deal that is agreed between the UK and the EU to a vote in both Houses of Parliament'. In its transference of European law into UK laws and domestic regulations, workers' rights would be 'fully protected and maintained'. The rights of EU nationals living in the UK would be guaranteed once this offer was 'reciprocated for British citizens in EU countries'. Throughout the Brexit negotiations, every effort would be made to 'strengthen the precious union between the four nations of the United Kingdom' and to maintain 'a Common

Travel Area with the Republic of Ireland while protecting the integrity of the United Kingdom's immigration system'.

The *Daily Mail* praised Theresa May's 'fighting talk', along with her 'gentle' reminder to the EU 'that a trade war would jeopardise its £500 billion investments in Britain' and 'put at risk millions of European jobs that are dependent on exports to the UK worth '£200 billion a year'. It went on to say that since the Brexit vote, Britain's economic performance had been 'phenomenal' and 'Donald Trump's promise of a quick trade deal could not have come at a more fortunate moment for her'.[23]

In contrast, the *Guardian* thought Theresa May's speech was 'a doubly depressing event'. It was 'a reality check' for the people who still believed 'the UK can stay in the single market at the same time as leaving the European Union'. It was, however, 'also shot through with unsupported optimism about UK economic performance, trade prospects and the readiness of the remaining EU–27 to strike the kind of deal that would suit the UK Government'. In this respect, the speech was 'riddled with its own streak of global fantasy'. May was also bluffing when she said that 'no deal would in the end be better than a bad deal'. And, in the longer term, 'the decision to allow migration to trump the single market' may make it harder to keep the economy on its growth trajectory.[24]

We cannot predict with any certainty the kind of impact Brexit will have over time on the UK economy's performance. If it falters, the prospects for British social policy will most certainly be adversely affected. With a neo-liberal Conservative Government in office, however, these prospects would still be bleak even if economic performance remained buoyant. The draconian cuts currently being imposed on our public sector will eventually trigger a major crisis across our welfare services. If, however, the Brexit negotiations leave the UK having to choose between a bad deal or no deal at all we will be left confronting, not only a sharp downturn in our economic and social welfare prospects, but the break-up of the United Kingdom itself.

The Supreme Court's rulings on Article 50

On 24 January, the Supreme Court delivered its ruling on the legal challenge brought against the Government by Gina Miller. It decided by eight votes to three to uphold the High Court's ruling that the Prime Minister could not trigger Article 50 without the prior approval of Parliament.

In delivering its ruling, the Supreme Court said that it was for the Government to decide on the kind of Parliamentary Bill that would now be needed before Article 50 could be triggered. The Supreme Court also ruled that it was not constitutionally necessary for the Government to obtain the consent of the devolved assemblies of Scotland, Wales and Northern Ireland before it triggered Article 50.

Immediately after the Supreme Court's ruling was delivered, Scotland's First Minister, Nicola Sturgeon, announced that she would be calling for a second referendum on Scottish independence. The SNP's Foreign Affairs Minister, Alex Salmond, said that in the meantime, his party would be tabling 50 substantive amendments to the Article 50 Bill when it was put before Parliament. In Wales, which voted for Brexit, its First Minister, Carwyn Jones, said that Labour and Plaid Cymru were drafting a joint plan to preserve Wales's access to the single market. In Northern Ireland, which voted for Remain, an election had been called following the breakdown of the Democratic Unionist's and Sinn Fein's power-sharing coalition Government. Fourteen of the 18 Northern Ireland MPs elected to Westminster take their seats in the House of Commons. The four Sinn Fein MPs refuse to do so. The eight Democratic Unionists, the two Ulster Unionists and the single Independent Unionist will probably vote in favour of triggering Article 50 while the three Social Democratic and Labour MPs will definitely vote against it.

Conclusion

On 26 January, the Government published its European Union (Notification of Withdrawal) Bill, confirming that the activation of Article 50 would be subject to the approval of Parliament. Five days were set aside for debate and scrutiny of the Bill by the Commons, after which it would be sent on to the Lords for further consideration. Prevarication of any kind, it was felt, would be seen by the general public as an intrinsically undemocratic response.

There is, however, nothing undemocratic in giving the electorate an opportunity to think again about the way in which they voted in a referendum. Referenda outcomes are not sacrosanct. They can be revised or revoked by electorates just as legislators revise or revoke statute laws when the need to do so arises.

Judging by the way in which the Bill was taken through its readings in the Commons, there are reasons for believing that the best interests of democracy will not be served when the terms of the final offer are debated two years hence. Both the Conservative and Labour MPs were required to vote under the restraint of three-line whips ordering them to back the Bill and show due respect for the wishes of the British people. The Bill passed its third reading in the Commons by 492 votes to 122. Three-line whips notwithstanding, 52 Labour MPs, including 11 junior shadow ministers and 3 whips voted against the Bill. Only one Conservative, the One Nation Tory Kenneth Clarke, had the courage and conviction to vote against the Bill.

Moreover, although the Government White Paper promised that Parliament would be allowed to vote on the exit deal before their counterparts in the European Parliament, it was soon made clear that they would only be able to do so on a 'take it or leave it' basis.[25] The Prime Minister made it clear that if the terms of the final offer on the table were unacceptable to Parliament she was not prepared to go back to the EU and try to negotiate a better deal. Theresa May had not been bluffing when she went on record to say that no deal with the EU was better than their offer of a bad deal. Faced with such a choice, the best option open to the UK would be for it to become a truly global trading nation, seeking out new trading partners under the rules of the World Trade Organization.

Only the ultra hard-core Brexiteers view such an option with equanimity and even enthusiasm. We can only speculate on the number of voters who – given the opportunity to do so – would opt for what Andrew Rawnsley describes as 'a very stark and high-risk version of Brexit'.[26] In October 2016, *The Independent* had cited UK Treasury documents that had been leaked to *The Times* in which the Government was warned that a hard Brexit of this kind would 'cost up to £66bn and slash UK GDP by almost 10%'. This loss of tax revenue would have a 'devastating' impact on the funding of our statutory social services. In the economy, lower levels of trade and investment would mean more 'businesses and jobs at risk'.[27] When Philip Hammond was interviewed by the German newspaper *Welt am Sonntag* in January 2017 he admitted that 'if Britain leaves the EU and loses access to the European Market it could suffer economic damage'. In order to regain competitiveness, 'the UK might have to cut corporation tax'. Asked whether the UK would eventually become an offshore tax haven, the Chancellor replied that 'if we are forced to be something different, then we will have to become something different'.[28]

The harder the final Brexit offer proves to be, the more compatible it will become with the values and aims of what is rapidly turning into an ultra neo-liberal Conservative Government. In ideological terms, the values in question are those of competitive market individualism. In such a context, the values and resources that underpin our statutory social services will be further undermined and marginalised. As the risks to our economic prosperity and social security increase, the institutional moorings of our welfare safety net will fall away.

The risks to the well-being of the United Kingdom, however, go far beyond the prospects for its economic and social policies. Any settlement that excluded continuing membership of the single market and the customs union will be likely to trigger the break-up of the UK, and the breakdown of the Good Friday Agreement in Northern Ireland. In the meantime the rights of EU member state nationals living in the UK and those of UK nationals living in the other 27 member states are left in jeopardy while negotiations proceed.

While the majority of Labour MPs and their supporters voted to remain in the EU, along with a growing number of One Nation Tories, they must all be viewing the prospect of an ultra-hard Brexit with grave misgivings. It certainly alarms Lord Kerr of Kinlochard who drafted the protocols embodied in Article 50 when he was serving as the UK's Ambassador to the EU in the 1990s. Lord Kerr warned his fellow peers on 20 February that the chances of the Brexit negotiations breaking down without a deal being agreed were 'well over 30 per cent'. He went on to say it was 'a sad fact that it wouldn't be those who got us into this sad fix who will suffer. The Bullingdon boys will be just fine. The country may not'.[29]

Nevertheless, in Lord Kerr's view, such an outcome need not mean that the country has to settle for 'a Hobson's choice of "deal or no deal" in a parliamentary democracy. Parliament should have the right to send the executive back to the negotiating table if it does not like an emerging deal; allow lawmakers a vote to extend the two-year deadline for Brexit to get the best outcome; and get ministers to admit that the UK could choose to stay in the EU even after exit negotiations have begun'.[30]

Unlike the Lord Chancellor, Lord Kerr believes that triggering Article 50 is a revocable act. In an earlier speech at the University of Bath, he warned the Prime Minister to be wary of making trade deals with the USA because 'our values are closer to European views than to Trump's tweets'. The UK was now facing 'a decade of uncertainty and disruption' as it dawned on the general public that 'leaving the EU single market won't increase our trading opportunities'. There was a possibility that, by 2019, there would be a sea change in public opinion after the British people had 'looked into the abyss and turned away'. They would have left the EU only to 'rejoin it immediately'. He declined an invitation to express this possibility in percentage terms.[31]

With all these uncertainties in mind, the House of Lords made two amendments to the Brexit Bill. First, they sought an assurance from the Government that those EU citizens living in the UK would be given the right to stay within three months of the date on which Article 50 was triggered. The terms of the second amendment were designed to give legal authority to the Government's verbal promise that parliament will have an opportunity to debate and vote on the final outcome of the Brexit negotiations. Such a 'meaningful vote' would empower parliament to prevent the 'UK from crashing out of the EU on World Trade Organization terms' without any deal at all. Both amendments were carried by substantial majorities in the Lords.[32]

The *Guardian* leader of 8 March contended that 'in spite of what conspiracy theorists like Lord Forsyth may say, parliament has a duty to decide on the terms. As Lord Kerr said yesterday, the mantra that the whole issue has been decided and cannot be revisited under any circumstances is the law of the lemmings'.[33] However, in the *Daily Mail*, Quentin Letts challenged these views regarding the sovereignty of parliament. In his opinion, the EU referendum was not 'a party political contest for election to Parliament. It was a "yes or no" vote on a greater scale, on a matter that has divided the people from most of their politicians. It was ultra-parliamentary, even uber-parliamentary. It was needed because the occupants of the Parliament were no longer willing to defend the people's sovereignty'.[34]

This, in essence, is the constitutional dilemma that divides opinion and explains the intensity of the passions that the debate about Brexit arouses. Within hours of playing a leading role in the House of Lords' Brexit rebellion, Lord Heseltine was sacked as one of the Government's senior policy advisers.

There will be other political casualties after the Commons votes to reject the two amendments submitted for their consideration by the Lords. Over the next two years, it remains to be seen whether the prospects for the UK's social policies as a whole will be numbered amongst these casualties.

Meanwhile, however, as a consequence of the outcome of the June 2017 General Election, the UK neoliberal Conservative government is governing with the support of Northern Ireland's Democratic Unionist Party's ten MPs. For fundamentally different ideological reasons, Theresa May, Jeremy Corbyn and their supporters view EU membership as an impediment to their long-term policy objectives. The new government remains committed to residualising the UK's public services sector while Labour's Corbynistas want to extend their remit in all directions. In their view, the EU's institutional values are too closely associated with those of competitive market capitalism to accommodate their radically socialist policies. In contrast, the government sees the EU as being insufficiently sympathetic to the 'high wage, low tax, low welfare' policies it wishes to pursue. The other main reasons why the government wants to leave the EU are set out in its Great Repeal Bill.

Four months on from the activation of Article 50, however, there are signs that more members of the British public are turning against any kind of hard and precipitate Brexit as they become more aware of the magnitude and complexity of the issues that must be resolved by March 2019. There are also welcome signs of a growing cross-party consensus regarding the need to seek a transition deal with the EU which extends the negotiating period beyond that date. Such a deal would give more time for careful attention to detail and consideration of possible options like some version of the Norway (EEA) model. It would almost certainly reduce the risk of a hard Brexit, and might even end in Parliament and the UK public voting to remain in the EU – assuming this option was still a possibility.

Notes

[1] Emmerson and Mitchell (2016).

[2] *Spectator*, 'Theresa May's first speech as Prime Minister: full text', 13 July 2016.

[3] 'Theresa May – her full Brexit speech to Conservative conference', 2 October 2016, http://www.independent.co.uk/news/uk/politics/theresa-may-conference-speech-article-50-brexit-eu-a7341926.html. See too May, J. (2016).

[4] Reilly and Newton Dunn (2016).

[5] Slack (2016), p 1, and Comment in same edition of *Daily Mail*, 4 November, p 16.

[6] Comment: 'We Must Get Out of The EU', in *Daily Express*, 4 November 2016, pp 1 and 2.

[7] Toynbee (2016).

[8] 'Voice of the *Daily Mirror*, Mrs May's lost control', *Daily Mirror*, 4 November 2016, p 8.

[9] May, T. (2016a).

[10] HM Treasury (2016), p 1.

[11] *Guardian* Leader, 'Britain's biggest foreign policy blunder cost the country dear', 24 November 2016, p 380.

[12] OBR (2016) and IFS (2016).

[13] Martin (2016).

[14] Littlewood (2016).

[15] Campbell and Morris (2017), p 1.

[16] Mason and Walker (2017).

[17] Campbell and Marsh (2017).

[18] May, T. (2016b).

[19] Crace (2017).

[20] Boseley (2017).
[21] Mason (2016).
[22] Quotations here are from Theresa May's Facebook page, 17 January 2017.
[23] Comment, in *Daily Mail*, 18 January 2017, p 14.
[24] *Guardian* Leader, 'May's speech: a domestic reality check and a European gamble', 18 January 2017, p 26.
[25] The White Paper was *The United Kingdom's exit from, and new partnership with, the European Union*, White Paper (Print), Cm 9417, HMSO (ISBN 9781474140652).
[26] Andrew Rawnsley, 'Parliament has diminished itself at this tirning point in our history', Observer, 12 February 2017, p 35)
[27] Withnall (2016).
[28] Withnall (2017).
[29] Gourtsoyannis (2017).
[30] *Guardian*, 'Brexit Britain: Peers can help make Parliament relevant to Britain leaving Europe', 22 February 2017, p 26.
[31] Kerr (2017).
[32] Mason and Asthana (2017).
[33] *Guardian*, 'The Lords are right, parliament must vote on the Brexit deal', 8 March 2017, p 26.
[34] Letts (2017).

References

Abel-Smith, B. (1964) *The Hospitals 1800–1948: A Study in Social Administration in England and Wales*, London: Heinemann.

Abel-Smith, B. (1994) *An Introduction to Health*, Harlow, Addison & Wesley: Longman Ltd.

Abel-Smith, B. and Titmuss, R. (1956) *The Cost of the National Health Service in England and Wales*, Cambridge: Cambridge University Press.

Abel-Smith, B. and Titmuss, K. (1987) *The Philosophy of Welfare: Selected Writings of Richard M. Titmuss*, London: George Allen and Unwin.

Abrams, P. (1978) 'Community care: some research problems and priorities', in J. A. Barnes and N. Connelly (eds), *Social Care Research*, London: Bedford Square Press for the Policy Studies Institute

Abrams, P. (1980) 'Social change, social networks and neighbourhood care', *Social Work Service,* 22, February: 12-23.

Abrams, P. (1984a) 'Realities of neighbourhood care', *Policy & Politics* 12, 4: 413-29.

Abrams, P. (1984b) 'Evaluating soft findings: some problems of measuring informal care', *Research Policy and Planning,* journal of the Social Services Research Group, University of Sheffield, 2, 2: 1.

Abrams, P. (1985) (ed. Martin Bulmer) 'Policies to promote informal care: some reflections on voluntary action, neighbourhood involvement and neighbourhood care', *Ageing and Society* 5: 1-18.

Alcock, P., Glennerster, H., Oakley, A. and Sinfield, A. (2001) *Welfare and Wellbeing: Richard Titmuss's Contribution to Social Policy*, Bristol: The Policy Press.

Alcock, P., Erskine, A. and May, M. (2003) *The Student's Companion to Social Policy*, Oxford: Blackwell.

Allan, G. (1983) 'Informal networks of care: issues raised by Barclay', *British Journal of Social Work*, 13, 417–33.

Ashford, D. (1986) *The Emergence of the Welfare States*, Oxford: Blackwell.

Audit Commission (1986), *Making a Reality of Community Care*, London: HMSO.

Baker, J. (1979) 'Social conscience and social policy', *Journal of Social Policy*, 8, 2: 117–206.

Baldock, J. (1999), 'Culture: the missing variable in understanding social policy?', *Social Policy and Administration*, 33: 4, 458–73.

Baldwin, P. (1990) *The Politics of Social Solidarity: Class Bases of the European Welfare State, 1875–1975*, Cambridge: Cambridge University Press.

Ball, C. and Ball, M. (1982) *What the Neighbours Say*, Berkhamsted: Volunteer Centre; Harmondsworth: Penguin Books.

Ball, C. et al (1988) *The Law Report: Teaching and Assessment of Law in Social Work*, London: Central Council for Education and Training in Social Work.

Bamford, T. (1990) *The Future of Social Work*, Basingstoke: Macmillan.

Barbalet, J.M. (1988) *Citizenship*, Open University Press, Milton Keynes.

Barclay Report (1982) *Social Workers: Their Role and Tasks*, London: Bedford Square Press.

Barry, B. (1973) *The Liberal Theory of Justice: A Critical Examination of the Principle Doctrine in A Theory of Justice by John Rawls,* Oxford: Clarendon Press.

Bauer, P.G. (1972a) *Dissent on Development: Studies and Debates in Development Economics*, London: Weidenfeld and Nicolson.

Bauer, P.G. (1972b) 'The Case Against Foreign Aid', *The Listener*, 21 September.

Bayley. M. (1973) *Mental Handicap and Community Care*, London: Routledge & Kegan Paul.

Bayley, M. (1980) 'Neighbourhood care and community care: a response to Philip Abrams', *Social Work Service* 22, February.

Bayley, M. (1982) 'Helping care to happen in the community', in A. Walker (ed), *Community Care: The Family, the State and Social Policy,* Oxford and London: Basil Blackwell and Martin Robertson, 179-82.

Beales, H.L. (1933), *The Early English Socialists,* London: Hamish Hamilton.

Beard, C. and Beard, M. (1927) *The Rise of American Civilization, Vol. I*, London: Jonathan Cape.

Beard, C.A. and Beard, M.R. (1944) *A Basic History of the United States*, Philadelphia: New Home Library, Blakiston Company.

Becker, S. and Bryman, A. (2012) 'Evidence-based policy and practice' in Becker, S., Bryman. A. and Ferguson, H. (eds), *Understanding Research for Social Policy and Social Work: Themes, Methods and Approaches*, 2nd edn, Bristol: Policy Press.

Beckett, J.C. (1971) *A short history of Ireland*, London: Hutchinson University Library.

Beech, M. and Page, R.M. (2015) 'Blue and Purple Labour challenges to the welfare state: how should "statist" social democrats respond?', *Social Policy and Society*, 14, 3: 341–56.

Beermann, R. (1958a) 'A Discussion on the Draft Law Against Parasites, Tramps and Beggars', *Soviet Studies*, IX: 2.

Beermann, R. (1958b) 'Laws Against Parasites, Tramps and Beggars', *Soviet Studies* IX: 2.

Beermann, R. (1961) 'The Parasite Laws', *Soviet Studies*, XIII: 2.

Berger, P. and Luckmann, T. (1966) *The Social Construction of Reality: A Treatise in the Sociology of Knowledge*, Garden City, New York: Anchor Books.

Berger, P.L. and Luckmann, T. (1967) *The Social Construction of Reality*, London: Allen Lane, The Penguin Press.

Beveridge, W. (1948) *Voluntary Action: A Report on Methods of Social Advance*, London: Allen and Unwin.

Berlin, I. (1980) *Concepts and Categories,* Oxford: Oxford University Press.

Berlin, I. (1990) *The Crooked Timber of Humanity,* London: John Murray.

Bevir, M. (1999) *The Logic of the History of Ideas*, Cambridge: Cambridge University Press.

Bierstedt, R. (1979) 'Sociological thought in the eighteenth century', in T. Bottomore and R. Nisbet (eds), *A History of Sociological Analysis*, Heinemann Educational Books.

Billis, D. (1981) 'At risk of prevention', *Journal of Social Policy*, 10: 3.

Birrell, W.D. (1972) 'Relative deprivation as a factor in conflict in Northern Ireland', *The Sociological Review*, 20, 3: 317–43.

Birrell, W.D. (2009) *The Impact of Devolution on Social Policy*, Bristol: Policy Press.

Birrell, W.D. and Murie, A.S. (1975), 'Ideology, conflict and social policy', *Journal of Social Policy*, 4, 3: 243–58.

Blake, R. (1970) *The Conservative Party from Peel to Churchill*, London: Eyre and Spottiswoode.

Blatchford, R. (1931) *My Eighty Years*, Cassell, London.

Boatright, M.C. (1968) 'The myth of frontier individualism' in R. Hofstadter and S.M. Lipset (eds) *Turner and the Sociology of the Frontier*, Harper Torchbooks.

Booth, C. (1902) *Life and Labour of the People in London*, 17 vols., London: Macmillan.

Boseley, S. (2017) 'Poverty is killing UK children, warns report', *Guardian*, 26 January, pp 1 and 4.

Bottomore, T. and Rubel, M. (eds) (1963) *Karl Marx: Selected Writings in Sociology and Social Philosophy,* Pelican Books.

Boulding, K.E. (1967) 'The boundaries of social policy', *Social Work*, 12: 3–11.

Boulding, K.E. (1968) *Principles of Economic Policy*, London: Staples.

Bray, J.F. (1931) *Labour's Wrongs and Labour's Remedy, or the Age of Might and the Age of Right,* London School of Economics Reprints No. 6.

Brebner, J. (1946) *North Atlantic Triangle*, New Haven: Yale University Press/ Toronto: Ryerson Press/London: Geoffrey Cumberlege, Oxford University Press.

Brewer, C. and Lait, J. (1980) *Can Social Work Survive?*, London: Temple Smith.

Briggs, A. (1967) 'The welfare state in historical perspective', in Schottland, C.I. (ed), *The Welfare State: Selected Essays*, New York: Harper and Row, 25–45.

Broady, M. (1972) *Social Administration: Some Current Concerns*, University of Swansea.

Brown, G. (2015) 'Britain's already fragile union is at risk – not from Scotland but its own Government', *Guardian*, 12 June.

Brown, P., Hadley, R. and White, K.J. (1982) 'A case for neighbourhood-based social work and social services', in Barclay Report, *Social Workers: Their Role and Tasks*, London: Bedford Square Press, Appendix A.

Bulmer, M. (1985) 'The rejuvenation of community studies? Neighbours, networks and policy', *The Sociological Review*, 33: 430–48.

Bulmer, M. (1986) *Neighbours: The Work of Philip Abrams*, Cambridge: Cambridge University Press.

Bulmer, M. (1987) *The Social Basis of Community Care*, London: Unwin Hyman.

Bulmer, M. and Rees, A.M. (eds) (1996) *Citizenship Today: The Contemporary Relevance of T.H. Marshall*, London: UCL Press.

Bulpitt, J. (1986) 'The Discipline of the New Democracy: Mrs Thatcher's Domestic Statecraft', *Political Studies,* XXXIV.

Bunyan, J. (1965) *The Pilgrim's Progress,* Harmondsworth: Penguin Books.

Burke, E. (1982) *Reflections on the Revolution in France,* London: Penguin Books.

Burke, H. (1987) *The People and the Poor Law in 19th century Ireland,* Littlehampton: Women's Education Bureau.

Butler, I. and Drakeford, M. (2011) *Social Work on Trial: The Colwell Inquiry and the State of Welfare,* Bristol: Policy Press.

Byrnes, R.F. (1968) *Pobedonostev, His Life and Thought,* Bloomington and London: Indiana University Press,

Campbell, D. (2015) '£3.8bn is not enough to secure NHS future, medical groups warn', *Guardian,* Spending Review and Autumn Statement 2015, 26 November, p 2.

Campbell, D. (2016) 'Hospitals told to shed staff as NHS funding crisis deepens', *The Guardian,* 30 January, p 1.

Campbell, D. and Marsh, S. (2017) 'Trusts declare emergency black alert amid unprecedented patient demand', *Guardian,* 12 January, p 4.

Campbell, D. and Morris, S. (2017) 'Humanitarian crisis in NHS says Red Cross', *The Guardian,* 7 January, p 1.

Cameron, D. (2015) Prime Minister's Speech, Runcorn, Cheshire, 22 June 2015: https://www.gov.uk/government/speeches/pm-speech-on-opportunity

Cameron, D. (2016) Foreword, in *The Best of Both Worlds: The United Kingdom's Special Status in a Reformed European Union,* London: HM Government.

Carr, E.H. (1969) *The Bolshevik Revolution 1917–1923, Vol. II,* London: Macmillan.

Carr-Saunders, A. (1964) *World Population, Past Growth and Present Trends,* London: Frank Cass.

Carrier, J. and Kendall, I. (1973) 'Social policy and social change: explanations of the development of social policy', *Journal of Social Policy,* 2, 3: 209–24.

Carrier, J. and Kendall, I. (1977) 'The development of welfare states: the production of plausible accounts', *Journal of Social Policy,* 6, 3: 271–90.

Carrier, J. and Kendall, I. (1986) 'Categories, categorizations and the political economy of welfare, *Journal of Social Policy,* 15, 3: 315–35.

Carrier, J. and Kendall, I. (1992) 'Law and the social division of welfare', *International Journal of the Sociology of Law,* 20: 61–87.

Carrier, J. and Kendall, I. (2016) *Health and the National Health Service,* Abingdon: Routledge.

Cecil, R., Offer, J. and St Leger, F. (1987) *Informal Welfare: A Sociological Study of Care in Northern Ireland,* Aldershot: Gower.

Challis, D. and Davies, B. (1981) *The Thanet Community Care Project: Some Interim Results,* Discussion Paper 194/3, mimeo, University of Kent: Personal Social Services Research Unit.

Challis, D. and Davies, B. (1985a) *Community Care for the Frail Elderly,* PSSRU: University of Kent.

Challis, D. and Davies, B. (1985b), 'Long-term care for the elderly: the community care scheme', *British Journal of Social Work*, 15, 6: 563–79.

Challis, D. and Davies, B. (1986a) *Case Management in Community Care*, Aldershot: Gower.

Challis, D. and Davies, B. (1986b) *Matching Resources to Needs in Community Care*, PSSRU, Aldershot: Gower.

Clark, D.A. (2005) 'Sen's capability approach and the many spaces of human well-being', *Journal of Development Studies*, 41: 8, 1339–68.

Clarke, K. (2016) *Kind of Blue*, London: Macmillan.

Coleman, T. (1972) *Passage to America*, London: Hutchinson.

Coll, B.D. (1972) 'Public assistance in the United States: Colonial times to 1860', in E.W. Martin (ed.), *Comparative Development in Social Welfare*, Allen and Unwin, London.

Collini, S. (1979) *Liberalism and Sociology: L. T. Hobhouse and Political Arguments in England 1880–1914,* Cambridge: Cambridge University Press.

Collins, A.H. and Pancoast, D.L. (1976) *Natural Helping Networks*, Washington: National Association of Social Workers.

Conquest, R. (1968) *Agricultural Workers in the USSR*, London: Bodley Head.

Conservative Party (2015) *Conservative Party Manifesto 2015: Strong Leadership: A Clear Economic Plan: A Brighter More Secure Future*, London.

Cooper, J. (1983) *The Creation of the Personal Social Services 1962–1974*, London: Heinemann.

Cooper, M. and Culyer, A. (1968), *The Price of Blood* (Hobart Paper No. 41), London: Institute of Economic Affairs.

Corcoran, M., Duncan, G.J. and Hill, M.S. (1984), 'The economic fortunes of children: Lessons from the Panel Study of Income Dynamics', *Signs: Journal of Women in Culture and Society*, vol 10, no 2, pp 232–48.

Crace, J. (2017) 'Corbyn tastes blood as he corners the Maybot over NHS', *Guardian*, 12 January, p 4

Crawford, R., Emmerson, C., Keynes, S. and Tetlow, G. (2015) *Post-Election Austerity: Parties' Plans Compared,* London: Institute for Fiscal Studies, Nuffield Foundation.

Curtis Report (1946) *Report of the Care of Children Committee* (Curtis Report), Cmd. 6922, London: HMSO.

Daly, M. (2011) *Welfare*, Cambridge: Polity Press.

Darby, J. and Williamson, A. (eds) (1978) *Violence and the Social Services in Northern Ireland*, London: Heinemann.

Davies, M. (1981) *The Essential Social Worker: A Guide to Positive Practice*, London: Heinemann.

Davies, N. (2000) *The Isles: A History*, London: Papermac/Macmillan.

Davis, J. (1922) *The Russian Immigrant*, Macmillan, New York.

Deacon, A. (2002) 'The dilemmas of welfare: Titmuss, Murray and Mead', in S.J.D. Green and R.C. Whiting (eds), *Boundaries of the State in Modern Britain*, Cambridge: Cambridge University Press.

Deacon, A. and Mann, K. (1999) 'Agency, modernity and social policy', *Journal of Social Policy*, 28, 3: 413–35.

Deacon, R., Lipton, N. and Pinker, R. (2010) *Privacy and Personality Rights: Commercial Exploitation and Protection*, Bristol: Jordans.

Deakin, N. and Wright, A. (1995) 'Tawney', in George, V. and Page, R. (eds) *Modern Thinkers on Welfare*, London: Prentice Hall/Harvester Wheatsheaf.

Dean, H. (2002) 'Social justice', in Alcock, P., Erskine, A. and May, M. (eds) *The Blackwell Dictionary of Social Policy*, Oxford: Blackwell, p 39.

Dean, H. (2010) *Understanding Human Need*, Bristol: Policy Press.

den Otter, S. (1996) *British Idealism and Social Explanation*, Oxford: Clarendon Press.

Dennis, N. and Halsey, A.H. (1988) *English Ethical Socialism: Thomas More to R.H. Tawney*, Oxford: Clarendon Press.

Department for Education (1992) *Choice and Diversity: A New Framework for Schools*, Cm 2021, London: HMSO.

Department of Health (1992) *The Patients Charter*, London: HMSO.

Department of Health (2012) *Caring for our Future: Reforming Care and Support*, Cm 8378, London: HMSO.

DHSS (Department of Health and Social Security) (1974) *Report of the Committee of Enquiry into the Care and Supervision Provided in Relation to Maria Colwell*, HMSO.

Dicey, A.V. (1962) *Law and Public Opinion in England During the Nineteenth Century*, London: Macmillan.

Dingwall, R. (1976) *Aspects of Illness*, London: Martin Robertson.

Donnelly, L. (2016) 'Waiting times behind sharp rise in patients' unhappiness with NHS', *Daily Telegraph*, 9 February, p 18.

Douglas, J. (ed) (1970) *Deviance and Respectability: The Social Construction of Moral Meaning*, New York: Basic Books.

Douglas, M. (1990) 'Foreword', in M. Maus, *The Gift*, Abingdon: Routledge.

Durbin, Elizabeth (1985) *New Jerusalems: The Labour Party and the Economics of Democratic Socialism*, London: Routledge and Kegan Paul.

Durbin, Evan (1940) *The Politics of Democratic Socialism*, London: Routledge & Sons.

Durkheim, É. (1967) *Socialism*, London: Collier-MacMillan.

Eagleton-Pierce, M. (2016) *Neoliberalism: The Key Concepts*, London and New York: Routledge.

Elias, N. (2000) *The Civilizing Process*, Oxford: Blackwell.

Eliot, G. (1959) *Middlemarch*, Dent Dutton.

Elkins, S. and McKitrick, E. (1968) 'A meaning for Turner's frontier: democracy in the Old North West' in R. Hofstadter and S.M. Lipset (eds) *Turner and the Sociology of the Frontier*, Harper Torchbooks.

Elliot, F. (2015) 'Higher wages and welfare cuts in Britain's new deal', *The Times*, 9 July, p 1.

Elliott, L. (2015) 'Tickling the electorate's tastebuds', *The Guardian Budget*, 9 July, pp 1 and 12.

Emmerson, C. and Mitchell, I. (2016) *The EU Single Market: The Value of Membership versus Access to the UK*, Institute for Fiscal Studies Report R119, 10 August.

Esping-Andersen, G. (1990) *The Three Worlds of Welfare Capitalism*, Polity Press, Oxford.

Evandrou, M., Falkingham, J. and Glennerster, H. (1990), 'The personal social services', in Hills, J. (ed), *The State of Welfare: The Welfare State in Britain since 1974*, Oxford: Oxford University Press, 206–73.

Evans, G. (1996) 'Northern Ireland during the cease-fire', in Jowell, R., Curtice, J., Park, A., Brook, L. and Thomson, K. (eds) *British Social Attitudes: The 13th Report*, Dartmouth and Aldershot: SCPR.

Evers, A. and Guillemard, A.-M. (eds) (2012) *Citizenship and Social Policy: The Changing Landscape*, Oxford: Oxford University Press.

Ferguson, A. (1966) *An Essay on the History of Civil Society, 1767*, Edinburgh: Edinburgh University Press.

Finch, D. (2015) *A Poverty of Information: Assessing the Government's New Child Poverty Focus and Future Trends*, London: Resolution Foundation.

Finch, J. and Groves, D. (1983) *A Labour of Love: Women, Work and Caring*, London: Routledge & Kegan Paul.

Fine, S. (1956) *Laissez-Faire and the General Welfare State: A Study of Conflict in American Thought 1865–1901*, Ann Arbor: University of Michigan Press/London: Geoffrey Cumberlege, Oxford University Press.

Finer, M. and McGregor, O.R. (1974) 'The history of the obligation to maintain', in *DHSS Report of the Committee on One-Parent Families, Vol 2*, Cmnd 5629–1, London: HMSO.

Finlayson, G. (1994) *Citizen, State and Social Welfare in Britain 1830–1990*, Oxford: Clarendon Press.

Fontaine, P. (2002) 'Blood, politics and social science: Richard Titmuss and the Institute of Economic Affairs, 1957–1973', *Isis*, 93: 401–34.

Forder, A. (1984) 'Neo-classical and micro-economic theory', in A. Forder, T. Caslin, G. Ponton and S. Walklate (eds) *Theories of Welfare*, London: Routledge and Kegan Paul, pp 26-53.

Forder, A., Caslin, T., Ponton, G. and Walklate, S. (1984) *Theories of Welfare*, London: Routledge and Kegan Paul.

Fowler, N. (1984) Secretary of State for Social Services' Speech to the Joint Services Annual Conference, Thursday, 27 September, press release.

Fox Piven, F. and Cloward, R.A. (1972) *Regulating the Poor: The Functions of Public Welfare*, London: Tavistock Publications.

Frankenberg, R. (1966) *Communities in Britain*, Harmondsworth: Pelican Books.

Fraser, T.G. (2000) *Ireland in Conflict 1922–1998*, London and New York: Routledge.

Freedman, R. (ed) (1962) *Marx on Economics*, London: Penguin.

Friedman, M. (1968) *Capitalism and Freedom*, Chicago: University of Chicago.

Froland, C., Pancoast, D., Chapman, J. and Kimboko, P. (1981) 'Linking formal and informal support systems', in B. Gottlieb (ed) *Social Networks and Social Support*, Beverly Hills: Sage.

Galbraith, J.K. (1970) *The Affluent Society*, Harmondsworth: Penguin.

Gallagher, T. (1991) 'Justice and the law in Northern Ireland' in Jowell, R., Brook, L. and Taylor, B. and Prior, G. (eds) British Social Attitudes: The 8th Report, Dartmouth and Aldershot: SCPR.

Garrard, J.A. (1971) The English and Immigration: A Comparative Study of the Jewish Influx 1880–1910, London: Institute of Race Relations, Oxford University Press.

Gay, P. (1973), The Enlightenment: An Interpretation, Vol. 2 The Science of Freedom, Wildwood House.

George, V. (2010) Major Thinkers in Welfare, Bristol: Policy Press.

George, V. and Page, R. (eds) (1995) Modern Thinkers on Welfare, Hemel Hempstead: Prentice Hall/Harvester Wheatsheaf.

George, V. and Wilding, P. (1976), Ideology and Social Welfare, London: Routledge and Kegan Paul.

Gerth, H.H. and Mills, C. Wright (eds) (1961), From Max Weber: Essays in Sociology, London: Routledge and Kegan Paul.

Giddens, A. (1982) Profiles and Critiques in Social Theory, London: Macmillan.

Gilmour, I. (1993) Dancing with Dogma: Britain Under Thatcherism, London: Pocket Books.

Ginsburg, N. (1979) Class, Capital and Social Policy, London: Macmillan.

Gish, O. (1971) Doctor Migration and World Health, London: G. Bell and Sons.

Glasby, J. (2015) '"The end of local government as we know it": what next for adult social care?', in Z. Irving, M. Fenger and J. Hudson (eds) Social Policy Review 27, Bristol: Policy Press, 73–89.

Glendon, M.A. (1991) Rights Talk: The Impoverishment of Political Discourse, New York: The Free Press.

Glennerster, H. (2014) 'Richard Titmuss: forty years on', CASE papers, CASE/180, London: Centre for Analysis of Social Exclusion (CASE).

Godbout, J.T. and Caille, A. (1998) The World of the Gift, London: McGill-Queens University Press.

Godwin, W. (1976) Enquiry Concerning Political Justice, Harmondsworth: Penguin Books.

Goffman, E. (1968a) Stigma: Notes of the Management of Spoiled Identity, Harmondsworth: Penguin.

Goffman, E. (1968b) Asylums: Essays on the Social Situation of Mental Patients and Other Inmates, London: Penguin Books, p. 15 passim.

Goodin, R.E. (1985) 'Self-reliance versus the welfare state', Journal of Social Policy, 14: 1, 25–47.

Goodwin, B. and Taylor, K. (1982) The Politics of Utopia: A Study in Theory and Practice, London: Hutchinson.

Gough, I. (1979) The Political Economy of the Welfare State, London: Macmillan.

Gourtsoyannis, P. (2017) 'Lord Kerr, Article 50 Author, warns Brexit talks may fail', Scotsman, 21 February.

Gray, J. (1931) A Lecture on Human Happiness, London School of Economics Reprints no. 2.

Gray, A. and Birrell, D. (2013) *Transforming Adult Social Care: Contemporary Policy and Practice*, Bristol: Policy Press.

Graycar, A. (1983) 'Informal, voluntary and statutory services: the complex relationship', *British Journal of Social Work*, 13: 379–93.

Green, D. (1993) *Reinventing Civil Society: The Rediscovery of Welfare without Politics*, London: Institute of Economic Affairs.

Griffiths, Sir Roy (1988) *Community Care: Agenda for Action*, London: HMSO.

Hadley, R. (1981) 'Social services departments and the community', in E.M. Goldberg and S. Hatch (eds), *A New Look at the Personal Social Services*, London: Policy Studies Institute.

Hadley, R. and Hatch, S. (1981) *Social Welfare and the Failure of the State*, London: Allen and Unwin.

Halevy, E. (1930) 'The World Crisis of 1914–1918: An Interpretation, being the Rhodes Memorial Lecture delivered in 1929', Oxford: Clarendon Press.

Hall, P. (1976) *Reforming the Welfare: The Politics of Change in the Personal Social Services*, London: Heinemann.

Halmos, P. (1967) 'The Personal Service Society', *British Journal of Sociology*, XVIII: 1, March.

Halsey, A.H. (1996) 'T.H. Marshall and ethical socialism', in M. Bulmer and A.M. Rees (eds) *Citizenship Today: The Contemporary Relevance of T.H. Marshall*, London: UCL Press.

Halsey, A.H. (2007) *Democracy in Crisis?*, London: Politico's.

Hammersley, M. (2012) 'Criticism of the evidence-based policy and practice movement' in S. Becker, A. Bryman and H. Ferguson (eds), *Understanding Research for Social Policy and Social Work: Themes, Methods and Approaches*, 2nd edn, Bristol: Policy Press.

Handlin, O. (1953) *The Uprooted*, Watts & Co., London.

Hansen, M.L. (1961) *The Atlantic Migration*, New York: Harper Torch-books.

Harris, D. (1987) *Justifying State Welfare*, Oxford: Oxford University Press.

Harris, J. (1992) 'Political thought and the welfare state 1870–1940: an intellectual framework for British social policy', *Past and Present*, 135: 116–41.

Harris, J. (2002) 'From poor law to welfare state? A European perspective', in D. Winch and P.K. O'Brien (eds), *The Political Economy of British Historical Experience 1688–1914*, Oxford: Oxford University Press, 409–38.

Hart, K. (2014) 'Marcel Mauss's economic vision, 1920–1925: anthropology, politics, journalism', *Journal of Classical Sociology*, 14: 1, 34–44, DOI: 10.1177/1468795X13494716.

Hart, K. and James, W. (2014) 'Marcel Mauss: A living inspiration', *Journal of Classical Sociology*, 14: 1, 3-10, DOI: 10.1177/1468795X13494725.

Hayek, F.A. (1982) *Law, Legislation and Liberty, Vol II*, London: Routledge and Kegan Paul.

Heath, A. and Evans, G. (1988) 'Working class conservatives and middle class socialists', in Jowell, R., Witherspoon, S., and Brock, L. (eds) *British Social Attitudes: The Fifth Report,* Aldershot: SCPR, Gower.

Heilbroner, R.L. (1986) *The Essential Adam Smith*, Oxford: Oxford University Press.

Hennessy, P. (2007) *Having It So Good: Britain in the Fifties*, London: Penguin Books.

Hennock, E.P. (1987) *British Social Policy and German Precedents: The Case of Social Insurance, 1880–1914*, Oxford: Clarendon Press.

Hewison, R. (1995) *Culture and Consensus*, London: Methuen.

Heywood, J.S. (1962) 'The public understanding of casework', *Social Work,* 19: 1, January.

Hick, R. (2012) 'The capability approach: insights for a new poverty focus', *Journal of Social Policy*, 43: 2, 291–308.

Hill, C. (1971) *Lenin and the Russian Revolution*, London: Pelican Books.

Hirschman, A.O. (1991) *The Rhetoric of Reaction*, Cambridge, MA, and London: Belknap Press of Harvard University Press.

HM Treasury (2016) *Policy Paper: Autumn Statement 2016*, 23 November.

Hobhouse, L. (1911) *Social Evolution and Political Thought*, New York, Columbia University Press.

Hofstadter, R. (1968) 'Introduction', in R. Hofstadter and S.M. Lipset (eds) (1968) *Turner and the Sociology of the Frontier*, Harper Torchbooks.

Hofstadter, R. and Lipset, S.M. (eds) (1968) *Turner and the Sociology of the Frontier*, Harper Torchbooks.

Hofstadter, R., Miller, W. and Aaron, D. (1959) *The American Republic, Vol. I to 1865*, Prentice Hall, New Jersey.

Holloway, M. and Lymbery, M. (2007) 'Editorial: Caring for people: social work with adults in the next decade and beyond', *British Journal of Social Work*, 37, 3: 375–86.

Holmyard, E.J. (1957) *Alchemy*, Harmondsworth: Penguin Books.

Hopkins, C.H. (1961) *The Rise of the Social Gospel in American Protestantism 1865–1915*, New Haven: Yale University Press.

Horton, J. (1966) 'Order and conflict: theories of social problems as competing ideologies', *American Journal of Sociology*, LXXI: 6, May: 713.

House of Commons (1984) *Second Report from the Social Services Committee, Session 1983–84: Children in Care, I, Report Together with the Proceedings of the Committee (Short Report)*, House of Commons Paper 360.1, London: HMSO.

Howe, D. (1990) 'The client's view in context', in P. Carter, T. Jeffs and M. Smith (eds) *Social Work and Social Welfare Yeabook 2*, Buckingham: Open University Press, 66–76.

Hume, D. ([1739] 1966) *A Treatise of Human Nature, Volume Two, with an Introduction by A.D. Lindsay*, London: Dent.

Hume, D. ([1748] 1955) *An Inquiry Concerning Human Understanding*, ed. C.W. Hendel, Indianapolis and New York: Bobbs-Merrill.

Hume, D. ([1751] 1998) *An Enquiry Concerning the Principles of Morals*, ed. T.L. Beauchamp, Oxford: Clarendon Press.

Hunter, D.J. and Judge, K. (1988) *Griffiths and Community Care: Meeting the Challenge*, Briefing Paper 5, London: King's Fund Institute.

Hutton, W. (2015) 'Everything we hold dear is being cut to the bone. Weep for our country', in *The Observer*, 22 November, p. 46.

IEA (Institute of Economic Affairs), Harris, R. and Seldon, A. (1965) *Choice in Welfare*, London: IEA.

IFS (Institute for Fiscal Studies) (2016) *Autumn Statement 2016 Analysis*, 16 November.

Ignatieff, M. (1984) *The Needs of Strangers*, London: Chatto and Windus.

Inman, P. (2015) 'A sigh of relief can be heard around Whitehall', *The Guardian*, Spending Review and Autumn Statement 2015, 26 November, pp 6-7.

Ionescu, G. and Gellner, E. (eds) (1996) *Populism, Its Meanings and National Characteristics*, London: Weidenfeld and Nicolson.

James–Davis, F. (1970) *Social Problems, Enduring Major Issues and Social Change*, New York: Free Press.

Janowitz, M. (1976) *Social Control of the Welfare State*, New York: Elsevier.

Jayasuriya, L. (1992) 'Citizenship and Welfare: Rediscovering Marshall', paper presented at the Conference on Beyond Economic Rationalism: Alternative Futures for Social Policy, University of Western Australia, Perth, 1992.

Jenks, L.H. (1938) *The Migration of British Capital to 1875*, Jonathan Cape, London.

Johnson, N. (1999) *Mixed Economies of Welfare: A Comparative Perspective*, Hemel Hempstead: Prentice Hall Europe.

Johnson, P. (1985) *Saving and Spending: The Working-class Economy in Britain 1870–1939*, Oxford: Clarendon Press.

Johnson, M. and Cooper, S. (1984) *Informal Care and the Personal Social Services*, London: Policy Studies Institute.

Johnson, J., Rolph, S. and Smith, R. (2010) *Residential Care Transformed: Revisiting 'The Last Refuge'*, Basingstoke: Palgrave Macmillan.

Jones, O. (2015) 'The Conservative case for the left is overwhelming', *Guardian*, 17 June, p 30.

Jones, R. (1980) 'Review of *The Idea of Welfare*', *British Journal of Sociology*, 31: 4.

Joubert, C. (1905) *Russia As It Really Is*, London: Eveleigh Nash.

Joyce, R. (2015) *Benefit Cuts: Where might they come from?*, London: Institute for Fiscal Studies, 26 May.

Kaim–Caudle, P.R. (1969) 'Selectivity and the Social Services', *Lloyds Bank Review*, April, 92: 45.

Kavanagh, D. (1990) *Thatcherism and British Politics: The End of Consensus?*, Oxford: Oxford University Press.

Kay, S. (1972) 'Problems of accepting means–tested benefits', in D. Bull (ed), *Family Poverty*, London: Duckworth, 29–36.

Keegan, W. (1993) *The Spectre of Capitalism: The Future of the World Economy after the Fall of Communism*, London: Vintage.

Keegan, W. (2016) 'Our Quixotic leader may need Labour to save him in Europe', *The Observer*, 21 February, p 40.

Kellner, P. (2015) 'Comment: Corbyn takes early lead in Labour leadership race', *The Times*.

Kerr, Lord (2017) 'Brexit, Will divorce be damaging, and could it be amicable?', Institute for Policy Research, University of Bath, 27 January.

Kidd, B. (1894) *Social Evolution*, Macmillan, London.

Klein, J. (ed) (1965) *Samples from English Cultures*, vols I and II, London: Routledge & Kegan Paul.

Klein, R. and Miller, J. (1995) 'Do-it-yourself social policy: searching for a new paradigm?', *Social Policy and Administration*, 29, 4, December.

Knapp, M. (1984) *The Economics of Social Care*, Basingstoke: Macmillan.

Knapp, M. (1989) 'Private and voluntary welfare', in M. McCarthy (ed) *The New Politics of Welfare: An Agenda for the 1990s?*, Basingstoke: Macmillan, 225–52.

Kuhn, T. (1996) *The Structure of Scientific Revolutions*, Chicago: University of Chicago Press.

Larkin, M. and Mitchell, W. (2016) 'Carers, choice and personalisation: what do we know?', *Social Policy and Society*, 15, 2: 189-205.

Lee, E.S. (1968) 'The Turner thesis reexamined', in R. Hofstadter and S.M. Lipset (eds) *Turner and the Sociology of the Frontier*, Harper Torchbooks.

Lee, P. and Raban, C. (1988) *Welfare Theory and Social Policy: Reform or Revolution?* London: Sage.

Le Grand, J. (2003) *Motivation, Agency, and Public Policy: Of Knights and Knaves, Pawns and Queens*, Oxford: Oxford University Press.

Le Grand, J. (2006) *Motivation, Agency, and Public Policy* (paperback edn), Oxford: Oxford University Press.

Leisering, L. and Leibfried, S. (1995) *Zeit der Armut. Lebensläufe im Sozialstaat*, Frankfurt am Main: Suhrkamp; also published in 1999 as *Time and Poverty in Western Welfare States: United Germany in Perspective*, Cambridge: Cambridge University Press.

Leisering, L. and Walker, R. (1998) *The Dynamics of Modern Society: Poverty, Policy and Welfare*, Bristol: Policy Press.

Lenski, G.E. (1966) *Power and Privilege: A Theory of Social Stratification*, McGraw-Hill.

Leonard, P. (1972) 'Review, Robert Pinker, *Social Theory and Social Policy*', *Journal of Social Policy*, 1: 1, 91–2.

Letts, Q. (2017) 'Unelected busybodies led by the vain old lion', *Daily Mail*, 8 March, pp 14-15.

Leventhal, F.M. (1990) '"The best for the most": CEMA and state sponsorship of the arts in wartime, 1939–1945', *Twentieth Century British History*, 1: 3.

Lewis, J. (1992) '"Providers", "consumers", the state and the delivery of health services in 20th century Britain', in A. Wear (ed) *Medicine in Society: Historical Essays*, Cambridge: Cambridge University Press, 317–45.

Lipsey, D., Shaw, A. and Willman, J. (1989) *Labour's Electoral Challenge*, Fabian Research Series 352, London: Fabian Society.

Lister, R. (1990) *The Exclusive Society*, London: Child Poverty Action Group.

Lister, R. (2012) 'Social citizenship in New Labour's new "active" welfare: the case of the United Kingdom', in A. Evers and A.-M. Guillemard (eds), *Citizenship and Social Policy: The Changing Landscape*, 121–49.

Littlewood, M. (2016) 'Article 50 will trigger economic pain', *Mail on Sunday*, 27 November, p 31.

Low, E. (2000) 'Class and the conceptualization of citizenship in twentieth-century Britain', *History of Political Thought*, 21: 1, 114–31.

Lund, B. (2007) 'State welfare', in M. Powell (ed), *Understanding the Mixed Economy of Welfare*, Bristol: Policy Press, 41–60.

Lyotard, J.F. (1984), *The Postmodern Condition: A Report on Knowledge,* Manchester University Press.

Madison, B. (1960) 'The organization of welfare services', in C.E. Black (ed) *The Transformation of Russian Society: Aspects of Change since 1861*, Cambridge, M.A.: Harvard University Press.

Malherbe, M. (1979) *Accreditation in Social Work: Principles and Issues in Context*, London: Central Council for Education and Training in Social Work.

Malthus, T. (1970) *An Essay on the Principle of Population,* Harmondsworth: Penguin Books.

Mann, K. (2009) 'Remembering and rethinking the social divisions of welfare 50 years on', *Journal of Social Policy*, 38: 1, 1–18.

Marcuse, H. (1964) *One-Dimensional Man*, Boston: Beacon.

Marshall, T.H. (1950) *Citizenship and Social Class*, Cambridge: Cambridge University Press.

Marshall, T.H. (1963) *Sociology at the Crossroads and other Essays*, London: Heinemann Educational Books.

Marshall, T.H. (1965a) *Social Policy*, London: Hutchinson.

Marshall, T.H. (1965b) 'Freedom as a Factor in Social Development', paper presented at the India International Centre, New Delhi, 1965; in India International Centre, *Freedom and Development,* Asia Publishing House.

Marshall, T.H. (1965c) 'The right to welfare', *The Sociological Review*, 13, 3: 261–72.

Marshall, T.H. (1966a) 'Welfare in the Context of Social Development', in J. Morgan (ed) *Welfare and Wisdom,* Toronto: University of Toronto Press.

Marshall, T.H. (1966b) 'Welfare in the Context of Social Policy', in J. Morgan (ed) *Welfare and Wisdom,* Toronto: University of Toronto Press.

Marshall, T.H. (1969) 'Reflections on Power', *Sociology*, 3: 2, May.

Marshall, T.H. (1970) *Social Policy in the Twentieth Century* (3rd edn), London: Hutchinson.

Marshall, T.H. (1972) 'Value problems of welfare-capitalism', *Journal of Social Policy*, 1: 1, 15–32.

Marshall, T.H. (1973a) 'Richard Titmuss: an appreciation', *British Journal of Sociology*, 24, 2: 138–9.

Marshall, T.H. (1973b) 'A British sociological career', *International Social Science Journal*, XXV: 1/2, 90-1.

Marshall, T.H. (1981) *The Right to Welfare and Other Essays*, London: Heinemann Educational Books.

Marshall, T.H. and Bottomore, T. (1992) *Citizenship and Social Class*, London and Concord, MA: Pluto Press.

Martin, D. (2016) *Mail Online*, 'Who are they trying to kid?...', 25 November.

Marx, K. (1963) *Karl Marx: Selected Writings in Sociology and Social Philosophy*, edited by T.B. Bottomore and M. Rubel, Harmondsworth: Penguin.

Marx, K. (1972) *Critique of the Gotha Programme*, Peking: Foreign Languages Press.

Marx, K. and Engels, F. (1959), *The Manifesto of the Communist Party*, Moscow: Foreign Languages Publishing House.

Marx, K. and Engels, F. (1998) *The Communist Manifesto*, edited and introduced by D. McClennan, Oxford: Oxford University Press.

Mason, R. (2015) 'Poor families likely to be hit unfairly by £12b welfare cuts, says thinktank', *Guardian*, 22 June.

Mason, R. (2016) 'John Major: NHS at risk from Brexit pythons', *Guardian*, 5 June.

Mason, R. and Asthana, A. (2017) 'Lords defeat May for second time on Brexit bill', *Guardian*, 8 March, p 4.

Mason, R. and Walker, P. (2017) 'NHS chief defies May over shortfall funding', *Guardian*, 12 January, pp 1 and 4.

Matza, D. (1967) 'The disreputable poor', in R. Bendix and S.M. Lipset (eds) *Class, Status and Power: Social Stratification in Comparative Perspective* (2nd edn), Routledge and Kegan Paul.

Mauss, M. (1990) *The Gift*, Abingdon: Routledge.

May, J. (2016) 'Theresa May's Conservative Conference Speech on Brexit', *Politics Home*, 2 October.

May, T. (2016a) Prime Minister's Speech to the Lord Mayor's Banquet: 14 November 2016, Prime Minister's Office, 10 Downing Street, https://www.gov.uk/government/organisations/prime-ministers-office-10-downing-street

May, T. (2016b) 'I'm determined to build the shared society for all', *Sunday Telegraph*, 8 December, p 17.

Mayer, J.E. and Timms, N. (1970) *The Client Speaks: Working Class Impressions of Casework*, London: Routledge and Kegan Paul.

McBriar, A.M. (1962) *Fabian Socialism and English Politics, 1884–1918*, Cambridge University Press.

McClelland, J.S. (1996) *A History of Western Political Thought*, London: Routledge.

McGauran, J.P. and Offer, J. (2015) 'Christian political economies, Richard Whately and Irish poor law theory', *Journal of Social Policy*, 44, 1: 43–61.

McGregor, O.R. (1957) *Divorce in England*, London: Heinemann Educational Books.

McGregor, O.R., Blom-Cooper, L. and Gibson, C. (1970) *Separated Spouses*, London: Duckworth.

Meacham, S. (1987) *Toynbee Hall and Social Reform, 1880–1914: The Search for Community*, New Haven and London: Yale University Press.

Mead, G.H. (1967) *Mind, Self and Society*, Chicago: University of Chicago Press.

Mead, M. (1986) *Beyond Entitlement: The social obligations of citizenship*, New York: The Free Press.

Medawar, P. (1984) *Plato's Republic*, Oxford: Oxford University Press.

Mencher, S. (1967) *Poor Law to Poverty Program*, University of Pittsburgh Press, Pittsburgh.

Miller, D. (1989) *Market, State and Community*, Oxford: Clarendon Press.

Milligan, S. (1969) 'The Petrograd Bolsheviks and social insurance 1914–17', *Soviet Studies*, XX, 3: 370–4.

Mishra, R. (1977) *Society and Social Policy:Theoretical Perspectives on Welfare*, London and Basingstoke: Macmillan.

Mishra, R. (1981) *Society and Social Policy* (2nd edn), London and Basingstoke: Macmillan.

Mishra, R. (1989) 'The academic tradition in social policy', in M. Bulmer, J. Lewis and D. Piachaud (eds) *The Goals of Social Policy*, London: Unwin Hyman.

Moller, H. (1964) *Population Movements in Modern European History*, MacMillan Company, New York/Collier-MacMillan, London.

Montgomerie, T. (2015) 'This so-called one-nation Toryism stinks', *The Times*, 21 May.

Montgomerie, T. (2016) 'Enough. I'm quitting the Conservative Party after 28 years membership', *The Times*, 18 February, p 29.

Moore, B.S., Jnr (1970) *Social Origins of Dictatorship and Democracy*, London: Penguin Books.

Morris, P. (1969) *Put Away*, London: Routledge and Kegan Paul.

Mulholland, M. (2002) *The Longest Conflict*, Oxford: Oxford University Press.

Murray, C. (1990) *The Emerging British Underclass,* London: Institute of Economic Affairs.

Myrdal, G. (1971) *The Challenge of World Poverty*, London: Penguin Books.

Nast, J. and Blokland, J. (2014) 'Social mix revisited: neighbourhood institutions as setting for boundary work and social capital', *Sociology*, 48: 3, 482–99.

National Audit Office (1987), *Community Care Developments*, London: HMSO.

Naughton, J. (2012) 'Fifty years ago, a physicist, wrote a book that completely changed the way we think about scientific progress …', *The Observer:The New Review*, 19 August, p 14.

Neal, S. and Murji, K. (2015) 'Sociologies of everyday life: editors' introduction to the Special Issue', *Sociology*, 49, 5: 811–19.

Needham, C. (2015) 'The spaces of personalisation: places and distance in caring labour', *Social Policy and Society*, 14, 3: 357–69.

Noble, D.W. (ed) (1965) *Historians Against History: The Frontier Thesis and the National Covenant in American History*, Minneapolis: University of Minnesota Press.

Nove, A. (1969) *An Economic History of the USSR*, London: Allen Lane.

Nozick, R. (1974) *Anarchy, State and Utopia*, Oxford: Blackwell.

Nussbaum, M.C. (2000) *Women and Human Development:The Capabilities Approach*, Cambridge: Cambridge University Press.

Oakeshott, M. (ed) (1946) Introduction, in Thomas Hobbes, *Leviathan,* Oxford: Basil Blackwell.

Oakeshott, M. (1951) Review of T.H. Marshall, *Citizenship and Social Class, The Cambridge Journal*, iv, 10: 629-30.

Oakeshott, M. (1975) *On Human Conduct,* Oxford: Oxford University Press.

Oakley, A. (1997) *Man and Wife: Richard and Kay Titmuss: My Parents' Early Years,* London: Flamingo/Harper Collins.

Oakley, A. (2014) *Father and Daughter: Patriarchy, Gender and Social Science,* Bristol: Policy Press.

OBR (Office for Budget Responsibility) (2016) *Economic and Fiscal Outlook, November 2016,* 23 November.

O'Connor, J. (1995) *The Workhouses of Ireland: The Fate of Ireland's Poor,* Dublin: Anvil Books/ Minneapolis: Irish Books and Media.

Offer, J. (1984) 'Informal welfare, social work and the sociology of welfare', *British Journal of Social Work,* 14, 6: 545–55.

Offer, J. (1999a) 'Idealist thought, social policy and the rediscovery of informal care', *British Journal of Sociology,* 50, 3: 467–88.

Offer, J. (1999b) *Social Workers, the Community and Social Interaction: Intervention and the Sociology of Welfare,* London: Jessica Kingsley.

Offer, J. (2006a) '"Virtue", "citizen character" and "social environment": social theory and agency in social policy since 1830', *Journal of Social Policy,* 35: 2, 283–302.

Offer, J. (2006b) *An Intellectual History of British Social Policy: Idealism versus Non-idealism,* Bristol: Policy Press.

Offer, J. (2010) *Herbert Spencer and Social Theory,* Basingstoke: Palgrave Macmillan.

Offer, J., St Leger, F. and Cecil, R. (1988) *Aspects of Informal Care: Some Results from a Study of a Small Town in Northern Ireland,* Belfast: DHSS (NI).

O'Leary, B. and McGarry, J. (1997) *The Politics of Antagonism: Understanding Northern Ireland,* London and Atlantic Highlands, NJ: Athlone Press.

Osborne, G. (2015) Speech by the Chancellor of the Exchequer, Mansion House, London, 10 June, https://www.gov.uk/government/speeches/mansion-house-2015-speech-by-the-chancellor-of-the-exchequer

Owen, R. (1991) *A New View of Society,* Harmondsworth: Penguin Books.

Page, R.M. (2010) 'The changing face of social administration', *Social Policy and Administration,* 44: 3, 326–42.

Parker, G. (1990) *With Due Care and Attention,* London: Family Studies Policy Centre,

Parker, J. (1975) *Social Policy and Citizenship,* London and Basingstoke: Macmillan.

Parker, R.A. (1974), 'Social administration in search of generality', *New Society,* 6 June.

Parker, R.A. (1983) 'The gestation of reform: the Children Act 1948', in Bean, P. and MacPherson, S. (eds) *Approaches to Welfare,* London: Routledge and Kegan Paul, 196–217.

Parry, G. (1991) 'Conclusion: paths to citizenship' in Vogel, H. and Moran, M. (eds) *The Frontiers of Citizenship,* London: Macmillan.

Pearson, G. (1983) 'Commentary on social policy', *Critical Social Policy,* 2, 3: 78–86.

Pearson, K. (1905) *National Life from the Standpoint of Science,* A. & C. Black, London.

Penna, S. and O'Brien, M. (1996) 'Postmodernism and social policy: a small step forwards?', *Journal of Social Policy*, 25: 1, 39–61.

P.E.P. (1961) *Family Needs and the Social Services,* London: Allen and Unwin.

Piachaud, D. (1981) 'Peter Townsend and the Holy Grail', *New Society*, 10 September.

Pierson, C. (1991) *Beyond the Welfare State*, Oxford: Polity Press.

Pinker, R.A. (1966) *English Hospital Statistics, 1861–1938*, London: Heinemann.

Pinker, R.A. (1971) *Social Theory and Social Policy*, London: Heinemann.

Pinker, R.A. (1973) *The Welfare State: A Comparative Perspective*, London: Bookstall Publications.

Pinker, R.A. (1974) 'Social policy and social justice', *Journal of Social Policy*, 3, 1: 1–19.

Pinker, R.A. (1977) 'Preface', in D. Reisman, *Richard Titmuss: Welfare and Society*, London: Heinemann, vii–xv.

Pinker, R.A. (1979), *The Idea of Welfare*, London: Heinemann.

Pinker, R.A. (1981) 'The contribution of T. H. Marshall', in *The Right to Welfare and Other Essays*, by T.H. Marshall, London: Heinemann.

Pinker, R.A. (1982a) 'Theory and ideology in social welfare', *SWRC Reports and Proceedings, 26*, Social Welfare Research Centre: University of New South Wales..

Pinker, R.A. (1982b) 'An alternative view', Appendix B in the Barclay Report (1982), 236–62.

Pinker, R.A. (1983) 'Social welfare and the education of social workers', in P. Bean and S. Macpherson (eds) *Approaches to Welfare*, London: Routledge and Kegan Paul.

Pinker, R.A. (1984) 'Populism and the social services', *Social Policy and Administration*, 18, 1: 89–98.

Pinker, R.A. (1985) 'Social policy and social care: divisions of responsibility', in Yoder, J.A., Jonker, J.M.L. and Leaper, R.A.B. (eds) *Support Networks in a Caring Community*, Dordrecht/Boston/Lancaster: Martinus Nijhoff, 103–21.

Pinker, R.A. (1986) 'Social welfare in Japan and Britain: A comparative view', in Øyen, E. (ed), *Comparing Welfare States and Their Futures*, Aldershot: Gower, 114–28.

Pinker, R. (1987) 'Opportunities for altruism', in T. Philpot (ed) *On Second Thoughts: Reassessments of the Literature of Social Work*, Wallington: Reed Business Publishing, 56–60.

Pinker, R.A. (1989) 'Social work and social policy in the twentieth century: retrospect and prospect', in Bulmer, M., Lewis, J. and Piachaud, D. (eds), *The Goals of Social Policy*, Unwin Hyman, London, 84–107.

Pinker, R.A. (1990) *Social Work in an Enterprise Society*, London: Routledge.

Pinker, R. (1991) 'On rediscovering the middle way in social welfare', in Wilson, T. and Wilson, D. (eds) *The State and Social Welfare: The Objectives of Policy*, London and New York: Longman.

Pinker, R.A. (1992) 'Making sense of the mixed economy of welfare', *Social Policy and Administration*, 26, 4: 273–84.

Pinker, R. (1993) 'Social policy in the post-Titmuss era', in R. Page and J. Baldock (eds), *Social Policy Review 5*, Canterbury: Social Policy Association, 58–80.

Pinker, R.A. (1995a) 'The place of freedom in the concept of welfare', in Barker, E. (ed) *Freedom*, London: University College Press.

Pinker, R.A. (1995b) 'Golden Ages and welfare alchemists', *Social Policy and Administration*, 29: 2, 78–90.

Pinker, R. (1995c) 'T.H. Marshall' in George, V. and Page, R. *Modern Thinkers on Welfare*, London: Prentice Hall and Harvester Wheatsheaf.

Pinker, R.A. (1996) 'The experience of citizenship – a generational perspective', based on T.H. Marshall Memorial Lecture at the University of Southampton, 30 April 1996.

Pinker, R.A. (1999) 'New liberalism and the middle way', in Page, R. and Silburn R. (eds) *British Social Welfare in the Twentieth Century*, Basingstoke: Palgrave, 80-104.

Pinker, R.A. (2000) 'Review of J.T. Godbout in collaboration with A. Caille, *The World of the Gift*, 1998', *Journal of Social Policy*, 29: 1, 150–52.

Pinker, R. (2003) 'The Conservative tradition in social welfare', in P. Alcock, A. Erskine and M. May (eds), *The Student's Companion to Social Policy*, Oxford: Blackwell/Social Policy Association, 78–84.

Pinker, R.A. (2004a, unpublished) 'The idea of welfare in a globalized world', paper presented at the conference 'Globalization of the Welfare State?', Hanse Institute for Advanced Study, Delmenhorst, Germany, 6–8 February 2004.

Pinker, R. (2004b) 'The role of theory in social policy research' in Becker, S. and Bryman, A. (eds), *Understanding Research for Social Policy and Practice*, Bristol: Policy Press.

Pinker, R.A. (2006a) 'From gift relationships to quasi-markets: an odyssey along the policy paths of altruism and egoism', *Social Policy and Administration*, 40, 1: 10–25.

Pinker, R.A. (2006b) 'Citizenship, civil war and welfare: the making of modern Ireland', *Twenty-first Century Society*, 1, 1: 23–38.

Pinker, R.A. (2008) 'Richard Titmuss and the making of British social policy studies', *Sosiologisk tidsskrift (Journal of Sociology)*, 16, 2: 167–84.

Pinker, R.A. (2011) 'Social inequality, poverty and social redistribution', *The Greek Review of Social Research, Special Issue 136 C*, Athens, 9–23.

Pipes, R. (ed.) (1968), *Revolutionary Russia*, Harvard University Press and Oxford University Press.

Pitcher, J.H. (1964) Understanding the Russians, London: Allen and Unwin.

Plant, R., Lesser, H. and Taylor-Gooby, P. (1980) *Political Philosophy and Social Welfare: Essays on the Normative Basis of Welfare Provision*, London, Basingstoke and Henley: Routledge & Kegan Paul.

Polanyi, K. (1977) *The Livelihood of Man*, New York and London: Academic Press.

Pope, R., Pratt, A. and Hoyle, B. (1986) *Social Welfare in Britain, 1885–1985*, Beckenham: Croom Helm.

Popper, K. (1978) *Objective Knowledge: An Evolutionary Approach*, Oxford: Clarendon Press.

Porter, R. (1992) *The Enlightenment,* Macmillan.

Powell, M. (ed) (2007) *Understanding the Mixed Economy of Welfare*, Bristol: Policy Press.

Preston, J. (2008) *Kuhn's The Structure of Scientific Revolutions*, Continuum International.

Prime Minister's Office (1991) *The Citizen's Charter: Raising the Standard,* Cm 1599, London: HMSO.

Putnam, H (1979) 'The "corroboration" of theories' in T. Honderich and M. Burnyeat (eds), *Philosophy As It Is*, Harmandsworth: Penguin.

Qureshi, H., Challis. D., and Davies, B. (1983) 'Motivations and rewards for helpers in a Kent community care scheme', in S. Hatch (ed) *Volunteers. Patterns. Meanings and Motives*, Berkhamsted: Volunteer Centre, 144–66.

Rawls, J. (1971) *A Theory of Justice*, Cambridge, MA: Belknap Press of Harvard University Press.

Rawnsley, A. (2015) 'The Corbynistas are already preparing their alibis for defeat', *Observer*, 24 October.

Rawnsley, A. (2017) 'Parliament has diminished itself at this tirning point in our history', *Observer*, 12 February, p 35.

Rees, A.M. (1995) 'The other T.H. Marshall', *Journal of Social Policy*, 23, 3: 341–62.

Rees, A.M. (1996) 'T.H. Marshall and the progress of citizenship', in M. Bulmer and A.M. Rees (eds) *Citizenship Today: The Contemporary Relevance of T.H. Marshall Today,* London, UCL Press, 1–24.

Reilly, J. and Newton Dunn, T. (2016) 'Who do you think you are? Loaded foreign elite defy will of British voters', *Sun*, 4 November, pp 1 and 9

Reisman, D. (1977) *Richard Titmuss: Welfare and Society*, London: Heinemann.

Reisman, D. (1984) 'T.H. Marshall and the middle ground', in Boulding, K.E. (ed), *The Economics of Human Betterment*, London: Macmillan.

Rex, J. and Moore, R. (1967) *Race, Community and Conflict: A Study of Sparkbrook*, Oxford: Oxford University Press.

Rhodes, R.A.W. (2014) 'Genre blurring in public administration: what can we learn from the humanities?', *Australian Journal of Public Administration*, 73, 4: 317–30. DOI: 10.1111/1467-8500.12085.

Ricardo, D. (1929) *The Principles of Political Economy and Taxation,* Dent Dutton.

Riddell, P. (1991) *The Thatcher Era and its Legacy,* Oxford University Press.

Richmond, A. (1969) 'Sociology of Migration in Industrial and Post-industrial Societies', in J.A. Jackson (ed) *Migration*, London: Cambridge University Press.

Rieger, E. (1992) 'T.H. Marshall's theory of citizenship rights revisited: social rights in the nation state and in the European Community', paper presented to the Conference on Comparative Studies of Welfare State Development, University of Bremen, September 1992.

Rimlinger, G.V. (1971) *Welfare Policy and Industrialization in Europe, America and Russia,* John Wiley, New York.

Roach, J.L. and Roach, J.K. (1972) *Poverty: Selected Readings*, London: Penguin Books.

Roberts, R. (1971) *The Classic Slum: Salford Life in the First Quarter of the Century*, Manchester: Manchester University Press.

Robertson, A. (1984) 'Social Services Planning and the Quality of Life', in Robertson, A. and Osborn, A. (eds) *Planning to Care*, London: Gower, 127–42.

Robertson, A. and Osborn, A. (eds) (1984) *Planning to Care*, London: Gower.

Rodgers, B.N. with J. Greve and J.S. Morgan (1968) *Comparative Social Administration*, Allen and Unwin, London.

Room, G. (2011) *Complexity, Institutions, and Public Policy: Agile Decision-Making in a Turbulent World*, Cheltenham, UK and Northampton, MA: Edward Elgar.

Room, G. and Williamson, A. (eds) (1983) *Health and Welfare States of Britain: An Inter-country Comparison*, London: Heinemann.

Rowntree, B.S. (1901) *Poverty: A Study of Town Life*, London: Macmillan.

Rowntree, B.S. (1941) *Poverty and Progress*, London: Longmans, Green.

Rowntree, B.S. and Lavers, G.R. (1951) *English Life and Leisure*, London: Longmans, Green.

Ruddick, G. (2015) 'Council tax tinkering not enough to safeguard care homes, say experts', *The Guardian*, Spending Review and Autumn Statement 2015, 26 November, p 3.

Runciman, W.G. (1966/1972) *Relative Deprivation and Social Justice*, Harmondsworth: Penguin.

Runciman, W.G. (1997) *A Treatise on Social Theory, Vol. 3: Applied Social Theory*, Cambridge, Cambridge University Press.

Russell, B.W.E. (1898) *One Who Has Kept a Diary: Collections and Recollections*, London: Smith, Elder.

Saint-Simon, C.H. de (1956) *The Doctrine of Saint Simon,* Boston.

Schram, S.F. (1993) 'Postmodern policy analysis: discourse and identity in welfare policy', *Policy Sciences*, 26: 249–70.

Schutz, A. (1972) *The Phenomenology of the Social World*, London: Heinemann.

Scott J. and Bromley, R. (2013) *Envisioning Sociology: Victor Branford, Patrick Geddes, and the Quest for Social Reconstruction*, Albany, State University of New York.

Seebohm Report (1968) *Report of the Committee on Local Authority and Allied Personal Social Services*, Cmnd 3703, London: HMSO.

Seldon, A. (1966) 'Which Way to Welfare?', *Lloyds Bank Review*, October.

Seldon, A. (1968) 'Commitment to Welfare: A Review Article', *Social and Economic Administration*, 2, 3: 196–200.

Seldon, A. (1990) *Capitalism*, London: Basil Blackwell.

Semmell, B. (1960) *Imperialism and Social Reform*, Allen and Unwin, London.

Sen, A. (1983) 'Poor, relatively speaking' in *Oxford Economic Papers*, 35, 2:153-62.

Sen, A.K. (1992) *Inequality Re-examined*, Oxford: Clarendon Press.

Sen, A.K. (1993) 'Capability and well-being', in M.C. Nussbaum and A.K. Sen (eds), *The Quality of Life*, Oxford: Clarendon Press, 30–53.

Sen, A.K. (1999) *Development as Freedom*, Oxford: Oxford University Press.

Seton-Watson, H. (1960) *The Decline of Imperial Russia 1855–1914*, London: Methuen.

Shannon, F.A. (1968) 'A post-mortem on the labour-safety-valve theory' in R. Hofstadter and S.M. Lipset (eds) *Turner and the Sociology of the Frontier*, Harper Torchbooks.

Sheard, S. (2013) *The Passionate Economist*, Bristol: Policy Press.

Sibeon, R. (1991) *Towards a New Sociology of Social Work*, Aldershot: Avebury.

Sinfield, A. (1970) 'Which way for social work? in P. Townsend et al (eds), *The Fifth Social Service: A Critical Analysis of the Seebohm Proposals*, London: Fabian Society.

Skidelsky, R. (ed) (1989) *Thatcherism*, Chatto and Windus.

Slack, J. (2016) 'Enemies of the People', *Daily Mail*, 4 November, p 1.

Smith, A. (1976a) *An Inquiry into the Nature and Causes of the Wealth of Nations*, (eds R.H. Campbell and A.S. Skinner), Oxford: Clarendon Press.

Smith, A. (1976b) *The Theory of Moral Sentiments*, (eds D.D. Raphael and A.L. Macfie), Oxford: Clarendon Press.

Smith, J. (2000) *Britain and Ireland: From Home Rule to Independence*, Harlow: Longman.

SNP (Scottish Nationalist Party) (2015) *Stronger for Scotland*, SNP Manifesto 2015, p 7.

Soper, T. (1969) 'Western Attitudes to Aid', *Lloyds Bank Review*, October, No 94.

Specht, H. (1981) 'British social services under siege: an essay review', *Social Service Review*, 55: 4, 593–602.

Spencer, H. (1910 [1893]), *The Principles of Ethics*, Vol. 2, New York: Appleton (the two volumes of *Ethics* were first published in London by Williams and Norgate in 1892 and 1893).

Spicker, P. (1993) 'Can European social policy be universalist?', in Page, R. and Baldock, J. (eds) *Social Policy Review 5*, Social Policy Association, University of Kent.

Spicker, P. (1999) 'Definitions of poverty: eleven clusters of meaning' in Gordon, D. and Spicker, P. (eds) *The International Glossary of Poverty*, London: Zed Books.

Spicker, P. (2006) *Liberty, Equality, Fraternity*, Bristol: Policy Press.

Stacey, M. (1969) 'The myth of community studies', *British Journal of Sociology* 20, 2: 134–47.

Stafford, W. (1987) *Socialism, Radicalism and Nostalgia: Social Criticism in Britain, 1775–1830*, Cambridge University Press.

Stephens, D. (1970) *Immigration and Race Relations*, Fabian Research Series 291.

Stephenson, G. (1969) *History of Russia 1812–1945*, Macmillan, London.

Stevenson, O. (1981) *Specialisation in Social Service Teams*, London: Allen and Unwin.

Stevenson, O. and Parsloe, P. (1978) *Social Service Teams: The Practitioners View*, London: DHSS.

Tawney, R.H. (1950) 'The war and the people', *New Statesman and Nation*, 22 April, 454-6.

Tawney, R.H. (1964) *Equality*, London: George Allen and Unwin.

Taylor, C. (1975) 'Neutrality in the university', in A. Montefiore (ed) *Neutrality and Impartiality in the University and Political Commitment*, Cambridge: Cambridge University Press, London, 128-48.

Taylor, M. (2016) 'Unions fear end of free health service', *Guardian*, 9 February, p 8.

Taylor-Gooby, P. (1981) 'The empiricist tradition in social administration', *Critical Social Policy*, 1, 2: 6–21.

Taylor-Gooby, P. and Dale, J. (1981) *Social Theory and Social Welfare*, London: Edward Arnold.

Taylor-Gooby, P. (1994) 'Postmodernism and social policy: a great leap backwards?', *Journal Social Policy*, 23, 3: 85–404.

Taylor-Gooby, P. (1995) 'Comfortable, marginal and excluded: Who should pay the higher taxes for a better welfare state?', in R. Jowell et al (eds) *British Social Attitudes: The 12th Report*, Aldershot: Dartmouth, 1–17.

Thane, P. (1982) *The Foundations of the Welfare State*, Harlow: Longman.

Thistlethwaite, F. (1955) *The Great Experiment*, Cambridge University Press, London.

Thistlethwaite, F. (1960) *Migration from Europe Overseas in the Nineteenth and Twentieth Centuries*, reprinted from Xle Congres International des Sciences Historiques, Stockholm, 1960, 'Rapports, V, Historic Contemporaine', Almquist and Wikell, Goteborg–Stockholm–Uppsala, 1960.

Thomas, B. (1954) *Migration and Economic Growth*, Cambridge University Press.

Thomas, W.I. and Znaniecki, F. (1958) *The Polish Peasant in Europe and America, Vol. I*, New York: Dover Publications.

Thompson, W. (1968) *An Inquiry into the Principles of the Distribution of Wealth*, New York: Burt Franklin.

Thornberry, C. (1964) *The Stranger at the Gate: A Study of the Law on Aliens and Commonwealth Citizens*, Fabian Research Series 243.

Thornton, A.P. (1963) *The Imperial Idea and its Enemies*, London: Macmillan.

Timms, N. (1962) 'The public and the social worker', *Social Work*, 19, 1: 3–7.

Tinker, A. (1992), *Elderly People in Modern Society*, London and New York: Longman.

Titmuss, R. (1950) *Problems of Social Policy*, London: HMSO and Longmans, Green and Co.

Titmuss, R.M. (1958a) 'The social division of welfare', in his *Essays on 'The Welfare State'*, London: Allen and Unwin.

Titmuss, R.M. (1958b) *Essays on 'the Welfare State'*, London: Allen and Unwin.

Titmuss, R.M. (1963), *Essays on 'the Welfare State'* (2nd edition), London: Allen and Unwin.

Titmuss, R.M. (1968) *Commitment to Welfare*, London: Allen and Unwin.

Titmuss, R.M. (1970) *The Gift Relationship: From Human Blood to Social Policy*, London: Allen and Unwin.

Titmuss, R.M. (1974) *Social Policy: An Introduction*, London: Allen and Unwin.

Titmuss, R. (1976) *Commitment to Welfare*, London: George Allen and Unwin

Titmuss, R.M. (1976b) *Essays on 'The Welfare State'* (3rd edn), London: Allen and Unwin.

Titmuss, R. and Titmuss, K. (1942) *Parents' Revolt: A Study of the Declining Birth-rate in Acquisitive Societies*, London: Secker & Warburg.

Tolstoy, L.N. (1957) *War and Peace*, Vol. 2, Book 4, Penguin Books.

Tönnies, F. (2001) *Community and Civil Society*, ed. J. Harris, Cambridge: Cambridge University Press.

Townsend, P. (1957) *The Family Life of Old People*, London: Routledge & Kegan Paul.

Townsend, P. (1962) *The Last Refuge: A Survey of Residential Institutions and Homes for the Aged in England and Wales*, London: Routledge and Kegan Paul.

Townsend, P. (1970) 'The objectives of the new local social service', in P. Townsend et al (eds), *The Fifth Social Service: A Critical Analysis of the Seebohm Proposals*, London: Fabian Society.

Townsend, P. (1979) *Poverty in the United Kingdom*, Harmondsworth: Penguin.

Toynbee, P. (2016) 'The court's ruling …', *Guardian*, 4 November, pp. 1 and 4

Treasury (1991) *Competing for Quality*, London: HMSO. Troyat, H. (1961) *Daily Life in Russia Under the Last Tsar*, London: Allen and Unwin.

Tunstall, J. (1966) *Old and Alone: A Sociological Study of Old People*, London: Routledge and Kegan Paul.

Turner, B.S. (1986) *Citizenship and Capitalism: The Debate over Reformism*, London, Boston and Sydney: Allen and Unwin.

Turner, F.J. (1962) *The Frontier in American History*, New York: Holt, Rinehart and Winston.

Twigg, J. (1994) 'Carers, families, relatives: socio–legal conceptions of care–giving relationships', *Journal of Social Welfare and Family Law*, 16: 3, 279–98.

Vaizey, J. (1983) *In Breach of Promise: Gaitskell, MacLeod, Titmuss, Crosland, Boyle. Five Men Who Shaped a Generation*, London: Weidenfield and Nicholson.

Veit-Wilson, J. (2000) 'States of welfare: a conceptual challenge', *Social Policy and Administration*, 34, 1: 1–25.

Venturi, F. (1964) *Roots of Revolution*, London: Weidenfield and Nicolson.

Vincent, A.W. (1984) 'The Poor Law Reports of 1909 and the social theory of the Charity Organisation Society', *Victorian Studies*, 27, 3: 343–63.

Von Clausewitz, C. (1940) *On War, Vol. iii*, London: Kegan Paul, Trench, Trubner and Co.

Von Laue, T. (1969) 'Problems of industrialization', in T.G. Stavrou (ed), *Russia Under the Last Tsar*, Minneapolis: University of Minnesota Press.

Vucinich, A. (1960) 'The state and the local community' in C.E. Black (ed) *The Transformation of Russian Society: Aspects of Change since 1861*, Cambridge, M.A.: Harvard University Press.

Walker, R. (2014) *The Shame of Poverty*, Oxford: Oxford University Press.

Walker, R. with Ashworth, K. (eds) (1994) *Poverty Dynamics: Issues and Examples*, Aldershot: Avebury.

Wallace, Sir D.M. (1912) *Russia*, London: Cassell.

Walvin, J. (1987) *Victorian Values*, London: Andre Deutsch.

Walzer, M. (1983) *Spheres of Justice: A Defense of Pluralism and Equality*, London: Martin Robertson/New York: Basic Books.

Warham, J. (1970) *Social Policy in Context*, London: Batsford.

Warham, J. (1973) 'Social administration and sociology', *Journal of Social Policy*, 2, 3, 193–207.

Warham, J. (1978) 'Social policy and social services', in *Introduction to Welfare: Iron Fist and Velvet Glove*, Milton Keynes: Open University Press.

Weale, A. (1980) 'Robert Pinker, *The Idea of Welfare*', *Journal of Social Policy*, 9, 2: 246–68.

Webb, S. and Webb, B. (1944) *Soviet Communism: A New Civilization* (3rd edn) Longman Green, London.

Weber, M. (1964) *The Theory of Social and Economic Organisation*, London: Free Press of Glencoe, Collier Macmillan.

Weiner, M. (1985) *English Culture and the Decline of the Industrial Spirit, 1850–1980*, Harmondsworth: Penguin Books.

Wellman, B. (1981) 'Applying network analysis to the study of support', in B. Gottlieb (ed) *Social Networks, and Social Support*, Beverly Hills: Sage.

Welshman, J. (2004) 'The unknown Titmuss', *Journal of Social Policy*, 33, 2: 225–47.

Wenger, G.C. (1981) *The Elderly in the Community: Family Contacts, Social Integration and Community Involvement*, Working Paper 18, mimeo, University College of Bangor.

Wilding, P. (1976) 'Richard Titmuss and social welfare', *Social and Economic Administration*, 10, 3: 147–66.

Wilding, P. (1983) 'The evolution of social administration', in Bean, P. and McPherson, S. (eds) *Approaches to Welfare*, London: Routledge and Kegan Paul, 1–15.

Wilding, P. (1995) 'Richard Titmuss', in George, V. and Page, R. (eds) *Modern Thinkers on Welfare,* London: Prentice Hall/Harvester Wheatsheaf.

Williams, F. (1989) *Social Policy: A Critical Introduction*, Oxford: Polity Press.

Williams, F. (2015) 'Towards the welfare commons: contestation, critique and criticality in social policy', in Z. Irving, M. Fenger and J. Hudson (eds), *Social Policy Review 27*, Bristol: Policy Press, 93–111.

Willmott, P. (1987) *Friendship Networks and Social Support: A Study in a London Suburb,* London: Policy Studies Institute.

Wincott, D. (2003) 'Slippery concepts, shifting contexts', *Social Policy and Administration*, 37, 3: 305–15.

Wincott, D. (2015) 'Original and imitated or elusive and limited? Towards a genealogy of the welfare state idea in Britain', in Beland, K. and Petersen, K. (eds) *Analysing Social Policy Concepts and Languages: Comparative and Transnational Perspectives*, Bristol: Policy Press, 127–42.

Wintour, P. and Elliott, L. (2015) 'Chancellor's £27bn U-turn', *Guardian*, 26 November, pp 1 and 9.

Withnall, A. (2016) '"Hard Brexit" could cost up to £66bn and slash UK GDP by almost 10%', *Independent*, 11 October.

Withnall, A. (2017) 'UK could become 'tax haven' of Europe if it is shut out of the single market after Brexit, Chancellor suggests', *Independent*, 15 January.

Yelloly, M. (1980) *Social Work Theory and Psychoanalysis*, London: Van Nostrand, Reinhold.

Young, M. and Willmott, P. (1957/1968) *Family and Kinship in East London*, London: Routledge & Kegan Paul.

Young, M. and Willmott, P. (1960) *Family and Class in a London Suburb*, London: Routledge & Kegan Paul.

Young, T. (2015) 'Why Tories should join Labour and back Jeremy Corbyn', *The Daily Telegraph*, 17 June.

Index

Toynbee, Polly 299
trust 140, 185
Turgot, Anne Robert Jacques 198
Turner, Bryan 120, 172, 259, 260, 262
Turner, F.J. 76, 77
Twigg, J. 9
two-parent family 44

U

UK (United Kingdom) 31, 195–6, 204, 269–309
 see also Britain
the underprivileged 148
unilateral nuclear disarmament 285, 287
unilateral transfers 98
unitarism 41, 42, 189
unitary model of social welfare 13, 20, 102, 107,
 216, 218, 249, 290
 and citizenship 42–3, 103, 217
United Irishmen 174
United States 74, 76–9, 83–4, 85, 86, 88
Universal Credit 282
universalist social service 42, 99–100
universality 41, 42, 102, 251, 253
'universal stranger' 99, 100, 104, 213
University of Kent 154
unmarried mothers 205–6
'The Uses of History in Sociology' (Goldthorpe)
 236
Utilitarians 189
utility 72, 73, 213

V

Vaizey, John 95, 111
value judgements 48, 49, 50, 52
'Value Problems of Welfare-Capitalism' (Marshall)
 243, 247, 249, 253, 262
Veit-Wilson, John 25, 58
'victim' thesis 29, 51, 52
Victorian Britain 199–200
vigilante associations 185
village commune 79
Vincent, A.W. 23
Violence and the Social Services in Northern Ireland
 (Darby and Williamson) 195
voluntary sector 154, 231–2
voluntary work 155

W

Wales 295, 306
Walker, Robert 30
Walvin, James 199
Walzer, M. 260
Warham, Joyce 22
wars 172–3, 178, 184, 185–6
wealth creation 56, 57, 58
Webb, Adrian 37
Webb, Sidney and Beatrice 16, 75, 118, 148
Weber, Max 1, 229–30
Weiner, Martin 152
welfare benefit cuts 276
'Welfare in the Context of Social Development'
 (Marshall) 252
'Welfare in the Context of Social Policy'
 (Marshall) 252

welfare pluralism 187, 188, 190, 195, 203–4, 287
 and Beech and Page 191
 compared with unitary system 189, 216
 definition 12, 269–70
 favoured by British voters 237–8
 and interdependence and dependency 102–3
 interdependence and dependency 217
 and Marshall 194, 261, 262
 and private sector providers 289
 and provision of better-quality social services
 218
 and Titmuss 99, 151, 192
 see also pluralism
welfare policy from below 21
Welfare Reform and Work Bill 278, 281
welfare rights 174, 177
welfare society 45, 82, 87–8
welfare spending cuts 272
welfare state 4, 5, 70, 71–85, 87–8, 229
welfare unitarism 190, 191
 see also unitary model of social welfare
welfare unitarist 99
Wellman, B. 11
Wenger, G.C. 154
Wilding, P. 23, 95, 255
Williams, F. 196, 260
Williamson, Arthur 184, 195
Willmott, Peter 151, 155
Wilson, Harold 31, 209
Wilson, Woodrow 78
Wincott, Daniel 25
'winter of discontent' 98
Witte, Sergei 79
women
 and Marshall 260
 and Titmuss 109, 110
Wootton, Barbara 201
The World of the Gift (Godbout and Caille) 14

Y

Yelloly, M. 125
Young, Michael 151
Young, Toby 278

Z

zemstvo reforms 80
Znaniecki, F. 77